THE MAKING OF THE MODERN COMPANY

This book adopts a historical perspective to highlight, and bring back into focus, the key features of the modern company. A central argument in the book is that legal personhood attaching to an entity containing a corporate fund seeded by shareholders is a direct and inevitable consequence of limited liability, and the company's status as a separate legal entity from its shareholders. Management by a board subject to legal duties to the company as an entity that can exist in perpetuity facilitates a long-term perspective that can accommodate both shareholder and stakeholder interests. These defining characteristics differentiate the modern company from other business forms.

The Making of the Modern Company applies a twenty-first century lens to the corporation through its history to identify turning points in its development. It sets out how key features emerged in the course of two separate developmental cycles in English corporate law: first with the English East India Company in the seventeenth century, and then with general incorporation statutes in the second half of the nineteenth century. The book's historical perspective highlights that the key features are part of the 'secret sauce' of modern companies.

Each cycle coincided with unparalleled periods of economic success associated with corporate activity.

This book will be of interest to corporate law and governance academics, theorists and practitioners, those who study the company from related disciplines, and anyone who questions why uncertainty still exists about the structure of a legal form that has been described as 'amongst mankind's greatest inventions'.

Contemporary Studies in Corporate Law

Series editors: Marc Moore, Christopher Bruner

Corporate law scholarship has a relatively recent history despite the fact that corporations have existed and been subject to legal regulation for three centuries. The modern flourishing of corporate law scholarship has been matched by some broadening of the field of study to embrace insolvency, corporate finance, corporate governance and regulation of the financial markets. At the same time the intersection between other branches of law such as, for example, labour, contract, criminal law, competition, and intellectual property law and the introduction of new inter-disciplinary methodologies affords new possibilities for studying the corporation. This series seeks to foster intellectually diverse approaches to thinking about the law and its role, scope and effectiveness in the context of corporate activity. In so doing the series aims to publish works of high intellectual content and theoretical rigour.

Titles in this series

Working Within Two Kinds of Capitalism: Corporate Governance and Employee Stakeholding: US and EC Perspectives
Irene Lynch Fannon

Contracting with Companies
Andrew Griffiths

The Law and Economics of Takeovers: An Acquirer's Perspective
Athanasios Kouloridas

The Foundations and Anatomy of Shareholder Activism
Iris H-Y Chiu

Corporate Governance in the Shadow of the State
Marc T Moore

Reconceptualising Corporate Compliance
Anna Donovan

Corporate Opportunities: A Law and Economics Analysis
Marco Claudio Corradi

The Making of the Modern Company

Susan Watson

•HART•
OXFORD • LONDON • NEW YORK • NEW DELHI • SYDNEY

HART PUBLISHING

Bloomsbury Publishing Plc

Kemp House, Chawley Park, Cumnor Hill, Oxford, OX2 9PH, UK

1385 Broadway, New York, NY 10018, USA

29 Earlsfort Terrace, Dublin 2, Ireland

First published in Great Britain 2022

A catalogue record for this book is available from the British Library.

A catalogue record for this book is available from the Library of Congress.

Library of Congress Control Number: 2022930179

ISBN: HB: 978-1-50992-362-5
ePDF: 978-1-50992-363-2
ePub: 978-1-50992-364-9

Typeset by Compuscript Ltd, Shannon

Preface

In the first class of my first company law lecture in 1992, I focused on *Salomon v Salomon & Co Ltd*. Nothing innovative or unique in that; every company law course in a Commonwealth jurisdiction begins the same way, I suspect. *Salomon* has variously been described as a seminal or foundational case, calamitous and, by Lord Cooke of Thorndon, as a turning point in the law. It may be all of those things. *Salomon* is seminal because the House of Lords, unexpectedly, set down that a company is a separate legal entity from its shareholders and, so long as the requirements of an incorporation statute are met, the company is a person at law.

In that same company law class, and again like many other teachers of company law, I told my students that a company is comprised of shareholders just as Shakespeare had a company of players. Separate from shareholders and yet comprised of shareholders? An internal contradiction exists at the heart of company law that plays itself out in every aspect of the principles that determine both company law and our understanding of the modern company. Understanding the source of the contradiction requires casting a lens back over the origins of the key features that make up the modern company. The sources are more diverse, interesting and significant than might be anticipated.

This book project began with a focus on England in second half of the nineteenth century and the transition from companies' being understood to be contractually based on shareholders in the mid-century to the outcome in *Salomon*. It became apparent, however, that the origins of the key features of the modern company were much earlier than previously thought. The first part of the book therefore focuses on developments in the structure and governance of the English East India Company in the second half of the seventeenth century. By 1657, the Company was an artificial legal person based on a corporate fund separate from all natural persons. Within 50 years, the English East India Company dominated the world. Lessons for modernity abound. The English East India Company achieved its greatest financial successes once it had acquired and utilised all the key features of the modern company. Over time, its impact on the world caused great harm.

Understanding the making of the modern company has profound implications for the form that is the beating heart of capitalism. The wealthiest people in the world are not human beings. Human beings benefit and prosper from the activities of companies. Engaging with the challenge of the impact of people on the planet compels us to understand the impact of artificial legal people too. The modern company has been described as mankind's greatest invention, with its impacts both egregious and enhancing. It may be that the most powerful feature of the corporation is its potential perpetuity, within which lies the potential to harness for good as well as to control for harm.

Acknowledgements

NO ONE IS an island and no book gets completed without tangible and intangible forms of support. I have been fortunate to receive both in the 10 years *The Making of the Modern Company* was in development.

Research assistants from Auckland Law School provided research skills and genuine enthusiasm and belief in this project. They are too many to mention by all by name, but I do single out Nick Goldstein, Michael Nuysink, Luke Taylor, Hayden Noyce, Sandy Guo and Beryl Tan as being especially enthusiastic and excellent. And in particular the talented Carter Pearce, who did some amazing research on the development of the modern company in the nineteenth century. Thank you to you all!

Dr Tim Bowley from Monash University provided brilliant support in helping me to draw out the themes of the book, making explicit what I had left implicit, as well as organising the project. Sincere thanks. Thank you also to Roberta Bassi from Hart Publishing, who believed in this book from the start and who patiently waited for it to come to fruition, and to Catherine Minahan, my copyeditor.

All academics have mentors and supporters, and I have been fortunate in having John Farrar as a mentor. Joe McCahery has been a great supporter, as has Randall Thomas, Jennifer Hill and Marc T Moore. I have also benefited from wonderfully collegial networks of scholars in corporate law, who seem to combine being the nicest people in academia with being rigorous academics. These include all the participants in CLTA (now ScoLa) and Daughters of Themis, as well as the network connected with Vanderbilt University and the leadership and governance group at my own University. And my thanks to colleagues at the University of Auckland, who may disagree at times with my ideas but who take time to engage – including Warren Swain, Chris Noonan, Arie Rosen, and Ljiljana Erakovic. I am also grateful to the University of Auckland, which has been my academic home for my entire academic career. Constraints are never placed on exploring ideas that may not fit mainstream thinking: instead they are supported. Truly what academic freedom is.

And finally to Christabel Pahl, Charlotte Pahl, Eoin Watson and Elizabeth Watson, my four favourite humans, who through help both tangible and intangible are the reason my dreams are realised.

Contents

Table of Cases

England and Wales

United States

Canada

Australia

Table of Legislation

United Kingdom

New Zealand

United States

France

1

Introduction

I. INTRODUCTION

In 1932, Berle and Means wrote:

> Briefly, the past century has seen the corporate mechanism evolve from an arrangement under which an association of owners controlled their property on terms closely supervised by the state to an arrangement by which many men have delivered contributions of capital into the hands of a centralized control.[1]

Justice Brandeis in *Liggett v Lee* said that

> the typical business corporation of the last century, owned by a small group of individuals, managed by their owners, and limited in size by their personal wealth, is being supplanted by huge concerns in which the lives of … thousands of employees and the property of … thousands of investors are subjected, through the corporate mechanism, to the control of a few men.[2]

The belief that the modern company started small based on its shareholders and then got bigger is widespread and not true. This book focuses the lens of history further back in time to demonstrate that the modern company first emerged in the middle of the seventeenth century. It started big, primarily as a vehicle for raising long-term capital.[3] The first modern companies were business corporations like the English East India Company and the Bank of England. The key features of those companies have contemporary significance. As Walter Werner said, 'I believe that corporation law must rest on an understanding of big corporations and how they became the organizations they are today'.[4]

This book focuses on the English East India Company as the first modern company. A key point in the lifecycle of the Company occurred in 1657. In the autumn of that year, Oliver Cromwell signed a new charter for the Company,

[1] AA Berle and GC Means, *The Modern Corporation and Private Property*, rev edn (Harcourt, Brace & World, 1968) 119.

[2] *Liggett v Lee* 288 US 517, 565 (1933).

[3] In its second cycle later in the 19th century, the form was initially adopted by small enterprises that had previously been operated as partnerships to take advantage of the benefits of limited liability.

[4] W Werner, 'Corporation Law in Search of its Future' (1981) 81 *Columbia Law Review* 1611, 1662.

granting it permanent capital. From its establishment at the end of the sixteenth century, the Company had been based on a series of royal charters. The ascendancy of the Protectorate following the English Civil War (1642–51) raised a significant question concerning the legitimacy of the Company, and the Company struggled to attract investors. The governing body had gone as far as resolving to close its business and sell its premises. Ultimately, however, Cromwell had become convinced that trade to India would benefit the nation most through a corporation based on one permanent joint stock. At this point, the English East India Company had acquired all the key features that made it the world's first modern company.

At the beginning, the elite majority shareholders who controlled the governance of the English East India Company operated the Company entirely in their own interests. The Company's small investing shareholders were a new breed of merchant drawn from the ship captains and shopkeepers of London whom Napoleon Bonaparte would later scorn. That 'generality', as they were called, would not invest unless they had a voice and unless the governance of the Company changed. The two groups of shareholders debated and shaped the governance and structure of the Company through the innovation of the quarterly general meeting. The sophistication of the capital and governance initiatives introduced would lay the foundations not just for the modern company but for modernity itself.

Significantly, the shift did not come by the investing shareholders' controlling the management of the English East India Company. The generality did not need to. Instead, their investment capital was combined in a permanent fund of capital held by the Company. The governing body was accountable to the shareholders for a return on that capital. Members of the governing body were regularly elected by the generality and swore an oath to manage the Company in the interests of all of the shareholders.

Chaudhari says:

> The organization of East India trade through joint-stock companies anticipated and perhaps even indirectly contributed to the eventual creation of modern business corporations and the abstract concept of the 'firm' as the main regulator through which the whole complex of economic production and exchange could take place.[5]

The English East India Company became a behemoth that dominated the world for 250 years. For much of its existence, it was an instrument of empire. But for a period it took the form of a modern company. In the hundred years after Cromwell granted its new charter and before its activities took a darker turn under Robert Clive, the Company grew rapidly, surpassing its rival the Dutch East India Company and all other companies trading into India. Just like the

[5] KN Chaudhuri, *The Trading World of Asia and the English East India Company: 1660–1760* (Cambridge University Press, 1978) 19.

modern companies of the gilded age of the late nineteenth century and the 'tech' industry giants of our second gilded age, the English East India Company was unstoppable unless or until the state intervened.

II. KEY FEATURES

What were the key features combined in the English East India Company? It was legally a corporation, so some were drawn from the 'old incidents of corporations' that had become accepted by the fifteenth century. These features were the rights of suing and being sued, of having a common seal, to enter into transactions as a corporation, of dealing with lands and making by-laws as internal rules.[6] The Company also had the benefit of perpetual succession.[7] Blackstone later poetically described perpetual succession in a corporation thus:

> [F]or all the individual members that have existed from the foundation to the present time, or that shall ever hereafter exist, are but one person in Law, a person that never dies: in like manner as the river Thames is still the same river, though the parts which compose it are changing every instant.[8]

The Company itself could exist potentially in perpetuity.

The most significant feature, relating to the ability to sue or be sued, and enter into transactions using a seal, was the fact that the English East India Company was a *persona ficta* or artificial legal person. Business corporations were a subset of the corporation form used for multiple public purposes. In 1612, in *The Case of Sutton's Hospital*,[9] Coke CJ had held that all common law corporations existed in the abstract separate from their members. Legal personhood was not based on the underlying members: the English East India Company as a business corporation was a *persona ficta* existing in the abstract as a legal person in its own right.

The Company was also based on another abstract concept – the Corporate Fund. The innovation of double-entry bookkeeping had entered England in the middle of the sixteenth century. Double-entry bookkeeping had the effect that the Joint Stock or Corporate Fund of the Company that was seeded by the capital of shareholders was separate from those shareholders for accounting purposes. As a result of its separate *persona ficta* status and double-entry bookkeeping, the English East India Company was therefore a separate legal and accounting entity from its shareholders.

[6] CT Carr, *Select Charters of Trading Companies, 1530–1707*, vol XXVIII (B Quaritch, 1913) xii.
[7] ibid xii.
[8] W Blackstone and J Chitty, *Commentaries on the Laws of England*, vol 1 (W Walker, 1826) ch XVIII 468.
[9] *The Case of Sutton's Hospital* (1612) 10 Co Rep 23a, 77 ER 960.

III. PROPERTY VERSUS SOCIAL ENTITY

Two long-standing conceptions dominate contemporary thinking about what a modern corporation or company is. Former Delaware Chancellor William T Allen described them as the property conception and the social entity conception.[10]

In Allen's property conception, the company is the private property of shareholders. This model is favoured by many law-and-economics scholars. According to Allen, 'The corporation's purpose is to advance the purposes of these owners (predominantly to increase their wealth), and the function of directors, as agents of the owners, is faithfully to advance the financial interests of the owners.'[11] The company itself is no more than a nexus of contracts between participants. Allen notes that the property model is currently the dominant academic paradigm of the corporation. '[I]n its most radical form, the corporation tends to disappear, transformed from a substantial institution into just a relatively stable corner of the market in which autonomous property owners freely contract'[12] with shareholders the residual owners of the firm.

In Allen's social entity conception, the modern company is not the private property of shareholders. The company is a social institution that is not wholly private as it also has a public purpose. Its existence depends on government concurrence through the act of incorporation. The attributes of a corporation, juridical or legal personality, limited liability and perpetual life are derived from the state rather than privately acquired through contract. This conception provides ballast to arguments that a company depends on a social licence to operate and is under a duty in some sense to all those interested in or affected by the corporation.

In the social entity conception, the corporation is capable of bearing legal and moral obligations:

> The corporation comes into being and continues as a legal entity only with governmental concurrence. The legal institutions of government grant a corporation its juridical personality, its characteristic limited liability, and its perpetual life. This conception sees this public facilitation as justified by the state's interest in promoting the general welfare. Thus, corporate purpose can be seen as including the advancement of the general welfare. The board of directors' duties extend beyond assuring investors a fair return, to include a duty of loyalty, in some sense, to all those interested in or affected by the corporation.[13]

As Allen concludes, '[t]o law and economics scholars, who have been so influential in academic corporate law, this model is barely coherent and dangerously wrong'.[14]

[10] WT Allen, 'Our Schizophrenic Conception of the Business Corporation' (1992) 14 *Cardozo Law Review* 261, 264.

[11] ibid 265.

[12] ibid (footnotes omitted).

[13] ibid.

[14] ibid.

Should the company be operated in the interests of shareholders (the property conception) or in its stakeholders' interests (the social entity conception)? Who ultimately has management decision rights: the directors, or the shareholders? Relatedly, is the company governed constitutionally through the general meeting or the board? Who owns the corporation: its shareholders, or does the corporation itself as a legal person have property rights? Is the modern company the private property of shareholders, or is the modern company a social entity and therefore not wholly private?

These dichotomous questions are long-standing. Other fundamental questions relate to the source of corporateness or corporate personality. Is the corporateness or status as a legal person of a modern company ultimately derived from and based on its shareholders, or is it derived from the state? If the former, does it follow that the company is the private property of shareholders? If the latter, is it a social entity that belongs to no one? Even more fundamentally, what sort of legal person is the modern company?

Entities used for business have always been an interweaving of the public and the private, even before recognition that there was such a thing as a public–private divide. Corporateness was originally regarded as political, with a requirement that it be derived from the Crown or Parliament through charters, letters patent or statutory instruments. As discussed in section II, Sir Edward Coke, in 1612 in *The Case of Sutton's Hospital*,[15] determined that corporations are *persona ficta*, artificial legal persons created through a concession by the Crown. A step in the transition to the modern company was the use of Joint Stock Funds in chartered trading corporations like the English East India Company, with the Joint Stock Fund becoming permanent capital. Those trading corporations were clearly public organisations chartered for a public purpose, and were therefore closer to the social entity conception.

Property conceptions dominated in the eighteenth and nineteenth centuries. The Bubble Act of 1720 made it difficult to obtain corporate charters and therefore for the company to be a *persona ficta* or legal person. Attempts were made to create companies using contracts, with the innovation of settling the Joint Stock or Corporate Fund on a trust through a deed of settlement. That settlement achieved legal separation of the Joint Stock Fund to some extent; one of the key features of the modern company. Even though legally they were always recognised to be a form of partnership, these contractual deed-of-settlement companies, rather than chartered business corporations, were the focus of the seminal case law in the period. That case law established the foundations of company law that remain with us today. Economically, the deed-of-settlement company and the chartered business corporation were essentially the same. Both forms were called companies in the period, causing confusion about the nature of the corporate form.

[15] *The Case of Sutton's Hospital* (n 9).

An understanding of the modern company as contractually based on and, therefore, the property of shareholders, persisted in the mid-nineteenth century when general incorporation statutes first made incorporation freely available. A company incorporated through a general incorporation statute was widely understood to be based on an association of shareholders. Incorporation, therefore, was not considered to create legal corporations like the chartered business corporations of the seventeenth and eighteenth centuries. However, by the end of the nineteenth century, the courts had formed the view that the combined effects of the process of incorporation and statutory limited liability for shareholders meant that the company was a separate entity from its shareholders for both accounting and legal purposes.[16] That is, English law reached the position that a company incorporated under general incorporation legislation was not simply an association of shareholders operating as a company, with legal personhood a fiction based on those shareholders. The *persona ficta*, the artificial legal person that is a separate legal entity from its shareholders at the moment of incorporation, had emerged again.

So what is a modern company? In 1992, when Allen wrote his paper, the social entity model was dominant. Allen nevertheless presciently foresaw a range of factors indicating that the property model might dominate how the company was conceived of in the future.[17] This has come to pass. An economic lens is applied to the modern company, with the contours of its legal form not considered significant. Contractually based law-and–economics theories, which envisage companies as the private property of current shareholders, dominate the discourse.

The recent rise of stakeholder capitalism, where boards are encouraged to look beyond maximising value for shareholders towards considering the interests of stakeholders and the environment, shows the pendulum is swinging back again. Prevailing certainties about the nature and role of the company were swept away by the disruption of the global financial crisis of 2008–09 and the coronavirus pandemic. Increasingly, the social entity conception is gaining dominance, with stakeholder capitalism apparently favoured by influential bodies like the CEO members of the American Business Roundtable[18] and influential individuals like Larry Fink of Blackrock[19] and Leo Strine, who

[16] See the discussions in PW Ireland, 'The Rise of the Limited Liability Company' (1984) 12 *International Journal of the Sociology of Law* 239; TL Alborn, *Conceiving Companies: Joint Stock Politics in Victorian England* (Routledge, 1998).

[17] Allen himself avoided saying which model he favoured. After he left the bench and moved to academia, his subsequent writings made it apparent that he was a supporter of the entity model. See WT Allen and LE Strine Jr, 'When the Existing Economic Order Deserves a Champion: The Enduring Relevance of Martin Lipton's Vision of the Corporate Law' (2005) 60 *The Business Lawyer* 1383, 1383–98.

[18] Business Roundtable, 'Statement on the Purpose of a Corporation' *Business Roundtable* (19 August 2019) at http://opportunity.businessroundtable.org/ourcommitment/.

[19] L Fink, '2021 Letter to CEOs' *BlackRock* (2021) at www.blackrock.com/corporate/investor-relations/larry-fink-ceo-letter ('The more your company can show its purpose in delivering value to

succeeded Allen as Delaware Chancellor.[20] The extent to which a real shift either has or should take place is contested. At the time of writing, evidence is emerging that value has not in fact subsequently been delivered to all stakeholders.[21]

The modern company can accommodate both conceptions. Through its historical perspective, this book highlights how the modern company incorporates public and private elements. The key public element is the social licence to operate as a *persona ficta* or artificial legal person. That artificial legal person is a subject of rights and duties. The private element is the Corporate Fund separated from shareholders and all other persons through double-entry bookkeeping. That Corporate Fund is seeded by the capital of shareholders.

Normatively, shareholders should be differentiated from other corporate stakeholders because shareholders seed the Corporate Fund with capital. Value can be extracted, transacted for, aggregated and generated by the *persona ficta* that becomes an entity as it operates in the world. Value can be valorised for the benefit of shareholders in the form of dividends. While the *persona ficta* exists, it has proprietary rights in the entity. If the company ceases to operate and the company is liquidated, the 'life' of the *persona ficta* ends. The financial value of the entity is realised for creditors, with any residual value in the Corporate Fund becoming the property of shareholders.

The modern company as a *persona ficta* can operate in the world potentially in perpetuity. A long-term perspective is possible, enhancing the opportunities to grow value over a lifespan that can extend beyond the lifespans of natural persons. The modern company, however, operates contextually and must be adaptable to maintain its social licence to operate. The company develops an externally perceived persona relating to its reputation and brand.[22] That persona has value, and it can also protect the company from regulation. Accommodating the interests of corporate stakeholders can be in the interests of the entity and Corporate Fund and, therefore, of the company in the long term.

This book shows how stakeholder capitalism can be incorporated into corporate governance. By focusing on the entity itself, stakeholderism's key pitfall can be sidestepped, namely, how a board attempts to mediate (and can easily be held accountable for mediating) the interests of diverse stakeholders.

its customers, its employees, and its communities, the better able you will be to compete and deliver long-term, durable profits for shareholders.').

[20] LE Strine Jr, 'Restoration: The Role Stakeholder Governance Must Play in Recreating a Fair and Sustainable American Economy – A Reply to Professor Rock' (2021) 76 *The Business Lawyer* 397.

[21] LA Bebchuk and R Tallarita, 'The Illusory Promise of Stakeholder Governance' (2020) 106 *Cornell Law Review* 91.

[22] MM Blair, 'Corporate Personhood and the Corporate Persona Persona' [2013] *University of Illinois Law Review* 785.

IV. THE AGENCY PROBLEM

Recognition of agency problems for shareholders inherent in the corporate form threads its way through the study of the history of the corporation. Adam Smith in 1776, in *The Wealth of Nations*,[23] identified the problem. Jensen and Meckling[24] in 1976 pathologised the apparent misalignment of the interests of current shareholders and corporate managers as the agency problem that the authors of *The Anatomy of Corporate Law* describe as a central focus of corporate law.[25]

Economic agency theory focuses primarily on the company from the perspective of shareholders. The legal form of the company itself is reduced to either a nexus of contracts, or a nexus for contracts. Much current law-and-economics thinking stems from legal realism where there is a scepticism about traditional legal concepts and baselines. However, explaining the modern company requires more than an economic analysis of the law that does not take the law itself seriously. The risk with ignoring the law is that the significance of key legal characteristics is not sufficiently recognised, including, in particular, the *persona ficta* concept. As one commentator points out, 'the challenges of managing complexity often calls for concepts that may seem more "metaphysical" than the Realists and their successors would countenance'.[26]

This book everts the law-and-economics perspective to bring back into focus the company as a legal entity in its own right. By focusing on the historical development of business corporations and Joint Stock Companies, and the evolution of their key characteristics, this book highlights a critical point regarding the company. A modern company is not merely a proxy for its shareholders. Tracing its development reveals that it did not evolve merely to prioritise current shareholders by incentivising governing bodies to equate their own interests with those of current shareholders. Instead, juridical personhood, the evolution of permanent share capital, the use of double-entry bookkeeping to separate and then identify and measure return on capital, combined with the shift to a board with significant management powers and a duty to act in the interests of shareholders as a whole, gave rise to a legally distinct commercial and legal entity based on a Corporate Fund. That entity was not equated with, and dominated by the interests of, its current shareholders.

The historical perspective adopted highlights the significance of Joint Stock or, as it is termed in this book, the Corporate Fund. Accounting principles also

[23] A Smith, *An Inquiry into the Nature and Causes of the Wealth of Nations*, vol 3, 5th edn (W Strahan and T Cadell, 1789).

[24] MC Jensen and WH Meckling, 'Theory of the Firm: Managerial Behavior, Agency Costs and Ownership Structure' (1976) 3 *Journal of Financial Economics* 305.

[25] R Kraakman et al, *The Anatomy of Corporate Law: A Comparative and Functional Approach*, 3rd edn (Oxford University Press, 2017).

[26] HE Smith, 'Complexity and the Cathedral: Making Law and Economics More Calabresian' (2019) 48 *European Journal of Law and Economics* 43, 46.

matter when we seek to understand the modern company. Pacioli's invention of double-entry bookkeeping enabled the Corporate Fund to be separated from the shareholders. It provided the architecture that isolates the Corporate Fund in the *persona ficta*.

V. *THE MAKING OF THE MODERN COMPANY*

The Making of the Modern Company argues for recognition that the modern company is an amalgam of key features drawn from antecedent forms. As such the modern company is neither wholly the private property of current shareholders, nor is it just a social entity. The hybrid nature of the modern company enables it to accommodate the two apparently dichotomous conceptions. This book will illustrate how the key features developed and came together in the course of two distinct historical cycles in Anglo company law, which ended up at a surprisingly similar point.

The first cycle was the development of the chartered business corporation in the first half of the seventeenth century. The English East India Company had by 1657 evolved into a modern company with permanent capital and a governing body of professional managers charged with acting in the interests of the company. The second cycle focuses on developments in the limited liability company in the second half of the nineteenth century following the enactment of the general incorporation statutes. By the beginning of the twentieth century, the Joint Stock Company contractually based on shareholders had transitioned to becoming an artificial legal person that was a separate legal entity from its shareholders based on a Corporate Fund.

The first 12 chapters of the book trace the source and integration of the key features over the two historical cycles. Chapters 13 to 16 draw on the historical analysis to highlight insights that bear significantly on contemporary debates over the nature, role and governance of modern companies.

Chapter 2 sets out business forms that emerged from the Middle Ages onwards. It highlights the key features derived from the legal forms of the business corporation and the contractual Joint Stock Company that were brought together in the English East India Company in 1657. The sources of those features are identified. There is particular focus on the two key features: the company as a *persona ficta* or artificial legal person, and the Joint Stock Fund separated for accounting purposes from shareholders.

In the following three chapters, discussion turns to the English East India Company. Chapter 3 traces the innovations in financing that took place in the Company in the first half of the seventeenth century. Chapter 4 shows how the investing generality as small shareholders used the innovation of the general meeting to drive through changes to the governance of the English East India Company that ensured accountability of the governing body to the interests of shareholders held in the Company. Chapter 5 describes what happened once the English East India Company had acquired all the key characteristics of a modern company: rapid and dazzling success in the first half-century, and then governance shortcomings and extensive private trade by employees at all levels, leading to its transitioning to becoming an instrument of government rather than a modern company.

This first set of chapters demonstrate how the modern company emerged sooner than is currently understood. In chapters 6 and 7, the discussion turns to the possible emergence, in the chartered business corporations, of modern features of the modern company at an earlier time than supposed. The focus of chapter 6 is on directors' duties, most particularly on the duty to act in good faith and the best interests of the company, which, arguably, has its origins in the oath directors swore on taking up office. Chapter 7 examines the liability of shareholders of business corporations, showing how a consequence of the corporation's being a separate legal entity to its shareholders, was that shareholders were not liable for the debts of the business corporation.

Chapter 8 moves to the eighteenth century with a focus on the deed-of-settlement company as a form of contractual company that became significant after the Bubble Act of 1720 made corporate charters for business difficult to obtain. Whilst acknowledging that the contractual form, modified by shareholders' settling assets on a trust through a deed of settlement, offered many of the advantages of the corporate form, the chapter concludes that the lack of comprehensive limited liability for shareholders, and challenges in holding directors accountable, made the contractual deed-of-settlement company a second-best form.

The focus in chapters 9 and 10 is on the general incorporation statutes, and the impact of the combination of incorporation and statutory limited liability on the corporate form. It is clear that the statutes were intended to legitimise the contractual form. Over the course of the second half of the nineteenth century, though, legal separation followed the separation for accounting purposes of capital in the company. *Salomon v Salomon & Co Ltd*[27] is rightly recognised as the end point of the process of recognition that the modern company had become a separate legal entity from its shareholders, not contractually based on those shareholders. Key milestones in that transition are set out in chapter 10.

In chapter 11, an economic lens is applied to the modern company, focusing on the nineteenth century and the financial success, through size and scale, of United States (US) and German corporations when compared with English companies. Chapter 12 sets out reasons why the transition to the modern form took longer in England, suggesting that a combination of factors, which included the financing structures, attitudes to limited liability and the legacy of the eighteenth century contractual form, may have contributed.

The first 12 chapters of *The Making of the Modern Company* thus focus on developments in England in the period leading up to the end of the nineteenth

[27] *Salomon v Salomon & Co Ltd* [1897] AC 22 (HL).

century and the recognition in *Salomon v Salomon & Co Ltd* that the modern company was a *persona ficta* and a separate legal entity from its shareholders. The concluding chapters of the book set out consequences of these insights.

Chapter 13 considers the key features of the modern company through theoretical lenses. The Corporate Fund, the *persona ficta* and corporate legal personality are considered in depth. In chapter 14, the discussion turns to the company as an entity, and its relationship to the firm and the organisation. Chapter 15 considers the significance of the insights for corporate governance and the role of the board of the modern company, adopting a constitutional framework. In chapter 16, the focus turns to the evolving debate around corporations and sustainability, with the perils and potential inherent in the modern company as a perpetual corporation considered.

The modern company has been termed 'among humanity's most ingenious inventions'.[28] Inherent in the modern company is the potential to vastly enrich both shareholders and stakeholders by the creation of value that may extend beyond the financial. Nobel Prize winner and President of Columbia University, Nicholas Murray Butler, famously described the limited liability company as 'the greatest single discovery of modern times … [e]ven steam and electricity … would be reduced to comparative impotence without it'.[29] Professor Gower, in the leading UK work on company law, similarly commented that '[u]nquestionably the limited liability company has been a major instrument in making possible the industrial and commercial development which have occurred throughout the world'.[30]

The Making of the Modern Company does not aspire to be a history of the modern company or a critique of the form. Instead, turning points in the historical development of the fundamental features and key characteristics of the modern corporate form are set out. The book highlights how the combination of these features enables the corporate form to reach its potential as an unparalleled aggregator and generator of value. To put it in more colloquial terms, these features are the 'secret sauce' of modern companies. At the same time, considering the company through both historical and contemporary lenses compels us to recognise its potency and potential as a force for harm as well as value creation.

[28] YN Harari, *Sapiens*: A Brief History of Humankind (Vintage Books, 2014) 32.

[29] WM Fletcher, *Cyclopedia of the Law of Corporations*, vol 1 (Callaghan, 1917–1920) pt 21.

[30] LCB Gower, DD Prentice and BG Pettet, *Principles of Modern Company Law*, 5th edn (Sweet & Maxwell, 1992) 70.

Part One

Development of the Modern Company

2

Persona Ficta *and Joint Stock*

I. TWO KINDS OF LEGAL ORGANISATION

LEGAL ORGANISATIONS EITHER are primarily based on the people who comprise them, or derive their corporate status from the state in some way. The distinction is of long standing. In Roman law there were two kinds of association: the *societas* and the *universitas*. The *universitas* derived its legal status from the state. The *societas* referred to a general category of contractual relationships between members.[1]

The assets of the *societas* were owned by its members based on the terms of the contract that bound them. The links between the *societas*, the modern partnership, and also the contractual and property conception of the company are apparent,[2] although it cannot be assumed that each form did not arise spontaneously and independently.

Also, the *societas* differed from the modern partnership in key aspects. A *societas* established obligations between contracting parties to make contributions towards a shared goal, but did not affect third parties. Each partner in a *societas* had to agree to a contract with a third party to be bound by that contract, so there was no mutual agency. Liability of partners was not joint and several; it was pro rata. Roman law did not distinguish between obligations and assets of the *societas* and those of its members.[3] Therefore, there was no weak form entity shielding of the assets held by the *societas*, as there is with the modern partnership,[4] where a 'fund' holds the assets of the partnership separately from the partners.[5]

[1] M Weber and L Kaelber (trs), *The History of Commercial Partnerships in the Middle Ages: The First Complete English Edition of Weber's Prelude to The Protestant Ethic and the Spirit of Capitalism and Economy and Society* (Rowman & Littlefield Publishers, 2003) 60.

[2] R Scruton and J Finnis, 'Corporate Persons' (1989) 63 *Proceedings of the Aristotelian Society, Supplementary Volumes* 239, 242.

[3] See the discussion in Weber and Kaelber (n 1) 54.

[4] H Hansmann, R Kraakman and R Squire, 'Law and the Rise of the Firm' (2006) 119 *Harvard Law Review* 1333, 1356, 1358. Unlike the *societas*, in the *peculiam* a master provided his son with assets. Unlike the *societas*, the *peculium* business exhibited a degree of asset partitioning.

[5] Weber and Kaelber (n 1) 56.

The *universitas*, as a legal entity, could hold property. It had rights and obligations that were distinct from those of its members.[6] The Romans had the idea of corporate separateness, which they may have derived from the Greeks.[7]

II. EARLY CORPORATE ENTERPRISES

A. Towns and Guilds

Legal systems of the Middle Ages enshrined a similar fundamental distinction between an enterprise with corporate separateness, on one hand, and an enterprise based on its constituent members, on the other hand. Roman law was drawn on, with what became corporations being called *universitas* for much of the period.

Loose associations of persons sought to be treated as collective entities and recognised as corporate and legal persons.[8] Examples were towns and guilds, with commercial corporate life beginning in towns as part of the struggle of private individuals to free themselves from ecclesiastical, feudal and political control.[9] Towns and old Saxon boroughs had franchises conferred on them by charter that could include the right of perpetual succession, the right to sue and be sued as a group, the right to use a common seal and the right to elect officials.[10] In the fourteenth and fifteenth centuries, 'the legal crystallization of these characteristics contributed heavily to the common law doctrine of corporations'.[11]

Guilds (or gilds) were societies of traders usually drawn from within a borough.[12] Members had the right to share in the trade at a sufficient level to earn a living by their own individual efforts.[13] Guilds were freely formed in Anglo Saxon times, with the dominance of agriculture in the period prior to the Crusades meaning there was little scope for other forms of business association.[14]

[6] Scruton and Finnis (n 2) 242.

[7] JK Angell and S Ames, *Treatise on the Law of Private Corporations Aggregate*, 7th edn (Little, Brown, 1861) 34–35.

[8] The doctrine of the German fellowship (*Genossenschaft*) developed, where corporate status can be obtained by a resolution of members given recognition by the Crown or the state. In the early Middle Ages, some corporations formed freely by their members were recognised as juridical persons. The City of London Corporation is the most famous example of a Corporation that exists without a known charter. AB Levy, *Private Corporations and their Control* (Routledge, 1950) 12. The real entity theory of the modern company expounded by Gierke and others is based on the recognition understanding of corporate personality: see ch 13 for further discussion.

[9] CA Cooke, *Corporation, Trust and Company: An Essay in Legal History* (Harvard University Press, 1951) 19.

[10] ibid 21. There was little standardisation in the charter until the Municipal Corporations Act (5 & 6 Wm IV, c 76).

[11] Cooke (n 9) 21.

[12] ibid 22.

[13] ibid.

[14] Levy (n 8) 13.

In England, guilds needed charters after the Norman Conquest.[15] Membership of a guild, which was the exclusive local organisation of a particular trade, carried with it the right to exercise the calling within the town limits. The main function of guilds was the supervision and protection of their members, with the activities of members closely regulated, meaning boroughs and guilds were regarded as synonymous forms of organisation by some.[16] Guilds were, however, economic organs that were subservient to the mayor and council as the governing bodies of the town or borough.[17]

B. The Early Corporation

The concept of a corporation with a separate pool of assets and separate legal personality is 'distinctly European', even though its precise origins are contested.[18] England in the Middle Ages was awash with forms of corporation used for ecclesiastical (religious) and lay purposes, with the latter further divided into eleemosynary (charitable) and civil purposes.[19] In the fifteenth century, words betokening corporateness became common.[20] The term 'corporation' appears in the Year Books from 1429, the word 'corporate' from 1408, 'incorporate' from 1439, and 'body corporate' in a 1481 report[21] as well as in a statute of 1461. That statute also contains the first use of the word 'corporation' in a statute.[22]

[15] ibid 13.

[16] Quoted in Madox: Firma Burgi, 29 (as cited in Cooke (n 9) 21, fn 7). An incorporated town and a 'gidated' town are regarded as synonymous. See the discussion in Cooke (n 9) 21–24.

[17] RR Formoy, *The Historical Foundations of Modern Company Law* (Sweet and Maxwell, 1923) 3.

[18] D Gindis, 'Conceptualizing the Business Corporation: Insights from History' (2020) 16 *Journal of Institutional Economics* 569.

[19] Cooke (n 9) 51. See also JP Davis, *Corporations: A Study of the Origin and Development of Great Business Combinations and of Their Relation to the Authority of the State* (GP Putnam's Sons, 1905) vol 1. Municipal and ecclesiastical corporations existed after the Middle Ages and were numerous throughout Europe. Levy (n 8) 12. The Edwardian Statutes of Mortmain, aimed at limiting the land held by corporate bodies, were extended during the reign of Richard II to include 'Mayors, bailiffs, and commons of cities, boroughs and other towns that have a perpetual commonalty'. CT Carr, *The General Principles of the Law of Corporations: (Being the Yorke Prize Essay for the Year 1902)* (Cambridge University Press, 1902) xii.

[20] Such as 'commonitas, perpetua, corpus political et corporatum'. Carr (n 19) xiii.

[21] Quoted in Mich 8 Hen 6, pl 2, fo 1a–1b (1429.086) (corporation); Mich 10 Hen 4, pl 5, fo 3b (1408.005) (corporate); Mich 18 Hen 6, pl 6, fo 21a–22a (1439.006) (incorporate); Pasch 21 Edw 4, pl 21, fo 7a–7b (1481.029) (body corporate) (as cited in DJ Seipp, 'Formalism and Realism in Fifteenth-Century English Law: Bodies Corporate and Bodies Natural' in PA Brand and J Getzler (eds), *Judges and Judging in the History of the Common Law and Civil Law: From Antiquity to Modern Times* (Cambridge University Press, 2012) ch 2, endnote no 11).

[22] Quoted in 1 Edw 4, ch 1 (1461) (as cited in Seipp (n 21) ch 2, endnote no 10). Seipp says '[w]hen distinguished from these collective bodies, we ordinary human beings were called bodies natural, private persons, singular persons, sole persons, natural persons, single persons, common persons, natural men, and material men'.

C. The Regulated Company

A charter bestowing incorporation and status as a legal person was petitioned for as a grant by the Crown.[23] Regulated Companies were chartered by the Crown, and legally were a form of corporation that preceded corporations operating with Joint Stock. Regulated Companies evolved from the guilds of merchants and craftsmen created through Royal Charters.[24] The evolution of the English wool trade contributed to the break-up of guilds, with national organisations, the Company of the Staple and, later, the Company of Merchant Adventurers, involved in cloth export, replacing local guilds. In Regulated Companies, each member traded on his own behalf subject only to the by-laws of the company itself.[25]

Regulated Companies did not trade themselves: they regulated the trade they were concerned with.[26] They had the public purpose of administering revenues.[27] Regulated Companies were not, therefore, similar to modern companies; they were more akin to guilds and, like the guilds, they were an instrument of control.[28] These chartered corporations regulated crafts such as shoemaking, masonry and carpentry.[29] At most, Regulated Companies were, therefore, part of the transition to the modern form, because the corporation form was used for purposes connected with commerce for the first time.

D. Business Corporation Charters

It took some time for grants to merchants to contain words that denoted incorporation proper for merchants and traders.[30] The first known charter of the Company of Merchant Adventurers was granted in 1407.[31] The Patent of Henry VII to the Merchant Adventurers at Calais is broadly similar to later charters for merchants and traders. Rather than creating a body politic and corporate, as later corporate charters did, the charter gives and grants 'unto our said Merchant Adventurers power, License, Libertie, and Authority' to meet in

[23] The grants were initially given by the Crown and later by either or both the Crown and Parliament. Incorporation could also be granted through letters patent, and in the 18th century by a discrete statute.

[24] Levy (n 8) 13. In Anglo-Saxon times, guilds could be freely formed without a charter, but after the Norman Conquest a charter was needed.

[25] Formoy (n 17) 4.

[26] Levy (n 8) 16.

[27] Cooke (n 9) 35.

[28] ibid 37.

[29] ibid 38.

[30] Carr (n 19) xii.

[31] Levy (n 8) 12–15.

Calais, assemble and choose a Governor, Deputy Governor and 24 Assistants to rule the Merchants. From their inception, therefore, and in common with other forms of corporation and with towns and boroughs, members had the power to elect their governing body.[32]

III. EARLY FUNDS

A. The Emergence of Investment Capital

The period between the fourteenth and sixteenth centuries saw the emergence of a commercial class and, by the sixteenth century, an increase in the amount of money available for business.[33] Mercantile families accumulated wealth over several generations that became funds available for investment.[34] Usury laws restricting lending meant the only way funds could be invested was through investors' taking on the risks and responsibilities of a partnership.[35]

Initially there was no concept of capital as something that should be kept intact,[36] with the word not used in relation to companies in the sixteenth century.[37] Business was treated as a system of 'contracts and expectancies'.[38] In a *societas* partnership, all partners contributed equally to losses and shared equally in profits, with all responsible equally for the debts of the firm.[39]

Individuals combining to create a fund that engaged in an enterprise and then divided up the profits was a different type of economic activity from the guild, which provided an umbrella for individual enterprise within a town or borough. The size of the partnership funds, whether based on money or tools or goods, led to an increase in the scale of business. The expansion of markets beyond towns and boroughs contributed to the breakdown of control by guilds. Guilds became private associations through the second half of the sixteenth century. The fraternal system of brotherhood based on the relationship of master and apprentice was replaced by master and servant, with a resulting disparity in wealth.[40]

[32] Quoted in Patent of Hen VII to the Merchant Adventurers at Calais (as cited in G Cawston and AH Keane, *Early Chartered Companies (AD 1296–1858)* (Edward Arnold, 1896) 250).

[33] Cooke (n 9) 40.

[34] ibid 41–42.

[35] ibid 45.

[36] WR Scott, *The Constitution and Finance of English, Scottish, and Irish Joint-Stock Companies to 1720*, vol 1 (Cambridge University Press, 1912) 60.

[37] Formoy (n 17) 6. See the discussion of the emergence of the term in accountancy treatises and in the early history of the English East India Company, in E Cannan, 'Early History of the Term Capital' (1921) 35 *Quarterly Journal of Economics* 469.

[38] Cooke (n 9) 40.

[39] ibid 46.

[40] ibid 37.

B. Early Privateers and Joint Stock

English company history has a colourful link with privateering. A privateer needed enough equipment and supplies for a six-month voyage,[41] so investing for a period was required. Even with small ships, a type of Joint Stock system of investment was used. Initially stock could be money, or it could be other forms of stock provided by investors, such as goods or even the supply of the ship itself. Over time the term 'stock' also came to mean the whole outlay.[42]

Men would work for their 'part', which consisted of a share of a base rate as well as 'pillage' upon completion (all goods and valuables found). The specific rules for how this would be split up were based on position and hierarchy, with rules for pillage that were broadly similar to modern rules relating to paying dividends to shareholders.[43]

Traders also required investment for more than a short period. Unless the investor went on the trading or privateering voyage, the investor could not be actively involved in the enterprise. Yet no distinction was made between active operating partners and inactive investing partners. The *societas* partnership was not, therefore, the ideal business form.

In a form of partnership called a *commenda*, used originally in Italian maritime trade, one of the partners supplied the capital either in goods or money without taking part in the venture, and the other partner operated the venture.[44] Despite the clear advantages of the *commenda* form for investors in trade, privateering and other ventures that endured over time, the form emerged or was adopted in England later than in some Continental countries. A clear advantage of the *commenda* form was the use of Joint Stock Funds separated from partners for accounting purposes through double-entry bookkeeping. Double-entry bookkeeping was adopted in England later than in Italy and Holland, arguably explaining the lag in English business practice.[45]

C. Double-Entry Bookkeeping and Joint Stock

Double-entry bookkeeping involves an accounting system that requires every entry in an account to have a corresponding entry in another account. Thus, investors' capital contribution would be shown in a capital or equity account, and a corresponding entry in an asset account of the firm would show an amount equal to the capital contributed as an asset of the firm. The business of the firm

[41] KR Andrews, *English Privateering Voyages to the West Indies, 1588–1595* (Cambridge University Press for the Hakluyt Society, 1959) 20.

[42] Scott (n 36) 60.

[43] Andrews (n 41) 26.

[44] Weber and Kaelber (n 1) 66–68.

[45] Cooke (n 9) 46.

is on the assets side. This system, therefore, draws a clear distinction between investors' investments, on the one hand, and the firm's financial resources, on the other hand. From a commercial and accounting perspective, the firm has a distinct financial existence.

Joint Stock Funds are one of the foundations of modern capitalism. The development of Joint Stock that was perpetual and separate from shareholders for accounting purposes[46] was facilitated by double-entry bookkeeping,[47] which emerged in Italy in the sixteenth century and was first used for forms of commercial partnership. Pacioli published *Summa de Arithmetica, Geometria, Proportioni et Proportionalita*, a 615-page work that set out the double-entry bookkeeping method, in 1494.[48]

In 2019 *The Economist* said:

> The book was revolutionary on more than one count. It integrated computation using Hindu-Arabic numerals with the logic of classic Greek geometry; it was written in the Italian of the marketplace rather than Latin; and it was circulated in large numbers thanks to the new technology of printing. Yet its greatest significance lay in a slim 'how to' chapter that described the double-entry accounting system used by Venetian merchants. With examples from dealers in butter to lemons to silk, Pacioli set out the method for tracking income and expenditure and the calculation of net profit or loss, which for the first time allowed an immediate snapshot of a firm's financial position. This slim section would facilitate the birth of the modern corporation.[49]

Summa de Arithmetica was not translated and published in England until 1543, delaying the use of Joint Stock Funds in England.[50] Joint Stock Funds were first used in partnerships. Double-entry bookkeeping was necessary for a separation of the accounts of the firm from the capitalist accounts of the capital partners.[51] Capital is creditor and cash is debtor.[52]

The concept of the firm entered European practice in the sixteenth and early seventeenth centuries. The use of double-entry bookkeeping meant that the firm as a business enterprise was considered in some ways as separate from the partners.[53] Max Weber writes about the separate fund of the partnership in European partnerships, and the relation of the separate fund to personal creditors and the partners' personal assets.[54] The form survives as the modern

[46] Weber and Kaelber (n 1) 26–27.

[47] ibid.

[48] Pacioli was a true Renaissance Man who worked with Leonardo Da Vinci on a book on perspective that informed Da Vinci's *The Last Supper*.

[49] 'A revolutionary treatise goes on the block: The first folio of finance' *The Economist* (London, 4 June 2019) at www.economist.com/books-and-arts/2019/06/06/a-revolutionary-treatise-goes-on-the-block.

[50] Cooke (n 9) 46.

[51] ibid.

[52] J Gleeson-White, *Double Entry: How the merchants of Venice shaped the modern world – and how their invention could make or break the planet* (Allen & Unwin, 2011) 156, 101.

[53] Cooke (n 9) 48.

[54] Weber and Kaelber (n 1) 115–25.

partnership. The protection provided to the partnership business as a fund has been termed 'weak form entity shielding', meaning that creditors of the firm have claims on the assets of the firm in priority to the personal creditors of the owners.[55]

IV. CONTRACTUAL JOINT STOCK COMPANIES

A. The Emergence of Contractual Joint Stock Companies

Societas, or partnerships based on the partners who comprised them, existed in parallel with *Universitas* or corporations in the Middle Ages. Partnerships that used double-entry bookkeeping to separate the partnership fund from the partners emerged in England in Elizabethan times. As private partnerships, they were not chartered by the Crown and were not, therefore, corporations. Although legally a form of partnership, they were called Joint Stock Companies. To distinguish them from chartered corporations, the form is described in this book as the contractual Joint Stock Company.

Contractual Joint Stock Companies differed from *societas* partnerships because of the separation for accounting purposes of a partnership fund from the partners as the stock of the business.[56] For partners as stockholders, the stock of each partner became a figure moving from 'balance sheet to balance sheet representing the claim of that partner to or the claim upon him of the firm's balance between assets and liabilities'.[57]

B. The Origin of the Joint Stock Fund

A contractual Joint Stock Company is legally a partnership based on a shared Joint Stock Fund. Some commentators, termed receptionists,[58] consider the

[55] J Armour et al, 'What Is Corporate Law?' in R Kraakman (ed), *The Anatomy of Corporate Law*, 3rd edn (Oxford University Press, 2017) 6.

[56] The separation was significant. As CA Cooke described the emergence and subsequent development, the firm's books were not the accounts of the partners as individuals. With the spread of the double-entry system, the notion of the balance sheet as a recurring statement of the assets and liabilities emerged around 1608, increasing the separation of the partner and the business. Cooke (n 9) 48.

[57] ibid 49.

[58] WS Holdsworth and others, *A History of English Law*, vol VIII (Sweet & Maxwell, 1903–72) 207; W Mitchell, 'Early Forms of Partnership' in *Select Essays in Anglo-American Legal History*, vol III (Little, Brown, 1909) 194; CT Carr, *Select Charters of Trading Companies, AD 1530–1707*, vol XXVIII (B Quaritch, 1913) xxi (also cited by M Schmitthoff, 'The Origin of the Joint-Stock Company' (1939) 3 *The University of Toronto Law Journal* 74, 74–75 fn 2, fn 3, fn 4); Levy (n 8) 8–9; RL Reynolds, 'Origins of Modern Business Enterprise: Medieval Italy' (1952) 12 *Journal of Economic History* 350.

English form of contractual Joint Stock Company was derived from the associations that were organised forms of commercial partnership emerging initially in Italy before spreading to the rest of Western Europe.[59]

St George's Bank of Genoa, founded in 1407 from the consolidation of the public debt of Genoa, exhibited some characteristics of a contractual Joint Stock Company. A fund that operated as a trading institution was created and divided into shares. Initially it preserved the character of a loan. In 1419, when the agreed 7 per cent interest rate could not be paid, 'lenders' accepted a lower rate varying according to the yield of the revenue. Receptionists argue that the Joint Stock principle was born.[60]

Evolutionists consider the contractual Joint Stock Company to be indigenous to England.[61] Schmitthoff argues that its development was a continuity leading from the guild to the Regulated Company and then to the Joint Stock form. That continuity drew on the Germanic concept of corporateness of a communal and self-governing group of citizens derived from guilds and boroughs, and the concept of joint action as seen in the medieval fellowship and then the civilian partnership. The English Joint Stock Company would therefore be a product of collectivism based on the people who are part of it. Schmitthoff contrasts the Joint Stock Company with the Italian *compera*, which is based on an association of individual bondholders.[62] As Schmitthoff saw it:

> The organisation of the English Joint Stock company was designed to afford concentration of means and powers to the explorers who set out to discover trade routes hitherto unknown. The compera never emancipated itself from its origin as an ingenious and well-secured money-lending device.[63]

Scott rejects Italian influence, because Italian commercial and financial relations had declined by the time the contractual Joint Stock Company emerged in England.[64] Schmitthoff argues that receptionists must prove a structural continuity between the Italian Genoan Bank and the English contractual Joint Stock Companies. He also asserts that[65] St George's Bank of Genoa was an organisation that had 'developed which was apt to become the nucleus of a fundamental

[59] See, eg, AB Levy, who says that when the Crusades led to a revival of trade with the Near East, greater capital resources were needed. The dominant business form became the partnership. Associations organised as forms of commercial partnership, emerging initially in Italy before spreading to the rest of Western Europe. Levy (n 8) 8–9.

[60] Schmitthoff (n 58) 74, 78.

[61] Scott (n 36); AA Berle, *Studies in the Law of Corporation Finance* (Callaghan and Company, 1928) 2–15; HW Ballantine, *Manual of Corporation Law and Practice* (Callaghan and Company, 1930) 2–7; Schmitthoff (n 58) 74.

[62] Schmitthoff (n 58) 74, 79. German fellowship (*Genossenschaft*) is based on an assumption that public bodies, guilds and voluntary associations could be formed freely, and obtain corporate status by resolution of their members: Levy (n 8) 12.

[63] Schmitthoff (n 58) 74, 80.

[64] Scott (n 36) 13.

[65] Schmitthoff (n 58) 74, 76.

and universal legal principle but which, owing to the peculiarities of its origin, remained an isolated and barren phenomenon'.[66]

Solinas shows that the link and source is, in fact, the Italian, particularly Genoese, merchant community, which was regarded as a commercial and financial aristocracy within the alien communities in London in the Middle Ages.[67] That Genoese community inevitably influenced English business practice. By the end of the thirteenth century, the Italians de facto carried on most of the financial operations in England. That dominant position also allowed them to take up a powerful position in English trade.[68] Trade based in Southampton utilised Genoese carracks until the fifteenth century, when increasingly the English owned ships themselves or in partnership.[69] All this suggests that the English learned business practice and techniques from the Italians.

C. Sixteenth-Century Contractual Joint Stock Companies

The associative or collective basis of the contractual Joint Stock Company may never have been significant, despite evolutionists' view of the form as a direct descendant of fellowships and guilds.[70] The key characteristic of contractual Joint Stock Companies was not the coordination of men but the combining in the holding of shares in a Joint Stock Fund.

Over time in England, therefore, contractual Joint Stock Companies became separate accounting entities because the books of the firm were not the accounts of the partners as individuals.[71] Crucially, the later legal separation of capital from investors, discussed in later chapters, was 'supported (or perhaps led) by the notion of the business as a separate accounting entity'.[72]

Between 1560 and 1580, privateers operated using Joint Stock Funds. The use of Joint Stock Funds occasionally extended over more than one voyage. Some voyages were chartered and therefore operating within the corporate structure, as discussed in the next section.[73] Capital for an expedition had to be locked up for a much longer period of time before goods obtained in the East or America could be brought back.[74] English trading was based on what Levy called 'private daring and enterprise'.[75]

[66] ibid 74, 79.

[67] See also M Solinas, *Legal Evolution and Hybridisation: The Law of Share Transfers in England* (Intersentia, 2014) 82.

[68] ibid 83.

[69] ibid 85.

[70] CA Cooke states that 'the joint stock fund subscribed for by the members was the very essence of their association'. Cooke (n 9) 142. The evolutionists discussed above include Schmitthoff, (Schmitthoff (n 58) 74), and WR Scott (Scott (n 36) 13).

[71] Cooke (n 9) 66, 48.

[72] ibid 48.

[73] ibid 57.

[74] Levy (n 8) 17.

[75] ibid 21.

Most famous are the privateering ventures of Frobisher and Drake. These were combinations of merchants, capitalists and sailors. Queen Elizabeth I, merchants, Drake and friends were involved in the expedition of 1557. Queen Elizabeth, as Drake's secret backer, contributed capital.[76] At the end of the voyage, provision was set aside for refitting ships, wages were deducted and then net proceeds were shared out in proportion to contributions.[77] In some instances voyages would be employed for dual purposes: trade as well as prize hunting.[78] A select few official 'Privateers', such as the Earl of Cumberland and Drake, were given permission by Elizabeth I to engage the Spanish on their own account during the Spanish War of 1585 to 1604.[79]

In mercantile expeditions, the merchants provided capital in vessels, wages and provision for crew, as well as goods for sale or barter. At end of the expedition, goods were distributed or sold, expenses were defrayed and the balance was divided in proportion to the share of each member.[80]

Merchants sought a more stable form, which was provided by Joint Stock.[81] Trading using Joint Stock differed from operating through the Regulated Companies discussed in section II.C. The business was carried on by officers in the company's name. It was easier to become a member of a Joint Stock Company than a member of a Regulated Company, as membership of a Joint Stock Company was primarily based on the purchase of shares.[82]

After the Spanish War ended in 1604, many London merchants formed Joint Stocks among themselves.[83] The men who continued to operate these ventures through the seventeenth century became very wealthy, and were some of the most successful business men of the era.[84]

As a financing device for long-term voyages, Joint Stock was an advance on the partnership, because, unlike partnerships, the capital contributed by shareholders could not be withdrawn at will. Only when the voyage or venture was completed was the Joint Stock divided. In terms of capital lock in, therefore, Joint Stock was an intermediate step between partnerships and modern companies. The innovation was that shareholders gave up the right to withdraw their capital while the voyage or venture was underway, but only for that limited period.

[76] ibid 22.

[77] ibid.

[78] Andrews (n 41) 18. Elizabeth I would provide Drake with a sum of money to bolster the original capital investment in equipment. The Queen would be guaranteed a fixed-sum return, as well as priority over prizes found. These prizes were allocated based on hierarchy within the crew and then divided up dependent on how many stockholders there were.

[79] Cooke (n 9) 6.

[80] Levy (n 8) 22.

[81] ibid.

[82] ibid 23.

[83] Andrews (n 41) 20.

[84] ibid 32. Not all were successful. Of 25 documented West Indian privateering ventures, 15 were financially successful, four were very profitable and five did not meet expenses.

V. BUSINESS CORPORATIONS

A. The Emergence of Business Corporations

'The idea of using corporate association for the private gain of the members' had also emerged.[85] During the reign of Elizabeth I, 'the outline of an incorporation of traders began to be fixed'.[86] From the beginning, the grant of a corporate charter to a group of individuals was dependent on their demonstrating some public benefit that would result from the grant. Corporate status was obtained by petitioners' citing their past industry and expense, that enterprise would be advanced by a Royal Charter, and their patriotic desire for commerce, civilisation and good government.

For a period, the corporation as a legal form was a framework within which Joint Stocks were constituted for single terminating ventures. The difference between operating ventures through the Regulated Company structure (discussed in section II.C), on one hand, and using Joint Stock Funds, on the other hand, was that Joint Stock ventures were carried on by the officers in the name of the corporation, rather than by the members themselves.

Participation was easier than in the Regulated Companies and the earlier guilds. In the Regulated Companies, certain individual traders could carry out their businesses either personally or through their factors within specified limits.[87] In a corporation operating using Joint Stock Funds, only a contribution of capital was needed by members.[88]

Joint Stock Funds, therefore, were a financial device learned from the Italians, either through the Genoans or through the recently translated book by Pacioli, that was then used within the existing form of the corporation. Whether independently, intentionally or inadvertently, therefore, 'the Dutch and especially the English followed the Genoese example of combining private investment with state-granted monopoly privileges'.[89] The combination of a legal form derived from the state with a private fund seeded by money provided by investors anticipated the modern company.

B. The Russia (Muscovy) Company

The Russia (Muscovy) Company was founded in 1553 and chartered in 1555. The English had observed the Portuguese and the Spaniards being vastly

[85] Cooke (n 9) 54–55.

[86] Carr (n 58) xiii.

[87] WR Scott, *The Constitution and Finance of English, Scottish and Irish Joint-Stock Companies to 1720*, vol 2 (Cambridge University Press, 1910) 36, 'the form of government, in its essentials, was copied from the regulated company [and] it was decided that, instead of each person participating by trading on his own capital, a joint stock should be established'.

[88] Levy (n 8) 23.

[89] Hansmann, Kraakman and Squire (n 4) 1376.

enriched through trade with new countries. The Russia Company was, therefore, established to discover a north-east passage to China. Scott speculates that a Regulated Company, where everyone traded on their own behalf, would not have been thought appropriate for such distant voyages, and that a combined enterprise and stock were needed.[90] The Russia Company may therefore have been the first business trading corporation based on shares in an enduring Joint Stock Fund, if the wording of the petition for the Charter – 'a joint and united stock' – is read literally.

On the other hand, the practice in the mid-sixteenth century was to plan to terminate funds at the end of voyages, even if that was not always possible.[91] Some evidence shows that the intention may have been to have a series of independent undertakings, to keep account of each voyage and not to mingle one voyage with another.[92] However, Scott shows how calls for additional contributions were made on the original contribution of £25 for a share that lifted the nominal amount of a share from £25 to £200.[93] At that time shareholders did not have limited liability to the Joint Stock to which they subscribed, so they could be subject to extra calls.

It was recognised that the business corporation form allowed traders to operate as if they were a single person. In 1604, a Parliamentary Commission said:

> The Muscovy Company, consisting of eight score, or thereabouts, have fifteen directors, who manage the whole trade; these limit to every man the proportion of stock he shall trade for, make one purse and stock of it all, and consign it into the hands of one agent at Musco, and so again, at their return, to one agent at London … A whole Company, by this means, is become as one man.[94]

The Russia Company did not continue to operate with Joint Stock. When early voyages failed to meet expectations, losses were covered by further calls made on shareholders in the 1550s and 1560s.[95] The contemporary State Papers state that:

> In 1564 it was urged in a petition to the Privy Council that such losses had been sustained it was necessary to call up £60 per share partly to make these good, partly

[90] Scott (n 87) 36.

[91] When the initial calls on shares did not cover the high costs of establishing the new trade and losses of ships and cargo, more calls were made on shares. Scott speculates that it may have been the original intention to wind up the joint stock at the first favourable opportunity and take subscriptions for new expeditions, meaning that the Joint Stock would not have been permanent. On the other hand, a literal reading of the wording of the petition for the Charter – 'a joint and united stock' – may mean that permanent joint stock was the aim. (SA Khan, *The East India Trade in the XVIIth Century in its Political and Economic Aspects* (S Chand & Co, 1923) 3).

[92] Scott (n 87) 39.

[93] ibid 39–40.

[94] Report of Committee on the Bill for Free Trade: *Journals of the House of Commons*, I, 218 (as cited in Cooke (n 9) 58).

[95] Scott (n 87) 44.

> to equip an expedition to Persia. The shareholders were then so discouraged that there was great difficulty in inducing them to pay the amounts due.[96]

As a result of the ongoing losses, in 1586 the Company was financially reorganised. The Company used short-term rather than perpetual capital, which was organised in several separate accounts, each for a period of one to three years. Beyond the difficulty in collecting from the original shareholders, this change stemmed from the intention to raise money from wider circles. It was also intended to give more discretion to traders, to pay dividends more frequently and to simplify accounting. By 1622 this process had been taken one step further, and the separate accounts were replaced by individual accounts. With this step the Russia Company was reorganised as a Regulated Company.[97]

The failure of the use of Joint Stock in the Russia Company can be attributed in part by the payment of proceeds as dividends without retaining a reserve fund.[98] As will be set out in the next chapter, similar problems arose in the early history of the English East India Company, with the solution found for the English East India Company in permanent capital.

C. Society of the Mines Royal

A charter was granted in 1568 to the Society of the Mines Royal. Although the importance of trade in the historical development of the modern company is well known and documented, the significance of mining enterprises is less well recognised, even though they were amongst the first chartered business corporations in England.

The English mining corporations adopted features of German mining companies. Records and by-laws of German mining companies exist from the end of the fifteenth century onwards, with a gradual evolution to a single unit on the common account with common profit and loss. Members had to make payments (*Zubusse*) when called on and were liable to creditors. Members could avoid further liability if they abandoned their shares. However, shares were transferrable, so these were capitalistic enterprises.[99]

Significantly, although much of the wording of the Mines Royal charter was similar to that of charters for regulated companies, membership of the Society of the Mines Royal was based on a definite holding of shares rather than

[96] Quoted in State Papers, Domestic, James I, viii 59 (as cited in Scott (n 87) 44).

[97] Formoy (n 17) 17. The Russia Company may also have been the first to refer to its governing body as 'directors'. A 1604 Parliamentary Commission said 'The Muscovy Company, consisting of eight score, or thereabouts, have fifteen directors who manage the whole trade; these limit to every man the portion of stock he shall trade for, make one purse and stock of it all.' Quoted in Report of Committee on the Bill for Free Trade, Journals of the House of Commons I, 218 (as cited in Cooke (n 9) 58).

[98] Scott (n 87) 64.

[99] Levy (n 8) 11–12.

admission to a society.[100] Mines Royal was therefore a chartered corporation, where membership was founded on a holding in a share in a Joint Stock Fund. Members had the benefit of a fraction of the licences granted to Mines Royal, with voting rights ('voice and suffrage') to some extent attached to how high a fraction of the licence a member held.[101]

Elizabeth I sought to replicate the mining success seen on the Continent by chartering two corporations to organise the prospecting, mining and smelting of copper and precious metals.[102] Mines Royal was established in England by a German called Hochsetter, who was backed by the great German mining firm Haug. Hochsetter's father had been principal surveyor and master of the mines of the realm during Henry VIII's reign.[103] In 1564, Hochsetter and Thurland, an Englishman, obtained a mining patent for several counties. Copper was found in several places, including near Keswick – 'the best in England'.[104] Thurland wrote to William Cecil, Queen Elizabeth I's chief adviser, arguing that while copper was plentiful, the costs of working were greater than anticipated. Hochsetter therefore petitioned for leave to erect his water-draining engines, asserted his mining skills and, to off-set his expenses, asked for a monopoly. Hochsetter 'hath determined to join with him in company divers others, and in that respect doth mean to make divident of the commodities and profits'.[105]

Of the 50 shares, Hochsetter proposed to retain some for himself, and

> some parts of goodwill and friendship to dispose freely unto others and of the rest to levy upon agreement of such as shall participate therein such sums of money as he shall think may answer to the travails and charges in that behalf sustained.[106]

Revealing the political context in which charters were sought, one of the free shares was offered to Cecil, and others to members of the aristocracy. The charter as letters patent gave licence to Hochsetter and Thurland, including the right to assign and convey licences and privileges for 'divers good considerations' from assignees like members of the nobility. Cecil and the other parties were granted 'divers parts and portions of the licenses powers authorities privileges and benefits and immunities aforesaid'.[107]

Recognising that the mineral works were 'to the likely benefit and commodity of this our Realm of England and Subjects of the same', and that therefore there was a public benefit, the Queen through the Charter ratified privileges in perpetuity.[108]

[100] Carr (n 58) xcv.
[101] Quoted in Mines Royal Charter, Patent Rolls, 10 Eliz pt v (as cited in Carr (n 58) 14).
[102] M Lynch, *Mining in World History* (Reaktion Books, 2002) 62.
[103] ibid 62.
[104] Carr (n 58) xciv.
[105] ibid.
[106] ibid xciv–xcv.
[107] Quoted in Mines Royal Charter, Patent Rolls, 10 Eliz pt v (as cited in Carr (n 58) 4–5).
[108] By 'We for Us our heirs and successors … to be construed and taken beneficially in the favour of the said Thomas Thurland, Danyell Houghsetter, their heirs and assigns and of the assigns of them and of every of them'. Quoted ibid.

The Charter also granted Mines Royal corporate status as a juridical or legal person. Mines Royal was 'one body politic in itself incorporate and a perpetual society of themselves both in deed and name'. The benefits of perpetual succession were recognised: incorporation prevented 'divers and sundry great inconveniences which by the several deaths of the [members thereof] or their assigns should else from time to time ensue'.[109] 'The term "body politic" (corps politique) had been introduced in the Year Books in Michaelmas in 1478, when Serjeant Starkey said that there was a distinction between bodies politic and natural bodies.'[110] Bodies politic were legal persons. The corporation could sue and being sued; it had a common seal (just as the Crown had the Great Seal); and it could deal with lands.[111]

The Society of the Mines Royal could exist in perpetuity. Perpetuity, a key characteristic, was very easily accepted to be a characteristic of corporations.[112] Henry Maine attributed the conception of perpetual succession in the corporation as equating with succession in families, where the death of an individual made no difference to the collective existence of the aggregate body.[113]

The Charter also gave Mines Royal powers that do not exist in modern companies. Those powers both echo back to the guilds and presage the public powers granted to later chartered business corporations like the English East India Company. They included the power to make statutes, acts and ordinances.[114] The Charter further granted Mines Royal the power to expel members deemed unworthy,[115] and the power to rule and govern labourers and workmen, and to impose penalties by fines and forfeitures.[116] Interestingly, employees were considered to be part of the corporation.

[109] 'But also for the better and more advancement of the said Mineral Works ... and by those presents for Us our heirs and successors do give and grant, to the aforenamed [names] that they by the name of *Governor Assistants and Commonalty for the Mines Royal* shall be from henceforth forever one body politic in itself incorporate and a perpetual society of themselves both in deed and name'. Quoted in ibid.

[110] Mich 18 Edw 4, pl 17, fo 15b–16a (1478.088) (as cited in Seipp (n 21) ch 2, endnote no 6) and see the discussion by Seipp (n 21) in n 112.

[111] Carr (n 58) 6.

[112] Seipp discusses cases from 15th-century Year Books that related to ecclesiastical corporations and were therefore affected by canon law. In a case in the Year Book for 1478, an abbot and covent (convent) of the abbey brought a writ of trespass for trees cut down in the time of the abbot's predecessor. The defendant pleaded the legal maxim that personal actions die with the person, so it was too late to sue about what happened in the time of the previous abbot. Before the case went off on the application of the Statute of Marlborough (1267) as to standing trees, Serjeant Starkey explained that the abbot and covent as a corporation, a body politic, unlike a natural body, could not die, could not be dead and so its personal actions would always survive. This point that corporations could not die had been made in 1465, and would be made again in four different cases in 1481 and 1482. Seipp (n 21) 46.

[113] See HS Maine, *Ancient Law: Its Connection with the Early History of Society, and its Relation to Modern Ideas: with an Introduction by Theodore W Dwight*, 3rd American, from 5th London edn (Henry Holt and Company, 1873) xlii, 178–79.

[114] Carr (n 58) 9 (footnotes omitted).

[115] ibid 10 (footnotes omitted).

[116] ibid 12 (footnotes omitted).

The Crown endowed the grantees with the 'old incidents of incorporation'.[117] Mines Royal had a name. It also had a governance body consisting of one or two Governors and six or more Assistants initially appointed on incorporation, and then elected from the Commonalty (members) through the ordinary Courts (meetings) and assemblies.

After 12 months of operations, the local landowner, the Earl of Northumberland, sent his retainers to seize the excavated ore, claiming that, as the mine was on his land, any produce must belong to him. The case was decided in favour of the Crown on the basis that, by common law, gold and silver mines were the property of the Crown, and on the mistaken belief that the mine had yielded gold and silver rather than copper.[118] Interestingly, and as an obiter finding because of the mistaken facts, the justices held, contrary to the Regalian laws in other lands, that while common law meant that gold and silver were the preserve of the sovereign, produce and profits of mines of other metals 'shall pass to the owner of the land'. The more liberal mining regime in England compared with other jurisdictions may have ultimately contributed to the success of the English mining industry.[119] Here we see the early glimmerings of capitalism.

VI. SEPARATE LEGAL ENTITY

In English law, corporate separateness was linked to the status of corporations as juridical or legal persons. Corporations were, therefore, separate legal entities. Less clear is at what point corporations were considered to be separate legal entities from their members.

The conception that a collective group, such as a family or a tribe, could exist as legally distinct from its members stretches back to antiquity. Maine writes about how the belief that families or tribes were solely based on familial lineage is repeatedly shown to be false, no matter what the society. Instead the powerful legal fiction of an association of kindred permitted family relations to be created artificially.[120]

Whether a legal person could exist separately from natural persons was debated in England in the fourteenth and fifteenth centuries. A nuisance action was brought in 1372 against both the Dean and Chapter of St Peter of Exeter, and also against a clerk named John Weliot. The record of the case records that

[117] ibid xiiii–xiv. The words used resembled existing words used for grants for municipal groups and religious bodies, remaining broadly consistent for 400 years before the general incorporation statutes rendered charters for enterprise obsolete in the mid-19th century.

[118] *R v Earl of Northumberland* (1568) 1 Plowden 310, 75 ER 472 (The Case of Mines).

[119] Lynch (n 102) 63.

[120] See the discussion in Maine (n 113) 20–42, 127, on the association of kindred.

the plea from the counsel for the defendants that Weliot was being sued twice because he was also a member of the chapter, was not allowed.[121]

In 1429, the mayor, bailiffs and commonalty of Ipswich, and also Jabe as an individual defendant, were sued for trespass.[122] The defendants pleaded that Jabe was being sued twice as he was one of the commonalty of Ipswich.[123] The court was divided: Justice Martin agreed that the writ should be thrown out, as if it were allowed, Jabe could be charged twice for the same wrong and Jabe's goods could be put in execution twice.[124] Chief Justice Babington and Justice Paston disagreed, on the basis that damages would only be collected from goods that were collectively owned.[125] Justice Strangeways agreed with Babington and Paston, saying that 'no individual person is the commonalty'.[126] Strangeways said '[s]ingular goods are not goods of the commonalty, and no person by himself is the commonalty, but "this aggregate and this body"'.[127]

'Maitland[128] saw here the first stirrings of limited liability, the separation of corporate assets from individual assets for some purposes …'[129] Clear evidence exists that some judges viewed the members as individuals separate from the commonalty.[130] In a jury challenge case involving Lincoln Cathedral,[131] Prat challenged the inclusion of a juror who was a brother of one of the canons of Lincoln Cathedral, and therefore a brother of one member of the chapter. The court was split. Four serjeants, one apprentice and one justice said that the canon's brother should not be struck off the jury.[132]

Four serjeants, four justices and one serjeant[133] pleaded that the canon's brother should be struck from the jury for presumed bias.[134] Even though the

[121] Quoted in Mich 46 Edw 3, pl 7, fo 23b–24a (1372.075); 46 Edw 3, Lib Ass 9, fo 306b–307a (1372.123ass) (as cited in Seipp (n 21) ch 2, endnote no 11).

[122] Seipp (n 21) 45–46.

[123] ibid 46.

[124] ibid.

[125] ibid.

[126] ibid.

[127] ibid.

[128] (1429) YB Mich 8 Hen VI, fo 1a–1b, pl 2.

[129] Seipp (n 21) 46.

[130] Quoted in Mich 8 Hen 6, pl 2, fo 1a–1b (1429.086); Mich 8 Hen 6, pl 34, fol 14b–15a (1429.118); Mich 9 Hen 6, pl 9, fo 36b (1430.056) (as cited in Seipp (n 21) ch 2, endnote no 13). See also (1429) Mich 8 Hen VI, fo 14b–15a, pl 32.

[131] A series of cases in the Yearbook Reports from 1478 to 1482 are described by Frederic Maitland as 'the most interesting cases in all the Year Books'. F Pollock and FW Maitland, *A History of English Law*, 2nd edn, vol 1 (Cambridge University Press, 1898) 491.

[132] Arguments put forward were 'that the dean-and-chapter as a collective entity could not have a brother or any other relative, that the canon himself was a stranger to the action and not a party or privy to it, that the canon's death or excommunication or a release from the canon would not affect the lawsuit, that if the collective body lost a judgment the canon's own goods would not be executed upon, as was said in 1429, and finally that the canon had no advantage or individual benefit or interest if the collective body won. The collective entity of dean-and-chapter was completely separate, completely estranged from the canons who made up the chapter.' Seipp (n 21) 47–48.

[133] Who became a justice while argument continued: ibid 47.

[134] ibid. 'Some of the arguments were that the canon was a party or privy to the action and not a stranger, that he had advantage by the collective body's recovery to their common use, and that the

justices said during argument that this question was evenly poised, four of the five justices favoured striking the canon's brother from the jury. Any other outcome would be counterintuitive: Seipp terms it the realist outcome.[135] In fact earlier Yearbook cases had struck brothers or other relatives of monks or nuns from juries when the abbot and convent were on trial.[136]

That the argument was considered tenable at all in the Lincoln case may be an indication that the concept of the corporation as a legal entity separate from the natural persons who comprised it was gradually taking hold in England.[137] Seipp considers the most obvious and proximate source of the arguments using the metaphor of a disembodied incorporeal yet corporate body composed of many natural bodies was the 'conciliarist' writing earlier in the fifteenth century by theologians and canonist lawyers, mostly in Paris, about the 'mystical body' (*corpus mysticum*) of the Church, based on 1 Corinthians chapter 12,[138] and the Church's *corpus politicum*.[139] These Church reformers sought to differentiate the Church as an ideal entity from the individual popes and prelates who led it at the time.[140]

VII. *PERSONA FICTA*

A. The *Persona Ficta* Concept

Corporations were a mechanism the Crown used to grant powers to cities, churches and universities. Only legal persons were capable of bearing rights and duties[141] (although legal persons do not automatically have rights and duties). Legal persons did not need to be natural persons nor even contain natural persons; they could be *persona ficta* or artificial legal persons. That idea was received into English law in the sixteenth century. Maitland was careful to term *persona ficta* 'the Italian Theory of the Corporation', recognising that, despite earlier glimmerings in the English Year Books discussed above, the concept did not develop in England until after the Middle Ages.[142]

canon's brother would be permitted to appear in court and give evidence (if he had any), as a family member not barred by the law of maintenance, so that as to the dean and chapter he was family.' The most common argument was 'simply that the brother of one of the canons could be presumed to be biased when the dean and chapter were a party'.

[135] ibid.

[136] Quoted in Trin 28 Hen 6, pl 17, fo 10a (1450.007); 34 Edw 3, Lib Ass pl 6, fo 203b–204b (1360.006ass) (as cited in Seipp (n 21) 47).

[137] Seipp (n 21) 46–47.

[138] 1 Corinthians 12:12 KJV: 'For as the body is one, and hath many members, and all the members of that one body, being many, are one body: so also is Christ.'

[139] Seipp (n 21) 49.

[140] ibid.

[141] PW Duff, *Personality in Roman Private Law* (AM Kelley, 1971) 1.

[142] O Gierke, *Political Theories of the Middle Age*, tr FW Maitland (Cambridge University Press, 1913) xiv.

The concept of the *universitas* or corporation as a *persona ficta* existing in its own right as an artificial legal person arguably originated with Pope Innocent IV (reigned 1243–54), who in a previous manifestation was the distinguished Italian jurist Sinibaldus Fliscus (also known as de Flisco or Fiesco). His discussion of the corporation was part of a 1246 commentary on the five books of decretals of an earlier Pope: Gregory IX.[143]

To Innocent IV, the *universitas* or corporation was a 'person' at law: 'the College is in corporate matters figured as a person'.[144] Whilst being aware a legal person is not the same as a human being – 'Corporation as well as Chapter, Tribe, and so on, are legal terms rather than names of persons'[145] – Innocent IV considered the legal person existed separately at law from the corporate body comprising natural persons, decreeing that a *universitas* could not be excommunicated even though wrongdoing monks who were 'members' of the *universitas* could be.[146]

The guardianship role was key. From Roger Scruton and John Finnis:

> Canon law described the corporate person as a persona ficta. Its corporators stood in law as guardians of property which belonged in fact to no-one, and guardianship, rather than agency, became the mark of legally competent association.[147]

German Friedrich Carl von Savigny, who favoured the *persona ficta* conception of the corporation, acknowledged Pope Innocent IV as the source of the common law *persona ficta* theory in his influential mid-nineteenth-century treatise on Roman law.[148] Real entity theorist Otto von Gierke, who opposed Savigny's theories of the corporation, also said Pope Innocent IV 'was the father of the dogma of the … fictitious … character of legal persons'.[149]

Whether *persona ficta* theory originated with Innocent IV or with the Romans is, however, disputed. According to Duff, the links are exaggerated.[150] Interestingly, David Siepp suspects the origin of the *persona ficta* theory may be in the lawyers' love of the counterintuitive result.[151] As Maitland put it, the Germanists, proponents of real entity theory, would

> tell us that a good deal of harm was done when, at the end of the Middle Ages, our common lawyers took over that theory from the canonists and tried, though often in a half-hearted way to impose it upon the traditional English materials.[152]

[143] M Koessler, 'The Person in Imagination or Persona Ficta of the Corporation' (1949) 9 *Louisiana Law Review* 435, 437.

[144] Quoted in Pierre Gillet, *La personnalité juridique en droit ecclesiastique* (Malines, 1927) 165 (as cited in Koessler (n 143)).

[145] Koessler (n 143) 438 (footnotes omitted).

[146] ibid 437–38.

[147] Scruton and Finnis (n 2) 242.

[148] FC von Savigny, *System des heutigen Romischen Rechts*, vol 2 (Veit, 1840).

[149] Gierke and Maitland (n 142) xxiv.

[150] Duff (n 141) 1.

[151] Seipp (n 21) 50.

[152] FW Maitland, 'The Corporation Sole' in HAL Fisher (ed), *The Collected Papers of Frederic William Maitland*, vol 3 (Cambridge University Press, 1911) 212. See the discussion in ch 13 of this volume on Gierke and real entity theory.

B. *The Case of Sutton's Hospital*

What is not contested is that Sir Edward Coke CJ, in his report on *The Case of Sutton's Hospital* in 1612, set out the classic exposition of the *persona ficta* theory of the corporation in the common law.[153] The references in the report to excommunication and to the absence of a corporate soul echo the words of Innocent IV, who at least adumbrated the Italian theory that Coke transplanted and developed.

The facts of *Sutton* may explain its outcome. Thomas Sutton was a sixteenth-century English civil servant and businessman who had coal-mining interests. He was also a large-scale moneylender to prominent men of his day, including William Cecil, chief adviser to Queen Elizabeth I, and to Coke CJ himself. Sutton was referred to by contemporaries as 'Croesus' and 'Riche Sutton'. During his lifetime, Parliament passed an Act creating a charitable corporation that would enable Sutton to establish a school and a hospital.[154] James I granted a licence for the school and the hospital for the needy in the grounds of the old charterhouse.[155]

Sutton left a portion of his estate to the charitable corporation. Sutton's heirs challenged the validity of the bequest because the date that the charterhouse building was purchased was after the date of the incorporation. The heirs argued that this order of events meant that the incorporation had failed, because nothing of the corporation existed physically on the putative date of incorporation.[156] The Court of Exchequer Chamber found against the heirs, holding that the incorporation was valid, as was the founding of the hospital and therefore the transfer of property to it.

In the statement most often quoted from the case, Coke CJ said that the corporation was 'invisible, immortal and rest[ing] only in intendment and consideration of the law'.[157] In a less quoted passage, useful for context, the statement was made to support the argument that

> an hospital in expectancy or intendment, or nomination, shall be sufficient to support the name of an incorporation when the corporation itself is only in abstracto, and rests only in intendment and consideration of the law; … and therefore … cannot have predecessor nor successor … They cannot commit treason, nor be … outlawed, nor excommunicate, for they have no souls, neither can they appear in person, but by attorney.[158]

The common law *persona ficta* corporation as conceived or adumbrated by Coke CJ is, therefore, a creation of the law that exists as an artificial legal person in the abstract. When considering the *persona ficta* conception of the

[153] *The Case of Sutton's Hospital* (1612) 10 Co Rep 23a, 77 ER 960.
[154] ibid 960.
[155] ibid.
[156] ibid 961.
[157] ibid 973.
[158] ibid.

corporation set out by Coke CJ, it is important to remember that the corporation that was the subject of the case was not a business enterprise. It did not contain a Joint Stock Fund.

VIII. CONCLUSION

By the early 1600s, with the business corporation, England found itself with a corporate form for business, albeit with its financing and capital arrangements at a formative stage. With the contractual Joint Stock Company, it also had an associative form that was similarly at a formative stage of development. Both utilised Joint Stock Funds.

The focus of the next stage of development of the business form is on the business corporation incorporated by means of a charter. The business corporation was the vehicle of choice for England's burgeoning overseas trade. It combined the key features of the corporation with Joint Stock Funds. Its evolution accelerated because of the growth of that trade, and its participants' desire for a more stable form of business enterprise.

From the beginning of the sixteenth century, the biggest strides in the development of the legal form for business therefore occurred in the business corporation, which will be the focus of chapters 3, 4 and 5. The contractual Joint Stock Company continued to exist in parallel. It was not until the Bubble Act 1720 made obtaining charters for joint stock enterprises difficult that the contractual Joint Stock Company became significant again.

3

The Transition to Permanent Capital in the English East India Company

I. INTRODUCTION

By the end of the sixteenth century, English traders sought a stable form of organisation.[1] It became clear that the challenges of competing with other ascendant European powers required a united effort. Ships trading through the new sea routes to India and America needed stronger concentrations of material power to protect their goods and themselves.[2] The Dutch combined six Amsterdam companies that had been in keen competition with each other, under the direction of the States-General, into the Dutch East India Company (*Vereenigde Oost Indische Compagnie* (VOC)) in 1602.[3]

When the first group of London merchants petitioned the Privy Council for permission to mount a voyage to the East Indies, they stated that the Dutch success had stirred them to 'no less affection to advance the trade of their native country than the Dutch merchants were to benefit their Commonwealth'.[4] Like all petitioners for corporate charters, the English East India Company needed a public purpose for its petition for incorporation to be received favourably. Elizabeth I granted the English East India Company its Charter near the end of her reign, on 30 December 1600. The date is auspicious, as the new century heralded a new age of emerging capitalism.

This chapter focuses on developments in the English East India Company in the first half of the seventeenth century. The Company transitioned from operating with series of single Joint Stock Funds to operating using permanent capital. Over time, by observing the VOC and learning from their own experience, the merchants and traders who invested in the English East India Company realised that permanent capital worked best. The development happened incrementally.

[1] AB Levy, *Private Corporations and their Control* (Routledge, 1950) 22.

[2] ibid 17.

[3] ibid 18.

[4] Quoted in H Stevens and G Birdwood (eds), *The Dawn of British Trade to the East Indies as recorded in the Court Minutes of the East India Company 1599–1603* (London, 1886) 8 (as cited in KN Chaudhari, *The Trading World of Asia and the English East India Company 1660–1760* (Cambridge University Press, 1978) 6).

A series of voyages using a Joint Stock was more advantageous than single voyages with proceeds divided up at the end of each voyage, primarily because of the advantages of investing in infrastructure for the longer term. In turn the corporation's being able to own infrastructure meant that trading through a perpetual corporation with a permanent capital was superior to a series of voyages using a Joint Stock.

When trading to distant lands, the combined investment of capital and the infrastructure in place meant the English East India Company with permanent capital was ultimately preferred by Cromwell and investors. The alternatives were either free trade, or each individual merchant's trading through the Company in the Regulated Company form. Financial innovations seen in the English East India Company, and also its trading rivals in Europe, meant mental horizons around investment were lengthened by the duration of voyages. Conflicting goals of power by monarchs and profits by merchants caused change by each.[5]

II. THE FIRST TWENTY YEARS

The English East India Company was conceived by a diverse group of Londoners, ranging from the Lord Mayor Sir Stephen Soame, through 'buttery Elizabethan burghers', including primary driver Sir Thomas Smythe, already wealthy through his trade through the Levant Company to grocers, and tradesmen, and even to mariners enriched by Elizabethan privateering adventures.[6] At a September 1599 meeting, 57 adventurers elected 15 committees (directors). The minimum subscription for shareholders was £200, and subscribers were not permitted to pay their subscriptions in kind using ships or goods (stock), as had been past practice.

The promoters applied for a charter. As trade to India was so remote, it was recognised that a 'joint and united stock'[7] was needed to undertake it, which would be open to all investors.[8] The Company had 218 subscribers, with management by the 'gouvernor and 24 committee men'.[9] The Charter gave the Company a 15-year monopoly on trade from the Cape of Good Hope to the Straits of Magellan,[10] later described as a monopoly granted over two-thirds of the trading world.[11]

[5] L Neal, *The Rise of Financial Capitalism: International Capital Markets in the Age of Reason* (Cambridge University Press, 1990) 8.

[6] W Dalrymple, *The Anarchy: The Relentless Rise of the East India Company* (Bloomsbury Publishing, 2019) 1–2.

[7] WR Scott, *The Constitution and Finance of English, Scottish, and Irish Joint-Stock Companies to 1720*, vol 2 (Cambridge University Press, 1910) 92. The term 'joint stock' did not have the meaning of an ongoing stock that it would later acquire.

[8] Dalrymple (n 6) 7.

[9] Scott (n 7) 92–93.

[10] RA Bryer 'The History of Accounting and the Transition to Capitalism in England: Part 2 Evidence' (2000) 25 *Accounting, Organizations and Society* 327, 345.

[11] Dalrymple (n 6) 9.

The English East India Company did not get off to a roaring start: initial calls on shares were not met, falling £8,000 short.[12] The Company passed a 'resolution which compelled each shareholder to add a further 10 per cent to his adventure, thus bringing the minimum holding, which came to be regarded as the share, to £220.'[13] An order was made by the Privy Council that those in arrears had to pay, under threat of imprisonment.[14] In 1601, in order to finance a voyage, another assessment of 10 per cent on the original capital subscribed was made, taking the financial input for a share from the initial £200 to £240.

Clearly, therefore, the shareholders did not have limited liability to the Company. However,

> the idea of the corporate entity evolved so rigidly that no liability on the part of the shareholders for the company's debts was considered possible. As a result, it was held that if a company became extinct and its reserves exhausted, creditors could not maintain actions against the shareholders. On the other hand the company itself could make calls and request additional payments in excess of the par value of the shares.[15]

Sailors were to be paid out of the proceeds of the voyage if the voyage was successful. If the voyage was unsuccessful, it was determined that there would be a further call on the adventurers (shareholders). Interestingly, sailors on the voyage were given shares;[16] an early form of Employee Share Ownership scheme and in line with the financial benefits given to crew of privateering vessels under Elizabeth I. The sum of £68,373 was raised, higher than any amount previously ventured in the East Indies trade.[17] Two months after the Charter was granted, the *Red Dragon* and its three small escort ships, the *Hector*, the *Susan*, and the *Ascension*, set off on the first voyage.[18]

Some evidence indicates that the ventures may have been intended to be single voyages each on a single stock, and with different investors for each voyage in the same way privateers operated. Previously, corporations had been used as a framework within which Joint Stocks were constituted for single ventures. The Joint Stock was wound up after ships returned and proceeds divided.[19] Had that happened, the English East India Company would have been a corporation within which a series of terminating Joint Stock Funds were operated. From a legal perspective, the English East India Company as a corporation would have had within it a series of contractual Joint Stock Companies. However, the exigencies of the period (plague leading to the need to send out a second voyage)

[12] Scott (n 7) 93.
[13] ibid 94.
[14] ibid.
[15] Levy (n 1) 25.
[16] Scott (n 7) 95.
[17] Bryer (n 10) 345.
[18] Dalrymple (n 6) 10–11.
[19] Levy (n 1) 23.

meant that investment from the first and second voyages was combined.[20] As the adventure continued past a single voyage, shares could be traded, although not free of the risk of future calls.

The difficulty of attracting investment, and perhaps the risk of further assessment for contributions being made on shareholders, meant a share that had cost the adventurer £240 (£200 plus assessments of £40) sold for £180 during this period.[21] Those adventurers who had previously agreed to provide investment for next two voyages would only provide funding for one, so the fourth voyage of 1608 had its own Joint Stock. That ship was lost, leading to diminished investment for the fifth voyage. Ultimately, though, the combined voyages proved profitable overall.[22]

In 1609, the English East India Company was granted a new Charter by James I, giving it sole rights to trade to the East Indies.[23] By 1613 there had been 12 voyages in total, all but one very lucrative.[24]

The year 1613 saw the first innovation in the financial structure of the English East India Company, with a subscription for four voyages to be paid over four years.[25] The idea of a series of expeditions with one capital was a natural development of the previous interrelation of two voyages. Possibly, the change of title may have been thought desirable to avoid associations connected with a 'thirteenth voyage'. Whatever the reason, instead of 'thirteenth voyage', the term 'Joint Stock' was used, and the whole series of expeditions was described as the 'First Joint Stock'.[26]

The next period was one of increased prosperity, attributed by some to the substitution of a Joint Stock Fund extended over several years for the previous annual voyages with single Joint Stocks. Unrealised property from one voyage was transferred and used as infrastructure for the next voyage.[27] With increased trade, the Company extended its basis of operations by the establishment of factories in the East Indies wherever possible.[28] The movement to raising funding over an extended time period made a longer-term perspective possible, and investment in the cost of those factories became financially viable.

[20] Scott (n 7) 97–98.

[21] ibid 96.

[22] ibid 100–01. £13,700 was obtained, which, combined with the proceeds from the third voyage, returned a 234% profit for investors.

[23] Bryer (n 10) 346.

[24] Scott (n 7) 101.

[25] The combination of voyages may not have been novel. Cooke refers to a 1622 source, where a capital stock for a privateering venture was used over two or more voyages, and where the ships themselves were valued and taken into the accounts. Malynes, *Consuetudo vel Lex Mercatoria* (1622) 169 (as cited in CA Cooke, *Corporation, Trust and Company: An Essay in Legal History* (Harvard University Press, 1951) 57). £418,691 was subscribed for by shareholders, with the payments by investors to be made over four years.

[26] Scott (n 7) 101.

[27] ibid 103.

[28] Bryer (n 10) 346.

The English East India Company developed centralised machinery for the regulation of trade, but at that time did not have the VOC's wide governmental powers.[29] The Company was not identified with the State in the same way as the VOC. The Company, nevertheless, frequently called upon State support by claiming its trade was more for public than private benefit. 'The State was now called upon to exercise functions which had hitherto been left to the initiative of private merchants.'[30]

The year 1614 also saw the introduction of capital accounting. For the first time, the English East India Company had a capital in which all investors in the new Joint Stock had an interest as shareholders. Although entrance conditions of admission for members were set down and entrance fees were payable, membership was based on holding shares.[31] Crucially, when identifying the emergence of capitalism,[32] at that time 'the word capital came to mean the total money advanced' to the enterprise.[33]

The Second Joint Stock issued in 1616 was used to purchase the assets of the First Joint Stock. The subscription was now called up in equal instalments, with profits reinvested and money borrowed.[34] The Company became widely held, with nearly 1,000 investing shareholders subscribing to the Second Stock[35] for a total of £1.6 million.[36] Investors were drawn from all walks of life, with courtiers, nobles and gentry investing,[37] as well as widows, clergymen, merchants and tradesmen.[38] The central significance of the English East India Company was recognised, with one contemporaneous leader commenting that it was 'composed of the greatest part of the Privy Council, of the nobility, of the Judges of the land, the gentry of the kingdom, and [was] furnished with an assured stock of sixteen hundred thousand pounds'.[39]

[29] SA Khan, *The East India Trade in the XVIIth Century in its Political and Economic Aspects* (S Chand & Co, 1923) 4.

[30] ibid 7.

[31] Cooke (n 25) 59. Shares were not freely transferrable, though. A share could not be transferred until the purchaser had bought his place in the Company.

[32] Bryer (n 10) 347: 'From 1614, instead of the word "stock", the company began to use the word "capital".' The reason for the use of the word capital rather than the word stock is that the word stock had come to have many different meanings including the money advanced by an individual, the commodities bought with it, the total money advanced to the enterprise and as another word for a share.

[33] ibid.

[34] Scott (n 7) 104.

[35] Cooke (n 25) 57–58.

[36] Dalrymple (n 6) 20. In 1617, £1,629,040 was subscribed for in the Second Joint Stock by 954 persons, which was to be called up in eight equal instalments of 12.5% each. By 1620, half was paid in. Between 1617 and 1620, £1,600,000 was expended, provided by calls on stockholders, profits on first and second expeditions reinvested, and money borrowed. Scott (n 7) 104.

[37] R Mishra, *A Business of State: Commerce, Politics, and the Birth of the East India Company* (Harvard University Press, 2018) 5.

[38] Cooke (n 25) 58.

[39] Mishra (n 37) 3 (footnotes omitted).

The Company engaged in trilateral trade, exporting bullion and importing commodities from the Indies, re-exporting commodities to Europe and re-importing bullion. The lucrative country trade involved the exchange of Indian textiles for spices. Small agile ships were built, and the Company set up shipyards and foundries on the Thames, becoming one of the major employers in the London area.[40]

III. THE SECOND TWENTY YEARS

In 1620, increased competition from the Dutch, dishonest factors and a general crisis in England meant the fortunes of the English East India Company declined. In November 1621, the Company was temporarily unable to pay its debts, with the winding up of the First Joint Stock causing losses to those who had paid high prices in the secondary markets for shares.[41] Nevertheless, the overall return for investors in the First Joint Stock, even after less successful later voyages, was 187.5 per cent.[42]

The VOC had long realised that frequent asset liquidations were inefficient. The Dutch Estates General in 1623 granted the VOC perpetual existence, meaning its capital was permanent.

> While shareholders lost their power to withdraw at will, they were compensated with a new right to sell their shares without the consent of other owners, a compromise that reconciled a company's need for fixed capital with a shareholder's need for liquidity.[43]

In the period, the VOC had expended considerable sums on building forts and other infrastructure in India, rather than focusing on the short term through single or series of voyages with division of the investment and proceeds to shareholders at the end.[44] Also, the practice of stationing ships in Asia to provide for a network of inter-Asia trade and to provide security for the trading fleet took place much earlier in the VOC than in other trading companies. The requirement to liquidate Joint Stock Funds at the end of every voyage or series of voyages created a challenge for the English East India Company. It meant that infrastructure assets had to be sold to the next Joint Stock, creating a hold-up problem and discouraging long-term investment.

By 1623, the English East India Company was £92,000 in arrears (the equivalent of around $24,000,000 in 2021).[45] Factors were experiencing difficulties in

[40] Bryer (n 10) 346.
[41] Scott (n 7) 107.
[42] Bryer (n 10) 346.
[43] H Hansmann, R Kraakman and R Squire, 'Law and the Rise of the Firm' (2006) 119 *Harvard Law Review* 1333, 1376–77.
[44] Khan (n 29) 4.
[45] E Nye, 'Pounds Sterling to Dollars: Historical Conversion of Currency' at www.uwyo.edu/numimage/currency.

purchasing commodities for shipping to England. By July 1624 it was believed that no man's adventure 'was now worth money'.[46] Many shareholders declined to provide further capital. The Company was forced to borrow abroad, including in Amsterdam.[47] By 1628, the English East India Company had been forced to revert to independent voyages.[48]

> It was only as a last resort to keep the charter alive and to recover the remaining assets of the Second Joint-Stock that this method of trading was adopted. More experienced adventurers recognized that the co-existence of separate stocks involved endless confusion.[49]

Nevertheless, existing investment in infrastructure meant that further outlay on factories, forts and a permanent staff in India was not needed as they were already in place. Single voyages were therefore profitable[50] and a pattern of single voyages continued.[51]

In March 1629, in the winding up of the Second Joint Stock, 'confusions' in the accounts that had arisen with the reversion to separate voyages appeared to spur the recombination of the capitals in the Third Joint Stock in 1633. The purchase by the Third Joint Stock of 'remains' from earlier ventures required the valuation of 'certain unrealised properties' – a significant process because of the linkage with the new concept of capital.[52] Attempting to keep the various capitals apart caused confusion, with many activities carried on in common with the different ventures often using the same ships. Bribing the same officials was the Company's biggest overhead. Difficulty existed in deciding which capital should be assigned costs, with the figures eventually assigned in a somewhat arbitrary way.[53]

The Third Joint Stock, due to terminate in 1636, did not in fact terminate until 1642. Attempts to raise a Fourth Joint Stock were initially unsuccessful, because investors had lost confidence in the English East India Company.[54] The Courteen Association, which had been supported by Charles I, had a royal grant to trade to India, with the Company's Royal Charter watered down by the King. The competition between the Company and the Courteen Association meant both 'the rivals had reached the brink of ruin'.[55] Although Courteen had been supported by Charles I, by the 1640s the Courteen Association's place as

[46] Scott (n 7) 108.
[47] G Dari-Mattiaci et al, 'The Emergence of the Corporate Form' (2017) 33 *Journal of Law, Economics and Organization* 193, 219.
[48] Scott (n 7) 109.
[49] ibid.
[50] WW Hunter, *History of India: The European Struggle for Indian Supremacy in the Seventeenth Century*, ed AVW Jackson (Grolier Society, 1907) 257.
[51] Bryer (n 10) 362–64.
[52] ibid 347.
[53] ibid 355; Scott (n 7) 111.
[54] Hunter (n 50) 257.
[55] ibid 266.

a competitor had been taken by West India free traders like Martin Noell, who was a friend of Oliver Cromwell,[56] and Maurice Thomson.[57]

IV. THE THIRD TWENTY YEARS

With the advent of the Civil War in 1642, it was no longer certain that the Royal Charter that had been granted to the English East India Company was valid. Despite uncertainty about whether it was able to mount voyages or still had exclusive privileges, the English East India Company considered itself as remaining subject to the responsibilities that came with the grant. For example, in 1647, during a period when the Company had lost its privileges, the Governor told the shareholders that '"Every man had liberty to go to India," but the Indian princes held the Company "liable for what depredations" any Englishman might there commit.'[58] The Company had to maintain the factories and other infrastructure. The interlopers and free traders were therefore free riders.

The Company had made a case to Parliament in February 1647 that it retain its monopoly,[59] arguing from long experience that the monopoly was needed to provide the scale of resources required to compete with the Dutch and Portuguese, to minimise internal conflict, and to share and minimise risks associated with long sea voyages.

A call was made for permanent capital. One Joint Stock was the best way to carry on the work with honour and profit to the nation. A coalition between Courteen's Association and the English East India Company, where the Company would have exclusive rights to trade in India, meant that in 1650 Parliament had resolved on trade to the East Indies with one company and one Joint Stock.[60] Nevertheless, money could not be raised for investment from shareholders: 'in vain the Company's beadle went round to the freemen with the subscription book'.[61] The financial position became so dire that by July 1651, the Company was considering whether it was worthwhile even electing a Governor and the other officers, since the Company had no other business than to pay its debts.[62] The Company limped on through the Civil War, which ended on 3 September 1651.[63]

Cromwell viewed the trade with India from a national standpoint, with the English East India Company one of several possible mechanisms that could be

[56] Khan (n 29) 89.
[57] ibid 83.
[58] Hunter (n 50) 258.
[59] Bryer (n 10) 364.
[60] Hunter (n 50) 265–67. It was agreed that the Association would retain its Assada factory at Madagascar and Asiatic and African trade. See also the discussion in Khan (n 29) 84.
[61] Hunter (n 50) 267.
[62] ibid 268.
[63] ibid 257.

utilised to carry out that trade.[64] The Navigation Act of 1651 was a model for winning English supremacy over the seas. Cromwell 'both strengthened and controlled the Company in regard to its foreign enemies'.[65] When the Company petitioned Cromwell for help against the Dutch for injuries it had suffered, those grievances were one of the contributing reasons for the 1652 war against the Dutch. In the 1654 peace treaty, the Dutch pledged to settle outstanding claims by the Company.[66]

Cromwell's 1651 Navigation Act increased desire for an open trade, with free traders mounting voyages. The Council of State, apparently with the sanction of Cromwell, began to issue licences for private trade to India. The English East India Company appeared to be doomed. The Amsterdam burghers claimed to have received advice that 'the Lord Protector will dissolve the East India Company at London, and declare the navigation and commerce to the Indies to be free and open'.[67]

Two sets of committees (directors) were elected for the two sets of shareholders, with the new United Stock eventually heavily subscribed for by investors like Maurice Thomson, who was elected a committee.[68] Thomson supported a return to the older system of regulated trade through a Regulated Company with increased state protection of foreign trade, as an alternative to the trade's being thrown open to the nation.[69] Individual members should be permitted to trade on their own behalf under the regulated system. If the Company was not in a position to send out ships, its members should be able to do so.[70]

The governing body initially responded by allowing members to trade in India if they paid a fee to the Company. They quickly realised, though, that such concessions would mean a change from the Joint Stock to the regulated system. In the autumn of 1654, a petition to the Council of State asked that trade to East India be carried on by a Regulated Company.[71] Committees appointed by the English East India Company to consider the issue voted 11:5 that Joint Stock was the most advantageous method. The Court of Committees (Board of Directors) determined in March 1654 that 'it is not in the power of this Court to give liberty to any private persons to trade to India; but if any do it, it is at their

[64] ibid 258.
[65] ibid 264.
[66] ibid 260–62. The settlement, set through arbitration by the Protestant Swiss Cantons, led to the VOC's being ordered to pay the English East India Company £85,000, as well as restoring the island of Pularoon to the English. Revealingly, in terms of Cromwell's perception of the public purpose of the English East India Company, Cromwell instructed the Company to 'plant and manage the island so that it may not be lost to the nation'. A treaty with Portugal in July 1654 gave English ships the right to trade to any Portuguese possession in the East Indies.
[67] ibid 272.
[68] Khan (n 29) 84.
[69] Hunter (n 50) 268–69.
[70] ibid 271.
[71] ibid 273.

own peril'.[72] The arguments advanced for Joint Stock were 'advantage' (more profitable) and 'security' (less risky).

Ultimately, evidence based on accounting practices utilising double-entry bookkeeping won the day. The Company accountant Jeremy Sandbrooke produced an account of the East India trade that gave a complete financial history of the Company, showing the rate of return on the initial capital invested for each voyage and each Joint Stock.[73] Separate voyages had been given up by the Company after a full trial, it was claimed. Also, the Company now had the factories and infrastructure necessary to protect the distant trade, and the responsibility for the conduct of all Englishmen in the East.[74]

Cromwell, in 1655, referred questions on the future constitution of the East India Company to the Council of State, in the meantime continuing to grant trade licences to individual free traders.[75] Nevertheless, in 1656 the Council of State said that 'the said trade will be managed with most advantage to the Commonwealth and to the secureity of itself by a united joint stocke under regulacion'.[76]

With no sign of further resolution, the Court of Committees of the English East India Company resolved in 1656 to sell its 'privileges and houses in India'.[77] The shareholders, through the General Court of Committees (general meeting), sent a further petition to Cromwell on 20 October 1656.[78] Cromwell on the same day referred the petition to eight advisers, led by Cromwell confidante Colonel Philip Jones.[79] The Jones Committee was charged with recommending 'in what manner the East India trade might be best managed for the public good and its own encouragement'.[80]

The choice of Jones and two other of Cromwell's close confidantes, and Cromwell's prompt response to the petition, indicate that Cromwell had already decided to grant the English East India Company its Charter.[81] The Protector's primary motivation, seen already in the earlier enactment of the Navigation Act 1651, was English naval supremacy throughout the known world. In 1655 he had established a Committee of Trade. Realising that a national fleet was not yet strong enough to support open trade, the only real choice was the English East India Company, either using Joint Stock or operating as a Regulated Company.

As discussed in chapter 2, section II.C, Regulated Companies were corporations that acted as a regulating body within which individual merchants operated. Regulated Companies had been the norm in the past, and the Turkey Company

[72] ibid 271.
[73] Bryer (n 10) 366.
[74] Hunter (n 50) 273–74.
[75] ibid 274.
[76] Bryer (n 10) 367.
[77] Hunter (n 50) 275.
[78] Khan (n 29) 90.
[79] ibid.
[80] Hunter (n 50) 276.
[81] ibid 275–76.

operated at that time as a Regulated Company.[82] But the Turkey Company's trading position differed from that of the English East India Company, as it was within the reach of English diplomacy.[83] The founders of the English East India Company 'had declared in 1599 "that the trade of the Indias being so far remote from hence cannot be traded but in a joint and united stock"'.[84] It was finally recognised that the rationale behind that declaration remained true. Within six weeks, the Jones Committee had recommended to the Council of State that 'the India trade should be carried on by one company on the basis of a United Joint Stock'.[85]

The Council of State received the Jones Committee Report on 18 December 1656, but still did not act. Seeking to trigger action, the Company resolved, on 14 January 1657, that unless a decision was made within the month, it would sell all of its factories, rights and customs in India, ordering Bills of Sale to be hung up in the London Exchange.[86] The Council of State reacted by advising Cromwell, on 10 February 1657, that a charter should be drawn up.[87]

Cromwell reluctantly intervened between the Company and its domestic rivals, only granting the Charter when he was convinced it was in the national interest to do so. The Protector's natural inclination may have been to favour free-trading small merchants over the Company elite with their Royalist connections. Other functions of government, however, left Cromwell little time for internal trade wrangles, with civil administration left to the Council of State.[88] In addition, former free traders who became shareholders in the English East India Company eventually favoured the state through the Company as the instrument through which trade to the East Indies could be carried out.[89]

To Cromwell, the India trade was an English interest conducted through a public corporation, with consequential benefits of treaties to the Company and its investors not a reason to grant the Charter. In return for support, Cromwell expected loans from the Company. Those loans were applied for public purposes and were repaid.[90] Consistently, Cromwell brooked no private diplomacy by the English East India Company; in 1657, at the same time he granted its Charter, Cromwell called the Company to task for attempting to negotiate directly with the Dutch Foreign Minister.[91]

[82] ibid 277.
[83] ibid 278.
[84] ibid 278–79. It is important to acknowledge that the meaning of the term 'joint and united stock' was different in 1599, when it meant a subscription for a single voyage with the accounts wound up and capital returned at the end of the voyage. As shown in this chapter, the use of joint stock for a series of voyages evolved over the first 50 years of the operation of the East India Company.
[85] ibid 276.
[86] ibid 281.
[87] ibid 282.
[88] ibid 264.
[89] Khan (n 29) 85. See also the view of pamphleteers of the day: ibid 86.
[90] Hunter (n 50) 262.
[91] ibid 264.

Oliver Cromwell's influence on the destiny of the English East India Company and also the form it would adopt was significant.[92] In 19 October 1657, in the last year of his life, and after long standing aloof from the domestic distresses of the English East India Company,[93] Oliver Cromwell granted the English East India Company a new Charter.[94] After the Restoration, the Charter disappeared from India House, and Cromwell's life was so crowded that 'his biographers have found no leisure for his dealings with the East India Company'.[95] As one historian puts it, 'the corporation passed, with little recognition of the change at the time, from its medieval to its modern basis'.[96]

V. THE 1657 CHARTER

No copy of the 1657 Charter survives. An order by Cromwell at Whitehall on 6 November 1657 in a shaky hand, suggesting the English form of malaria he would succumb to the following September, does survive: 'We recommend the answering of this petition to the Council of our Admiralty desiring them to do herein what they may for the incouragement of the East India Trade.'[97]

The text of the Charter is also known because much of it was adopted in the later Charter granted to the Company by Charles II after the Restoration.[98] Cromwell promised Parliamentary sanction in the next session. He died before this sanction could occur.[99] Cromwell had the power to recall the Charter if he saw cause and, in common with the 1650 Parliamentary grant, a degree of government control was possible.[100]

Most significantly, the India Trade was to be reconstituted in 'one joint stock' – words that did not appear in any of the previous Royal Charters. The notion of continuing joint stock had developed in the English East India Company by the combination of voyages and by observation of the VOC's success. The concept of capital had emerged in the earlier 1650 Parliamentary grant. The Company, under Cromwell's Charter, developed it further by the use of a continuous Joint Stock Fund as permanent capital.[101] As Hunter points out, the 'change was wrought not by Cromwell alone, but by Cromwell representing the spirit of the times'.[102]

[92] GL Beer, 'Cromwell's Policy in its Economic Aspects' (1901) 16 *Political Science Quarterly* 582.
[93] Hunter (n 50) 259.
[94] Scott (n 7) 128; Hunter (n 50) 282.
[95] Hunter (n 50) 251–52.
[96] ibid 252–53.
[97] Lebrecht Music & Arts and Alamy Stock Photo, 'Autograph Note of Oliver Cromwell to a Petition of the East India Company, Given at Whitehall on 6 November, 1657' at www.alamy.com/stock-photo-autograph-note-of-oliver-cromwell-to-a-petition-of-the-east-india-83336422.html.
[98] Khan (n 29) 90 (footnotes omitted). The new Charter ratified James I's earlier Charter, with some modifications and additional privileges granted.
[99] Hunter (n 50) 282–83.
[100] ibid 282.
[101] ibid 283.
[102] ibid.

In October 1657, on the day the Charter was granted, at a General Court (general meeting) held at India House,[103] the English East India Company appointed committees (directors) that drew up the preamble for the subscription. The minimum subscription was £100, with a £500 subscription required for a vote and a £1,000 subscription to become eligible to become a committee (director). Voting rights were thus linked to holding capital, rather than to membership as a freeman of the Company.[104] Small shareholders able to combine their holdings in order to have a vote.[105]

Freedom, or membership, of the company was thrown open to the public for the sum of £5. There was no requirement to subscribe for shares, although that would have been the motivation to become a member. Membership was also open to the members of the old East India Company, the rival Assada (formerly Courteen Association) merchants, and any other Merchant Adventurers and private traders in India who were willing to throw in their possessions at a fair valuation.[106] Membership was not without its obligations though. Members could not engage in private trade on their own account; if they did, they would forfeit any shares they held to the other shareholders.[107]

The capital was permanent. There were to be six calls. Those calls were payments of instalments on subscribed capital, rather than the requirement to contribute further capital over the initial subscription that had been in place for the early Company voyages at the beginning of the century.[108] Shareholders therefore had limited liability to the Company, making the shares in the Company more freely tradeable. The Joint Stock Fund was not to be wound up, but at the end of seven years assets would be valued and subscribers entitled to the estimated equivalent of their original subscription. At that time a new subscriber could join the company,[109] with the Joint Stock to continue as the capital of the company.[110] '[D]ivisions were for the future to be made in money only'[111] rather than in commodities[112] (a response to the debate of several decades earlier discussed in chapter 4), and shipping, bullion and goods transferred to new stock at valuation. Capital of £739,782 was subscribed for.[113]

Permanent capital linked shares with one of the critical characteristics of the corporation: perpetual succession. Some contemporary commentators

[103] ibid.
[104] Scott (n 7) 129.
[105] Hunter (n 50) 285.
[106] ibid 283–84.
[107] ibid 286. See the discussion on the debate over private trade in chs 4 and 5.
[108] First two of 12.5% then 18.75% calls over just two years.
[109] Scott (n 7) 129.
[110] Hunter (n 50) 285. In fact, as the Company prospered, the appraisements became statements of assets that enabled stockholders and the public to regulate their dealings.
[111] EB Sainsbury, *A Calendar of the Court Minutes etc of the East India Company, 1655–1659* (Clarendon Press, 1916) xxii.
[112] Hunter (n 50) 286.
[113] ibid 285.

consider 'perpetual existence' to be 'misleading', meaning no more than that 'the corporation lasts until dissolved'.[114] Others regard perpetual succession as an insignificant aspect of corporate personality that can be replicated through contracting.[115] Entity shielding of the permanent capital as the Corporate Fund of a corporation is more effective with perpetual succession.[116] Andrew Schwartz links the existence of the company in perpetuity with adopting a long-term perspective: 'This perpetual nature of the corporation means that it must plan for an infinite future and therefore strive to enhance value over the long term.'[117]

The English East India Company was a business corporation that initially operated with a series of terminating Joint Stock Funds. By 1657 it had developed to become the first company with all of the fundamental characteristics of the modern company, including shifting from operating with a series of terminating Joint Stock Funds to using permanent capital, termed, in this book, the Corporate Fund. Since the English East India Company was legally a corporation, characteristics such as the Company's being a legal entity separate from its members and the shareholders' not being liable for the Company's debts were in place in the Company before Cromwell's 1657 Charter. Double-entry bookkeeping and changes in accounting practice reflected societal changes in mid-seventeenth-century England, where the rate of return on capital (whether in land or enterprise) became the purpose of economic life.[118]

[114] FH Easterbrook and DR Fischel, *The Economic Structure of Corporate Law* (Harvard University Press, 1991) 11 (as cited in AA Schwartz, 'The Perpetual Corporation' (2012) 80 *George Washington Law Review* 764, 775).

[115] Hansmann, Kraakman and Squire (n 43) 1394.

[116] L Macgregor, 'Partnerships and Legal Personality: Cautionary Tales From Scotland' (2020) 20(1) *Journal of Corporate Law Studies* 237, 238, 261.

[117] Schwartz (n 114) 766.

[118] Bryer (n 10) 328: 'What was driving the development of the EIC's system of accounting were escalating socio-economic conflicts within the company mirroring conflicts in society. Resolving these conflicts ultimately required a bourgeois revolution in Marx's sense. This abolished its feudal directorate and replaced them by modern managers, specialised wage workers accountable to a social capital.'

4

Corporate Governance in the English East India Company

I. INTRODUCTION

THE FIRST HALF of the seventeenth century saw a battle for control between two factions[1] in the English East India Company that reflected the unrest in the period leading up to and during the Civil War of 1642 to 1651. On one side were the elite feudal merchants who, with the grant of a Royal monopoly and privileges, operated the Company trade in their own, and Royal, interests. The elite were majority shareholders who controlled the Company's governing body. On the other side were the generality: small investing shareholders. The generality was made up of the commercially minded landed class represented in Parliament, lesser gentry, yeoman farmers, independent new merchants trading with North America and the Caribbean, ships' captains, London shop keepers, and manufacturers. All had money to invest and were keen to participate in the new trading opportunities. To fund voyages, the Company and the elite merchants needed investors.

Governing bodies for corporations pre-date general meetings for investing shareholders. Regular general meetings for shareholders were an important innovation first seen in the English East India Company, from its inception at the beginning of the seventeenth century. Central to the debates that led to the 1657 Charter with permanent capital was the battle for the rights of the small investing shareholders in the Company against the elite merchants who controlled the governing body. The conflict between the generality and the elite led to the modernisation of the English East India Company, culminating in 1657 when the new age of corporate capitalism really began.

As discussed in chapter 3, over time, observation of the Dutch East India Company (VOC) and their own experience taught the merchants and traders who invested in the English East India Company that the advantages of a permanent Joint Stock Fund outweighed the advantages of terminating stock funds wound up after either a single voyage, or a series of voyages. There was also growing realisation that trading through a corporation with a permanent capital

[1] RA Bryer, 'The History of Accounting and the Transition to Capitalism in England: Part 2 Evidence' (2000) 25 *Accounting, Organizations and Society* 327, 344.

was superior to free trade. Those advantages were not, however, immediately apparent, with the Court Books recording sophisticated debates over issues such as the agency problem for shareholders and the obligations of the governing body. The governance and internal rules and practices of the English East India Company changed during the seventeenth century – in particular after 1640. The Charter of 1657 was different in key respects to the founding charter.

The decision to grant a new charter to the English East India Company ended a long battle of wills between those who favoured free trade to India, either independently of the Company or through the Company's using the Regulated Company form, and those who favoured permanent capital.

The battle lines were blurred. Through the first half of the seventeenth century, smaller investing shareholders in the Company, as members of the generality, became frustrated with how the major shareholders, who were elite merchants and members of the governing body, favoured their own interests over the interests of the Company and therefore all its shareholders. Some members of the generality became interlopers, trading on their own behalf as free traders, with the number of interlopers peaking in the 1640s.[2] Once Cromwell, driven by the threat to English trade posed by the Dutch, was convinced to grant a new charter to the English East India Company based on a permanent capital, concessions made by the elite members of the governing body meant the role of the governing body had shifted.

The small shareholders were not empowered by increasing control over the management of the Company. Instead, shareholder influence and constitutional rights through the General Court (general meeting) led to increased obligations on the governing body. Practices that favoured elite merchants, such as dividends paid by commodities, and the elite merchants' purchasing of commodities at favourable rates, ended. The elite accepted that they did not have a permanent right to control the Company. They also accepted that the role of the governing body, supported by sworn oaths, was to act in the interests of all of the shareholders. That obligation, therefore, related more to the permanent capital contributed by all investing shareholders than the actual shareholders themselves. From operating the Company in their own private interests, the governing body was obligated and entrusted to manage the English East India Company in the interests of all the shareholders. In practice this meant the interests of the Joint Stock Fund of the entity itself, seeded by the capital contributed by shareholders.

The governing body changed into the modern managers the Company's generality had long demanded. This change involved a transition. The transition was away from personal accountability for property and consumable surplus to

[2] G Dari-Mattiacci et al, 'The Emergence of the Corporate Form' (2017) 33 *The Journal of Law, Economics, and Organization* 193, 222. The word 'interloper' emerged in that period to describe free traders who competed with monopolisitic business corporations like the English East India Company.

individual investors, towards economic accountability for a return on capital. For that purpose, the Company recognised the need to distinguish capital from revenue: 'the greatest of accounting's responsibilities is to hold management accountable for the rate of return on capital employed'.[3]

II. DEVELOPMENT OF GOVERNANCE STRUCTURES IN EARLY BUSINESS CORPORATIONS

Governance by a body broadly equivalent to a modern board was a feature of early business corporations. The body comprised a Governor (gouvernor) and others, who were called assistants, committees or directors. A Parliamentary Commission referred to the 'directors' of the Russia (Muscovy) Company in 1604,[4] and the 1618 Charter of the Africa Company called for a board of 12 'directors'.[5] The use of the term 'director' did not become widespread, however, until after the chartering of the Bank of England in 1694.[6]

Early governance bodies of corporations also had roles different from those in modern corporations. The Merchants of the Staple, engaged in the export of wool, and the Merchant Adventurers, engaged in the export of cloth and manufactured goods, were the first companies of English merchants that were organised for overseas trade. Each was a Regulated Company, where the 'role of the board was to enact and enforce rules governing the activities of individual merchants, rather than manage a business'.[7]

Henry VII, in 1505, granted a Charter to The Company of Merchant Adventurers. The Charter authorised the election of 'Four and Twenty of the most sadd [steadfast] discreet and honest Persons of divers [various] fellowships' to be 'Assistants' to the Governor.[8] The role of the Governor and the Assistants was administrative; to resolve disputes that arose between merchant members and to enact ordinances that regulated the members of the company.[9] 'Instead of having an oversight function, the role of the board in these earliest trading companies was legislative (passing ordinances to regulate the membership) and adjudicative (hearing disputes involving the members).'[10]

[3] Bryer (n 1) 368.

[4] Quoted in Report of Committee on the Bill for Free Trade, *Journals of the House of Commons* I, 218 (as cited in CA Cooke, *Corporation, Trust and Company: An Essay in Legal History* (Harvard University Press, 1951) 58).

[5] FA Gevurtz, 'The Historical and Political Origins of the Corporate Board of Directors' (2004) 33 *Hofstra Law Review* 89, 110, fn 97; RR Formoy, *The Historical Foundations of Modern Company Law* (Sweet & Maxwell, 1923) 21.

[6] Gevurtz (n 5) 110; WR Scott, *The Constitution and Finance of English, Scottish, and Irish Joint-Stock Companies to 1720*, vol 1 (Cambridge University Press, 1912) 151–52, 205.

[7] Gevurtz (n 5) 123.

[8] ibid 125.

[9] ibid. This echoed the judicial function of medieval parliaments: ibid 110.

[10] ibid 169.

'Committee' was the word used for 'director' in some early corporations. The role of committees in corporations with Joint Stock funds differed from the role of assistants in Regulated Companies. In the English East India Company, in the period before permanent capital was introduced in 1657, the Governor and committees had regulatory and administrative functions that related to complying with the corporate charter and the subsidiary by-laws that could be passed by the membership. The role of a committee was broader, though. The basis of election of committees to the governing body differed from the basis of the appointment of assistants, who were chosen solely to carry out administrative functions.

As discussed in the previous chapter, and in common with other business corporations of the period, separate Joint Stocks were created for separate voyages or series of voyages, with the Joint Stocks operating sequentially or sometimes concurrently. Not every member of the English East India Company therefore subscribed to every Joint Stock.

Shareholders of each Joint Stock elected committees to represent the interests of that particular Joint Stock. Thus, in addition to their regulatory and compliance functions, committees represented their own interests as shareholders, and the interests of a particular Joint Stock in which they held shares. In periods when there were multiple Joint Stocks, separate meetings were held of the committees representing each Joint Stock.

The committee men involved in governing the English East India Company may have therefore viewed their role differently from the role of assistants on the governing bodies of Regulated Companies. The committees may have seen themselves, at least in part, as representatives of their shareholder' constituencies, and of the interests of those shareholders held in the Joint Stock. In a dispute with the generality comprising small shareholders in the 1620s, the Court of Committees of the English East India Company 'signified that the Governor, Deputy, and Committees were not the Company's Officers, but their neighbours, friends and fellow adventurers, and chosen by themselves'.[11]

Even in these early business corporations, the political climate surrounding the corporation influenced how the role of the governing body was perceived. By the time the English East India Company sought a charter from Cromwell in the 1650s, members of the Court of Committees had conceded that the role of the governing body could not be perpetual or hereditary. Instead, it was to manage:

> [I]f any failure is attributed to the managers … it may be for the future be managed by those who have lived and are well versed in these parts, with the help of others of known ability and integrity, and be chosen by the adventurers themselves, their posts not being perpetual or hereditary.[12]

[11] WN Sainsbury (1964d) *Calendar of state papers, colonial series, East Indies, China and Japan, 1625–1629* (HMSO, 1884), reprinted Vaduz, Kraus Reprint Ltd, 523 (as cited in Bryer (n 1) 353–54).

[12] EB Sainsbury, *A Calendar of the Court Minutes etc of the East India Company, 1655–1659* (Clarendon Press, 1916) 128.

In common with other words connected with the development of the modern company, the word 'management', which was used in corporations' statutes and charters from the sixteenth century,[13] had at that time a meaning different from the modern meaning. Up until the beginning of the twentieth century, 'to manage' meant the same as 'to direct' and 'to supervise'.[14] It was in the twentieth century, with the emergence of management science, that the word 'manage' took on the meaning that we now understand it to have. Thus, it was never the role of boards of directors or the equivalent to 'manage' a corporation in the modern sense of day-to-day involvement in the running of the company; the words 'direct' and 'supervise' capture much more the flavour of the role.[15]

In the English East India Company, tension between the representative roles of committees and their governance roles emerged the first half of the seventeenth century. Debate took place through the Courts (meetings) of the Company. There were Courts of Committees (meetings of boards of directors), and also General Courts; meetings of the generality comprising all the shareholders. Successive Courts of Committees were primarily comprised of elite merchants, who at that time ran the Company in their own personal interests rather than in the interests of the investing generality or the interests of the Company itself.

The General Court (meeting) of shareholders was an English East India Company innovation, which became part of the governance models for companies from that point on. The Governor, Deputy Governor and committees (directors) were elected, and fundamental resolutions were passed. Minimum qualification holdings for voting were in place, and the Company, through the General Court, had autonomy to pass by-laws subject to the Charter.[16] The General Court was the primary battleground for the two factions, shaping the governance not only of the English East India Company but also of the emerging modern company.

III. SHAREHOLDER ACTIVISM IN THE ENGLISH EAST INDIA COMPANY

Many of the elite merchants had become wealthy by trading successfully through the vehicle of the Levant Company. The Levant Company was a Regulated Company. The elite merchants were led by Sir Thomas Smythe, Auditor of the

[13] For example, 'to order, manage and direct the Affairs and Business of the said Corporation'. *The Charter of the Corporation of the Amicable Society for a Perpetual Assurance-Office* (Geo Sawbridge, 1710) 1.

[14] 'Manage, v.' *Oxford English Dictionary* (June 2021) at www-oed-com.ezproxy.auckland.ac.nz/view/Entry/113210?result=3&rskey=JYVU13&.

[15] The role of the board in 'management' is also discussed in PL Davies (ed), *Gower and Davies: Principles of Modern Company Law*, 8th edn (Sweet & Maxwell, 2008) 367: '[I]t is perhaps surprising that the model article for public companies refers to "management" quite generally, since it is clear that, in a large company, the totality of its management is something beyond the grasp of even the most talented set of directors.' But understanding management as akin to direction or supervision addresses this issue.

[16] AB Levy, *Private Corporations and their Control* (Routledge, 1950) 26.

City of London, who had made his fortune importing spices from Aleppo and currants from the Greek Islands.[17] The elite merchants would have preferred for it to be possible for the English East India Company to be operated as a Regulated Company, allowing each member to trade commodities on their own account. The risk and scale of investment required meant, however, that subscriptions were needed from outside investors. Those outside investors became the small shareholding generality. Although the Company operated through investment in shared voyages from its inception, it retained, in its first Charter, some of the characteristics typical of a Regulated Company, including the ability of members, including members who were part of the governing body, to trade on their own account.[18]

Around 1617, differences between the two shareholding groups in the English East India Company emerged in a manner not divorced from the changing political climate. The elite group had long controlled foreign trade. Charters contained a 'mere merchant' clause that restricted access by other groups who were not part of the merchant class.

The Company's need to raise high amounts of capital to fund voyages had meant, however, that non-merchants were able to obtain small stakes in the Company. The Company became widely held, with nearly 1,000 investing shareholders subscribing to the Second Stock, drawn from all strata of society.[19] For most of the early part of the seventeenth century, the feudal system of voting remained in place in the Company, with each shareholder having a vote so long as they held a qualifying number of shares. This system meant that even shareholders with a relatively small stake as members of the generality attending the General Court could be involved in and influence decision making.

Losses made it difficult to collect instalments from investors in the Second Joint Stock.[20] The main task of the Court of Committees, dominated by the elite merchants, became to persuade the small shareholder members of the generality to continue to invest in the Company. In 1619, at the insistence of the generality, auditors were appointed.[21] The laws required the appointment of two 'auditors general' (in addition to auditors for the generality), who had to ensure that accounts were true (factual) and fair (unbiased).[22] 'Negligences' in the accounts were discovered. The auditors claimed the surplus was understated by £50,000. The Court of Committees responded that the Company's business was carried on fairly.

[17] W Dalrymple, *The Anarchy: The Relentless Rise of the East India Company* (Bloomsbury Publishing, 2019) 1–2.

[18] Bryer (n 1) 344–45.

[19] Cooke (n 4) 57–58.

[20] WR Scott, *The Constitution and Finance of English, Scottish, and Irish Joint-Stock Companies to 1720*, vol 2 (Cambridge University Press, 1910) 107.

[21] Bryer (n 1) 348.

[22] ibid 351. The terms 'true' and 'fair' have survived to be used in modern accounting.

Central to convincing the generality of the merits and fairness of the investment was the development of a system of accounting for the capital of the Company.[23] Accounting laws were subsequently adopted based on a feudal idea of surplus as the excess of income over expenditure. The 'Accompts Proper' provided a summary of the state of the capital and the 'Accompts Currant' provided a detailed catalogue and summary of the movement of capital through the year.[24]

In 1623 the generality were told to anticipate that an instalment of £200,000 would be demanded from them. The generality responded that their expectation was for '"thicker dividends" rather than more payments'.[25] In 1624 the Company made a substantial distribution, but combined the payment with a motion that there be no further dividends until debt was reduced. Lessons learned from another venture were used as an illustrative lesson: 'Russia Company had failed to show prudence in its finance and "had smarted for its neglect".'[26]

Despite auditors' having been appointed and other steps taken to placate the generality, disputes between the elite and the generality continued through the 1620s. These disputes centered on the ways distributions were made, and later the methods used by the elite-controlled Court of Committees to determine distributions.

Initially, when a Joint Stock was terminated the surplus of commodities, such as pepper or calico and any cash, was divided. This practice disadvantaged those shareholders who were not merchants and could not dispose of commodities easily. Many of the elite merchants who controlled the Court of Committees could sell on the commodities through their retail networks, whereas members of the generality, who were often not merchants, could not. In 1629, 'in order to give contentment to the gentry,' (the generality) it was decided that distributions would be made in money.[27]

As the payments were based on the wholesale price of the commodities,[28] the system continued to favour the controlling elite. The elite merchants acquired commodities as cheaply as possible from the Company, and then sold them on through their retail networks at retail prices.[29] Stung by criticism, the elite, through the Court of Committees, signified that they were in fact representing all the shareholders.[30] That argument was not accepted by a faction of the generality represented and led by Thomas Smethwike, who argued that the trade depended on the capital contributions of the generality. It was inequitable to favour the interests of a few at the expense of those who provided the capital.

[23] ibid 346.
[24] ibid 348.
[25] Scott (n 20) 107 (footnotes omitted).
[26] ibid.
[27] Quoted in Court Book, xi, 16 January 1629 (as cited in Scott (n 20) 110); Bryer (n 1) 352.
[28] Bryer (n 1) 345.
[29] ibid 352.
[30] ibid 353–54 (footnotes omitted).

It was also dangerous to the cohesion of the totality. The elite were taking the Company's goods at their own prices and were attempting to 'engross the whole trade and stock into the hands of a few'.[31] The Governor had to concede that Smethwike was well informed: 'Mr Smethwike … is perfecter in the books than the Governor himself.'[32]

In the 1630s the Company appears to have shifted to a system of double-entry bookkeeping in order to demonstrate an equal return on equal capital contributed. This crucially significant shift in accounting practice meant members of the generality were able to get an exact balance whenever they wanted to.[33] References to Balance of the Estate in the minute books may be references to a balance sheet typical of double-entry bookkeeping systems from the middle of the sixteenth century.[34] The feudal practice of divisions made from capital remained in place, however, as capital was terminable.[35]

Despite concessions made by the elite merchants in their roles as committees (directors), the generality continued to assert that the Court of Committees had not been required to commit to their demands for accountability.[36] When in 1640 the Governor of the East India Company rebuked the generality for their failure to subscribe, the response recorded in the Court Book was 'Until they shall see something *acted* by the King and State, men will not be persuaded to underwrite a new stock.'[37]

The elite controlled the Court of Committees as the majority shareholders of the English East India Company. As merchants, their own interests were not served by the concessions. Why did the elite take account of the views of the minority generality? First, the costs involved in mounting voyages meant that the elite needed the capital contributed by the investing generality. Second, even though the generality held small blocks of shares, they had a high degree of power, because of the feudal principle of one vote for one member. Even though in practice the generality usually accepted the advice of the Court of Committees rather than attempting to remove the committees from office, the generality had the power to refuse to provide further capital investment for future Joint Stocks, and for that reason were influential.[38]

[31] ibid 354 (footnotes omitted).

[32] Sainsbury (n 11) 523 (as cited in Bryer (n 1)).

[33] Bryer (n 1) 355.

[34] BS Yamey, 'Closing the Ledger' (1970) 1 *Accounting and Business Research* 71, 72; Bryer (n 1) 357.

[35] Bryer (n 1) 365.

[36] ibid 357–59. A Committee looked at the Company's whole estate and, in 1634, to head off the 'ravelling and diving' of Thomas Smithwicke and his friends into the Company's books, the Auditors were said by the Governor to be within two weeks of 'making up a general account of the Joint Stock … the first general account since 1628'.

[37] WW Hunter, *History of India: The European Struggle for Indian Supremacy in the Seventeenth Century*, ed AVW Jackson (Grolier Society, 1907) 252.

[38] Bryer (n 1) 359.

The Court of Committees was obliged to concede, therefore, what the generality had long demanded: that the committees' role was as managers (in the historic and broader sense of the term), responsible for the capital contributed to the Company and accountable to the shareholders.[39] The committees acknowledged that they would be out of office unless re-elected by the generality. Concessions were made to the members of the generality because of the capital they contributed. The generality, however, began to lose power over decision making. Voting rights began to transition to being attached to shares and therefore capital contributed rather than to individual members. It was proposed by one set of large investors, the Assada merchants (previously Courteen's Association), that '[n]one with an adventure under £500 to have a voice in election, but those who have adventured so much to have "a ball in the balanceing box" in the event of any question, that "soe the Stocke may governe the Stocke"'.[40] The intention of the Assada merchants was clear: the only way in which the 'Stocke may govern the Stocke' – that Joint Stock capital could reign – was if every £500 of capital had one vote.[41]

IV. MAURICE THOMSON AND THE EMERGENCE OF DIRECTORS' DUTIES

Maurice Thomson may well be the most under-recognised architect of the modern company, even though he did not personally favour Joint Stock. He was born into an established Hertfordshire family at the same time as the inception of the English East India Company, around 1600, and his fortunes became inextricably linked with the Company.

By the time he was 17 years old, Thomson was a ship's captain involved in the lucrative trade between England and Virginia provisioning the new colony. By 1626 he was a free-trading interloper,[42] attempting to encroach on the Company's trade into East India.[43] By the early 1630s, Thomson was London's greatest tobacco merchant and trader, and a privateer in raids against the Spanish in the Caribbean. As part of Courteen's Association sanctioned by Charles I, Thomson competed with the Company. During the English Civil War he worked to dismantle the Company's monopoly.[44]

As a member of the generality, Thomson later argued that the English East India Company should become a Regulated Company rather than operating

[39] ibid.

[40] EB Sainsbury, *A Calendar of the Court Minutes etc of the East India Company, 1644–1649* (Clarendon Press, 1912) 371.

[41] ibid.

[42] For the origins of the word 'interloper', see n 2.

[43] R Brenner, *Merchants and Revolution: Commercial Change, Political Conflict, and London's Overseas Traders, 1550–1653* (Verso, 2003) 174–76.

[44] PGE Clemens, 'Review of "Merchants and Revolution: Commercial Change, Political Conflict, and London's Overseas Traders, 1550–1653"' (1993) 21 *Reviews in American History* 575, 576.

with Joint Stock funds. In the period leading up to the Cromwellian Charter, Thomson highlighted various deficiencies in the existing structure and form of the English East India Company. Nevertheless, Thomson became the first Governor of the English East India Company after it acquired its Charter with permanent capital in 1657.

In the 1620s, Thomson and other interlopers traded freely in the East Indies. They were, therefore, opposed to a monopolistic Charter for the English East India Company that would restrict their ability to trade. Creation of corporations was covered by the royal prerogative, with the consent of Parliament required for monopolistic privileges after the Statute against Monopolies was enacted in 1623.[45] Some interlopers were Anabaptists or Levellers, who favoured the separation of Church and State and who opposed the authority derived from a Charter.[46]

The interlopers generally came from outside London, beginning their careers as shopkeepers, or ships' captains, or as emigrants to the colonies. Acutely aware of the profit potential from commerce and colonisation, they were opposed to its restriction by monopolistic charters:[47] 'they considered that the prohibition was absolutely against the national liberties'.[48] Thomson himself was a religious independent and a leader in the London 'City Revolution' that led to the English Civil War.[49]

Support of free trade had been shared by William Cecil, Queen Elizabeth I's chief adviser at the time of the privateers. Cecil had denounced those who would take away an Englishman's right to trade.[50] An exception was made possible for corporations through the Statute of Monopolies, on the basis that the ostensible purpose of corporations had to relate to public goods. In a sense that became a loophole for merchants to gain or retain monopolistic rights through a chartered corporation.

Interlopers encroached on the charter rights of the English East India Company over the years, and the Company at times lost its exclusive privileges. Free traders then mounted voyages to India. Competition in the period from 1640 and during the English Civil War increased in the period from 1653 to 1656 once Cromwell had control, and when questions about the validity of the Charter meant that there was in effect free trade.[51]

[45] Statute of Monopolies 1623 (21 Jac 1 c 3). There was strong public feeling against monopolies. Monopolies granted by the King without the consent of Parliament were void at common law. The Crown argued that this did not extend to trading companies, but Parliament ultimately prevailed, with settlement in 1698 in relation to the English East India Company: 9 & 10 Will III, c 44 (as cited in Levy (n 16) 24).

[46] SA Khan, *The East India Trade in the XVIIth Century in its Political and Economic Aspects* (S Chand & Co, 1923) 82.

[47] Brenner (n 43) 685.

[48] Quoted in Public Record Office, CO 77, vol vii, no 6 (as cited in Khan (n 46) 83).

[49] Clemens (n 44) 575.

[50] Khan (n 46) 83.

[51] See the discussion in Brenner (n 43) 176–79.

The case against Joint Stock had been based on abuse of power by the elite who controlled the Company through the Court of Committees and operated the Company in their own private interests.[52] The generality camp was a coalition of the disaffected; the Levellers, the City merchants excluded from the English East India Company – all 'would unite in condemning a Company that had been founded on a charter granted by a king, and that excluded every other English merchant from a share in the trade'.[53]

In what could be called an early elucidation of agency theory,[54] Maurice Thomson argued that no one should trust another with their capital:

> It is against the rule of merchants to commit the disposal of their stock to the will of a few men … [and, therefore] [a] general stock managed only by a few, in which those who adventure largely can give no assistance, is very discouraging to personal endeavours and contrary to the custom of those companies who trade by particular stocks …[55]

If there was to be a chartered corporation for trade to India, Thomson argued in favour of the Regulated Company form, claiming:

> A general stock is slow in motion and attended by great charges, which devour much of the stock, whereas the government of a company like the Merchant Adventurers, the Muscovia and Turkey merchants is far less chargeable, though their respective stocks much exceed the joint stock of the East India Adventurers.[56]

The Governor of the English East India Company initially argued the controlling elite merchants as the founders of the Company were deserving of the benefits of its success:

> In free trade every merchant makes his own rules, but the Company is not guided by the example of merchants alone, for the foundation of the East India trade was laid at the charge not only of merchants but of the nobility, gentry, and others, who have borne its great burden: therefore it belongs to them and their successors as well as to the merchants.[57]

Thomson, in response, argued that capital would circulate more quickly if Joint Stock were not used. Also, free trade would benefit entrepreneurial men of small means, whereas 'it is not to the interest of a young man to leave his stock to the management of others and sit still in expectation of a tedious and slender gain'.[58]

[52] In fact, the most profitable voyages were those where the elite merchants operated their own capital, where they worked to minimise costs and ensure that turnover of capital was as speedy as possible.

[53] Khan (n 46) 85.

[54] MC Jensen and WH Meckling, 'Theory of the Firm: Managerial Behavior, Agency Costs and Ownership Structure' (1976) 3 *Journal of Financial Economics* 305.

[55] EB Sainsbury, *A Calendar of the Court Minutes etc. of the East India Company, 1650–1654* (Clarendon Press, 1913) 354. See also the discussion in Brenner (n 43) 179–81.

[56] ibid 354.

[57] ibid 358.

[58] ibid 369.

Thomson also identified the other problem for small investing shareholders in the English East India Company. The elite as merchants could extract greater value from the trade than the small investors. Thomson argued that free trade would prevent engrossing of pepper and other goods to keep them at a high price. 'Only those who have such designs in view will subscribe any more to a joint stock, and the profit made by it cannot be encouraging …'[59]

Although the English East India Company did not become a Regulated Company, and free trade arguments did not ultimately prevail, investors like Thomson, as members of the generality, succeeded in driving through key changes in the governance of the English East India Company. In doing so they prevailed against the elite merchants who were the major shareholders, the wholesale customers of the Company, and members of its governing body.

By the time the English East India Company sought a charter from the Protector, the elite merchants had shifted to conceding that the role of the governing body could not be perpetual or hereditary. The presumption had previously operated that those who had borne the greatest burden in the past were entitled to the greatest benefit. The role of a governing body shifted to management of the capital, with selection of the committees to be made by the shareholders with voting rights attached to capital held rather than membership.[60]

On Thomson's access objection, the Company argued that Joint Stock in fact potentially provided access to a wider range of investors than free trade, where every free trader had to be a merchant.[61] 'If it is settled in a joint stock, it is open to all who adventure in it, but if in an open trade, all who are not merchants will be excluded.'[62]

Changes brought about by the investing generality activism included a requirement that the controlling Court of Committees swear oaths to act in the interests of all the shareholders. The practice of favourable pricing for the elite merchants had ended. In the 1657 Charter granted by Cromwell, the oath[63] to be taken by the Governor, Deputy and 24 committees on their election required committees (directors) to be faithful and true to the interests of the adventurers (shareholders) in the current stock, including that 'an equall and indifferent hand be carried in the government of this fellowship and in the affaires thereof to *all* the adventurers that shall adventure or putt in stocke'.[64] No longer could the elite merchants, by controlling the governing body, run the Company in their own interests.

Maurice Thomson became Governor of the East India Company. As a member of the investing generality, Thomson had a powerful influence on the

[59] ibid.
[60] Sainsbury (n 12) 128, and accompanying text.
[61] Scott (n 20) 122.
[62] Sainsbury (n 12) 128.
[63] ibid 186–87.
[64] ibid 187 (emphasis added).

Charter of 1657, no doubt leading to the concessions to the generality. Thomson had set out all the disadvantages of trading using a Joint Stock, including the agency problem for investors. Nevertheless, Thomson and other members of the generality became founding investors of the English East India Company in its modern form. Although debates continued to rage over the desirability of free trade compared with investing through a monopolistic corporation, some of the generality of the English East Company had come around. Why?

Several reasons can be identified. First, the disadvantages of leaving trade open had become apparent following a fair trial of that form of trade in the preceding decades.[65] If things did not go well for the Company during the free-trade period early in the Protectorate, they also did not go well for the interlopers, the free traders who ignored the monopoly rights in the Charter. As Samuel Lamb later recounted, there was

> a great lowering of English commodities and advancing of Indian commodities, an increase of presents [bribes] to governors, etc, to such an odious excess that at length the very private traders themselves, being without union or protection, were the forwardest petitioners for a return to joint stock.[66]

The fact that free trade resulted in a reduction in the price of commodities for all participants, with trade to India becoming unprofitable, was used by proponents of the Charter and of Joint Stock to argue that permitting free trade would be disastrous for English trading interests to India.[67]

Second, the payment of dividends in cash rather than commodities, and the requirement that the committees run the Company in the interests of all the shareholders rather than in their own personal interests, expunged the chief grievances of the generality.

Third, and as discussed in the previous chapter, the establishment of permanent capital meant the governing body comprised managers charged with looking after the interests of the shareholders combined in the Joint Stock as the permanent capital of the English East India Company.[68] The VOC had permanent capital from 1623. Its success, the comparative success of combined voyages through single Joint Stock for the English East India Company, and the advantages in having permanent infrastructure in a distant land, were all factors that strengthened the case for permanent Joint Stock.

Finally, the members of the governing body conceded that their committees' roles were not as of right. With the shift to voting rights being attached to a share in the initial capital contributed, the small shareholding generality lost some of their voting power and influence. The trade-off for the enfranchisement

[65] ibid xii.

[66] Quoted in 'Seasonable Observations for the Encouraging of Foreign Commerce 1657' (as cited in G Cawston and AH Keane, *The Early Chartered Companies (AD 1296–1858)* (Edward Arnold, 1896) 103).

[67] Khan (n 46) 147. See the discussion below.

[68] Bryer (n 1) 367.

of capital at the expense of individual members may have been increased opportunities for the generality to participate in governance. In common with earlier charters, the 1657 Charter setting out the constitution of the English East India Company stated it was to have a Governor, Deputy Governor, Treasurer and 24 committees.[69] But, in a break from the past, rather than a permanent governing body drawn solely from the elite merchants with large holdings, eight committees were required to retire by rotation each July, and Governors and Deputy Governors could serve for a maximum of two successive years.

The VOC dominated the India trade in the first half of the seventeenth century. Once it also acquired permanent capital in 1657, the English East India Company had an advantage over the VOC. Unlike the VOC, through double-entry bookkeeping, the capital of the English East India Company was separate for accounting and legal purposes from the investing shareholders. This meant managers were accountable for a measurable return on capital. The impact of this innovation is discussed in chapter 5.

[69] Hunter (n 37) 285.

5

The Rise and Fall of the English East India Company

I. THE ENGLISH EAST INDIA COMPANY WITH PERMANENT CAPITAL

THE ENGLISH EAST India Company with permanent capital did not prosper immediately. During the period of the Cromwellian charter, straitened times meant that only 50 per cent of the capital was called.[1] The English East India Company borrowed £40,000 and no dividends were paid.[2]

A new charter was granted in 1661 after the 1660 Restoration.[3] Sole trade was granted to the English East India Company 'for ever hereafter', subject to revocation if the Company was unprofitable.[4] In return for Royal favour, the Company loaned money to Charles II at favourable rates. Some commentators attribute the success of the English East India Company in the eighteenth century to the relationship of the Company to public finance and the Crown, seen in the loans and then repayments made to the King during the period.[5] Both Cromwell and the Stuarts granted charters with provisions allowing the charters to be recalled,[6] meaning loans and payments to Cromwell or the King were deemed essential to ensure the continuing existence of the Company.

[1] WW Hunter, *History of India: The European Struggle for Indian Supremacy in the Seventeenth Century*, ed AVW Jackson (Grolier Society, 1907) 285. Hunter noted that £369,891 was paid up.

[2] WR Scott, *The Constitution and Finance of English, Scottish and Irish Joint-Stock Companies to 1720*, vol 2 (Cambridge University Press, 1910) 130.

[3] *The East-India companies charter, granted by the Kings most excellent Majesty Charles the second, under the great seal of England, dated the third day of April, in the 13th year of his Majesties reign, 1661* (The Making of the Modern World, 1759) at www.link.gale.com/apps/doc/U0101110584/MOME?u=learn&sid=bookmark-MOME&xid=d168a42a&pg=1 accessed 2 July 2019.

[4] Scott (n 2) 131.

[5] R Harris, *Industrializing English Law: Entrepreneurship and Business Organization, 1720–1844* (Cambridge University Press, 2000) 53–59. Robins highlights Sir Josiah Child's becoming a favourite at Court and transferring 10,000 of Company shares to James, brother of King Charles II: N Robins, *The Corporation that Changed the World: How the East India Company Shaped the Modern Multinational*, 2nd edn (Pluto Press, 2012) 51; SA Khan, *The East India Trade in the XVIIth Century in its Political and Economic Aspects* (S Chand & Co, 1923) 148–50; WR Scott, *The Constitution and Finance of English, Scottish and Irish Joint-Stock Companies to 1720*, vol 2 (Cambridge University Press, 1910) 143.

[6] Scott (n 2) 129.

In 1662, the Company declared a 20 per cent dividend. At that time, shares were selling at a 10 per cent discount to the paid up amount. Due to low paid up capital, the Company devoted profits for first four years to the development of trade. The Company was able to borrow additional funds on bonds at favourable rates.[7] The stable equity structure brought about by permanent capital facilitated a sharp increase in investment.[8]

The capitalist system of return on capital was in place. When declaring the dividend, the governor and committees laid out the principle that these distributions would, from that point on, not be divisions where capital and income were not distinguished, as had been the practice in the past.[9] When the first dividend was declared, the Governor stated that 'a division of twenty per cent in money may be made without touching the capital'.[10]

Between 1664 and 1667, the company returned amounts equivalent to two-thirds of its paid-in capital of £500,000 to shareholders. Crucially, however, the Governor and committees of the Company had realised the concept that the amount of money paid in by shareholders in subscriptions was not the same as the permanent Joint Stock or the Corporate Fund of the Company. Capital contributed could be returned to shareholders, and capital contributed did not have to be invested in fixed assets.[11]

The Company's governing body transitioned away from being personally accountable for property and consumable surplus to individual investors, and instead became responsible for a financial return on capital. For that purpose, the Company recognised the need to distinguish capital from revenue: 'the greatest of accounting's responsibilities is to hold management accountable for the rate of return on capital employed'.[12]

The English East India Company experienced an economic boom over the next three decades, completing 104 voyages between London and the East Indies between 1658 and 1688. In that period, sales increased eight-fold.[13] Profits after the formation of the permanent Corporate Fund were considerable.[14] Generous gifts to Charles II ensured widening powers in the Company's subsequent corporate charters.[15] By the end of the seventeenth century, the value of the English

[7] ibid 132.

[8] G Dari-Mattiaci et al, 'The Emergence of the Corporate Form' (2017) 33 *The Journal of Law, Economics and Organization* 193, 220.

[9] Scott (n 2) 131–32.

[10] EB Sainsbury, *A Calendar of the Court Minutes etc. of the East India Company, 1660–1663* (Clarendon Press, 1922) 131.

[11] RA Bryer, 'The History of Accounting and the Transition to Capitalism in England: Part 2 Evidence' (2000) 25 *Accounting, Organizations and Society* 327, 368: 'Permanent clearly did not mean that the capital would not return to the shareholders, or that it would be invested in fixed assets. The transition from terminable capital meant that management was now accountable to a social capital for the value of the capital advanced …'.

[12] ibid 368.

[13] Dari-Mattiaci et al (n 8) 236.

[14] AB Levy, *Private Corporations and their Control* (Routledge, 1950) 28.

[15] Khan (n 5) 148–50.

East India Company's trade was fast catching up with that of the Dutch East India Company (VOC). Between 1657 and 1691, proprietors received 840 per cent in dividends on their original investment: 50 per cent dividends were paid in 1680, 1682, 1689 and 1691.[16] The Company's share price quadrupled from £60–£70 in 1664 to £245 in 1677 and £300 in 1680.[17] In 1682, the original permanent capital was doubled by the issue of bonus shares.[18] Personnel sent to Asia increased from around 5,000 in 1657 to 10,000 in the first years of the eighteenth century.[19]

As the Company had paid dividends of 60 per cent in the first seven years of permanent capital, few, if any, owners of shares in the original united Joint Stock wanted to be bought out after seven years, as the Charter had made possible. Shares had become transferable,[20] and a secondary market for shares had developed. The Company became widely held, with the largest holding being £4,000 in nominal value of shares.

The remaining vestiges of the Regulated Company system disappeared in this period. In 1657, the members of the generality were the freemen of the Company, also called adventurers. In the 1657 Charter, it remained possible to be a freeman or member of the Company without holding shares. A shareholding requirement was introduced in the 1661 Charter. By 1693, purchasers of shares were no longer required to swear the oath of admission to the Company.[21] The Company had completed the transition away from membership by payment of an admission fee, which had been the practice in business corporations, including Regulated Companies. Now membership was based entirely on a holding of shares.

Voting continued to be attached to a minimum holding of shares in the permanent Joint Stock Fund; £500 or more of nominal value shares equalled one vote.[22] Those who had less than £500 in holdings were able to join their holdings for a vote.[23] From 1693 it was determined that there should be one vote for every £1,000, up to a maximum of 10 votes for £10,000.[24]

The victories won by the generality in the previous century were maintained. Quarterly meetings of the 'little Parliaments' met to hear directors' reports and to vote on corporate policy. In practice the General Court rarely refused to follow the proposals of the governing body.[25] The annual meeting

[16] Robins (n 5) 49.
[17] ibid 48–49.
[18] Levy (n 14) 27.
[19] Dari-Mattiaci (n 8) 233.
[20] Levy (n 14) 28.
[21] CA Cooke, *Corporation, Trust and Company: An Essay in Legal History* (Harvard University Press, 1951) 59.
[22] Levy (n 14) 27.
[23] Bryer (n 11) 368 notes one commentator who says that this was the first time this form of voting right had been incorporated in the Charter. However, see ch 2 and the discussion of the Mines Royal, where that form of voting may have been possible.
[24] Levy (n 14) 28.
[25] ibid 40.

in April regularly attracted over a thousand shareholders, brought together to elect 24 directors to office for 12 months, with those directors then electing the Governor.[26] (Provisions for rotation of directors were never, however, applied, with some directors and governors holding office for long periods.[27])

It was not all plain sailing for the English East India Company. Attacks continued from many quarters, in particular from those who continued to favour free trade, and from rival companies like the Turkey Company that traded using the Regulated Company system. In 1681, the Turkey Company claimed that the English East India Company excluded young merchants by failing to issue new shares.[28] In a case brought through the courts, it was argued that the English East India Company restrained all but its own shareholders from trade in India and that it was not therefore a company that maintained trade. The grant of monopoly rights to the Company was, therefore, against the Magna Carta and other Statutes, and also contrary to the common law right of all Englishmen to trade freely.[29] Trade through companies such as the Turkey Company (a Regulated Company) was open to all on payment of £25, whereas the English East India Company was open only to the few: 'the invisible East India Merchant, the Body Politick, countenances some few among them to engross, buy and sell at their own Rates, and excludes all others from the great and excessive Advantage of the few'.[30] Sir Josiah Child, who, as noted, had previously transferred 10,000 shares to Prince James and who was now Governor of the Company, responded that Joint Stock was more inclusive since 'noblemen, gentlemen, shopkeepers, widows, orphans and all other subjects' could buy shares, whereas only merchants who had served an apprenticeship to a particular trade could become members of a Regulated Company.[31]

The presiding judge, Judge Jeffreys, detected the free-riding weakness in these arguments from the Turkey Company. Jeffreys enquired:

> [I]s it fair after they [the English East India Company] have reduced it into so good a condition at a vast expense and trouble, for other particular persons to come and say 'let us have the benefit of it that have had nothing of the burden and charge?'.[32]

The disastrous experiences of the previous century, when competition meant that both the English East India Company and the Courteen merchants, and then the interloping free traders, lost money, led to wide acceptance that trade in the Indies could only be carried on by monopolistic chartered companies with

[26] Robins (n 5) 27.
[27] Levy (n 14) 28.
[28] Khan (n 5) 181.
[29] ibid.
[30] *Wherein are shewn The Disadvantages to a Nation, by confining any Trade to a Corporation with a Joint-Stock* (J Walthoe, 1730) as cited in Khan (n 5) 147–48.
[31] Scott (n 2) 142.
[32] TB Howell, *Howell's State Trials* (vol x, 371–554) as cited in Khan (n 5) 181–82.

permanent capital. As Khan points out, a Regulated Company would not have succeeded in India:

> Concentration of all the materials on a definite object, and its consistent pursuit through failure and success, were the essential qualities required in an English Company in India. These could not have been supplied by a Regulated Company … the real reason for the advancement of monopoly laid in the impossibility of carrying on the East India trade by any other method.[33]

As was later demonstrated by Josiah Childe, who led the Company through its next period, freedom of trade would have led to the English being expelled from the East by the Dutch, French and Danes.[34]

The Privy Council in 1681 responded to the claims of lack of freedom of access by requiring an enlargement of stock in the Company by the issue of more shares. The Joint Stock principle was strongly maintained.

After 1688, interlopers and free traders swayed public and parliamentary opinion against the English East India Company. A 5 per cent tax was imposed on the value of the capital.[35] A group of competitors was granted its own monopoly; however, the new Company was eventually combined with existing English East India Company in 1709, resulting in the first merger in company law history.[36]

Predicting modern capitalism, it was allegedly Josiah Child, through an anonymous pamphlet, who recognised in 1701 that the East India trade could become an instrument of capital accumulation that would act as a stimulation for industrial development and higher productivity.[37] Child termed it a 'Fund of Wealth'.[38]

II. THE IMPACT OF THE LEGAL STRUCTURE

It is well known that Adam Smith was a trenchant critic of the English East India Company,[39] as well as of the viability of the Joint Stock company form, whether incorporated or unincorporated. As Chaudhuri remarked:

> When Adam Smith, writing in the third quarter of the eighteenth century, castigated the East India Companies as the repository of monopoly power and economic

[33] Khan (n 5) 188.
[34] ibid 212.
[35] Levy (n 14) 28.
[36] ibid 28–29.
[37] J Child, *The Great Honour and Advantage of the East-India Trade to the Kingdom, Asserted* (Thomas Speed, 1697) at https://quod.lib.umich.edu/e/eebo/A32830.0001.001/1:3?rgn=div1;view=fulltext.
[38] ibid 4–5.
[39] For Adam Smith's views of the East India Company's monopoly, see A Smith, *An Inquiry into the Nature and Causes of the Wealth of Nations*, vol 2, eds R Campbell and A Skinner (Clarendon, 1976) 343–485.

> inefficiency, he was to remain unaware that the end of the chartered companies not only did not presage the disappearance of the particular form of their corporate structure but that their commercial monopoly was to be replaced by the monopoly of capitalism.[40]

By the time Smith wrote about the Company, the extent of private trade by employees of the Company meant it was no longer a monopoly in reality. An important additional factor that contributed to the Company's success, however, was its structure.

The introduction of permanent capital in the Company as a perpetual corporation facilitated a long-term focus by the governing body. It made the development of multidivisional administrative structures possible; and it made size and scale possible. It also led to the separation of shareholders, who became owners of shares with rights attached to them, from management of the Company by the governing body – a phenomenon in modern companies later identified by Berle and Means as separation of ownership from control.[41] The tools of accounting meant, however, that return on capital could be measured, making the governing body accountable to shareholders. Shareholders were also empowered through the regular Courts (meetings), where they could find out about and vote on corporate policy. As discussed in previous chapters, neither a measure of return on capital nor regular meeting of shareholders was a tool available to shareholders in the English East India Company's primary rival, the VOC. Finally, 'Like the modern corporation, the Company's share price was its heart-beat, communicating to the world the market's estimates of its future prospects.'[42]

In the 100 years after the 1657 Charter, the fortunes of the English East India Company were transformed. A company that had previously limped along, surviving precariously from voyage to voyage through the first half of the seventeenth century, and which had intended to disband only a year before the 1657 Charter, became the most enduring and wealthiest corporation the world has ever seen. As one commentator put it, 'Under [Cromwell's] charter the East India Company transformed itself from a feeble relic of the medieval trade-guild into the vigorous forerunner of the modern Joint-Stock Company.'[43] Another commentator observed that 'the reason for its great commercial and political strength must be sought at a deeper level, in the underlying structural system created by the Company's entrepreneurial and managerial committees'[44] (ie directors).

[40] KN Chaudhuri, *The Trading World of Asia and the English East India Company: 1660–1760* (Cambridge University Press, 1978) 19–20.

[41] AA Berle and GC Means, *The Modern Corporation and Private Property*, rev edn (Harcourt, Brace & World, 1968).

[42] Robins (n 5) 24–25.

[43] Hunter (n 1) 290–91.

[44] Chaudhuri (n 40) 21.

The most rapid development of the English East India Company was from 1660 to 1700. Import and export quantities grew significantly in absolute and relative terms.[45] As discussed in section I, the success of the Company during this period is usually attributed to its monopoly over trade to India and its political connections. The contribution of its legal structure to its success is not usually recognised beyond the acknowledgement that it was the first English corporation to have permanent capital.

Did the legal structure that had developed by 1657 contribute to the business success of the English East India Company? Increased ease of raising capital, efficiencies in transferring property, vertical integration leading to decreased costs, and decentralisation are advantages of the legal structure of the Company. These are advantages also offered by the modern multinational corporation.[46] Economists recognise that the English East India Company was, in fact, the first multidivisional firm.[47] Alfred Chandler and Oliver Williamson both identified the significance of the invention of the multidivisional firm. However, they identified the 1920s as the time and the United States as the place where the modern corporate form first emerged.[48] But the English East India Company had all the key features of the modern company by 1657 and became a multidivisional firm after 1657. Is the development of the modern corporate structure a precondition for a corporation's becoming a multidivisional firm, and for size and scale to develop? First legal structure and then financial success?

The English East India Company integrated permanent capital into the *persona ficta* corporation. The *persona ficta* corporation had existed in the abstract, separate from all natural persons, since the concept was introduced into the common law by Coke CJ.[49] Did that form make possible enclosure and generation of value as an entity over the long term? Did permanent capital rather than ownership by current shareholders facilitate longevity, and permit systems and structures to develop? Certainly, double-entry bookkeeping allowed the separation of the Corporate Fund in the Company as a separate legal entity from existing shareholders in their private capacities. In addition, the use of double-entry bookkeeping made it possible for investing shareholders to make the governing body accountable for a return on capital on their investment in the Company. In short, arguments about the importance of the legal form of the corporation combined with its accounting treatment are buttressed by the striking success of the English East India Company after 1657, when it had acquired all the characteristics of the modern company.

[45] ibid 82–90.

[46] E Erikson, *Between Monopoly and Free Trade: The English East India Company, 1600–1757* (Princeton University Press, 2014) 18–21.

[47] GM Anderson, RE McCormick and RD Tollison, 'The Economic Organization of the English East India Company' (1983) 4 *Journal of Economic Behaviour & Organization* 221.

[48] AD Chandler Jr, *The Visible Hand: The Managerial Revolution in American Business* (The Belknap Press, 1977); OE Williamson, *Markets and Hierarchies: Analysis and Antitrust Implications* (The Free Press, 1975).

[49] *The Case of Sutton's Hospital* (1612) 10 Co Rep 23a, 77 ER 960.

Monopoly rights, however, remain the most common reason given for the unprecedented success of the English East India Company. Contemporary supporters argued that the Company needed monopoly rights to support the development and maintenance of infrastructure. The 1813 and 1833 Acts rescinding monopoly were seen as an ideological break from the mercantilist past, with the English East India Company viewed as a primary example of the evil.[50]

Some inconvenient truths derogate from the narrative that the success of the English East India Company during the period after 1657 can be attributed wholly or even primarily to its monopoly rights. First, whilst the Company did indeed have monopoly rights in England, all other organisations trading into Asia during this period, including the VOC, were granted similar monopoly rights from their own countries. The Company thus competed with other European organisations in Asia on a level playing field. Also, the monopoly had limits even in relation to other English companies: for example, the English East India Company competed with the Levant Company, which had overland rights. Finally, allowing private trade by employees was debated in the English East India Company from the period it became a modern company in 1657. Views are split on whether free trade benefitted the Company by retention of key employees, or harmed it by employees' focusing on their own businesses. Ultimately, though, as discussed in section III, private trade by employees harmed the English East India Company.

III. PRIVATE TRADE IN THE ENGLISH EAST INDIA COMPANY

Private trade may have contributed to an astonishing tale of boom and bust in less than a decade in the English East India Company, which was described by the nineteenth-century economist Walter Bagehot as 'quiescence, improvement, confidence, prosperity, excitement, overtrading, CONVULSION, pressure, stagnation, ending again in quiescence'.[51]

Private trade was a live issue in the English East India Company for a long time. Employees of the Company engaging in their own trade had been identified as an issue when the oaths for admission to membership of the Company were debated in 1657. When a General Assembly of the New Subscribers to the permanent Joint Stock in the English East India Company met on 11 November 1657, the members were 'informed that by the charter of His Highness no person is to trade to the East Indies until he has been admitted to the freedom of the East India Company and taken the customary oath.'[52]

[50] Erikson (n 46) 2.
[51] Robins (n 5) 100.
[52] The form of the oath, and whether it needed to be taken according to the rule of the Charter, was debated. The 24 committees were asked to prepare draft oaths 'for the admission of all freemen, and

In late 1657, John Evelyn, the parliamentarian and diarist, wrote to a friend that he was now a 'merchant adventurer', offering a prayer, 'upon putting in a stock into the East India Company', that his investment might return safely and 'be employ'd to the uses of Charity, the provisions for my Relatives, the Comfort of my Life and honest subsistence of my family'.[53] Two weeks later, on 26 November 1657, John Evelyn went to a Court (meeting) of the English East India Company. He recorded in his diary that there was 'much disorder by reason of the Anabaptists, who might have the adventurers obliged only by an engagement, without swearing that they still might pursue their private trade; but it was carried against them'.[54] Although the religious convictions of the Anabaptists meant they could not swear an oath, as free traders many wanted to hold shares in the Company and also continue with their own private trade.

On 3 December 1657, Evelyn wrote to Dr Edward Reynolds, the leading Puritan clergyman of his day, about the sermon Reynolds was due to give to the East India Merchants the following Friday. Evelyn asked Reynolds, whom he did not know, to impress upon the East India Merchants 'the Sacrednesse of that sollemm Oath which hath bin taken by Us'.[55] 'I suppose Sir, you have bin informed by the obstructions in our first Assembly, how triflingly, yet how industriously the Anabaptistical Spirit appeared against an Oath, the expresse directions of our Charter, and so essential to the Consolidations of Communities …'[56]

Evelyn pointed out to Reynolds that these men were quite happy for the Governor and committees to take the oath, which could only mean that 'whilst others were obliged to transact uprightly, a few of those (who were to be principal Agents abroad) might enjoy the immunity of Free-Trade'.[57] Evelyn highlights a conflict of interest. Many shareholders in the Company who wanted to continue their own private trade would also be employed to act on its behalf as its agents (meaning employees at that time) in the East India trade.

In asking Reynolds to press the sacredness of the oath, Evelyn as a shareholder highlighted the problem inherent in these men's trading on their own behalf:

> I observe men too apt and diligent in contriving how they may equivocat, and evade it, which must needes end in the total Subversion of this hopefull deesigne, and the universal detriment of many innocent and well meaning Adventurers, who shall concredite their Tallent to faithlesse and negligent stewards.[58]

for the Governor, Deputy, and Committees when they enter upon the management'. EB Sainsbury, *A Calendar of the Court Minutes etc of the East India Company, 1655–1659* (Clarendon Press, 1916) 184.

[53] G Darley, *John Evelyn Living for Ingenuity* (Yale University Press, 2006) 149.

[54] J Evelyn, *The Diary of John Evelyn*, vol 1, ed W Bray (M Walter Dunne, 1901) 318.

[55] DDC Chambers and D Galbraith (eds), *The Letterbooks of John Evelyn*, vol 1 (University of Toronto Press, 2014) 215.

[56] ibid.

[57] ibid.

[58] ibid.

Debate over the form of the oath to be taken by members raged over several meetings. Evelyn attributed the reluctance of some members to take the oath solely to their own self-interest and desire to continue to operate as free traders to the East whilst acting as agents of the company. This may be too harsh. For some subscribers, taking the oath conscientiously was not possible because of their religious beliefs, and others could not take the oath in its existing form while they still had ships trading in the East. The final agreed form of oath allowed for the return of those ships.[59]

Evelyn's objection related more to the fact that many shareholders were also agents, in the sense of employees of the company. Evelyn was prescient when he highlighted the issues that would emerge for the Company when agents of the company also traded on their own behalf.[60] One of the objections to the Company made to the Privy Council in 1681 was that influential members sent home the choicest goods on their own private accounts, harming other shareholders.[61] In 1693, the East India Patent provided that private trading was forbidden,[62] but that ban did not endure.

As the eighteenth century progressed, private trade became widespread, extending even to the directors. Private trade by management and employees at all levels was permitted by the English East India Company.[63] The Company's overseas staff received a minimal salary and the right to conduct private trade on their own account in Asia.[64] This gave employees an incentive to stay in India while maintaining the Company's monopoly over exports to Europe. To compensate for the poor salary, ambitious Company men used their positions as a platform for patronage and private trade. This hunger for perks drove the executives to adventurism when opportunity allowed. Private trade made staff both executives and entrepreneurs in their own right, creating a tier of divided loyalties. The most senior figures in the English East India Company engaged in private trade and inside dealing, ensuring that they prospered as well as the Company.

Some commentators consider private trade was positive for the English East India Company, contributing to the Company's overcoming the VOC and

[59] Sainsbury (n 52) xxi.

[60] No copy of the 1657 Charter exists. In the 1661 Charter, which is reportedly similar in wording, there was a requirement that freemen (members) of the English East India Company swear an oath 'before they shall be allowed or admitted to Trade or Traffick as a freeman of the said Company'. *The East-India companies charter, granted by the Kings most excellent Majesty Charles the second, under the great seal of England, dated the third day of April, in the 13th year of his Majesties reign, 1661* at 3–4 www-proquest-com.ezproxy.auckland.ac.nz/docview/2240900996/fulltextPDF/6219C73EA02D4204PQ/1?accountid=8424.

[61] *The allegations of the Turky Company and others against the East India Company relating to the management of that Trade* [1681] Brit Mus, as cited in Scott (n 2) 140.

[62] Cooke (n 21) 59.

[63] Chaudhuri (n 40) 74–77.

[64] Levy (n 14) 41.

other rivals[65] through employees' being expressly permitted to trade on their own account.[66] 'Monopoly rights were not the key to Company success; it was the partial abrogation of those rights that sustained England's commercial success in Asia.'[67] Private trade allowed infusion of capital by employees.[68] Organisational decentralisation and intertwining of private and company interests encouraged exploration of new market opportunities, and also an internal network of communication. That interrelationship between private trade and monopoly rights was increasingly ignored as the debate over monopolies became more polarised. A central pillar of the English East India Company's success, at least initially, may have been that decentralisation.[69]

As Erikson places it:

> Given that the trajectory of the modern firm is understood currently as going from centralized administrative behemoths to decentralized multidivisional firms to the increasingly networked, global firms of the twenty-first century, the East India Company is also novel in a contemporary sense, because of the way it incorporated decentralized elements into the larger administrative hierarchy.[70]

Certainly, the private trade of employees was tolerated differently in different organisations,[71] with the English East India Company loosening up at a time others tightened up.[72]

IV. THE FALL OF THE ENGLISH EAST INDIA COMPANY

Adam Smith was critical of the English East India Company. It is less well known that Smith considered the English East India Company before 1748 to be an example of a Joint Stock company that functioned well:

> Their capital, which never exceeded seven hundred and forty-four thousand pounds, and of which fifty pounds was a share, was not so exorbitant, nor their dealings so extensive, as to afford a pretext for gross negligence and profusion, or a cover to gross malversation. Notwithstanding some extraordinary losses, occasioned partly by the malice of the Dutch East India Company, and partly by other accidents, they carried on for many years a successful trade.[73]

Evidence exists that the members of the governing body, at least initially, adopted some of the precepts of Reynolds and others about their broader obligations.

[65] Erikson (n 46) 13–14.
[66] ibid 1.
[67] ibid 2.
[68] ibid 14.
[69] ibid 3.
[70] ibid 15–16.
[71] ibid 13.
[72] Chaudhuri (n 40) 74–77.
[73] Smith (n 39) 747.

Directors focused on the moral welfare of employees abroad, cracking down on intemperance. Shareholders were encouraged to give money to the English East India Company's Poplar Almshouses,[74] which were founded to care for disabled Company seamen. The Poplar Fund was maintained by a levy on employee wages.[75] Employees who gave valiant service were rewarded financially.[76] On dealings in India, representatives were urged to make revenue from customs and rents sufficient for settlement's expenses and 'to carry it so civilly and justly to the natives as to beget in them a good esteem of their fair dealing'.[77]

At the same time, Josiah Child, as the Company's Governor and biggest shareholder, drove the Company forward on a mission of commercial dominion. The seeds of a desire for domination were planted.[78]

Up until 1748, the English East India Company relied on a powerful class of Indian merchants (called banians) to act as intermediaries between the Company and local traders. The banians arranged for the purchase of commodities, interpreting, making loans and brokering. A cold war raged in India between the French East India Company and the English East India Company.[79] In 1748, the key date identified by Smith, the Treaty of Aix-la-Chapelle ended the First Carnatic War in India between France and India.[80]

At a time when English colonialism was celebrated, Robert Clive (Clive of India) was recognised as a founder of empire. Under his leadership in the 1757 Battle of Plassey, the English East India Company won a victory over the Nawab of Bengal and his French allies. That battle, which took place 100 years after Cromwell's 1657 Charter, marks a clear shift in direction for the English East India Company. As Adam Smith described it, 'the spirit of war and conquest seems to have taken possession of their servants in India, and never since to have left them'.[81] The English East India Company, by triumphing over its last remaining rival in India had, for the first time, a true monopoly in India and greater power over the peoples of India.

After 1748, Smith considered that the focus of the English East India Company had shifted from being a trading enterprise to engaging in systematic extortion in India.[82] At that point, the private trade by company employees and others extended to extortion at all levels of the organisation, from directors

[74] Scott (n 2) 194.

[75] 'Poplar High Street: The East India Company almshouses' in H Hobhouse (ed), *Survey of London*: vols 43 and 44, *Poplar, Blackwall and Isle of Dogs* (British History Online, 1994) at www.british-history.ac.uk/survey-london/vols43-4/pp107-110.

[76] Scott (n 2) 194–95.

[77] ibid 198.

[78] See the discussion in Robins (n 5) 49–57.

[79] See discussion in GM Anderson and RD Tollinson, 'Adam Smith's Analysis of Joint-Stock Companies' (1982) 90 *Journal of Political Economy* 1237, 1250.

[80] ibid.

[81] Smith (n 39) 749.

[82] 'Smith recognized that the East India Company was not paradigmatic of joint-stock business organization; he objected to the deflection of company activities from productive trade to unproductive wealth transfer': Anderson and Tollinson (n 79) 1251.

like Lord Clive, Governor of Bengal, who died the richest man in England, to employees and factors based in India.[83] Smith considered that these developments affected growth in both India and England.

Whilst permitting private trade may have contributed to the success of the Company for some of the period before 1748, ultimately the fact that the trade extended to all levels of the organisation, including the governing body, contributed to the downfall of the English East India Company, at least as a modern company.

In 1657, Evelyn had objected to shareholders refusing to take the oath because he believed those shareholders would engage in private trade while acting as agents or employees of the Company. By 1757, employees and shareholders engaged in private trade, and directors did too. Nick Robins attributes problems that arose for the English East India Company after the mid-eighteenth century to the fact that directors and employees traded on their own behalf, combined with directors' failure to act in the long-term interests of the Company.[84] At the same time, the English East India Company eliminated the competition in India that it had previously faced from the VOC and from the French East India Company. The unintended consequence of the threats by the British Government to expropriate the Indian territories of the English East India Company led to a short-term focus by the governing body.[85]

The Company became a malign entity in India. Following the turning point of the 1757 Battle of Plassey, and with an absence of competitors for their products, Bengal's weavers were hard hit. The weavers were reduced to a position of near slavery, unable to sell to anyone but the English East India Company, and therefore with no choice other than to accept whatever price the Company offered.[86] The Company in 1765 also acquired *diwani* – the right to collect taxes. In the next six years, the English East India Company would collect over £20 million, generating a surplus of £4 million, a substantial sum at the time.[87] As Smith identified, most of the Company's revenues now resulted from activities that were not related to foreign trade.[88]

The English East India Company is often criticised for being a monopoly: until 1748, whilst the Company was a monopoly in England, it still needed to compete with French East India Company and the VOC, which were each monopolies in their own jurisdictions. After Plassey, the English East India Company had a true monopoly in India.

Private trade became increasingly corrosive for the Company. Discipline around bribery was never perfect, but sufficient to get by when the Company

[83] ibid 1250–51.
[84] Robins (n 5).
[85] See the discussion in Anderson and Tollinson (n 79) 1249–50.
[86] Robins (n 5) 80.
[87] ibid 79.
[88] Smith (n 39) 750.

was just one of many competing for the Asia trade, and local rulers retained some control. After Plassey, there was no restraining force on the Company at all, and the intensification of corruption was driven by the leaders of the Company, who enjoyed lavish lifestyles.

Another contributing factor was that the governing body was no longer acting in the long-term interests of the entity. As identified by Smith, control was exercised by shareholders voting in the Court of Proprietors (the general meeting) to appoint directors, who would not act in the interests of the company either in the short term, by the payment of dividends to investing shareholders, or in the long term, by caring about the value of the shares. Smith commented:

> Frequently a man of great, sometimes even a man of small fortune, is willing to purchase a thousand pounds share in India stock, merely for the influence which he expects to acquire by a vote in the court of proprietors. It gives him a share, though not in the plunder, yet in the appointment of the plunderers of India; the court of directors, though they make that appointment, being necessarily more or less under influence of the proprietors, who not only elect those directors, but sometimes over-rule the appointments of their servants in India. Provided he can enjoy this influence for a few years, and thereby provide for a certain number of his friends, he frequently cares little about the dividend; or even about the value of the stock upon which his vote is founded.[89]

This behaviour was epitomised by Robert Clive, as Governor of the English East India Company. After Plassey, Clive was handsomely rewarded with an endowment of land, making him the landlord of the English East India Company in Bengal. When he was challenged by director Laurence Sullivan, Clive broke the rules limiting each shareholder to a single vote, by splitting his holding into separate chunks. Although Sullivan narrowly defeated Clive by splitting his holding in turn, Clive soon mobilised support to overthrow Sullivan, reinstating his endowments.[90]

Clive also engaged in insider trading, purchasing large amounts of the Company's shares as well as privately trading, despite a directorial ban on involvement in Bengal's internal market. Public opinion back in London was incensed by his actions and the placing of his own interests above that of the Company. While Clive indulged his interests, he also cracked down on the perks enjoyed by others, generating a vast store of bitterness. Clive persistently overestimated the value of his acquisitions, creating unrealistic expectations in London of the financial revenue flowing into the Company.[91]

Despite the governance shenanigans, the English East India Company boom initially proved irresistible for both British and foreign investors, and demand for shares rose dramatically, perhaps driven by company employees seeking control

[89] ibid 752.
[90] Robins (n 5) 87–88. Clive spent £50,000 purchasing votes: Anderson and Tollinson (n 79) 1252.
[91] Robins (n 5) 89–90.

over trade rather than the fundamental strength of the company. Macaulay described it as a time of 'feverish excitement', driven by 'an ungovernable impatience to be rich' and a 'contempt for slow, sure, and moderate gains'.[92]

Executives in India lost sight of their commercial purpose and embezzlement became widespread. Astute observers at the time saw that the Company's aggressive acquisitions overwhelmed its management capabilities, with competing shareholder forces irreconcilable with collective interest. By the end of the 1760s, the Company's directors were recognising the hollowness of the Bengal victory and what the boom had in fact cost them. By December 1770, news of the Bengal famine, where it was estimated that around one-third of Bengalis starved to death, had reached London, provoking horror and outrage across the country.[93]

The governing body was no longer willing or able to act in the interests of the shareholders, held by the Company in the Corporate Fund, and therefore of the Company itself as an entity in either the short or the long term. The philosopher politician Edmund Burke saw India being 'radically and irretrievably ruined' because of the Company's 'continual Drain' of wealth.[94] The word 'loot' originated in India and entered the English language in this period. At this time, the Company fundamentally transformed from being a business corporation and the world's first modern company to becoming the centre of administration of empire.[95]

V. CONCLUSION – THE ENGLISH EAST INDIA COMPANY IN CONTEXT

The English East India Company is historically significant for a multitude of reasons that extend beyond its structure. It is also significant in the making of the modern company. Nick Robins, in his wonderful book about the Company, *The Corporation that Changed the World*, puts it well:

> [I]n its financing, structures of governance and business dynamics, the Company was undeniably modern. It may have referred to its staff as servants rather than executives, and communicated by quill pen rather than email, but the key features of the shareholder-owned corporation are there for all to see.[96]

The English East India Company was not the only chartered corporation with permanent Joint Stock or capital. Other business corporations with permanent capital included the Bank of England (1694),[97] the Hudson Bay

[92] ibid 90.
[93] ibid 98.
[94] Ninth Report, in Marshall, *Writings and Speeches of Burke*, V, 226 in Robins (n 5) 5.
[95] Levy (n 14) 29.
[96] Robins (n 5) 5.
[97] Levy (n 14) 30–36.

Company (1670),[98] which still exists today, and the South Seas Company (1711).[99] Although these corporations had all the key features of the modern company, acquiring those features was not a right that could be exercised by following a process set out in a general incorporation statute. The process for obtaining a charter, which included requirements of a public purpose and state approval for specific commercial privileges, was laborious and expensive, meaning that at any one time there were only about 20 business corporations.[100] Contractual Joint Stock Companies continued to exist in parallel, with 'A rush of speculative ventures towards the end of the seventeenth century [resulting] in over 140 joint stock companies by 1695.'[101]

The contractual form was, however second-best, because it lacked many of the key features that came with incorporation. The two great chroniclers of the development of the modern company highlight the key features and attractiveness to business of the business corporation. From Hunt:

> [I]n the seventeenth century the commercial advantages flowing from and incident to incorporation were becoming clear: perpetuity, or at least continuity of existence (and management) independent of that of members; transferable shares; unlimited divisibility of the equities; and the distinct demarcation of liability for the debts of a corporation, as well as of that for the debts of its shareholders.[102]

And from Dubois:

> It is difficult to convey how a study of the documents themselves makes one realize the great sense of conviction business men had that, for large-scale enterprise, the corporation was par excellence the legal device of proved utility and efficacy. Incorporation was definitely a privilege to be sought and prized.[103]

In addition, the governance structure that evolved in the English East India Company was essentially constitutional, even if power was ultimately abused. The governing body was responsible for the management of the Company but was required to present reports and policy to quarterly general meetings (Courts) of shareholders. The Company was, at least in the early period, democratic,[104] with general meetings called 'little Parliaments'. Performance could be measured by return on capital and also by the price of shares on secondary markets.

[98] ibid 30.
[99] ibid 36–40.
[100] Robins (n 5) 32.
[101] ibid 32.
[102] BC Hunt, *The Development of the Business Corporation in England 1800–1867* (Harvard University Press, 1936) 3.
[103] AB DuBois, *The English Business Company after the Bubble Act, 1720–1820* (Commonwealth Fund, 1938) 93.
[104] H Bowen, 'The "Little Parliament": The General Court of the East India Company, 1750–1784' (1991) 34 *The Historical Journal* 857.

6

The Early Emergence of Directors' Duties

I. INTRODUCTION

ORGANISATIONS WITH ALL the key features of the modern company had emerged by 1657 in business corporations like the English East India Company. Joint Stock as a permanent fund of capital (termed in this book 'the Corporate Fund') became part of the long-established form of the corporation. Like a cuckoo in the nest, the existence of the Corporate Fund led to a body of law that altered accounting, legal, and social relationships and obligations within the modern company. 'The eighteenth century wrestled hard with the new importance of a fund in place of people.'[1] In particular, private interests were developed relating to the relationships between shareholders and directors, and their obligations[2] as they related to the Corporate Fund.[3]

The long-standing framework of corporation law survived. The concept that the corporation was a separate legal entity from its members in their private capacities was upheld in the business corporation. The common seal and the deed as expressions of corporate will, with formal requirements separate from members, are evidence of this continuation of 'corporation' law principles.[4] By-laws became more internally and constitutionally focused, and[5] therefore more similar to modern corporate constitutions.

The business corporation held the Corporate Fund. The business corporation was increasingly treated as akin to a trust for those purposes.[6] Although the concept of the business corporation as a trust did not survive, its aftermath lingered in the law in concepts such as shares' being increasingly treated as personalty rather than real property[7] as the growth in significance of intangible forms of value began. The concept that the obligations of directors

[1] CA Cooke, *Corporation, Trust and Company: An Essay in Legal History* (Harvard University Press, 1951) 79.
[2] ibid.
[3] ibid 69.
[4] ibid 68.
[5] ibid 69; *Child v Hudson's Bay Co* (1723) 2 P Wms 207, discussed ibid 69.
[6] *Child v Hudson's Bay Co* (n 5), as discussed in Cooke (n 1) 69.
[7] See the discussion in Cooke (n 1) 69–72.

related to the interests of shareholders in the Corporate Fund rather than to current shareholders themselves may also originate in the conception of the business corporation as a trust. In the foundational case on directors' duties, *The Charitable Corporation v Sutton*,[8] discussed in this chapter, an action was brought against directors 'to have satisfaction for a breach of trust'.[9] This chapter suggests that *Charitable Corporation* may have been more an incremental development than a leap.

II. EMERGING OBLIGATIONS OF THE GOVERNING BODY OF THE ENGLISH EAST INDIA COMPANY

Leaders of the generality group in the English East India Company who had been free trade supporters were often younger sons of the English gentry. It was a period when the teaching of Latin meant notions of virtuous civic service were permeating through society, 'with an understanding of and commitment to classical political ethics'. These generality leaders are likely to have been exposed to ideas from Plato and Aristotle of community, justice, citizenship, freedom and equality.[10]

In addition, leading members of the generality who were elected to the governing body – and in the case of Maurice Thomson, elected as Governor in 1657 – were Puritans, who would have been influenced by Protestant ethics. Value was attached to hard work, thrift and efficiency. Max Weber identified the link between the religious ideas of groups like the Calvinists and the emergence of modern capitalism.[11]

John Evelyn, the diarist, was a secret Royalist. As an investor and a member of the generality, he was aware of the changes in the English East India Company. He described the Company as having 'newe oaths, new orders a mixt committee & I thinke so reformed as that if Warrs with Holland (which we feare) doe not decompose us, it is likely to prove one of the most profitable secure & hopefull trades in Europe'.[12]

The 'mixt committee' referred to by Evelyn clearly relates to the fact that the governing body of the Company was (in the context of its times) more diverse, no longer being drawn just from elite merchants but also from the less established and affluent members of the generality.

On 11 November 1657, a General Assembly of the New Subscribers to the permanent Joint Stock in the English East India Company met[13] and asked the

[8] *The Charitable Corporation v Sutton* (1742) 2 Atk 400, 26 ER 642.

[9] Cooke (n 1) 75.

[10] JE Farnell, 'The Social and Intellectual Basis of London's Role in the English Civil Wars' (1977) 49 *The Journal of Modern History* 641, 656.

[11] M Weber, *The Protestant Ethic and the Spirit of Capitalism*, tr T Parsons (Routledge, 2001).

[12] G Darley, *John Evelyn Living for Ingenuity* (Yale University Press, 2006) 149.

[13] The members of the generality were the freemen of the Company, also called adventurers. (In the 1657 Charter it remained possible to be a freeman or member of the Company without holding stock, although the shareholding requirement was introduced in the 1661 Charter.)

24 committees to prepare a draft oath 'for the Governor, Deputy, and Committees when they enter upon the management'.[14]

John Evelyn records in his diary that, on 4 December 1657, he attended the sermon to the company given by Dr Raynolds (Reynolds), on Nehemiah, xiii. 31, showing, 'by the example of Nehemiah, all the perfections of a trusty person in public affairs'.[15] The word 'trusty' may relate to general obligations around being entrusted to a position.[16] It is notable that governance of the English East India Company as a business corporation is still viewed as relating to public affairs. The trusty persons in public affairs were the new Governors and Committees of the English East India Company, giving an insight into how the obligations of governing bodies of business corporations were conceived of in 1657.

Nehemiah, governor of Persia in the fifth century BC, was known for being 'a wise and valiant Manager of great and honourable Actions'.[17] Through a review of the character of Nehemiah, Reynolds set out all of the characteristics of a good manager.[18] The obligations of good managers, which resonate with a contemporary reader and that extend to corporate stakeholders, included requiring an awareness of risk by the governing body,[19] that the governing body should take advice from gatekeepers,[20] and that the governing body consider the interests of the community.[21]

[14] EB Sainsbury, *A Calendar of the Court Minutes etc of the East India Company, 1655–1659* (Clarendon Press, 1916) 184.

[15] W Bray, *Memoirs Illustrative of the Life and Writings of John Evelyn* (Henry Colburn, 1818) 254.

[16] The online etymology dictionary traces the meaning of 'trusty' as 'reliable, to be counted on' as from the 14th century.

[17] Reynolds would send those who 'goe about great undertakings, to the reading of this Book of Nehemiah', as there were many things that such men could observe in him for their 'special direction'. E Reynolds, *The Comfort and Crown of Great Actions Preached, December 4, 1657, Before the Honorable East-India Company* (The Ratcliffe for George Thomason, 1659) 2 at www-proquest-com.ezproxy.auckland.ac.nz/docview/2264193406/fulltextPDF/49261CB7F61549DFPQ/1?accountid=8424.

[18] Recall that during the period the term 'manager' had the wider meaning of 'direction'. The printed sermon, *The Comfort and Crown of Great Actions*, is dedicated to the Gouvernor and Committees of the East India Company. He was 'persuaded that the great and good example of Nehemiah might still be before your eyes': Hon Edward Reynolds, To the Honorable The Governor and Committee of the *East-India* Company, ibid. The Book of Nehemiah in the Old Testament relates to the rebuilding of the walls of Jerusalem by Nehemiah, who was a Jew and a high official at the Persian Court.

[19] 'There was never any great enterprise without special opposition … and therefore men that engage in great works, must ever have their eyes ranging to and fro to discover dangers, that they may prevent them …': ibid 5 (citations omitted).

[20] 'Great business being full of variety of incidentall and circumstantial contingencies, will frequently call for further resolutions and renewed consultations, will like great Vessels many times spring a leak, and require immediate application of remedies. And therefore it is a part of necessary wisdom, as in great Cities, so in great Actions, to have Phisicians always within call, who may timely advise upon all needfull expedients for safety …': ibid 6 (citations omitted).

[21] 'Men of great and publick undertakings, should not look onely after narrow and domestical interests, but should make use of their own greatness, power, wealth, prevalency with patent persons to do reall offices of Love and Service to the poor Church of God … Nature hath implanted even in senseless and inanimate creatures, such a love of community … to preserve them whole from violence or reproach. How much more should we lay to heart publick evils, even then when our own condition may seem prosperous?': ibid 4.

Reynolds continues to relate graphically how diligence could be demonstrated:

> A man of either [fearful?] or sluggish principles, is very unfit for the management of any arduous and weighty affairs. It was a great businesse but one would think a sad one, for a man to sacrifice his beloved Son, and yet Abraham rose up early to go about it.[22]

Interestingly, the governing body is asked to consider employee interests, which was honoured in the Poplar charity established for former Company seamen discussed in chapter 2:

> [E]ven amongst those who serve you in these expeditions; sick Mariners; desolate Widows, poor Children: it would be a work of sweet favour to God, to have a steady stock going for the advantage of these, as well as of the Merchants. Their prayers may be wind in your Sails, and bring down a blessing on all your undertakings.[23]

Another obligation, also reflected in the oath, requires the Governor and committees not to act in their own self-interest when making decisions:

> Covetousness is not only a bar and obstruction to all honourable undertakings, but doth miserably corrupt and spoil them by a self-seeking management, when men drive on and interweave domestical interests, under the specious pretence of publick good.[24]

The final obligation in the sermon relates to how the governing body might operate as a collective decision-making body that is flexible and compromises.[25] Dr Reynolds says:

> Lastly … In great companies, and great businesses, it is hardly possible to carry things on in so smooth and regular a way, but that some differences of judgments may arise, and cause difficulties, breaches, and obstructions in the whole work … so may we of companies and undertakings, that divisions will endanger their standing. … In which case, wise and prudent men … will use their utmost indeavours to heal breaches, to close up divisions, to prevent mistakes, to finde out expedients, wherein all may readily agree for the preventing of evils, which differences of judgement, if not timely cured, may be likely to produce. In which case, there is nothing more conducent than mutual mildnesse [and] meeknesse …[26]

Interestingly, Reynolds in 1657 suggested humility in leadership, which aligns to modern principles of servant leadership:

> Certainly meeknesse is a very great ornament, and a very great instrument of power. We may think we show our power by our stiffnesse and inflexiblinesse; but is a greate

[22] ibid 6.
[23] ibid 6–7.
[24] ibid 7, 8. Also family members should not be employed: 'Since it is impossible for great actions to be managed without much concurrence, singular care is to be used that good and faithfull men, by whose care, and prudence, and prayers, they may be promoted, be employed in the transaction of them, that even near relations, do not prevaile with us, to entrust great works in the hands of weak or wicked men. Consanguinity hath a strong byais even with good men.'
[25] ibid 10–11.
[26] ibid 10.

> evidence of power to be of an yielding and meek disposition. It shews, first, a great power which a man hath over his own Spirit, which is a work of more power sometimes than the taking of a City ... Secondly, it shews great humility and self-denial ... A wise man will sometimes deny his own judgment, in order to a greater good ... To be ready to make it appear unto other men, that I am more desirous to please them upon the account of their profit, than to offend them upon the accompt of my own.[27]

The governing bodies of corporations always swore an oath. This practice extended to early business corporations. Under the original Charter of the English East India Company in 1600, the Governor and members of the Court of Committees as the governing body swore an oath 'faithfully to perform their said Office'.[28] Members were to swear any oath 'reasonably' imposed on them by management.[29]

The 1661 Charter of the Company, which was almost identical to the 1657 Charter,[30] required committees to swear an oath on election 'that they and every of them shall well and faithfully perform their said office of Committees in all things concerning the same'.[31] The Meeting of 17 November 1657 of the

[27] ibid 11.

[28] *Charter granted by Queen Elizabeth to the East India Company* (Parliament of England, 1600) at https://en.wikisource.org/wiki/Charter_Granted_by_Queen_Elizabeth_to_the_East_India_Company. A later 17th-century oath had the wording 'you will be faithful to the Governour, his Deputy and Company of Merchants of London, trading onto the East-Indies, in the management of their Trade'. 'A[n] old document containing the oath of fidelity to the East India Company also known as EIC ...' *Alamy* (2014) at www.alamy.com/a-old-document-containing-the-oath-of-fidelity-to-the-east-india-company-also-known-as-eic-the-honourable-east-india-company-heic-east-india-trading-company-eitc-the-british-east-india-company-or-informally-as-the-john-company-company-bahadur-or-simply-the-company-it-originally-traded-as-governor-and-company-of-merchants-of-london-trading-into-the-east-indies-and-traded-cotton-silk-indigo-dye-salt-spices-saltpetre-tea-and-opium-it-began-trading-circa-1600-and-was-absorbed-by-the-british-indian-government-in-1858-image351454087.html.

[29] J Shaw, *Charters Relating to the East India Company: From 1600 to 1761* (R Hill at the Government Press, 1887) 21–22. In 1628, a similarly worded oath – 'for the due and faithful performance of their duty' – was taken by the management of the Massachusetts Bay Company. *A copy of the Kings Majesties Charter for Incorporating the Company of the Massachusetts Bay in New England in America* (Printed by S Green for Benj Harris, 1689) 16 at www-proquest-com.ezproxy.auckland.ac.nz/docview/2248552679/fulltextPDF/B6C83DCDF9BB4A93PQ/1?accountid=8424. The Charter makes no mention of members, although all colonists had to take the oaths of supremacy and allegiance. See ibid 21. In 1670, members of the Hudson Bay Company were obliged to take an oath before being admitted. Committees (directors), the Governor and his deputy swore to 'well, truly and, faithfully perform his said Office'. *The Royal Charter for Incorporating the Hudson's Bay Company* (Printed by R Causton & Son, 1816) 5.

[30] 'Charters of the East India Company with related documents: the parchment records' (The National Archives, 1600–1947) at https://discovery.nationalarchives.gov.uk/details/r/16e42ef9-0b6c-4f6e-acb6-27cac99de0b4. After the Restoration in 1660, all copies of the 1657 Charter of the English East India Company were apparently destroyed in an attempt to expunge Cromwell's legacy. Nevertheless, contemporary accounts record that the 1661 English East India Company Charter gave greater powers to the Company, but was otherwise similar to the 1657 Charter.

[31] *The East-India companies charter, granted by the Kings most excellent Majesty Charles the second, under the great seal of England, dated the third day of April, in the 13th year of his Majesties reign, 1661* at www-proquest-com.ezproxy.auckland.ac.nz/docview/2240900996/fulltextPDF/6219C73EA02D4204PQ/1?accountid=8424 at 4.

Committees for the New Stock decided that the wording of the oath to be taken by the Governor, Deputy and 24 committees on their election to manage the affairs of that Stock would be as follows:[32]

> [Y]ou shall sweare to be faithfull and true during the tyme of your place of Governour, or Deputy, or trust as one of the Committees to the Fellowship or Company of the Merchaunts of London trading into the East Indies, and their successors; the good estate of the adventurers in this present Stocke you shall favour and affect; and the priviledges graunted unto them (to your power) endeavour to maintaine and preserve. You shall be carefull to see and provide that an equall and indifferent hand be carried in the government of this fellowship and in the affaires thereof to all the adventurers that shall adventure or putt in stocke; and that an equall division from tyme to tyme be made to all the adventurers according to the proportion of their several stocke duly paid in.[33]

Several aspects of the 1657 oath sworn by the Governor and committees of the English East India Company are striking. First, the obligation to 'the good estate of the adventurers in this present Stocke',[34] read in context with the rest of the oath, supports arguments that the duty is owed to the *interests* of shareholders held in the Company as permanent capital, rather than being owed to the current shareholders themselves.

Second, the requirement to be 'carefull to see and provide that an equall and indifferent hand be carried in the government of this fellowship and in the affaires thereof to all the adventurers that shall adventure or putt in stocke'[35] required that shareholding committees (directors) no longer favour their own interests above the interests of all of the stockholders (shareholders) in the permanent capital of the English East India Company. As discussed in chapter 3, although the practice of distributions by commodities had ceased before 1657, the controlling elite, who comprised the governing body and who were also wealthy merchants, had previously purchased commodities from the Company at rates favourable to themselves. The merchants had established retail networks where they were able to sell on those commodities. The commodities were often sold through the Levant Company, in which many were also major shareholders.

The requirement that

> an equall and indifferent hand be carried in the government of this fellowship and in the affaires thereof to all the adventurers that shall adventure or putt in stocke; and that an equall division from tyme to tyme be made to all the adventurers according to the proportion of their several stocke duly paid in ...[36]

supports assertions that by 1657 the English East India Company was essentially a capitalist enterprise focused on a return on capital contributed by shareholders,

[32] Sainsbury (n 14) 186–87.
[33] ibid.
[34] ibid 187.
[35] ibid.
[36] ibid.

rather than being focused on individual shareholders. The governing body was expected to consider 'the affaires' or interests of the shareholders, rather than the shareholders themselves.[37]

Finally, the obligation to be 'faithfull and true' mirrors, or may even be the original source of, the obligation of modern directors to act in good faith. It also echoes the use of the word 'faithful' in earlier forms of oath, including the oath taken by the governing body when the English East India Company was founded in 1600.[38]

In summary, therefore, the wording of the oath and also the way the obligations and roles of the governing body were conceived of by contemporaries are strikingly modern.

III. ROLE OF THE OATH IN THE OBLIGATIONS OF GOVERNING BODIES

Petitioners for charters of incorporation of business corporations followed the same formula from their beginning in the sixteenth century to the Victorian era. Petitioners cited their past industry and expense, and pleaded that their enterprise would be advanced by a charter. The public aspect was their patriotic designs for commerce, civilisation and good government.[39] The grantees were endued with all the old incidences of incorporation (right of perpetual succession, right to sue and be sued, common seal for acts of the corporation, powers to deal with land and to make by-laws).[40] Governors and officers had to acknowledge the charter and 'be aiding',[41] meaning to help or give support to something. The fundamental obligation of members of governing bodies as officers of the Company was, in common with all forms of corporation, therefore, to comply with the provisions of the charter and any corporate by-laws. By taking office, the Governor and committees assumed this obligation.

Committees (directors) of business corporations like the English East India Company did not have to swear the oaths of Allegiance and Supremacy that the Corporation Act 1661 required of officers of municipal corporations. They were also not obliged to take the sacrament.[42] But directors still needed to swear an oath.

[37] ibid.

[38] See n 28 and comment.

[39] CT Carr, *Select Charters of Trading Companies, AD 1530–1707*, vol XXVIII (B Quaritch, 1913) xiv.

[40] ibid xiii.

[41] ibid xiv.

[42] The sacrament referred to was the sacrament of Holy Communion. It was laid down in the Corporation Act 1661 that all municipal officeholders had to receive the sacrament of Holy Communion in accordance with the rites of the Church of England. The purpose was to exclude from public office Roman Catholics, followers of the Jewish faith and Protestant dissenters like Anabaptists. The Act was passed a year after the Restoration.

The South Seas Company is mentioned by Lord Hardwicke in his speech in *The Charitable Corporation v Sutton*.[43] It is the Company linked with the Bubble Act 1720. In 1717, the directors of the South Sea Company swore the following oath:

> I do faithfully promise, that in the office of director … I will give my best advice and assistance for the support and good government of the said company, and I will faithfully and honestly demean my self, and execute the said office accordingly, to the best of my skill and understanding. So help me God.[44]

In the Charitable Corporation, the directors were required to swear:

> [Y]ou will duly and faithfully perform the trust of a committee man of the Charitable Corporation, to the best of your knowledge and judgment for the benefit and advantage of the said corporation, so long as you shall continue in the said trust.[45]

This oath to perform one's duty faithfully was common at the time. Yet it almost never appears in litigation, meaning it may not have been legally enforceable. Although that part of the oath had clearly been breached in the Charitable Corporation, Lord Hardwicke did not address that breach in the case itself. What, therefore, was the significance of oaths sworn by directors of business corporations in seventeenth-century and eighteenth-century England?

Prior to the sixteenth century, adding an oath to a promise would effectively create two simultaneous legal obligations. The promisee could sue for 'perjury or breach of faith' in an ecclesiastical court, and enforce the underlying promise or contract in a regular court.[46] But by the sixteenth century, jurisdiction over perjury had shifted to the King's Bench,[47] with oaths almost never being litigated.[48] Contemporary thinking on oaths was 'cynical'; in the words of Selden, 'now oaths are so frequent, they should be taken like pills swallow'd whole, if you chew them you find them bitter, if you think of what you sweare twill hardly goe down'.[49] As another contemporary writer put it, 'the world is divided between those who would swear to nothing and those who would swear to anything'.[50]

[43] *The Charitable Corporation v Sutton* (n 8).

[44] South Sea Company and Great Britain, *An abstract of the several acts of Parliament, commission for taking subscriptions, charter, and by-laws of the honourable South-sea company* (Richard Mount, 1718) 26.

[45] *A Short History of the Charitable Corporation* (A Millar, 1732) 21.

[46] RH Helmholz, *The Oxford History of the Laws of England: The Canon Law and Ecclesiastical Jurisdiction from 597 to the 1640s*, vol 1 (Oxford University Press, 2004) 358.

[47] RB Outhwaite, *The Rise and Fall of the English Ecclesiastical Courts, 1500–1860* (Cambridge University Press, 2006) 19–20.

[48] B Shapiro, 'Law and the Evidentiary Environment' in L Hutson (ed), *The Oxford Handbook of English Law and Literature, 1500–1700* (Oxford University Press, 2017) 259–60.

[49] FE Pollock and Edward Fry (eds), *Table Talk of John Selden* (Quaritch, 1927) 85–87, 146, cited in C Robbins, 'Selden's Pills: State Oaths in England, 1558–1714' (1972) 35 *Huntingdon Library Quarterly* 303, 303.

[50] Robbins (n 49).

Despite this cynicism, oaths continued to be used frequently. According to Pufendorf, oath takers added moral obligations to pre-existing legal ones:

> Oaths in themselves produce no new and distinct obligation, but come in as a kind of accessory bond to an obligation already valid in itself. For in the taking of an oath we presuppose something, upon the non-fulfilment of which we call down upon our heads the punishment of God.[51]

Therefore, for business corporations like the English East India Company, the oath supported the fundamental obligation to comply with the Charter.

The supporting nature of the oath did not mean that oaths were pointless, as 'all men except atheists believe that God punishes the violation of promises'.[52] Oaths were particularly useful where 'fear of men did not seem effective enough',[53] and where there was a risk of 'lack of confidence, unfaithfulness, ignorance and passion'.[54]

According to Condren, oaths of office were not seen as binding contracts but as entailing a 'heavy ethical reciprocity'.[55] As oaths were not legally binding, there was a genuine risk that someone who did not believe in the sanctity of oaths would not be bound by them. This argument was made to deny public offices to Catholics.[56] Quakers who wished to replace oaths with solemn declarations 'also argued that if we, contrary to our principles and consciences were forced by penalties to swear allegiance … it might well be suspected of us, that at opportunity we would breach such oaths'.[57]

The idea of a dual moral and legal duty is evident in the wording of corporate oaths of office. Good faith does not appear by itself. Instead, directors swear to faithfully perform a duty: 'faithfully to perform their office',[58] and 'for the due and faithful performance of their duty',[59] to 'well and faithfully perform their said office'[60] and 'in the execution of the said office of director, I will faithfully and honestly demean my self'.[61] In other words, good faith relates to the performance of the office or duty.

[51] S Pufendorf, *De Jure Naturae et Gentium Libri Octo*, vol 2, trs CH Oldfather and WA Oldfather (Clarendon Press, 1934) 501.

[52] ibid.

[53] ibid 492.

[54] ibid 494.

[55] C Condren, *Argument and Authority in Early Middle England: The Presupposition of Oaths and Offices* (Cambridge University Press, 2006) 240.

[56] ibid 237.

[57] E Burrough, *A just and righteous plea presented unto the King of England and his Council, being the true state of the present case of the people, called Quakers* (Robert Wilson, 1661).

[58] Shaw (n 29) 21–22.

[59] *A copy of the Kings Majesties Charter for Incorporating the Company of the Massachusetts Bay in New England in America* (n 29) 16.

[60] *The Royal Charter for Incorporating the Hudson's Bay Company* (n 29) 2.

[61] Bank of England, *A Copy of the Charter of the Corporation of the Governor and Company of the Bank of England* (Printed by H Teape, 1758) 15.

The 1694 Charter of the Bank of England, another significant business corporation of the period, required both directors and shareholders to swear oaths of loyalty. Directors swore that they owned £2,000 of stock in the bank (the minimum) and

> do swear that in the office of a Director of the corporation or company of the Bank of England, I will be indifferent and equal to all manner of persons, and I will give my best advice and assistance, for the support and good government of the said corporation. And in the execution of the said office of director, I will faithfully and honestly demean my self, according to the best of skill and understanding.[62]

Directors were clearly officers and, mirroring the wording always used in petitions for charters, their role derived from the Crown and related to good government. These points are explored further in the next section.

In summary, therefore, the fundamental obligation of the members of governing bodies of business corporations was to exercise powers in accordance with the charter granted to the corporation. The oath sworn by members of the governing body created a moral duty that supported the legal duty, and also expanded upon the evolving nature of the role of a director of a business corporation holding permanent capital as the Corporate Fund in relation to that Corporate Fund. Directors swore to perform their office or their duty in good faith. The wording of the oaths and the inclusion of the wording that the 'good estate of the adventurers in this present Stocke you shall favour and affect' may be significant in understanding the source of the modern duty of directors to act in good faith and the best interests of the company.[63]

IV. *CHARITABLE CORPORATION v SUTTON*

The concept of being entrusted with a legal power is apparent in the wording of the 1657 oath for the members of the governing body of the English East India Company, with the words 'trust' and 'trusty' used in connection with the committee men.

In 1692, in the Charter of the Greenland Company, the position of committees was referred to as one of 'trust', as well as directors' swearing an oath to be faithful, to preserve the joint stock of the company and to treat all members equally:

> You swear to be faithful and true during the time of your place of trust as one of the committees to the Company of Merchants of London trading to Greenland … the good Estate of the Adventurers in this present Joynt Stock you shall favour and affect and the Priviledges granted unto them (to your power) endeavour to maintaine

[62] ibid.
[63] Sainsbury (n 14) 186–87.

> and preserve. You shall be carefull to see and provide that an equal and indifferent hand be carried in the Government of the Company.[64]

Charitable Corporation v Sutton[65] is regarded as a foundational case for modern directors' duties. Pamphleteers writing about the Charitable Corporation itself before the case was decided in 1742 were unsure about the boundaries of the directors' duties. One author tried to

> examine seriously the nature of that trust which is reposed in the directors, and by what limits they are restrained, with whatever else naturally belongs to the decision of this question, of which hitherto we may justly say, that it has been as little known as it has been much talk'd of.[66]

Directors clearly had a duty to manage the Corporation, supervise those beneath them, and inspect warehouses and accounts.[67] They were 'sworn to the due and faithful execution of this duty', and had they done it, the Corporation would have suffered no loss.[68]

There is some confusion amongst the cases from the time (which invariably dealt with municipal corporations). In *R v Richardson*, reported in 1758, prosecutors considered that the wording of a burgess's oath was so legally unimportant they did not set it out in pleading.[69] Instead, the pleading emphasised the taking of the oath, rather than the oath itself,[70] presumably because the oath supported the fundamental legal duty.

Lord Mansfield disagreed, saying 'such an offence [non-attendance at meetings] was against their oath of office: and consequently, this oath of office ought to be set forth'.[71] Lord Mansfield set out three categories of offence that could call for an officer's removal: offences against corporate duty and common law; offences not against corporate duty but 'of so infamous a nature' that the offender should not hold public office; and offences that are 'against his oath, and the duty of his office … and amount to breaches of the tacit condition annexed to his franchise or office'.[72] In other words, an officer could not be removed for breach of oath, but could be removed for breach of oath *and duty*. The 'tacit condition' relating to the duty of office Mansfield is referring to is unclear, but presumably relates to attendance at meetings being both a legal and moral duty.

This conflation can be seen in other cases where an oath is included in addition to and supporting a director's duty. In *Rex v The Corporation of Wells*,

[64] Greenland Trade Act 1692, s 11.
[65] *The Charitable Corporation v Sutton* (n 8).
[66] *A Short History of the Charitable Corporation* (n 45) 16.
[67] ibid 1–2.
[68] ibid 2.
[69] *R v Richardson* (1758) 96 ER 1115 (KB).
[70] ibid [93].
[71] ibid [88].
[72] ibid [118].

reported in 1767, attendance at meetings by a director was required by 'the nature and duty of his office, and also his oath'.[73] *James Bagg's Case* concerned an offence 'against the duty and trust of his freedom, and to the public prejudice of the city or borough, whereof he is free, and against his oath'.[74] In *Basingstoke Corporation v Bonner*, a burgess 'voluntarily refused to obey several orders and law … for the good of the said borough made, contrary to the duty of his office of capital burgess, and contrary to the tenor of his oath, contrary to the trust reposed in him'.[75]

Some commentators consider that the role of directors of corporations evolved so that they became akin to trustees for current shareholders. DuBois says that '[i]n the eighteenth century viewpoint of a director's powers and responsibilities, the catchword was "trustee"'.[76] DuBois reports that it was repeated endlessly that the directors were trustees for the proprietors (shareholders).[77] The authority DuBois cites and the examples he uses do not necessarily support his assertion. One example used, Norwich Union Assurance Office, involves a deed of settlement of a contractual Joint Stock Company rather than a corporation.[78]

In the variation of the contractual Joint Stock Company that arose after the Bubble Act 1720, assets were settled on a trust through a deed of settlement. Trustees were appointed. The roles of director and trustee were distinct and distinguished, even though in many instances, the same persons were trustees and directors. These companies were known as deed of settlement companies. So, in a deed of settlement company, trustees were trustees for beneficiary shareholders, but directors were not.

The second authority DuBois uses involves the wording of a proposed charter where the directors could be removed for 'Misbehavior, Breach of Trust, or any other just Cause'.[79] Extrapolating from the meaning of the word 'misbehaviour', breach of trust must have the meaning seen in the oaths, rather than the technical meaning applying to a trustee of a trust. It also does not state or follow that the directors were trustees for the current shareholders.

DuBois' final authority is drawn from a memorial relating to an investigation of the York Building Company, where it was stated that Sir John Meres had been guilty of a very great breach of trust in misrepresenting the true state of the affairs of the company to its General Court (meeting). Again, the meaning relating to being 'trusty' in the sense of being reliable, to be counted on, may

[73] *Rex v The Corporation of Wells* (1767) 4 Burr 1999 (KB) 2002.

[74] S Kyd, *A Treatise on the Law of Corporations*, vol 2 (Garland Publishing, 1811) 52.

[75] *Basingstoke Corporation v Bonner* (1729) 2 Ld Raym 1567.

[76] AB Dubois, *The English Business Company after the Bubble Act, 1720–1800* (The Commonwealth Fund, 1938) 293.

[77] ibid.

[78] ibid.

[79] ibid.

be appropriate, rather than suggesting a role that is akin to being a trustee for beneficiary shareholders.

As his primary authority, DuBois cites the 1742 leading case *Charitable Corporation v Sutton*.[80] Directors, through a grossly negligent failure to supervise servants (employees) of the corporation, allowed fraudulent loans to be made. Half the capital of the corporation was lost.

Charitable Corporation v Sutton is a foundational case on the role of directors. The statement by Lord Hardwicke that directors are agents is most often excerpted from the case and can be used to support arguments that Lord Hardwicke considered directors to be agents of the current shareholders of the company, with the term 'agent' given its modern meaning. That statement should be read in context, however, in light of the first three paragraphs, and the first two sentences in particular, which are supported by the prior discussion in this chapter:

> I take the employment of a director to be of a mixed nature. It partakes of the nature of a public office, as it arises from the charter of the crown. But it cannot be said to be an employment affecting the public government; and for this reason none of the directors of the great companies, the Bank, South-sea &c, are required to qualify themselves by taking the sacrament. Therefore committee-men are most properly agents to those who employ them in this trust, and who empower them to direct and superintend the affairs of the corporation … By accepting of a trust of this sort a person is obliged to execute it with fidelity and reasonable diligence …[81]

Charitable Corporation v Sutton is not authority for the role of directors as being akin to that of trustees for current shareholders. Nor is it authority for directors to be considered the legal agents of the current shareholders. It is suggested that the use of the term 'agent' should not be interpreted as meaning that the directors were the legal agents of the shareholders as we would understand that relationship in the twenty-first century. Agency did not emerge as a separate concept in the modern form until the nineteenth century.[82] The sense in which Lord Hardwicke is applying agency is different.

[80] *Charitable Corporation v Sutton* (n 8).

[81] ibid 644, per Lord Hardwicke.

[82] '[I]t must never be forgotten that agency did not become a single or significant subject until (very roughly) the turn of the nineteenth century … Its modern history … will fully unfold … doctrine by doctrine, the nineteenth century developments.' W Müller-Freienfels, 'Legal Relations in the Law of Agency: Power of Agency and Commercial Certainty' (1964) 13 *The American Journal of Comparative Law* 193, 197. The only reference to the term 'agent' in Giles Jacob's 1729 *New Law-Dictionary* is to agent and patient, where it refers to 'a Perfon [who] is the Doer of a Thing, and the Party to whom done'. The example of a man who makes a creditor his executor is used. G Jacob, *New Law-Dictionary: Containing, the Interpretation and Definition of Words and Terms Used in the Law* (London, 1729) xxix. By 1829, in James Whishaw, *New Law Dictionary*, the modern meaning of 'agent' as 'a person appointed to transact the business of another' had emerged. J Whishaw, *New Law Dictionary; Containing a Concise Exposition of the Mere Terms of Art, and Such Obsolete Words as Occur in Old Legal, Historical and Antiquarian Writers* (J & WT Clarke, 1829) 12.

Cooke considers the directors were trustees towards the corporation as a membership group, rather than towards the shareholders as shareholders.[83] What does Cooke mean? Lord Hardwicke distinguished loss arising from actions of directors that are based on faulty policy. Here the fault lies with the shareholders who appointed the board. In that constitutional sense, the directors are the agents or trustees of the membership group that elects them. It is a constitutional understanding of the governance of the company.

Whereas Lord Hardwicke does not consider that directors will incur liability for actions based on faulty policy, he does consider that directors will incur liability if they do not act with fidelity and reasonable diligence. Directors are then liable for breaches of trust committed by other directors. *Charitable Corporation v Sutton* is classified by Geltzer as a case where 'fiduciary office was identified as a category running alongside trusteeship of property', where Lord Hardwicke 'assimilated nonfeasance in failing to supervise with misfeasance of office'.[84]

Getzler also considers the fact that all were made liable, despite all breaching their duties in different ways, as evidence of 'a key step in the use of fiduciary relations to construct entities in law'.[85] A simpler and additional explanation is possible: that the entity already existed and Lord Hardwicke made explicit what had been implicit since the English East India Company acquired permanent capital in 1657. That step made the abstract *persona ficta* Coke CJ had considered in the earlier *Sutton Hospital Case*, discussed in chapter 2, an entity based on that permanent capital as a Corporate Fund.

Charitable Corporation v Sutton therefore can be seen as less foundational and more as judicial recognition of what had been one of the obligations of members of the governing bodies of business corporations with permanent capital since 1657. The 1657 oath carried moral rather than legal weight, but it set out the underlying obligation of trustiness 'to be faithfull and true ...; the good estate of the adventurers in this present Stocke you shall favour and affect'.[86] In other words, the modern duty that directors act in good faith and in the best interests of the company as an entity had begun to emerge in 1657, and was given judicial recognition nearly 100 years later. The moral obligation assumed to be trusty to the interests of shareholders held in the company as the Corporate Fund became the fiduciary obligation assumed by all directors when becoming directors of a modern company.

Directors were entrusted with the role to watch over the affairs of the Corporation. The wording of the 1661 Charter of the English East India Company makes this clear:

> Twenty four of the said Company to be Elected and appointed in such form as hereafter in these presents is expressed, which will all be called the Committees of the said

[83] Cooke (n 1) 74–75.

[84] J Getzler, 'Rumford Market and Genesis of Fiduciary Obligations' in A Burrows and A Rodger (eds), *Mapping the Law: Essays in Memory of Peter Birks* (Oxford University Press, 2006) 595.

[85] ibid 596.

[86] Sainsbury (n 14) 186–87.

> Company, who together with the Governor of the said Company for the time being, shall have the direction of and for the said Company.[87]

Although it is not stated, presumably those who entrusted the directors were the shareholders who elected the directors to the governing body.

The role of director was mixed. It still retained a public aspect that related to the corporate charter. Lord Hardwicke said the role of director is a public office arising from the charter. Despite the qualification around the role's not being wholly public, the business corporation remained a type of corporation. Crucially, directors were *also* entrusted with a power (the vestiges of the public nature of the office derived from early corporations' law). Although a public office, Lord Hardwicke said it was not of public government, as directors do not have to take the sacrament. The duty to comply with the charter, however, continued to apply. This duty may easily be aligned with the obligation of directors of modern companies to exercise powers for a proper purpose, meaning the purpose for which the power is granted or conferred.[88] If the wording in the charter was in conflict with interests of shareholders held in the Corporate Fund, which duty would prevail?

An anonymous pamphlet, published in the wake of the collapse of the Charitable Corporation but before the case was decided, may give clues about how directors' duties had come to be viewed in the period immediately before Lord Hardwicke's judgment.[89] The author, like Lord Hardwicke, views directorship as a 'mixed office', so the interpretation also assists in understanding the case itself. The Charitable Corporation was founded with 'the publick Advantage of the nation into our View'.[90] The charter was granted because of this public benefit: 'A charter was *accordingly* granted by her late majesty …'.[91] But the company was also intended to benefit its shareholders. As 'publicke Utility was thus mix'd with the private emolument [of shareholders] … it was highly reasonable to suppose, that they should soon be supported by a publick Sanction'.[92]

The author suggests two duties. The first is to consider the charter and the *purpose* for which it was granted by the Crown.[93] The second is to act in the best interests of the shareholders: 'a man ought to reflect whence he had that trust … when the proprietors chose him into that charge, it was that he might direct their affairs to the best advantage'.[94] Directors were indeed seen as both public servants and privately elected 'agents', in the sense that directors were elected and entrusted to the role by the shareholders. But, crucially, where those duties conflicted, the *purpose* of the corporation won out: 'In most cases the design and interest of the proprietors is to pursue that purpose [of the charter],

[87] *East India Company Charter* (1661) 2.
[88] *Howard Smith Ltd v Ampol Petroleum Ltd* [1974] AC 821 (PC).
[89] *A Short History of the Charitable Corporation* (n 45) 7.
[90] ibid.
[91] ibid.
[92] ibid.
[93] ibid 17 (emphasis added).
[94] ibid 20.

and their directors ought *therefore* keep this continually in View …'.[95] Directors were acting in the interests of the company as identified by the purpose as set out in its charter. All this has a modern flavour!

In summary, Lord Hardwicke in *Charitable Corporation v Sutton* affirmed that an aspect of the role of directors related to public office. The public office presumably extended to ensuring compliance with the Corporation's charter. Lord Hardwicke set down judicially for the first time the fiduciary duty that directors were charged with acting in the interests of those who empowered them to direct the affairs of the corporation. The interests of the shareholders were held in the Corporate Fund that became an entity. An argument can at least be advanced that the new fiduciary obligation had its origins in the pre-existing oath that had moral but not legal force. That oath was sworn by directors of companies with permanent capital, to 'be faithfull and true … [to]; the good estate of the adventurers in this present Stocke'.[96]

V. DEVELOPMENT OF DUTIES AROUND CONFLICT OF INTEREST

Directors of chartered business corporations like the English East India Company founded on permanent capital were considered to have obligations in their roles. John Evelyn expressed concerns to Reynolds about the risks of private trade. Reynolds, in his sermon on Nehemiah (see section II), exhorted the governing body of the East India Company to act with probity.

By 1694 (the year the Bank of England was founded), pamphleteers were already calling for reform. One writer noted that giving a quorum of directors the power to make decisions for the company rendered 'so small a number subject to the temptation of corruption'.[97] This prediction came true less than three years later. Directors were sent to Flanders to help fund the salaries of English troops during the Nine-Years War. The deal was prolonged 'for the particular profit of the *Antwerp*-Directors, without the least gain to the Bank', who also took three times the usual commission.[98] The loss was not apparent to shareholders, as the directors failed to report to the General Court (meeting) 'though being so essential a part of their trust, and a guide to the members'.[99]

The author blamed 'secret transactions' for private advantage.[100] He advised greater transparency, and that directors should not have potential conflicts of interest, requiring

> directors, that may have more regard to the good of the corporation than private advantage … nor committee men of other corporations (especially of the East India

[95] ibid 17.
[96] Sainsbury (n 14) 186–87.
[97] *Observations upon the constitution of the Company of the Bank of England, with a narrative of some of their late proceedings* (London, 1694) 1.
[98] *Considerations upon the management of the Bank of England* (1697) ii.
[99] ibid ii.
[100] ibid iii.

> Company), nor those whose times are taken up in Court Employments, or have too great transactions with the state: for these may possibly create to themselves separate and distinct opinions from what may be for the true interest, benefit and glory of the Bank of England.[101]

At the beginning of the seventeenth century, it was expected that directors would not have conflicts of interest. By-laws from the Bank of England, English East India Company and South-Sea Company include self-dealing and no-profit rules. Some pamphlets suggest that these were not general fiduciary rules but contractual responses to specific crises, although, unfortunately, there is very little information available surrounding these events. Most of the pamphlets were written anonymously: the copy of *Considerations upon the Management of the Bank of England* comes with a handwritten note 'I have not been able to find any reference to this probably unique tract, nor to the extremely interesting report which it contains.'[102]

In 1694 the Bank of England passed several by-laws. Though not explicitly a response to the Antwerp scandal, this was implied: 'Whereas it has been found *by experience*, that many incertainties and inconveniences have happened for want of a due and regular Method of Proceedings at General Courts of Election, for Remedy whereof in Time to come …'.[103]

The rules required the declaration of any dealings with the company, for the stated purpose of preventing fraud:

> [F]or the prevention of fraud and deceit in all and every the transactions of this corporation, it is resolved and ordained that in all cases whatsoever … [if] any of them, shall have any dealing or business with this corporation, upon their own account … in every such case, such governor, deputy-governor and director … shall at the time of his or their negotiating or transacting the same, declare and publish to the sub-committee for the time being, fully, fairly and clearly, such his share and interest.[104]

Whilst implicitly a response to the Antwerp scandal, the requirement that directors disclose their interests is strikingly similar to the requirements of disclosure of conflicts of interests that re-emerged in the nineteenth century.

Another by-law seems aimed directly at the Antwerp directors, but might be seen as a precursor to the modern no-profit rule. No director or officer

> shall presume directly or indirectly to receive or take any fee, gratuity or reward of any sort, kind, or quality whatsoever for the doing or dispatching, or the not doing or delaying, any business or affair belonging to this corporation, or for any other reason or colour, or upon any account relating to his or their respective employment,

[101] ibid iv.
[102] ibid title page.
[103] Bank of England, *Rules, orders, and by-laws; for the good government of the corporation of the governor and company of the Bank of England* (Bank of England, 1697) 3 (emphasis added).
[104] ibid 12–13.

> or otherwise concerning this corporation howsoever, from any persons whatsoever, other than only from this corporation, or by order thereof, or of the court of directors.[105]

Finally, the by-laws responded to the issue of transparency by requiring the keeping of a minute book.[106]

By-laws were passed by the English East India Company in 1694. These required directors to declare self-dealing to the board, unless the self-dealing just consisted of buying goods from the Company:

> That in all cases, wherein the Governour, Deputy, Committees, or any other Officer of the Company, shall in his own Right, or jointly with others, be concerned in Buying or Selling of Goods, or driving any Bargain with the Company, every such Person at the time of such Negotiation, shall make known to the Court of Committees, or Sub Committees, with whome such business is to be transacted, how far each of them are concerned therein … but by this Clause, none of the aforesaid Persons are obliged to declare how far they are concerned in Buying Goods at the Company's Candle.[107]

The by-laws included financial penalties for their breach – provided the director was first convicted of a crime.[108]

In 1712, the South Sea Company printed similar by-laws. This was one year after its founding, suggesting that these rules may have become almost default for new corporations. The 9th by-law was 'against concealing the dealings of the … directors with the corporation'.[109] Any director considering an interested transaction had to

> declare and publish to the court of directors … How much and in what manner or measure he is directly or indirectly concerned or interested in the goods proposed to be bought or sold, or other matters or affairs then negotiating, or in any other matter wherein he shall be directly or indirectly interested or concerned.[110]

Directors were unable to vote on debates concerning transactions in which they had an interest:

> If any debate shall thereupon arise, the person concerned, having first been heard, shall afterwards withdraw during such debate, and when the question is put. Provided that nothing in this by-law shall be understood to oblige any … director to declare, whether he is concerned or interested in goods bought by himself, or others for him, at any publick sale.[111]

[105] ibid 18.
[106] ibid 20.
[107] East India Company, *Abstract of by-laws made by the general court of adventurers of the East India company, the 17th January* (East India Company, 1694).
[108] ibid.
[109] South Sea Company, *By-laws, orders and rules, for the good government of the Corporation of the governor and company of merchants of Great Britain, trading to the South Seas and other parts of America, and for encouraging the fishery, and for the better carrying on and managing the trade of the said company* (J Barber, 1712) 3.
[110] ibid.
[111] ibid.

The 11th by-law prevented directors from profiting from their office: 'no officer … Shall directly or indirectly take any fee, reward, or present, other than such as shall be allowed, permitted or prescribed by the Court of Directors … and exposed to publick view'.[112]

The rules were expressed as by-laws rather than emerging through the Courts. Nevertheless, directors' obligations that are strikingly similar to contemporary directors' duties emerged in the period after 1657.

[112] ibid.

7

Liability of Shareholders of Business Corporations

I. INTRODUCTION

WAS PROTECTION FROM liability a feature of chartered business corporations with terminating Joint Stock Funds?[1] With permanent capital? Gower considered that incorporation seems

> at first to have been valued mainly because it avoided the risk of the company's property being seized in payment of the member's separate debts, rather than as a method of enabling the members to escape liability for the company's debts.[2]

As discussed in chapter 2, after Coke CJ's pronouncements in *The Case of Sutton's Hospital* in 1612, in the common law the corporation existed as a *persona ficta* or artificial legal person, separate from its members in their private capacities. Coke CJ was pronouncing on corporations in general, not business corporations with Joint Stock Funds or permanent capital. Considering the effect of a permanent capital on the liability of members of the business corporations of the late seventeenth century onwards raises two pertinent questions. First, did business corporations with permanent capital remain legally separate from members who were also shareholders? Second, in what circumstances could shareholders be compelled to pay further capital to the corporation? Finally, could shareholders be compelled to pay sums to meet the obligations of the corporation to third-party creditors?

The small number of business corporations formed during the period makes answering these questions challenging. Only 10 charters were granted in the period between 1630 and 1680.[3] With the focus on public purpose, petitioning successfully for charters for business concerns was challenging.

[1] See generally J Goebel Jr, *Cases and Materials on the Development of Legal Institutions* (The Vermont Printing Company, 1946) 428 at the end of the 18th century; cf CA Cooke, *Corporation, Trust and Company: An Essay in Legal History* (Harvard University Press, 1951) 77, which firmly established corporate debts were not debts of the members.

[2] LCB Gower, *Gower's Principles of Modern Company Law*, 4th edn (Sweet & Maxwell, 1979) 26.

[3] S Williston, 'History of the Law of Business Corporations Before 1800' (1888) 2 *Harvard Law Review* 105, 111–12, as cited in H Hansmann, R Kraakmann and R Squire, 'Law and the Rise of the Firm' (2006) 119 *Harvard Law Review* 1333, 1378.

II. LIABILITY OF SHAREHOLDERS TO THIRD-PARTY CREDITORS

The final question posed in section I is considered first. In what circumstances could shareholders be compelled to pay sums to meet the obligations of the corporation to third-party creditors?

The default rule for all forms of corporation was that members were not liable for debts of the corporation to third parties. As Levy describes it:

> The idea of the corporate entity evolved so rigidly that no liability on the part of the shareholders for the company's debts was considered possible. As a result, it was held that if a company became extinct and its reserves exhausted, creditors could not maintain actions against the shareholders.[4]

Early corporations were not business corporations and were unlikely to incur debt.[5] The issue of liability of shareholders of business corporations did arise from time to time when corporations with Joint Stock Funds incurred debt. The Virginia Company was chartered by James I in April 1606 to colonise the eastern coast of North America. It was a chartered corporation with Joint Stock. The minutes of the Court Book of the Virginia Company record a lively debate in 1622.[6] On one side, and in line with established principles of corporations' law, it was argued that members were not liable in their private capacities. Men's private estate was separate from the property of the Corporation, with only the goods of the Corporation liable for the debts:

> And touchinge the engagement of mens private estate hereby: therein was no danger; it beinge cleare by lawe that only the goode of the Corporation are lyable to the debte thereof, Concerninge which he [Mr Carswell] said he had taken aduise of most sufficient Lawyers: And Mr Carswell said that Mr White the Lawyer (who newly was departed out of the Court) having hearde this disputation did affirme that private mens estate could not be lyable to the debte by the Seale of the Corporation but onely the Goode of the Corporation it selfe.[7]

On the other side it was argued that members could be liable in their private capacities:

> Mr Wrote still persisted in his former opinion … that he could not be pswaded but each member of the Companie (upone grant of the Seale for Securytie) was bound to make this good, out of his owne private estate, alledginge that he had likewise askede Counsel of Lawyers …[8]

[4] AB Levy, *Private Corporations and their Control* ((Routledge, 1950) 25.

[5] As the discussion of the English East India Company in ch 3 illustrates, shareholders were, however, clearly liable to pay calls on their subscribed capital when required to do so by the governing body.

[6] SM Kingsbury (ed), *The Records of the Virginia Company of London: The Court Book, from the Manuscript in the Library of Congress*, vol 2 (Washington Printing Office, 1906) 165.

[7] ibid.

[8] ibid.

The example of the Russia (Muscovy) Company was given, where 'divers Brothers' of that company were sued for its debt through a levy.[9]

The Russia (Muscovy) Company, founded in 1553, was discussed in chapter 2 as an example of a corporation that shifted from operating using a Joint Stock Fund to operating as a Regulated Company. In 1620 it was resolved that the Russia Company would be wound up. Calls that had been made on shares were in arrears from many shareholders. A new undertaking was formed that would operate as a Regulated Company, where every member traded on his own behalf. That undertaking took over the assets and liabilities of the old Company for £12,000. Money was to be recovered from the Dutch as debtors, and there were also some other outstanding liabilities.

At the beginning, the new Russia Company did not raise enough capital and incurred loans at high interest rates. An Order in Council gave the company immunity from arrest for debt. In relation to further liability, Scott records that, on 17 December 1621, the debts of the previous company were ascertained to be £24,000 in total. It was determined that amount should be paid by adventurers (shareholders) from the previous Company who continued to be shareholders in the new Company.[10]

As it was now a Regulated Company, members of the new Russia Company were able to trade on their own account, with debts owing not necessarily relating to any past Joint Stock Funds in the Company but rather to the private obligations of those members. The private brothers (as the members of the new Russia Company as a Regulated Company were called) were, by order of the Council, acquitted and exempted from former debt.[11]

The Virginia Company, where the debate mentioned above took place, was not a Regulated Company. Even if the members of the Russia Company had been forced to pay debts they had incurred, or any former shareholders had been required to pay arrears in calls (and ultimately they were not), any precedent around liability incurred in the Russia Company was not relevant to members of the governing body or shareholders in the Virginia Company. Mr White the lawyer prevailed with the argument 'that private mens estate could not be lyable to the debte by the Seale of the Corporation but onely the Goode of the Corporation it selfe'.[12]

In early cases, it was also held that the debts of the corporation were not the debts of its members.[13] The separation of the liability of the corporation from the liability of its members was recognition that the corporation was a separate

[9] ibid 165–66.

[10] WR Scott, *The Constitution and Finance of English, Scottish, and Irish Joint-Stock Companies to 1720*, vol 2 (Cambridge University Press, 1910) 57–58. Note the levy on members did not take account of value of debt owed by the Dutch, so ultimately it was not collected.

[11] ibid.

[12] Kingsbury (ed) (n 6) 165.

[13] *Anon* (1441) YB 19 Hy VI 80; *City of London* (1680) 1 Ventr 351, as cited in Cooke (n 1) 77.

legal entity from its members. As discussed in chapter 2, that principle may have entered the common law as early as the fifteenth century, and was laid down in 1612 by Lord Coke in *The Case of Sutton's Hospital*.[14]

In 1680 in *City of London*,[15] the Court said that the shareholders' being made personally responsible for corporate debts was inconsistent with the nature of a body corporate. The default position was that corporate debts were not the debts of members in their private capacities.[16] Kenyon MR expressed similar views in 1788 in the famous case *Russell v The Men of Devon*.[17] Granted, *Russell* involved a public corporation.[18] However, four years earlier, in 1784, Lloyd Kenyon had opined privately that in the event of incorporation, 'the Corporate Stock alone would be answerable to the engagements, and the individuals who may compose the Corporation could not be liable in their private characters'.[19]

Some commentators argue that the holding in *City of London* in 1680 could have meant no more than the debts of a corporation could only be paid through the corporation itself, rather than creditors' being able to sue shareholders directly.[20] Shareholders may have been indirectly liable to creditors of the company, meaning, functionally, liability to third-party creditors. The 1671 case *Salmon v The Hamborough Company*,[21] where the principle of 'leviation' was set out, is often used as an example of this form of indirect liability. On appeal, the House of Lords apparently held that the members were obliged to answer to the corporation for the debts of the corporation to third parties dealing with it. If the company did not pay within a certain period, the House of Lords ordered the directors to

> make such a Leviation upon every Member of the said Company as is to be contributary to the Publick Charge, as shall be sufficient to satisfy the said Sum to be decreed to the Plaintiff in that Cause, and to collect and levy the same, and to pay it over to the Plaintiff as the Court shall direct.[22]

The case is not authority for the indirect liability of shareholders to creditors of the corporation in the early history of the business corporation.[23] The action was against the Governors, Assistants and Fellowship of the Merchant

[14] See the discussion in ch 2; Cooke (n 1).

[15] *City of London* (n 13), as cited in Cooke (n 1) 77.

[16] See Cooke (n 1) 77, which firmly established corporate debts were not debts of the members; AB DuBois, *The English Company After the Bubble Act, 1720–1800* (Octagon Books, 1971) 98, where it seemed reasonably well settled that there was no procedure by which a creditor of a corporation could proceed against a member for the corporation's debts.

[17] *Russell v The Men of Devon* (1788) 100 ER 359, 672.

[18] ibid.

[19] Lord Kenyon, Case of Opinion of 29 January 1784, Boulton & Watt Mss, Birmingham Collection, Assay Office, as cited in DuBois (n 16) 95–96.

[20] Cooke (n 1) 77.

[21] *Salmon v The Hamborough Company* (1671) 22 ER 763 (HL).

[22] ibid 764.

[23] D Jenkins, 'Skinning the Pantomine Horse: Two Early Cases on Limited Liability' (1975) 34 *Cambridge Law Journal* 308, 318.

Adventurers of England, commonly called the Hamborough Company. The Company of Merchant Adventurers was the corporation discussed earlier in chapter 2, which was chartered by Henry VIII in the period before Joint Stock Funds were utilised in England for business ventures. In 1776, in *The Wealth of Nations*, Adam Smith wrote of how, in the middle of the previous century, the Hamborough Company subjected trade to restraint and regulation with admission to the company by a fine (fee), not a purchase of shares:

> About the middle of the last century, the fine for admission was fifty, and at one time one hundred pounds, and the conduct of the company was said to be extremely oppressive.[24]

Significantly, therefore, the Hamborough Company did not have Joint Stock or permanent capital; it was a Regulated Company. It was because there was no Corporate Fund from which creditors might recover, and because the company refused to levy members to raise further capital, that Dr Salmon brought the action.

Dr Salmon, a prominent London doctor who was physician to Charles I, invested in other business corporations, including the English East India Company, which by that time had permanent capital.[25] Salmon was one of the nine creditors who brought the attention of the House of Lords to the activities of the Hamborough Merchants, as they were known.[26] Dr Salmon also brought his own action.

Dr Salmon had petitioned against the security of the common seal of the corporation. In relation to their own liability, the members argued in part that 'No single member of the Company ever derived any private benefit from money borrowed on the common seal.'[27] The members also argued that '[a]ll lenders to the Company should have ascertained that it had neither common stock nor any lands'.[28] Both arguments supported the separation of liability of the members in their private capacity from the corporation.[29]

The Report stated that as the Company had no capital fund, the plaintiff wanted members to be levied.[30] According to the case report, to repay debt the Corporation had in the past levied members. The Governor and Assistants refused to do so to repay the £2,000 owing to Dr Salmon. Claiming it had nothing that could be distrained, the Company did not appear. But members who 'served in their natural Capacities, did appear and demur, for that they were not in that Capacity liable to the Plaintiff's Demands'.[31] In other words, the

[24] A Smith, *The Wealth of Nations*, ed A Skinner (Penguin, 1970) 308.

[25] LL Peck, *Women of Fortune: Money, Marriage and Murder in Early Modern England* (Cambridge University Press, 2018) 65.

[26] Jenkins (n 23) 313.

[27] ibid 314.

[28] ibid.

[29] ibid.

[30] *Salmon v The Hamborough Company* (n 21) 763.

[31] ibid.

members argued that in their private or natural capacities, they were not liable for the debts of the corporation; it was a separate legal entity from them in their private capacities.

It follows, therefore, that the creditors would have been expected to rely on the capital of the company if the company had in fact issued shares. As a Regulated Company the Hamborough Company did not have Joint Stock or permanent capital against which Dr Salmon could claim. *Salmon v The Hamborough Company* demonstrates the enforcement challenges for creditors of corporations without permanent capital: Dr Salmon no doubt regretted his investment.

Commentators derive three points from *Hamborough*. First, even without an express provision permitting leviations, a corporation appears to have had the power to levy members.[32] If the corporation could levy assessments on its members, some commentators consider *Hamborough* provides evidence that creditors could force officers to do so for their benefit. If levies were not paid, some commentators consider there is also some evidence that creditors could proceed against the members in their individual capacities.[33]

Hamborough is one of a small number of cases that are used to support arguments that shareholders in corporations were not always protected from liability to creditors of the company. For example, Gower says:

> [M]any charters expressly conferred a power on the company to make leviations (or calls) on the members and it was by no means clear that a company did not have this power in the absence of an express provision. This being so limited liability was illusory; the company as a person was, of course, liable to pay its debts and in order to raise money to do so it would make calls on its members. Moreover [citing *Salmon v The Hamborough Company*] the creditors by a process resembling subrogation, could proceed directly against the members, if the company refrained from taking the necessary action.[34]

However, as Jenkins points out, it must have been implied that a Regulated Company had the power to make leviations because it could not otherwise have financed its operations.[35] That argument does not apply to a corporation with Joint Stock or permanent capital.

Salmon v The Hamborough Company, therefore, cannot be used as authority for the argument that shareholders in business corporations with Joint Stock or permanent capital did not always enjoy protection from liability to creditors of the company. Since *Hamborough* concerned a Regulated Company, it is not

[32] DuBois (n 16) 98.

[33] FG Kempin Jr, 'Limited Liability in Historical Perspective' (1960) 4 *American Business Law Association Bulletin* 11, 13–14; Cooke (n 1) 77, which states '[i]t was held by the Lords that there was an obligation on the members that they would answer to the corporation for its debts to the outside world'.

[34] Gower (n 2) 26, citing *Salmon v The Hamborough Company* (n 21).

[35] Jenkins (n 23) 317.

authority for creditors' being able to force the governing body to call up capital or proceed against members in their own capacity if the corporation had capital or Joint Stock against which creditors could claim.

Second, and relatedly, the principles governing leviations on members of Regulated Companies were not the same as the principles governing calls on shareholders of corporations with Joint Stock Funds or permanent capital. Jenkins argues leviation should properly be equated in modern parlance with a levy.[36] Although the liability of members of the Regulated Company was separate from the corporation itself, members would have joined knowing they could be levied by the Company.[37] Functional limited liability did not therefore exist in Regulated Companies, creating uncertainty both for members of these corporations and for the creditors who dealt with them.

Finally, the point that creditors could proceed against the members in their individual capacities if the company did not pay is not supported by the authority cited. As Jenkins points out, if *Hamborough* was authority for that point, it would have been followed in subsequent cases. *Hamborough* was not followed in eighteenth-century English cases, and when it was cited in 1852 in *Hallett v Dowdell*, all three Judges declined to follow it.[38]

Cooke, when discussing *Hamborough*, notes that the leviations on members of the Company were in fact made according to a note to another case.[39] Jenkins shows that those words should not be interpreted as meaning that the Chancery decree was carried into effect:[40] in fact Dr Salmon returned to the House of Lords on 14 March 1672 to complain that Hamborough was evading its obligation to him. Even though there was some suggestion the company might be dissolved, no record of any effective action beyond a reorganisation of the company remains.[41] The decree provided that an action for contempt was possible against the equivalent of the board (the Gouvernor, Deputy Gouvernor and 24 Assistants) but not against the members.

Whilst there is no real authority stating that shareholders of companies could be made liable to third-party creditors, there is also no authority definitively stating that they could not be made liable. Direct references to liability are rare.[42] It may have been assumed no liability was possible because the principle was of such long standing. Creditors of failed corporations discussed in this book, like the Charitable Corporation or the York Building Company, never proceeded against the personal estates of shareholders.[43] In 1721, the Commissioners of

[36] ibid 316.
[37] ibid 319.
[38] *Hallett v Dowdell* (1852) 18 QB 2, 35–36, as cited in in Jenkins (n 23) 320.
[39] *Harvey v East India Company* (1700) 2 Vern 396 (Ch), as cited in in Jenkins (n 23) 319.
[40] ibid.
[41] Jenkins (n 23) 319.
[42] DuBois (n 16) 94.
[43] ibid 95.

the Treasury considered that a special Act of Parliament would be required to make it possible to proceed in the future against shareholders of the proposed Bank of Ireland.[44] The Carron Company stated that while the capital stock and fund of the corporation would be answerable for the debts of the corporation in the first instance, if those amounts were insufficient to satisfy creditors, the shareholders would then be answerable as if 'their successors and assigns had not been incorporated into a Body Politic and Corporate and as if this present charter had never been granted'.[45]

III. COULD SHAREHOLDERS BE COMPELLED TO CONTRIBUTE CAPITAL TO THE COMPANY?

The second set of questions, discussed in this section, relate to the circumstances in which shareholders could be compelled to pay sums of capital to the company. Dubois comments that, whist it was reasonably well settled that creditors could not proceed against shareholders for the debts of the corporations, the issue of whether the General Court (meeting) could levy a shareholder for the benefit of the corporation must still be considered.[46] As we have seen, the authority, scant as it is, supports the argument that shareholders in corporations with Joint Stock Funds did not have to pay leviations or levies on their shares. Members of Regulated Companies who traded in their private capacities were levied. Clearly, a shareholder in a Joint Stock Fund or a corporation with permanent capital had to pay calls on their shares when called upon to do so.[47] But were the calls up to an agreed amount, the subscribed capital, or could the calls be made whenever the company required an injection of funds, meaning that shareholders did not have limited liability to the company?

Whilst commentators mostly concur that shareholders of corporations with permanent capital had limited liability to the corporation by the late eighteenth century, they differ about when limited liability of shareholders to the business corporation first emerged.[48]

With the advent of permanent capital, evidence shows that subscribing shareholders could be required to pay instalments on their subscribed capital, but no more. As seen in chapter 3, in the discussion of the English East India

[44] ibid 94.

[45] Inventories of Warrants, 15 July 1773, Bundle 65, 1872, Register House, Edinburgh (as cited in DuBois (n 16) 97, fn 79).

[46] DuBois (n 16) 98–99. Cooke (n 1) 77, is stronger, '[i]t was, of course, firmly established that the debts of a corporation were not the debts of its members', citing *Anon* (1441) YB 1 Hy VI, 80.

[47] See *Child v Hudson's Bay Co* (1723) 2 P Wms 207, where Lord Macclesfield used the example of the common by-laws of companies to deduct calls out of the stocks of the members refusing to pay their calls as an analogy when the validity of a by-law to place restrictions on stock was questioned – the statement is therefore strictly obiter.

[48] Goebel Jr, *Cases and Materials* (1946) 428; cf Cooke (n 1) 76–79. Cooke bases much of his argument on *Salmon v The Hamborough Company*, but see the discussion of that case in section II.

Company, in the period before it had permanent capital shareholders were required to contribute extra amounts above their initial subscriptions to the Company. For example, £200 was the minimum subscription in 1600.[49] When initial calls on shares were not met,[50] the Company required each shareholder to pay a further 10 per cent. The minimum holding, which came to be regarded as the share, became £220, and then £240.[51] The Privy Council threatened imprisonment of those who did not pay.[52] In the early seventeenth century, the modern concept of capital had not emerged. Had the concept existed, the extra payments might have been regarded as increases in capital.

Over time, shares were subscribed for, with payments to be made in instalments. By 1616, with the issue of a Second Joint Stock, subscribers made payments to be called up in eight equal instalments of 12.5 per cent each.[53] When the capital was made permanent in 1657, there were to be six calls over two years. At that time the original investors could have exited after seven years, with the capital wound up but valued and subscribers entitled to the estimated equivalent of their original subscription. At that time, it was intended a new subscriber could join the company[54] with the Joint Stock to continue as the capital of the company.[55] Therefore evidence exists that only in the initial period of the life of the English East India Company could subscribing shareholders be required to contribute more than the original capital they subscribed for. Once there is evidence of double-entry bookkeeping, payments appear to shift to instalments on capital subscribed for, which would appear on the Company side of the ledger. After the advent of permanent capital in 1657, most commentators consider that payments beyond instalments as part of subscriptions could not be required.[56]

A related question is whether governing bodies of corporations could be forced by creditors to make calls on shareholders for debts owing by the corporations. The Governor and Company for raising the Thames Water at York Buildings obtained its charter in 1690. The York Building Company was a chartered corporation with a permanent capital. In 1719, speculators purchased its charter, raising a joint stock of £1,200,000.

[49] Scott, *Constitution and Finance* (n 10) 92. Where the term 'joint stock' did not have the meaning of an ongoing stock that it would later acquire.

[50] ibid 93.

[51] ibid 94.

[52] ibid.

[53] ibid 104.

[54] ibid 129.

[55] WW Hunter, *History of India: The European Struggle for Indian Supremacy in the Seventeenth Century*, ed AVW Jackson (Grolier Society, 1907) 285. In fact as the Company prospered, the appraisements became statements of assets, which enabled stockholders and the public to regulate their dealings.

[56] DuBois (n 16) 99–104.

After a chequered history of speculative and failed ventures and stock manipulation, creditors asked the Court to order the York Building Company to make a call on its shareholders. Lord Hardwicke LC laid down:

> Where the companies are obliged to make calls, this court will not decree them to make such a call, upon a bill brought by a creditor for that purpose, in favour of that particular creditor, unless under very extraordinary circumstances.[57]

The concept of an equitable fund for creditors developed, although it may have depended on particular facts being present. In 1673, in *Naylor v Brown*,[58] Naylor lent money to the Company of Woodmongers. Sir William Wild declared a trust of £620 to several members of the company. In an action brought for the return by shareholders of the property of a dissolved chartered corporation, the Court held that 'there was still an equitable fund appertaining to the company for the benefit of creditors'.

> The Court was of Opinion that the Declaration, of the Trust by Sir Wm Wild was utterly void as to the said £620, for that the Corporation did not join therein, nor give him any Authority under their common Seal, or by any corporate Act to make such a Declaration.[59]

The Chancery Court ordered that the debts be paid before debts owed to the shareholders were repaid – the doctrine of equitable subordination. The Court said:

> Distribution of that Sum amongst particular Members of the Company was injurious to such Creditors who were not Members thereof; it being more reasonable, that if Losses must fall upon the Creditors, such Losses should be born by those who were Members of the Company, who best knew their Estates and Credit, and not by Strangers who were drawn in to Trust the Company in the Credit and Countenance it had from such particular Members; and which in this Case was more remarkable, because several of the principal Members of the Company had set their Names to the Plaintiffs Bond of £500 under the common Seal, which though it did not legally bind them in their private Capacities, yet it was certainly an Inducement to the Plaintiffs to lend their Money.[60]

Interestingly, Bainbridge and Henderson link the subordination of shareholders' claims as creditors in *Naylor* to the control of shareholders over the capital in the company.[61] Jenkins considers the facts indicate 'the presence of something very like fraud'.[62] Certainly, the fact that the shareholders were best placed

[57] *The Case of the York-Buildings Company* (1740) 2 Atk 57, 26 ER 432 (Ch).
[58] *Naylor v Brown* (1673) Cas temp Finch 83, 23 ER 44.
[59] ibid 44.
[60] ibid 45.
[61] See the discussion in SM Bainbridge and MT Henderson, *Limited Liability: A Legal and Economic Analysis* (Edward Elgar Publishing, 2016) 28.
[62] Jenkins (n 23) 311.

to have information about the operation of the company, combined with their inducing Naylor and others to lend money, probably led to their subordination to other creditors on dissolution in *Naylor*. DuBois considers that the concept that a corporation was a person distinct from its members probably influenced the decision.[63]

The facts in *Naylor* resemble those the House of Lords encountered in *Salomon v Salomon & Co Ltd*, 200 years later.[64] The difference in outcome may relate to the differences in the facts: there was evidence that Sir William Wild and others were more culpable than the hapless Mr Salomon. Although the debenture over the assets of Salomon & Co Ltd was in favour of Mr Salomon, who was a member of the company, at the time of liquidation of Salomon & Co Ltd Mr Salomon had sold the debenture to a third party and ploughed the proceeds back into the company. On such apparently minor differences of facts the law can turn …

IV. SHIFT IN FOCUS TO THE CONTRACTUAL JOINT STOCK COMPANY

As explained in chapter 2, the contractual Joint Stock Company form was long-standing. It was, however, eclipsed by the business corporation in the sixteenth and seventeenth centuries. The wider adoption of the chartered corporation was stymied in the early decades of the eighteenth century, as a result of the enactment of the Bubble Act 1720. There was a resulting growth in the significance of the contractual Joint Stock Company. The focus, therefore, in chapter 8 shifts to the contractual form, and how it came to exert influence on the development of company (and corporate) law.

[63] DuBois (n 16) 94, fn 47.
[64] *Salomon v Salomon & Co Ltd* [1897] AC 22 (HL).

8

The Significance of the Deed of Settlement Company

I. INTRODUCTION

THE FOCUS OF this chapter is on the emergence during the eighteenth century, and ultimate significance, of a variance on the contractual Joint Stock Company known as the deed of settlement company. The form is clearly significant in at least two ways. Its historical importance is that it sign-posts the point when the English form, law and governance diverged from those in the United States. During the period, the accountability mechanisms available to shareholders in English companies reduced, clearly led by practice in deed of settlement companies. Also, the apparent success of the form is used to bolster contemporary assertions that the modern company is based on contract.

II. THE BUBBLE ACT

The story of the speculative bubble in share prices in Joint Stock Companies in the early decades of the eighteenth century is a well-documented one.[1] A bull market emerged. Shares in Joint Stock Companies, whether incorporated or unincorporated, were believed to be a sure path to wealth. Shares in ventures such as making salt water fresh, a wheel for perpetual motion, and even '"[f]or an undertaking which shall in due time be revealed"' attracted investment.[2]

Speculative investment in the shares of contractual Joint Stock Companies alarmed the board of the South Seas Company, a business corporation supported by many Members of Parliament. Prices of all shares followed the rising price of the shares of the South Sea Company, but the board wanted all investment to be in the South Seas Company. The corrupt South Seas Board was able to

[1] See AB DuBois, *The English Business Company after the Bubble Act, 1720–1800* (Octagon Books, 1971) 1–83; CA Cooke, *Corporation, Trust and Company: An Essay in Legal History* (Harvard University Press, 1951) 80–83; R Harris, *Industrializing English Law: Entrepreneurship and Business Organization 1720–1844* (Cambridge University Press, 2000) 60–81; BC Hunt, *The Development of the Business Corporation in England 1800–1867* (Harvard University Press, 1936) 1–13.

[2] Cooke, *Corporation, Trust and Company* (1951) 81.

push through the Bubble Act.[3] A 'panic stricken Parliament issued a law which even when we now read it, seems to scream at us from the Statute book' was Maitland's depiction of the passage of the Act.[4] The ostensible and long-standing objection was not to Joint Stock per se; it was to stock jobbing – frauds on the public and wild speculation in shares. In 1696, the Commissioners for Trade and Plantations had complained of 'the pernicious art of stock-jobbing [which had] so wholly perverted the end and design of companies and corporations'.[5]

The Bubble Act prohibited the formation of contractual Joint Stock Companies, and had a chilling effect on the granting of corporate charters. As intended, the Act killed off many existing contractual Joint Stock Companies. The unintended consequence, with a degree of poetic justice, was a wave of share selling that affected the South Seas Company itself. The South Seas Board caused the South Seas Bubble: ironically, 'in opening the eyes of the deluded multitude, they took away the main prop of their own tottering edifice'.[6]

III. THE DEED OF SETTLEMENT COMPANY

Incorporation could only legally be achieved by charters granted by the Crown or by private Acts of Parliament.[7] Corporations therefore fell under state control. The primary intent of the Bubble Act 1720 was to put a stop to the use of Joint Stock Funds by unincorporated associations that did not have charters.[8] In other words, no more contractual Joint Stock Companies. Even though there was only one prosecution under the Act in the eighteenth century, officers of the Crown were more reluctant to grant charters. When charters were granted, restrictions were often placed on the use of the corporate form.[9]

Unlike the general incorporation statutes enacted 300 years later, the modern corporate form was not made widely available to all entrepreneurs, with only a few corporate charters granted in the first half of the eighteenth century. Manufacturing companies rarely obtained them.[10] To be granted charters, the long-standing requirement was that petitioners demonstrate public benefit. Public benefit would have been easier to show with an infrastructure project

[3] Bubble Act 1720 (6 Geo 1 c 18).

[4] FW Maitland, 'Trust and Corporation' in HAL Fisher (ed), *The Collected Papers of Frederic William Maitland*, vol 3 (Cambridge University Press, 1911) 390.

[5] *House of Commons Journals*, XI (1696), 595 (as cited in Hunt (n 1) 6).

[6] Coxe, *Memoirs of Walpole* (1820) II, 19 (as cited in Hunt (n 1) 8). For discussion, see Cooke (n 1) 80–83.

[7] DuBois (n 1) 15.

[8] ibid 215. The Bubble Act 1720 was also intended to stop corporations raising more capital than their charter permitted.

[9] A Televantos, *Capitalism Before Corporations: The Morality of Business Associations and the Roots of Commercial Equity and Law* (Oxford University Press, 2021) 35–36.

[10] H Hansmann, R Kraakman and R Squire, 'Law and the Rise of the Firm' 119 (2006) *Harvard Law Review* 1333, fn 142.

like a canal than a manufacturing concern. There was a widespread belief that shareholders were morally liable for obligations to third parties dealing with their enterprises, meaning that there was general caution around granting incorporation freely for wholly private ventures.

The Bubble Act did not prevent the creation of and investment in Joint Stock Funds. A private contractual form for large ventures that was legally a partnership was designed, to mirror endowed business corporations like the English East India Company as much as possible.[11] This was done, as the legal historian FW Maitland put it, 'without troubling King or Parliament, though perhaps we said we were doing nothing of the kind'.[12] This form of contractual Joint Stock Company was known as a 'deed of settlement company'.

The intention of the parties was to acquire features of the endowed business corporation through the common law of contract and the mechanism of the trust.[13] The deed of settlement was drafted, as much as possible, to exclude the normal rules of partnership that differentiated the partnership from the corporation. Adam Smith described Joint Stock Companies as 'always managed by a court of directors'.[14] Clauses were inserted to ensure that the rule that investing shareholders were legally partners who could bind each other was negated. Deeds of settlement were drafted so that investing shareholders were not partners who combined the ownership of capital with its direction and management. Shareholders were contractually removed from management. A typical deed of settlement made it clear that the board of directors had responsibility for the 'entire management and superintendence over the affairs and concerns of the company', with the obligation to act in conformity with the laws and regulations in the deed of settlement.[15]

Contractual Joint Stock Companies had existed in parallel with business corporations since the sixteenth century. The novel aspect of the deed of

[11] See DuBois (n 1) 216–18; WW Bratton Jr, 'The New Economic Theory of the Firm: Critical Perspectives from History' (1989) 41 *Stanford Law Review* 1471; J Gleeson-White, *Double Entry: How the merchants of Venice shaped the modern world – and how their invention could make or break the planet* (Allen & Unwin, 2011) 216.

[12] Maitland (n 4) 283.

[13] Cooke (n 1) 95.

[14] A Smith, *An Inquiry into the Nature and Causes of the Wealth of Nations*, vol 3, 5th edn (W Strahan and T Cadell, 1789) 123.

[15] The excerpt is from a clause in the deed of settlement for the London Ale Brewing Company, found in the appendix to J Collyer, *A Practical Treatise on the Law of Partnership: With an Appendix of Forms* (S Sweet, 1832). A typical clause in a deed of settlement vested management power in the directors of the company. For example, the deed of settlement of the Halifax Joint Stock Banking Company dated 1831 states 'That the entire management of the business, concerns and affairs of the Company shall be, and is hereby vested, and reposed in the several persons, parties, hereto of the first part, as the first Directors of the Company, and in all future Directors, to be nominated at the times and in manner hereinafter expressed; and the present and all future Directors shall have the sole and exclusive control, management, and disposal of the Capital Stock, funds, estate property, revenue, affairs and concerns of this Company; and shall and may regulate and determine the mode and means of carrying on and transacting the business of the said Company, and all other matters and things whatsoever connected with or relating to the business and affairs of this Company.'

settlement form that distinguished it from earlier types of contractual Joint Stock Company was the settling of the Joint Stock Fund on a trust. Mutual covenants between the shareholders as partners and the trustees selected by them were set out in the deed of settlement. The trustees covenanted to observe all the terms of the deed and to apply the Fund settled on them for the specified purposes.[16]

The office of director was a separate office from the office of trustee, with the first directors appointed in the deed of settlement and granted their powers in the deed. Deed of settlement companies had trustees administering the trust, and a board of directors, who were sometimes, but not always, also the same people as the trustees.[17] Chancery was more efficient than the common law courts in dealing with the concept of funds, with the equitable rights of the members as beneficiaries firmly established.[18] As Andreas Televantos highlights, this 'is strong evidence that eighteenth-century lawyers were comfortable with the notion of trusts of circulating trade assets to be used in a business'.[19]

IV. THE EFFICACY OF THE DEED OF SETTLEMENT COMPANY

The disadvantages inherent in not being treated as a juridical person by the common law made the deed of settlement company form ultimately less efficacious than the chartered business corporation. Challenges around the liability of shareholders to third parties, and around suing were the most significant drawbacks of the form.

Some other perceived disadvantages may have been less significant in practice. The clear disadvantage of the rules relating to the dissolution of partnership with any change in partners was avoided through hiding the ownership structure behind the trust.[20] Thus, deed of settlement companies fuelled by multiple investing shareholders were a viable option.[21] Second, the disadvantage that the form was not sanctioned by the law did not prove entirely problematic in practice. The courts showed a willingness to accommodate merchants using the form, at least until the nineteenth century. Televantos has shown that Lord Eldon, long regarded as an opponent of liberalism and hostile to the deed of settlement form, was in fact influential in the development of English commercial law in a

[16] Cooke (n 1) 88.

[17] DuBois (n 1) 217–19.

[18] ibid.

[19] Televantos (n 9) 37, citing DuBois (n 1) 115–16; M Freeman, R Pearson and J Taylor, *Shareholder Democracies? Corporate Governance in Britain & Ireland before 1850* (University of Chicago Press, 2012) 56.

[20] Televantos (n 9) 38.

[21] Televantos notes that 'deed of settlement companies could face difficulties in both finding and replacing trustees, especially in light of the restrictive law governing trustees' duties, remuneration, delegation powers, and unlimited liability': ibid 38, fn 58, citing DuBois (n 1) 222 and Harris (n 1) 137–59.

way that accommodated the form to some extent.[22] While not overtly endorsed, by the late eighteenth century deed of settlement companies were tolerated by the courts, with the Bubble Act largely forgotten during that period.[23]

Finally, the challenges of raising capital for investment without access to the corporation form were counterbalanced by the tendency for capital markets in the period to be 'local and personal rather than national and institutional'.[24] Shareholders in deed of settlement companies were liable to third parties for debts of the company. That potential liability was not the disadvantage it might seem, as personal liability for business debts was considered morally and ethically desirable.[25] Business corporations, where shareholders were not liable to third parties, were generally regarded as less trustworthy,[26] being 'widely associated with fraud, speculation, monopoly and inefficiency, and not generally looked upon in a favourable light'.[27]

On the other hand, the potential liability of shareholders of deed of settlement companies to third parties was a significant challenge for those shareholders. Shareholders would only be contractually liable to pay their share of the Joint Stock – an apparent limitation of liability to the company. Indeed, a typical provision in deeds of settlement that distinguished that form from a mercantile partnership was the clause stating that each shareholder was only liable to the extent of his own share in the capital stock. The limitation of liability of shareholders of these companies was contractual, though, so only applied to the parties to the contract: the company and each shareholder. Even after the repeal of the Bubble Act in 1825, the courts consistently treated deed of settlement companies as legal partnerships,[28] with shareholders as partners

[22] See the discussion in Televantos (n 9) 9–10; see in particular 'one commentator was able declare "Indeed, there is no branch of the law in which the exceeding merit of Lord Eldon is more strongly exhibited than this [partnership law], in which with the most painful and patient attention he laboured to obviate and overcome the difficulties of the subject, and by a particular examination and careful adoption of the customs of merchants, to established such principles as would eventually bring the law and practice of the courts of equity into conformity with the necessities of an extended commerce: and we find his repeatedly lamenting the strange rules so obviously at variance with mercantile customs with which he had to contend"': ibid 9, citing I Cory, *A Practical Treatise on Accounts*, 2nd edn (W Pickering, 1837) 70.

[23] Televantos (n 9) 38: 'The position began to change in the early nineteenth century, and deed of settlement companies began to attract official attention. Newspapers and journals were filled with promotions for shares in companies, many of which appeared to be dubious; use of company articles purporting to create limited liability and transferable shares had become more common; and the Bubble Act had been largely forgotten.'

[24] ibid 29, citing M Daunton, *Progress and Poverty: An Economic and Social History of Britain 1700–1850* (Oxford University Press, 1995) 245.

[25] Televantos (n 9) 29.

[26] ibid 29–30.

[27] P Ireland, 'Capitalism Without the Capitalist: The Joint Stock Company Share and the Emergence of the Modern Doctrine of Separate Corporate Personality' (1996) 17 *Journal of Legal History* 41, 43 (citations omitted).

[28] *Burnes v Pennell* (1849) 2 HLCas 497, 520–21; 9 ER 1181, 1191.

remaining liable for the debts of the company.[29] The most significant and insurmountable disadvantage of the deed of settlement company compared with the incorporated form was, therefore, the potential liability of shareholders to third parties dealing with the deed of settlement company.

Another significant disadvantage was restrictions on the ability of the deed of settlement company to litigate. A deed of settlement company could not sue without all shareholders, who were partners in the common law partnership, joining in the action. Exceptions existed to that principle, meaning some commentators consider that, in practice, it did not apply.[30] Trustees were permitted to sue on behalf of deed of settlement companies during the period.[31] Chancery, however, required all shareholder-beneficiaries to join in actions against the company itself, in effect rejecting jurisdiction over the form[32] and making it difficult for managers and directors to be held to account by shareholders.[33]

V. THE BUSINESS CORPORATION IN THE EIGHTEENTH CENTURY

In a treatise on corporations,[34] which Stewart Kyd wrote in 1793,[35] a corporation remained a political institution, in the sense it owed its existence to the state through a concession, with no other capabilities other than those for which it was established. Corporations were, therefore, juridical persons, but corporations were not regarded as existing separately from their members. Instead, corporations were considered to be 'a collection of many individuals … with the capacity of acting, in several respects, as an *individual*'.[36] Similarly, in *Blackstone's Commentaries*, corporations were characterised as individuals

[29] Televantos (n 9) 43. See also Ireland (n 27) 42–47; DuBois (n 1) 40.

[30] J Morley, 'The Common Law Corporation: The Power of the Trust in Anglo-American Business History' (2016) 116 *Columbia Law Review* 2145, 2183–91.

[31] See Televantos (n 9) 38, fn 54, '*Metcalf v Bruin* (1810) 12 East 400, 405; 104 ER 156, 158 (per Lord Ellenborough CJKB, "We could not, indeed, invert the rules of law to enable persons to sue as a body or company who are not a corporation; but here the bond has been given to trustees [ie not in the name of the shareholder-partners], who are under no difficulty of suing upon it in their own names …"). The point is not mentioned in Campbell's shorter report of the same case, (1810) 2 Camp 422, 170 ER 1204.'; see Televantos (n 9) 23, fn 55, '*Ex p Cobham* (1784) 1 Brown Ch Cas 576, 577; 28 ER 1307; noted in Notes of Cases in Chancery and Exchequer 1780–1788, held by Georgetown Law Library within the Lord Eldon Collection, 327 ("Thurlow C said he was aware that [not allowing joint creditors to prove against the separate estate] was the constant practice but it did not seem founded on any Principle – for it was clear a joint Creditor was a Creditor on all the Partners & on each"); and *Ex p Copland* (1787) 1 Cox 420, 29 ER 1230 (BC). See also Eldon's notes on *Ex p Kensington* (1808) …: Eldon wrote that Lord Hardwicke had said that joint creditors could not prove against the separate estate, but that "Lord Thurlow thought otherwise", Eldon Notebook 1807–1809 p 3.'

[32] Televantos (n 9) 48–49.

[33] ibid 47–49, citing *Ellison v Bignold* (1821) 2 Jac & W 503, 37 ER 720.

[34] S Kyd, *A Treatise on The Law of Corporations*, vol 1 (J Butterworth, 1793).

[35] ibid ii.

[36] ibid 13. This passage was quoted in Cooke (n 1) 66.

consolidated and united into a corporation, with those individuals and their successors considered one person at law.[37]

Kyd opined that the parts of the corporate body were bulky and visible and seen by all but the blind, and '[w]hen, therefore, a corporation is said to be invisible, that expression must be understood, of the *right* in many persons, collectively, to act as a corporation, and then it is as visible in the eye of the law, as any other right whatever'.[38]

To Kyd, the corporation was the collective of natural persons who had the right to act like a corporation. There was nothing incorporeal about a corporation made up of natural persons. He seemed to have little time for the *persona ficta* concept, concluding:

> [O]n this principle we may account, in a satisfactory manner, for many of the incapacities attributed to a corporation aggregate, without having recourse to the quaint observations frequent in the old books, '*that it exists merely in idea, and that it has neither soul nor body*'.[39]

Kyd appears to be referring unfavourably to *The Case of Sutton's Hospital*,[40] or at least the conception of the corporation as an artificial legal person existing in the abstract that stemmed from Coke CJ in the common law.[41]

[37] W Blackstone, *Commentaries on the Laws of England, in Four Books*, vol 1, 14th edn (A Strahan, 1803) 468.

[38] Kyd (n 34) 16.

[39] ibid 71 (footnotes omitted) (emphasis added).

[40] *The Case of Sutton's Hospital* (1612) 10 Co Rep 23a, 77 ER 960.

[41] Kyd's understanding of the corporation may align more closely with the wording used in the 18th century to grant charters to enterprises with Joint Stock Funds. The Charitable Corporation, incorporated during the reign of Queen Anne and discussed in ch 6, was a Joint Stock Company that was a moneylender to the poor. The wording of the grant stated 'For us, our heirs and successors do grant constitute declare and appoint [list of names] and all and every other person and persons who shall be a subscriber or subscribers to the fund or joint stock … shall be and be called one body corporate and politic of themselves in deed and in name by the name of The Charitable Corporation for Relief of Industrious Poor …'. One explanation may be that the form of words used to incorporate in a charter had changed from creating a body politic, the entity, to coordinating natural persons in the period between *The Case of Sutton's Hospital* and when Kyd wrote his treatise. In an early charter such as the form of words used to incorporate the Mines Royal in 1568, 'one body politic in itself incorporate and a perpetual society of themselves both in deed and name', the Crown appears to be creating a body politic. The wording for the grant for the Newfoundland Company, founded in 1610, two years before *The Case of Sutton's Hospital*, said, 'they shall be one body or communalty perpetual and shall have perpetual succession and one common seal to serve for the said body or commonalty and they and their successors shall be known called and incorporated', which appears to support the corporation's being comprised of its members. Later, the words 'one body corporate in deed fact and name', used for the African Company in 1660, became the standard form of words for incorporation until the 19th century. With the prevalent form of words from the beginning of the 18th century onwards being 'one body corporate in deed fact and name', it is difficult to argue against Kyd and Blackstone's interpretation that incorporation had become, in the words of Maitland, the law coordinating men. In the Charitable Corporation, the wording refers to 'one body corporate and politic of themselves'. Kyd's interpretation may therefore be inescapable and revert to an earlier understanding of a corporation as being comprised of its members, which was in place before the intervention of the Italian theory by Coke CJ in 1612.

Kyd diminished the significance of the 1612 innovation in conception brought about by *The Case of Sutton's Hospital* and the introduction of the *persona ficta* into the common law. Dubois describes Kyd's work as dominated by the medieval point of view, with discussion of municipal and eleemosynary corporations, but with chartered business corporations ignored:

> One might suppose from Kyd's attitude of intense scholasticism that no business of consequence was conducted in his time by chartered companies, or that the Bubble Act had legislated many companies out of existence … [A] casual conversation with almost any group of London lawyers would have enlightened Kyd how a large portion of the profession, and certainly how some of its distinguished members, were continually occupied with problems of 'corporation law' as it affected large commercial enterprises.[42]

Corporations' law and business practice in the period were shaped by the opinions of lawyers advising business units, rather than by court cases. As DuBois points out, the force of the common law of precedent disseminated through case law is such that the business life developed through business corporations in the eighteenth century is largely ignored.[43] Although these opinions were largely pragmatic rather than theoretical, Dubois says that in the rare instances when theory was thought necessary, *The Case of Sutton's Hospital* was cited as authority.[44] Lawyers were acutely aware of the distinction between business corporations and deed of settlement companies, but case law and precedent of the time were driven by the contractual deed of settlement form. This was simply because cases on deed of settlement companies found their way to the courts.

Business corporations and eighteenth-century deed of settlement companies were different legal forms, with the latter being a type of partnership and the former being a type of corporation. Since the documents relating to the deed of settlement form were drafted to make the deed of settlement company as close as possible to the business corporation, economically and functionally, the two forms were nevertheless similar:

> A joint-stock company, or simply 'company', was an association with certain distinctive economic characteristics: most notably, a relatively large number of members, a separation of management and ownership and more or less freely transferable shares. In contrast, the typical partnership was a highly personal association based around a few specifically defined and closely related people, many of whom were likely to be involved in the running of the concern. However, while to describe an enterprise as a joint-stock company conveyed much of its economic nature, it spoke nothing of its legal status. Companies were distinguished from partnerships – as they are today – but the distinction was made on economic, not legal, grounds.[45]

[42] DuBois (n 1) 84.
[43] ibid 85.
[44] ibid 86.
[45] Ireland (n 27) 42–43.

Ireland discusses an English partnership law treatise where the differentiation of partnerships and companies was on a purely economic basis, as public and private partnerships:

> Public partnerships were 'usually called companies or societies' and 'generally consisted] of many members' carrying on 'some important undertaking for which the capital and exertions of a few individuals would be insufficient. These companies were sometimes incorporated, sometimes not. While this did not affect their economic nature – they were still joint-stock companies or 'public partnerships' – legally, it was crucial. While incorporated companies were 'not … to be considered as partnerships within any of the legal principles applicable to partnerships formed by the voluntary agreement of individuals', joint stock companies 'not confirmed by public authority' were, legally speaking, mere partnerships, distinguishable only by the fact that 'the articles of agreement between [their members were] usually very different'.[46]

In that context, it is not surprising the two legal forms were conflated by some, with others[47] considering business corporations, like partnerships, to be comprised of their shareholders. Language may have exacerbated that conflation. The terminology for both the business corporation and the deed of settlement company implied both were based on their shareholders. David Ciepley posits that the English East India Company copied the form of the Dutch East India Company's structure while retaining the language of contractual Joint Stock Companies and merchant guilds, resulting in an ongoing theoretical misclassification of common law incorporated companies as being based on shareholders. Although shareholders were described at that time as 'proprietors', rather than the investors or shareholders they had become, Ciepley suggests the terminology remained in place in part because the change was gradual.[48] That terminology, therefore, masked the actual critical characteristics of the business corporation as a modern company; in particular that it was a separate legal entity from its shareholders.

The distinction was entirely clear at law. The incorporated form, the business corporation, was a form of corporation on one hand; and the unincorporated form, the deed of settlement company, was a partnership on the other. The courts, particularly the Chancery Court presided over by Lord Eldon, consistently treated deed of settlement companies legally as partnerships.[49] The courts

[46] ibid 44 (footnotes omitted), cited in Televantos (n 9) fn 13.

[47] 'James Grant, writing in 1850, also characterised the corporation as a "body of persons associated together for specific purposes", as did Nathaniel Lindley in his treatises on the law of partnership': Ireland (n 27) 46 (footnotes omitted); and see discussion ibid 44–46.

[48] D Ciepley, 'Corporate Directors as Purpose Fiduciaries: Reclaiming the Corporate Law We Need' (2019) 41 *Social Science Research Network* at papers.ssrn.com/sol3/papers.cfm?abstract_id=3426747.

[49] Televantos (n 9) 43, 'courts of the Regency era, especially Lord Eldon's Chancery, refused to treat deed of settlement companies as anything other than partnerships: the trust played only a minor role in their constitution, and did not oust most of the partnership law rules'.

tolerated the desire of entrepreneurs to trade using deed of settlement companies as if they were separate legal entities,[50] without departing from a fundamental position that these enterprises were partnerships at law, not corporations.[51]

Most significantly, shareholders were not protected from liability to third parties. As Televantos puts it:

> What is perhaps most remarkable about the law of the time is how it balanced these different political, economic, and ethical considerations. The courts gave effect to traders' presumed expectation that partnerships and trusts had an existence separate from the partners and trustees, by shielding the partnership or trust assets from the private wealth and creditors of the partners or trustees. At the same time, the law made clear that partners and trustees took personal responsibility for debts they contracted in their own name – whether as partner, trustee, or personally.[52]

VI. THE RELATIVE ADOPTION OF THE TWO CORPORATE FORMS

A business corporation in the United States always shared critical characteristics with early business corporations like the English East India Company: an 'incorporated company was viewed as a product of legislative action; the state's creation and empowerment of an entity'.[53] The deed of settlement company was never significant in the United States, where the Bubble Act 1720 did not apply after the American Revolution.[54] The fact that the traditional nomenclature linked to business corporations was used throughout, with terms such as 'stockholder' and 'corporation' rather than 'company' and 'shareholder', supports arguments that there was less divergence in the United States than in England. The complications of two different corporate forms were avoided.

The development of English company law was driven by the contractual deed of settlement form. English company law and norms influenced US corporate law, in particular around the liability of shareholders. As will be discussed in chapter 11, for a period charters were also difficult to obtain in the United States, particularly for manufacturing corporations. Charters were issued for limited periods, and often with clauses that made shareholders liable for the debts of the corporation. However, once general incorporation arrived, the transition back to the business corporation form used by the English East India Company happened more quickly and easily in the United States than in England. As also

[50] ibid 51.

[51] ibid 173.

[52] Televantos (n 9) 173.

[53] D Kershaw, 'The Path of Corporate Fiduciary Law' (2012) 8 *New York University Journal of Law & Business* 395, 404.

[54] The divergence in paths between England and the United States is usually attributed to the Bubble Act of 1720, which was not repealed in England until 1825. The Bubble Act was repealed (6 Geo 4 c 91) as 'unintelligible and impossibly severe'. *Hansard* HC Deb 2 June 1825, vol 13, col 1019 (as cited and discussed in Hunt (n 1) 41).

discussed in chapter 11, the earlier re-utilisation of the key features inherent in the corporate form may have had an enormous economic impact.

In *The Wealth of Nations*, Adam Smith argued that the corporate form was most suited for only a limited number of enterprises, such as banking, insurance, canals and water supply, that required high capital input, a public benefit or utility, and those enterprises where 'all the operations are capable of being reduced to what is called a Routine, or to such a uniformity of method as admits of little or no variation'.[55] Joint Stock Companies for enterprises without these characteristics were unlikely to be able to compete successfully with other enterprises.

The success of the modern company as the vehicle of choice for most business enterprises is evidence that Smith was not ultimately correct in his predictions about the limitations of the corporate form. But for quite some time Adam Smith seemed to be right. In an analysis of a selection of 290 corporations incorporated by charter or special statute in the United Kingdom in the period 1720 to 1844 (when the first general incorporation statute passed into law), only five companies were incorporated for manufacturing purposes. Railways became increasingly common in the latter part of the period. The vast majority of incorporations, though, were for infrastructure companies: water, gas, harbours, bridges and canals. All these are either undertakings identified by Smith as suiting the corporate form, or undertakings that can be seen to fit the Smith formula.[56]

This distribution of incorporations might be attributed to the Bubble Act 1720, which was enacted to limit speculation in rash and sometimes fraudulent ventures. Obtaining consent for incorporation of business ventures was challenging in the century it was in force, in particular for wider business purposes like manufacturing that did not offer a clear public benefit.

An analysis of 224 deed of settlement companies formed during the period shows a similar but not identical distribution of business types. There were 29 manufacturing companies, 57 insurance companies and 63 banking companies. All these are enterprises for which it would be more difficult to demonstrate public utility, but all, except manufacturing, fit the Smith formula of routine.[57]

In the United States, when the Bubble Act no longer applied in the post-colonial period, only 335 charters were granted, with a 'mere handful' established

[55] Smith (n 14) 447.

[56] Of 291 incorporated companies, the majority were for infrastructure projects, ie 39 water, 1 banking, 34 bridges, 59 canals, 6 colonial, 27 gas, 26 harbours, 6 manufacturing, 21 property, 59 railways and 5 shipping. These figures are derived from an analysis, carried out by the author, of information extracted from a database: Robin Pearson, Mark Freeman and James Taylor, *Constructing the Company: Governance and Procedures in British and Irish Joint-Stock Companies 1720–1844* (Ms Excess and Access versions, 49, 152 cells of data) and Summary of Variable Codes (booklet, 27-page introduction to the database) (study no 5622, deposited with the AHDS, January 2007) at beta.ukdataservice.ac.uk/datacatalogue/studies/study?id=5622.

[57] ibid.

for manufacturing purposes during the same period.[58] As in England, many corporations were formed to fund the types of enterprises favoured by Smith. Nevertheless, incorporation through a charter from the State legislature was relatively easy to obtain. There was a shift away from petitions and towards a system of equality of rights of access to incorporation. That shift was the beginning of a move towards incorporation as a right.

General Acts of incorporation for sectors like fire companies in the late eighteenth century were followed by a general act of incorporation for manufacturing enterprises in New York State in 1811.[59] The full benefits of the incorporated form with perpetual life were not yet realised, with charters or incorporation granted only for a limited period[60] – in the New York general incorporation Act, for 20 years.[61] The perpetual business corporation in the form of the English East India Company in the period after 1657 was not made widely available or utilised by enterprise.

VII. CORPORATE GOVERNANCE IN DEED OF SETTLEMENT COMPANIES

Chapter 4 set out the fight by the small investing generality of the English East India Company through the general meeting to make the governing body accountable in its management of the company. That accountability was achieved in part through the constitutional mechanism of the General Court (meeting), as well as via the development of directors' duties, accountability for a return on capital through accounting mechanisms and, finally, a secondary market in shares based on perceptions of actual and future value of the company.

Any organisational form is only as strong as the people who occupy and operationalise it – in particular its governing body. As shown in chapter 5, many of the gains made by the generality in the shift of power were lost by the short-sighted greed of Clive and others in the English East India Company in the eighteenth century. Nevertheless, the constitutional empowerment of small investing shareholders through the innovation of the regular general meeting survived in the business corporation: 'it was the public forum in which all interests in the company, large and small, came together to exercise their will'.[62]

In both business corporations and deed of settlement companies, powers to manage, in the sense of directing and superintending the company, rested with

[58] LM Friedman, *A History of American Law*, 3rd edn (Simon & Schuster, 1973) 130–32. See also AA Berle and GC Means, *The Modern Corporation and Private Property*, rev edn (Harcourt, Brace & World, 1968) 11.

[59] Statute of 22 March 1811, New York Statutes, VII, 233 (as cited in Cooke (n 1) 94).

[60] Bratton (n 11) 1485.

[61] Cooke (n 1) 94.

[62] Freeman, Pearson and Taylor (n 19) 240.

the board. Indeed, although legally a deed of settlement company was a partnership, functionally the allocation of the power to manage to a board was a characteristic that distinguished a deed of settlement company from the private mercantile partnership.

In *Burnes v Pennell*,[63] the House of Lords, considering the deed of settlement company form, opined:

> [O]n the principle which regulates the liability of common parties, a distinction must be made between a member of a common mercantile partnership and a shareholder in a joint stock company. No one will contend that a joint stock company would be liable on a bill of exchange, drawn, accepted, or indorsed by any one shareholder. Why? Because it is known that the power of carrying on the business of the company, and of drawing, accepting, and indorsing bills of exchange, is vested exclusively in the directors. This shews that, although a joint stock company is a partnership, it is a partnership of a different description and attended with different incidents and liabilities from a partnership constituted between a few individuals who carry on business jointly, with equal powers and without transferrable shares. All who have dealings with a joint stock company know that the authority to manage the business is conferred upon the directors, and that a shareholder, as such, has no power to contract for the company. For this purpose, it is wholly immaterial whether the company is incorporated or unincorporated.

In both the deed of settlement form and the business corporation form, the General Court (meeting) also had decision-making powers. These could relate to policy or major changes. The issue of additional shares or purchase of extensive property were often decisions for the General Court.[64] The source and nature of the powers of the two decision-making bodies, the General Court and the Court of Committees (board of directors), differed. For a business corporation, it was constitutional. It would be the charter or by-laws, or the incorporating statute if it was a business corporation formed through a discrete statute as a private Act of Parliament. (That mode of incorporation became more common later in the eighteenth century.[65]) For a deed of settlement company, the allocation would be made in the deed of settlement, so could be viewed as contractual. In both cases, it was understood that shareholders could not overrule decisions of boards other than through the General Court. Shareholders were understood to be bound by the terms of the charter, act of incorporation or deed of settlement.[66]

Boards of directors were accountable to shareholders through the General Court, and since general policy was set by shareholders, the General Court could in theory overrule measures taken by directors. It was also recognised, however, that directors owed duties to the company and that the General Court,

[63] *Burnes v Pennell* (n 28).
[64] DuBois (n 1) 291.
[65] Cooke (n 1) 91.
[66] DuBois (n 1) 303.

comprising shareholders, and the company were not necessarily the same. A governor of the South Seas Company expressed it thus:

> That altho' it is our general duty to follow your orders in doing which We shall ever be legally justified, We should nevertheless in a moral sense betray our Trust by implicitly putting in execution orders that may really be, or which to our judgment upon mature deliberation may seem to be improper.[67]

The authors of *Shareholder Democracies?* show empirically the reduction in collective powers of shareholders through the eighteenth and early nineteenth centuries. That reduction was led by practice in private deed of settlement companies and then followed by practice in business corporations. The reduction of shareholder powers in deed of settlement companies related to who drafted the constitutional documents. Rather than being a charter or incorporating Act of Parliament creating a statutory corporation, deeds of settlement were drafted by founding directors and their solicitors.[68] One merchant wrote, 'the directors, when they have the deed of settlement drawn up, take good care to give the shareholders as little power as possible'.[69]

A barrister who prepared deeds of settlement commented that directors aimed to maximise their powers and minimise their responsibilities at the expense of shareholders. 'The most extraordinary clauses' could be inserted, because 'the parties who become shareholders in very many cases never think of reading the deed of settlement, and indeed are not very competent to understand it'.[70]

Shareholder Democracies? characterises the powers of shareholders that were reallocated to directors as participatory but, it is suggested, many of these powers of shareholders exercised in the general meeting do not relate to direct management control. Instead, they relate to general policy, and to constitutional oversight and accountability. For example, a common clause in incorporating Acts for business corporations divided powers constitutionally by giving the board of directors the power to run the company as it saw fit, subject to the examination and control of the general meeting. That clause was less common in deeds of settlement.[71]

The study shows that shareholder and general meeting powers were much higher, and in fact increased, in business corporations in the eighteenth century compared with deed of settlement companies, with shareholder participation in both forms converging to a lower level by 1835.[72] The size of boards decreased and the terms of office for directors increased. The number of active shareholders was reduced, with some lessening of general-meeting powers over the appointment of salaried officers and casual board vacancies. There was a

[67] Minute of the General Court, Addit MS, 25,500 in fn 124 (as cited in DuBois (n 1) 298–99).
[68] Freeman, Pearson and Taylor (n 19) 60.
[69] Evidence of 'A B' SC on Joint Stock Companies, BPP (1844) VII, 104 (as cited ibid 60–61).
[70] ibid.
[71] Freeman, Pearson and Taylor (n 19) 128.
[72] ibid 242 and figure 9.1.

shift from the feudal system of voting based on individual shareholders towards votes based on capital contributed. Voting caps were increasingly abandoned, empowering major shareholders at the expense of small investors. Less access to account books by shareholders and the general meeting was led by the practice in deed of settlement companies.[73] The emergence of proxy voting might be seen as enhancing shareholder power, but, unsurprisingly, boards were able to manipulate proxy voting to achieve desired outcomes.[74]

VIII. CONCLUSION

The contractual Joint Stock Company form, even when combined with the innovative use of the deed of settlement to settle assets on trust for separation of the capital fund, did not offer all the advantages afforded by the modern company. The deed of settlement company form could not provide investing shareholders with comprehensive protection from liability to third parties.[75] The deed of settlement company could contractually limit the liability of subscribing shareholders to the deed of settlement company itself. As common law did not recognise the trust that held the capital, however, shareholders were not protected from claims by third parties. Shareholders and the companies themselves struggled to use the courts, Chancery in particular,[76] where they were tolerated more than sanctioned. The deed of settlement company was not a legal person, so it could not sue, or be sued, as a juridical person. Nor could shareholders readily litigate against the company.

Significance is attached to the apparent success of the deed of settlement company in the eighteenth century. Some commentators consider that modern companies are also contractual.[77] Others recognise the role of organisational law, but do not resile from considering the modern company to be primarily contractual.[78] Evidence of a form based on contract operating successfully provides ballast to arguments that the statutory components of organisational law, particularly legal personality and limited liability, are just an efficient way of bestowing characteristics on the modern company that are also available contractually, albeit less efficiently.

Assets were protected 'almost as though they belonged to a distinct entity', but the deed of settlement company was not a separate legal entity at common law. The practical barrier that all shareholders had to join in actions against the

[73] ibid 241.

[74] ibid 241–42.

[75] Televantos (n 9) 43; Dubois (n 1) 223–26.

[76] Televantos (n 9) 49.

[77] FH Easterbrook and DR Fischel, 'The Corporate Contract' (1989) 89 *Columbia Law Review* 1416; FH Easterbrook and DR Fischel, *The Economic Structure of Corporate Law* (Harvard University Press, 1991).

[78] J Armour et al, 'What Is Corporate Law?' in R Kraakman (ed), *The Anatomy of Corporate Law*, 3rd edn (Oxford University Press, 2017) 5.

deed of settlement company, made litigation by shareholders against the deed of settlement company impracticable.[79] Shareholders may have had a form of limited liability to the company itself for some of the period,[80] but, as the deed of settlement companies were partnerships at common law, shareholders were liable to third parties.[81]

Finally, the instability of the deed of settlement company that was legally a partnership form with lack of functional and legal separation of partners from the entity, restricted the ability to raise capital beyond personal networks of partners:

> Partnership's tie to the personality of the partners limited its effectiveness as a means of raising and locking in capital, and so corporations and depersonalised markets for shares were needed in the nineteenth century as capital demands increased with the scale of production.[82]

Trusts, Maitland's 'blessed back stair' of the law,[83] have several disadvantages compared with the modern company. First, a company can exist from the moment of incorporation, with the promise by shareholders through subscription to provide seed capital. Some form of assets must be settled on a trust for it to exist. Associations with no specifiable purposes, and no beneficial ownership of property, fall outside the domain of trusteeship altogether. The outcome of *The Case of Sutton's Hospital*[84] in 1612 would have been different if it had involved a trust rather than a corporation.

Also, as was recognised before the introduction of the general incorporation statutes, in instances where the rights of beneficiaries are unknowable, trusts are not able to safeguard the interests of shareholders as beneficiaries. And if a primary advantage of the modern company lies in its potential existence in perpetuity, creating a mechanism for growth of value in the long

[79] *R v Dodd* (1808) 9 East 516, 103 ER 670 (KB).

[80] Morley (n 30) 2183.

[81] Take *R v Dodd* (n 78), which involved a deed of settlement company with a multitude of shareholders. Lord Ellenborough said 'As to the subscribers themselves, indeed, they may stipulate with each other for this contracted responsibility; but as to the rest of the world it is clear that each partner is liable to the whole amount of the debts contracted by the partnership.' (See the discussion in Televantos (n 9) and compare Morley (n 30).) Also, as Televantos highlights, the entity shielding separating the personal wealth of partners from the assets of the firm may not have been as strong as is currently believed: '[T]he priority claim partnership creditors had to partnership assets did encourage creditors to deal with the firm, in that they could assess its solvency without investigating the private affairs of the partners, as Hansmann, Kraakmann, and Squire argue. However, … this is only part of a more complicated story … Hansmann, Kraakmann, and Squire overlook limitations on partnership law's ability to preserve business assets for business creditors. Business creditors might have no protected claim against business assets in cases where a partnership had continued trading after the death or retirement of a partner – a complicated area which very much vexed the courts.' Televantos (n 9) 144.

[82] Televantos (n 9) 28.

[83] O Gierke, *Political Theories of the Middle Age*, tr FW Maitland (Cambridge University Press, 1913) xxxi.

[84] *The Case of Sutton's Hospital* (n 40).

term, it was not an advantage shared by the trust. The potential longevity of the modern company links to its legal separation from the natural persons who are its shareholders. In the deed of settlement form, separation of capital was achieved through settlement of capital on the trust. At common law, however, the company was contractually based and legally a form of partnership. It is for that reason that the deed of settlement company was often called second best.

The ultimate significance of the contractual deed of settlement form may relate most to the influence it has had on how the modern company is understood, in particular in English law. As earlier chapters have shown, although the contractual form always existed in parallel with the endowed corporation, the contractual form enhanced by the use of deeds of settlement to settle assets on a trust was widely utilised in the eighteenth and early nineteenth centuries. The deed of settlement form, existing as it did at the edges of the law, was also widely litigated, leaving a legacy in the case law that informed the understanding in the nineteenth century of the companies incorporated pursuant to general incorporation statutes. These points are picked up in the following chapters. Also discussed is how the contractual form strengthened the economic perspective of the company, meaning that the legal form adopted was given less significance.

Finally, deeds of settlement shifted the constitutional balance between shareholders acting through the general meeting and boards, relating to general policy and constitutional oversight and accountability. Some of those shifts were eventually followed in the business corporation form, which continued to operate in parallel throughout the period. Many of those constitutional checks and balances had been hard won in the seventeenth and eighteenth centuries, as discussed in chapter 4. The constitutional basis of the governance of the modern company will be picked up in the discussion in chapter 15.

9

General Incorporation Statutes

I. INTRODUCTION

GENERAL INCORPORATION WAS permitted initially in the Joint Stock Companies Act 1844 to control rather than facilitate access to Joint Stock Funds.[1] However, the subsequent general incorporation acts of 1856 and 1862 were facilitative, with statutory limited liability for shareholders becoming the default position.

Companies incorporated pursuant to these statutes were initially understood to be based on their shareholders and, like contractual Joint Stock Companies, akin to partnerships. In the second half of the nineteenth century, the consequences of incorporation and statutory limited liability saw a gradual recognition that the modern company was in many ways a form of corporation. Like earlier business corporations such as the English East India Company, these modern companies were separate legal entities from their shareholders, based on a Joint Stock or Corporate Fund.

II. THE JOINT STOCK COMPANIES ACT 1844

The Joint Stock Companies Act 1844 was restrictive rather than facilitative. The authors of the Report that led to the development of the first piece of legislation permitting general incorporation by registration included that Victorian multitasker William Gladstone.[2] Those Report authors, like Adam Smith, considered that only a limited number of enterprises, such as banking, insurance, canals

[1] As Televantos puts it, 'This insight that general incorporation was only introduced to allow companies to be better regulated is an important one today, where the issue of whether corporate personality is a natural right of profit-making joint stock companies, or a privilege granted by the state which should be qualified in the public interest, remains hotly contested.' A Televantos, *Capitalism Before Corporations: The morality of business associations and the roots of commercial equity and law* (Oxford University Press, 2021) 174–75.

[2] Gladstone was brought in to head a Select Committee on Joint Stock Companies that was established to identify measures to prevent fraud: The Gladstone Committee, *First Report of the Select Committee on Joint Stock Companies; together with the Minutes of Evidence (taken in 1841 and 1843), Appendix, and Index* (HC 1844, 119-VII). For discussion, see R McQueen, *A Social History of Company Law: Great Britain and the Australian Colonies 1854–1920* (Ashgate Publishing, 2009) 43–45.

and water supply, were suited to the corporate form. These enterprises required large amounts of capital, were high-risk and had long amortisation periods.

In the first quarter of the nineteenth century, the renewed enforcement of the Bubble Act by the courts[3] led deed of settlement companies to seek private acts of incorporation. Lord Eldon considered that the Bubble Act was drafted too badly to be useful, but an unincorporated body acting as a corporate body was an offence at common law.[4] The subsequent repeal of the Bubble Act in 1825 led to concerns from Lord Eldon and others that raising large sums of money by selling freely transferrable shares was usurping Crown and parliamentary privileges, and that another speculative bubble would ultimately burst, harming English interests. Joint Stock was linked with gambling mania and corruption, with that perception strengthened by a market crash in 1825.[5] Lord Eldon still considered raising sums by selling shares to be illegal, despite the repeal of the Bubble Act.[6]

The 1844 Joint Stock Companies Act was introduced, therefore, at a time when companies were still viewed with suspicion. The Report of the Select Committee set out various modes of deception adopted by deed of settlement companies. The Report argued for legislation that would tackle these practices.[7] Robert Lowe, the architect of the later and more facilitative Joint Stock Companies Act 1856, said that the Select Committee appeared to have 'conducted its deliberations in a state of mental perturbation',[8] and

> the headings of the different sections of what one would generally expect to be a very demure and quiet sort of document running thus:- 'Form and Destination of the Plunder,' 'Circumstances of the Victims,' 'Impunity of the Offenders,' and the like; so that a hurried glance at the contents might make a man fancy he was reading a novel instead of a blue-book.[9]

As Televantos puts it, '[t]he long eighteenth century strategy of allowing such companies to exist on the periphery of legality was deemed to have failed – because of the market crashes and frauds company promotions seemed to encourage.'[10]

Registration of deed of settlement companies through the 1844 Act was a form of state or public control of the private form.[11] Incorporation was a two-stage process. Provisional registration was required for both existing deed of

[3] *R v Dodd* (1808) 9 East 516, 103 ER 670 (KB). See the discussion in CA Cooke, *Corporation, Trust and Company: An Essay in Legal History* (Harvard University Press, 1951) 97–99.

[4] *Kinder v Taylor* (1824–1826) LJR Ch 68, cited in Cooke (n 3) 99 and see the discussion ibid 99–102.

[5] Televantos (n 1) 39–42.

[6] *Kinder v Taylor* (n 4), cited in in Cooke (n 3) 99 and see the discussion ibid 99–102.

[7] The Gladstone Committee (n 2) (communicated by the Commons to the Lords: HL 1844, 65-XX).

[8] *Hansard* (HC 1856, 140) cols 111–26.

[9] ibid col 117.

[10] Televantos (n 1) 174.

[11] McQueen (n 2) 43–51. See also Televantos (n 1) 43.

settlement companies and new companies, before proceeding to a second stage of final registration and incorporation.

Existing deed of settlement companies were brought under the umbrella of the law through registration. New companies were initially formed following the same process in the first stage as the process used for the formation of deed of settlement companies. Provisional registration of deed of settlement companies gave them a form of recognition by the law prior to the perfection of incorporation in the second stage of registration. The 1844 Act therefore both ensured complete legal recognition of deed of settlement companies if the registration process was completed, and permitted incorporation of new companies if the two-stage process set out in the statute was followed.

The 1844 statute did not give the shareholders of the incorporated companies limited liability. Requirements such as minimum capitalisation and publicity, the two-stage registration process and enforcement difficulties meant that 76 per cent of companies were abandoned before completing the second stage of registration in the period the Act was in force between 1844 and 1856.[12]

Cooke clearly considered that the 1844 Act transformed the deed of settlement company into a modern company. It had been

> clothed in the garments of rectitude; it had achieved incorporation, limited liability, power to acquire land for its purposes under general Acts of Parliament. That incorporation which was once the gift of the Sovereign to the few had become the statutory right of the multitude.[13]

Certainly, promoters were no longer required to petition, setting out a public purpose, for incorporation to be granted, as had been the long-standing requirement for grant of a corporate charter.[14] The competitive business unit could be incorporated for entirely private enterprises like manufacturing. Certainly, if the two-stage registration process was followed through to its conclusion, incorporation was guaranteed. But it was the 1856 Act that included statutory limited liability for shareholders as the default. The Companies Act 1862, which expanded on the 1856 Act, remained in force, with some amendments, for the rest of the nineteenth century and provided the statutory framework for modern English company law. The 1844 Act has little lasting significance beyond its being the first English general incorporation statute.

III. THE JOINT STOCK COMPANIES ACT 1856

The Joint Stock Companies Act 1856, and the subsequent Companies Act 1862, were facilitative rather than restrictive. Lowe believed incorporation should be

[12] For discussion see Televantos (n 1) 43–44.
[13] Cooke (n 3) 187. Limited liability for companies incorporated pursuant to the 1844 Act became possible when the Limited Liability Act 1855 was enacted.
[14] ibid 102.

freely available and that the benefits of investing in companies should be made available to the middle classes.[15] Business initially responded to the availability of the new form with statutory limited liability. As a writer in *The Shareholders' Guardian* commented in 1864:

> [W]hen it was perceived that limited liability would be accepted even in the circles of the banking community, scarcely any bounds were placed to the animation which followed, and limited liability soon became patronized not only by banks but by every other conceivable kind of undertaking, financial and industrial.[16]

It was also commented in relation to the new companies that not only their numbers, but also the nature of their business 'would have staggered Adam Smith'.[17] The growth was most notable in manufacturing – a form of enterprise that did not fit the Smith formula as manufacturing companies did not necessarily require large amounts of capital, might not be high risk and did not have long amortisation periods. No ostensible public benefit attached to incorporation of a manufacturing company. In the period between 1863 and 1866, 876 new companies offered shares to the public. Of those companies, 283 were involved in manufacturing and trading, with the next largest group being mining enterprises.[18]

IV. LIMITED LIABILITY

Statutory limited liability of shareholders to the company and to third parties dealing with the company became the default position for companies from 1856. Statutory limited liability was not a nineteenth-century innovation, although default limited liability was, as one of the attributes acquired as of right on incorporation. Statutory companies formed by discrete statutes for infrastructure projects in the period before the general incorporation statutes of the mid-nineteenth century could be granted statutory limited liability. *Hansard* says 'the rule had been to grant them only in cases where the enterprise, from its magnitude, demanded a very large capital, and where the benefit to the nation from the undertaking was evident'.[19]

[15] For a discussion, see SM Watson, 'The Significance of the Source of the Powers of Boards in UK Company Law' [2011] *Journal of Business Law* 597.

[16] *Shareholders' Guardian* (1 March 1864), as cited in BC Hunt, *The Development of the Business Corporation in England 1800–1867* (Harvard University Press, 1936) 148–49.

[17] *The Times* (20 June 1864), as cited in Hunt (n 16) 149, fn 20.

[18] Hunt (n 16) 150.

[19] *Hansard* (HC 1853, 129) cols 1598–99 states 'There was power in special cases for the Queen in Council to grant charters with limited liability. The practice with respect to these charters was this: They were sent to the Committee of Privy Council for Trade. Those consisting of financial questions-for instance, colonial and banking charters-were disposed of under the responsibility of the Treasury. Charters, neither commercial nor financial, were under the responsibility of the Home Office, and the ordinary charters were disposed of under the Committee of Privy Council for Trade.

Use of discrete statutes to form statutory companies for large-scale infrastructure projects such as canals and railroads became common with the onset of the Industrial Revolution. The liability of shareholders was often limited to the nominal value of their shares.[20] The limitation of liability led to the legal separation of these statutory corporations from shareholders; a legal separation that also developed in the modern company by the end of the nineteenth century. In 1837, clearly adopting the *persona ficta* conception, Alderson B said of the shareholders in a statutory company that 'the individual members of a corporation are quite as distinct from the metaphysical body called "the corporation", as any others of his Majesty's subjects are'.[21] As discussed in chapter 2, early corporations were considered to be separate legal entities from their members in a similar way. As discussed in chapters 3 and 7, once the concept of permanent capital had developed, evidence exists that shareholders were not considered to be liable for the debts of business corporations to third parties dealing with the company, because the business corporation was a separate legal entity from its shareholders.

In the deed of settlement company form, the Joint Stock Fund was held in a trust created for business purposes. The title to trust assets was held by the trustees. By the end of the eighteenth century, a clause was commonly inserted stating that 'each shareholder was only to be liable to the extent of his own share in the capital stock'.[22] These clauses would not necessarily have been legally effective; a point Gower says 'was probably not clearly grasped by lawyers and certainly not by investors'.[23] Such clauses could not apply to persons dealing with the deed of settlement company as third parties. However, the trust agreement could also contain a clause freeing the beneficiaries from liability to third parties for debts incurred by the trustee on behalf of the trust. The clause was regarded as effective in a series of early-nineteenth-century cases involving insurance companies that put the limitation of shareholder liability clause in their insurance contracts. Chancery also recognised that shareholders, as beneficiaries, had limited liability so long as third parties were given sufficient notice of the claimed exemption from liability at the time they extended credit

With respect to those charters, the rule had been to grant them only in cases where the enterprise, from its magnitude, demanded a very large capital, and where the benefit to the nation from the undertaking was evident. That rule was not of easy application, and the course of precedent had not been uniform. The present Government had only granted charters in two classes of cases-one the Australian Voyage, and the other the Submarine Telegraph. He found that charters had been obtained by the following companies:-Royal Mail Pacific Steam, Peninsular and Oriental, Indian and Australian, General Screw, Eastern Steam, South American General, African Royal Mail, and Liverpool and Australian.'

[20] JB Baskin and PJ Miranti Jr, *A History of Corporate Finance* (Cambridge University Press, 1997) 139.

[21] *Bligh v Brent* (1837) 2 Y & C Ex 268, 295.

[22] This clause was commonly inserted in the deeds of settlement of insurance companies and became common at the end of the 18th century and beginning of the 19th century: Cooke (n 3) 87; see *Re European Assurance Society* (1875) 1 Ch D 307 (CA) and the cases cited therein.

[23] LCB Gower, *Principles of Modern Company Law*, 4th edn (Sweet & Maxwell, 1979) 26.

to the trust.[24] Maitland went as far as asserting that the deed of settlement form '(in effect) enabled men to form joint-stock companies with limited liability, until at length the legislature had to give way'.[25]

This advantage, if it existed at all, did not persist following the outcome of *Waugh v Carver* in 1793.[26] By the time the introduction of statutory limited liability was debated in 1854, it was stated at the outset that it was assumed that every partner (as shareholders in deed of settlement companies were called) had unlimited liability and that the law had been settled since *Waugh v Carver*.[27] One of the arguments in the debate in the 1850s leading to statutory limited liability was that it would create equity for partners in private partnerships with partners in public partnerships – the incorporated form. In the debate that led to the enactment of the facilitative Joint Stock Companies Act 1856, Robert Lowe, reprobated the state of the law, saying that it would have been better if *Waugh v Carver* had been decided the other way, and saying that what was to become the Joint Stock Companies Act 1856 would overrule that judgment.[28]

The US experience provided a potential model for the inclusion of limited liability in the Companies Act 1862.[29] Legislators to varying extents had drawn on the US experience when the Limited Liability Act 1855 was drafted.[30] Also, many legislators were cognisant of the competitive advantage forms of limited liability offered the commercial interests of the French[31] and the Americans.[32] That realisation was not universal. One Lord said in 1855, somewhat sniffily and not at all presciently, that he doubted

> the principle was so successful in the United States as was pretended; compare the commercial character, the state of credit, and the transactions on the Broadway at New York and in England, and he would ask which of the two countries stood the highest in respect to all that characterised its commercial men?[33]

[24] FG Kempin Jr, 'Limited Liability in Historical Perspective' (1960) 4 *American Business Law Association Bulletin* 11, 12–13; *Re Waterloo Life Assurance Co* (1864) 33 Beav 542.

[25] FW Maitland, 'The Unincorporate Body' in HAL Fisher (ed), *The Collected Papers of Frederic William Maitland*, vol 3 (Cambridge University Press, 1911) 278–79.

[26] *Waugh v Carver* (1793) 126 ER 525.

[27] See the discussion of the relatively short duration of unlimited liability in England in *Hansard* (HC 1854, 134) cols 752–60 (Mr Collier). Morley argues that shareholders of deed of settlement companies were only seen as partners from the 1820s. See J Morley, 'The Common Law Corporation: The Power of the Trust in Anglo-American Business History' (2016) 116 *Columbia Law Review* 2145, 2176. But see the discussion of authority by Televantos (n 1) 43–46, which refutes this assertion.

[28] *Hansard* (n 8) col 114. The statutory requirement that creditors be alerted to the limited liability of beneficiary shareholders is the origin of the use of the word 'limited' in English companies; there is no equivalent requirement in the United States, or in civil law jurisdictions. The reason for the divergence may be that the deed of settlement form did not exist in a significant way in the United States, and did not exist at all in civil law jurisdictions.

[29] Kempin (n 24) 14.

[30] *Hansard* (HL 1855, 139) cols 2039–42.

[31] In the limited partnership called *partnership en commandite*.

[32] *Hansard* (n 30) col 2040.

[33] ibid.

The benefits to enterprises of all sizes brought about by limited liability, combined with having the status of a juridical person as a consequence of incorporation, may have been an unintended consequence of the general incorporation statutes. The motivating factor for the legitimation of incorporation by registration was apparently to facilitate wider investment. As such, it embodied liberal principles of freedom of contract and unlimited association. There is no evidence from that time of recognition either that shareholders' having an automatic right to limit their liability changed the relationship of shareholders to the company, or that the Joint Stock or Corporate Fund would provide protection for shareholders as investors and protection for the company itself from creditors of shareholders.

Lowe may have inadvertently delayed the realisation of full benefits of incorporation with limited liability in England. He did not favour requirements then in place around paid-up capital, since paid-up capital was not seen to be of benefit to the company. Evasion of the requirement was, he opined, 'as easy as lying'.[34]

V. WAS THE MODERN COMPANY A PARTNERSHIP OR A CORPORATION?

The motivating factor for the legitimation of incorporation by registration was to facilitate investment by a wider range of investors. The driving motivation of proponents behind the Joint Stock Companies Act 1856[35] was the enactment of legislation that would embody liberal principles of freedom of contract and association.

Parliamentarians of the day may have considered the modern company incorporated pursuant to the 1856 Act to be a continuation in form of the eighteenth-century deed of settlement company, and therefore legally a form of partnership. Robert Lowe was the chief architect of the 1856 and 1862 legislation.

[34] *Hansard* (n 8) col 126 (Robert Lowe): 'Taking the Limited Liability Act as it now stands, it is required that 20 per cent of the amount subscribed shall be paid up, and that the fact of such payment having been made shall be proved by a declaration made by two of the promoters. Now, in the case of bona fide companies I can imagine nothing more embarrassing than this. It involves such companies in a great deal of difficulty; and I have had strong complaints from various quarters of the trouble and embarrassment which have been experienced in forming bona fide companies from this cause alone. This provision was not meant to hit the honest, but the fraudulent; but it is evident that fraudulent companies can easily evade it, for they have nothing more to do than to get two of their promoters to make a declaration to the effect that the amount of capital required by the Statute has been subscribed – it is, as Hamlet says, "as easy as lying," – it is only required that the declaration shall be made, no power being given to inquire whether it really has been subscribed or not. So that while you are annoying and embarrassing bona fide concerns, you are not in the least degree placing a check upon those that are fraudulent. On the contrary, if they succeed in satisfying the Government requisitions, they obtain a spurious merit to which they are by no means entitled. By this enactment also you are taking the business of people out of their own hands. It is often a disadvantage to a concern to start with a great amount of paid-up capital.'

[35] Joint Stock Companies Act 1856 (19 & 20 Vict c 47).

In the *Hansard* debates leading to the enactment of the Joint Stock Companies Act 1856, Lowe consistently referred to Joint Stock Companies as private partnerships, asking at the outset of the debate 'how shall the principle of limited liability be extended to private partnerships?'[36] Indeed much of the focus was on the advantages of limited liability to sleeping partners in the French law of *commandite* (without seeking to emulate the form), rather than discussion of the advantages of limited liability then in place in the American corporation.[37]

Although the debates in *Hansard* consistently refer to private partnerships, the contractual Joint Stock Company was differentiated by some parliamentarians from the mercantile partnership. For example, Mr Bouverie said there was more than a technical distinction between Joint Stock Companies (meaning deed of settlement companies) and private partnerships. The shares in a company were transferable at the will of the holder; in the partnership it was otherwise. Whilst seeing a deed of settlement company as a partnership carried on with a high number of members (as indeed it was at law), the bond of union in contractual Joint Stock Companies was different from that in private partnerships. In contractual Joint Stock Companies those involved needed to have no mutual knowledge of each other.[38]

The general incorporation statutes referred to the subscribers' forming themselves into an incorporated company and did not spell out the consequences in any detail.[39] As a learned commentator in the *Law Quarterly Review* of 1897 stated, 'Our Legislature … delivered itself on the Companies Acts in its usual oracular style, leaving to the Courts the interpretation of its mystical utterances.'[40]

A business corporation in the time of the English East India Company was not contractually based on its shareholders. Maitland writes of 'Contract, that greediest of legal categories, which once wanted to devour the state, resents being told it cannot painlessly digest even a joint-stock company.'[41]

In 1867, in *Oakes v Turquand and Harding*, Lord Cranworth explained that 'The course of legislation was to rear up the company into a separate persons with certain powers and privileges, but without conferring on it in an unqualified manner all the attributes of a perfect corporation.'[42] As the nineteenth century progressed, it became apparent that the modern company was a legal

[36] *Hansard* (n 8) col 111.
[37] ibid; see also *Hansard* (HC 1855, 139) cols 310–20.
[38] *Hansard* (n 37) vol 139, col 320.
[39] Joint Stock Companies Act 1856, s 3.
[40] Anon (1897) 13 *Law Quarterly Review* 6. For useful recent discussions of the economic and legal background to the case, see P Ireland, 'Triumph of the Company Legal Form 1856–1914' and GR Rubin, 'Aron Salomon and His Circle' in J Adams (ed), *Essays for Clive Schmitthoff* (Professional Books, 1983). The case was also the subject of Lord Cooke of Thorndon's Hamlyn Lecture in 1996: CA Cooke, *Turning Points of the Common Law* (Sweet & Maxwell, 1997).
[41] O Gierke, *Political Theories of the Middle Age*, tr FW Maitland (Cambridge University Press, 1913) xxiv–xxv.
[42] *Oakes v Turquand and Harding* (1867) 2 LR HL 325 (HL) 374.

form different from the contractually-based deed of settlement company, which was legally a partnership.

But where did the balance of attributes sit? Was the modern company a separate legal entity from its shareholders like a corporation, or was it based on its shareholders in the same way as a deed of settlement company was, therefore remaining a variant on the partnership?

Robert Lowe did not want the Joint Stock Companies Act 1856 to be seen as creating corporations. Ironically, given the path the law ultimately took, in the debate leading to the enactment of the 1856 Act Lowe said:

> One method would be to carry the present law of limited liability into these partnerships, and to say that any number of persons, however small – even to one, and there could not be a much smaller number than that – that he or they shall be entitled to be formed into a corporation, and to enjoy, as such, the privilege of limited liability. To that proposition I am not disposed to accede; and for this reason – that it appears to me that there is something incompatible and inconsistent between the character of a man acting as a principal in trade, and that of a person being corporator, and whose liability as such shall be limited. There would be a constant ambiguity whether such a person was trading as a principal or as a private individual. There is nothing inconsistent with the character of limited liability in the position of an agent such as a director or manager, but the position of a principal carrying on such business would be ambiguous and uncertain; many of his acts would bear a double construction, and there would always be a struggle on the part of creditors to fix him with individual liability, and on his own part to refer his acts to his corporate capacity. Individual partners would have to guarantee their own partnerships. These difficulties would increase as the partnerships grew smaller, till in the case of little tradesmen they would become absolutely intolerable. Everything would always be said to have been done by the corporation and nothing by the individual, and a door to vexation, quibbling, and perjury would be opened which it is most desirable to keep closed.[43]

Lowe failed to predict the inevitable effect the 1856 Act and the process of incorporation would have on the private form. Once incorporated, these private forms acquired the key characteristics of a corporation, including perpetuity and status as a juridical person, with the attributes of being able to sue and be sued and transact as a legal person. Because Lowe did not consider the process followed in the 1856 Act led to the formation of a corporation, a company formed pursuant to the 1856 Act was considered at the time to be based on its shareholders. Shareholders of incorporated companies were not considered to be separate from the company in their private capacities. Therefore the de facto position was that shareholders would be otherwise liable for the debts of the company, meaning statutory limited liability became the default. However, statutory limited liability led to the eventual accounting and then legal separation of

[43] *Hansard* (n 8) col 113.

shareholders from the company, in the same way that shareholders were legally separate from the business corporation.

Based on what we know about the operation of modern companies, and in particular the challenges around 'one man' companies, Lowe is prescient in foreseeing the issues that could arise once Joint Stock Companies were viewed as corporations. Forty years later, the seminal case *Salomon v Salomon & Co Ltd*[44] established that a company just like the one Lowe had described was legally a statutory corporation.

The transition of the English company from being based on its shareholders to being legally separate from its shareholders can be traced through the nineteenth-century treatises of writer and jurist Nathanial Lindley, later Lindley LJ of the English Court of Appeal, the Judge who was overturned by the House of Lords in *Salomon v Salomon & Co Ltd*.[45] Lindley's treatise on company law started life as an 1863 supplement to his treatise on partnership law,[46] with Lindley's seeing company law as a branch of partnership law subject to its principles.[47] In the text he describes companies as partnerships incorporated by registration and companies as a form of partnership.[48] In the introduction to the text Lindley defined a company as an 'association of many persons who contribute money or money's worth to a common stock and employ it for some common purpose'.[49]

Lindley did nevertheless recognise the hybrid basis of the modern company, saying in an earlier 1860 edition of his partnership treatise:

> Companies are associations of persons intermediate between corporations known to common law and ordinary partnerships, and partaking of the nature of both; and the law relating to companies depends as well on the principles which govern ordinary partnerships, as on those which are applicable to corporations strictly so called.[50]

By the third edition of his treatise in 1873, and as the form and the law surrounding the company evolved, Lindley acknowledged the implications of incorporation of a modern company; that it was a separate legal entity from its shareholders: '[A] company which is incorporated, whether by charter, special act of Parliament, or registration, is in a legal point of view distinct from the persons composing it,'[51] concluding 'and is therefore regarded by lawyers somewhat as

[44] *Salomon v Salomon & Co Ltd* [1897] AC 22 (HL).

[45] *Broderip v Salomon* [1895] 2 Ch 323 (CA); *Salomon v Salomon & Co Ltd* (n 44).

[46] N Lindley, *Supplement to a Treatise on the Law of Partnership Including its Application to Joint-Stock and Other Companies*, 5th edn (W Maxwell, 1863).

[47] N Lindley, *A Treatise on the Law of Companies, considered as a branch of the Law of Partnership*, 5th edn (Sweet & Maxwell, 1889).

[48] ibid 8.

[49] ibid 1.

[50] N Lindley, *A Treatise on the Law of Partnership: Including its Application to Joint-Stock and Other Companies,* vol 1 (T & JW Johnson, 1860) 67.

[51] N Lindley and S Dickinson, *A Treatise on the Law of Partnership Including its Application to Companies*, vol 1, 3rd edn (W Maxwell, 1873) 227.

a firm is by non-lawyers.'[52] Lindley may have been somewhat Delphic, because on the face of it the separation of shareholders from the modern company made inconsistent assertions he continued to make elsewhere in his treatise that a company was an association of shareholders.[53]

VI. *SALOMON v SALOMON & CO LTD*

Aron Salomon was a leather merchant and hide factor, wholesale and export boot manufacturer, and government contractor, operating as a successful sole trader in Whitechapel in the East End of London for over 30 years. Salomon's six sons applied pressure on him to give them a share in the business, and Salomon wished to extend the business. Salomon formed a company and sold his business to the company. At the time, the legislation required a company to have a minimum of seven members. Salomon himself and six members of his family, who held one share each as nominees, were the shareholders of A Salomon and Co Ltd. In substance, if not form, the company was a 'one-man company'.

The price paid by the company for the transfer of the business was £39,000, 'a sum which', as Lord Macnaghten said in the House of Lords, 'represented the sanguine expectations of a fond owner rather than anything that can be called a businesslike or reasonable estimate of value'.[54] Although worthy of comment, this fact ultimately had no bearing on the outcome, and at that time there were no rules in place around prices of sales of existing businesses to companies.

The company paid £30,000[55] of the purchase price out of money as it came in. Salomon immediately returned that funding to the company in exchange for fully-paid shares, £10,000 in debentures. The balance (except for £1,000) was used to pay debts. The debentures were an acknowledgement of indebtedness by the company to Salomon, secured on the property and effects of the company. Salomon received about £1,000 in cash, £10,000 in debentures and half the nominal capital of the company in issued shares.

The company fell upon hard times brought about by a depression and strikes. Contracts with public bodies were farmed out amongst different firms. Salomon attempted various strategies to get the company back on its feet. He and his wife lent the company money, and he mortgaged his debentures to obtain funds, which he then loaned to the company. The mortgagee was registered as the holder of the debentures. Still the company did not prosper; it was placed into receivership and then liquidation, resulting in a forced sale of its assets. The sale was enough to enable the liquidator, if he wished, to pay the mortgagee of the

[52] ibid.

[53] See P Ireland, 'Limited Liability, Shareholders Rights and the Problem of Corporate Irresponsibility' (2010) 34 *Cambridge Journal of Economics* 837.

[54] *Salomon v Salomon & Co Ltd* (n 44) 49.

[55] Lord Macnaghten's speech in *Salomon v Salomon & Co Ltd* (n 44) seems wrong on this point.

debentures, but not enough to repay the debentures in full or the unsecured creditors. In the course of the liquidation, the mortgagee of the debentures brought a claim against the company. The liquidator attempted to resist the claim by arguing that the debentures were invalid on the ground of fraud.

Vaughan Williams J in the lower court had held that the company was an agent for Salomon.[56] If in fact the liquidator had been a trustee for the bankruptcy of Salomon, the Statute of Elizabeth would have applied as the sale would have been by Salomon to himself.[57] Vaughan Williams J clearly considered a company and its shareholders were one and the same, saying at one point that 'a man may become … a private company'.[58]

Vaughan Williams J, a bankruptcy expert,[59] looked upon Salomon and his six sons with a jaundiced eye. He disapproved of the 'one-man' company, which was then a new practice,[60] and thought he detected fraud. He held that the company was merely acting as Salomon's nominee and agent, and therefore Salomon as principal had to indemnify the company's creditors himself. Salomon appealed to the Court of Appeal, which turned down his appeal, largely on the differing ground that the company was set up for an illegitimate purpose that the legislature had not intended.[61] Both Vaughan Williams J and the members of the Court of Appeal considered that a one-man company was an abuse of the Companies Act 1862.[62]

The case worked its way up through the English judicial system in the 1890s at *Jarndyce v Jarndyce* speed.[63] A different outcome was expected in the House of Lords than the one that ultimately transpired. The first major review of the Companies Act 1862 was underway at the same time. The Davey Report, which was written before *Salomon* reached the House of Lords but after the judgments of the Court of Appeal were delivered, was wide-ranging – perhaps the first work of comparative corporate governance contrasting English company law with corporate law in European jurisdictions and with the United States.[64] The Report dealt with issues that are still live today, such as when to impose civil or criminal liability on directors for wrongdoing, and the extent to which creditors might expect protection when dealing with companies.

[56] *Broderip v Salomon* (n 45) 330.
[57] ibid 330.
[58] ibid 331.
[59] Vaughan Williams J was author of Sir Ronald L Vaughan Williams et al, *The Law and Practice in Bankruptcy, comprising the Bankruptcy Acts, 1883 to 1890; the Bankruptcy Rules and Forms, 1886, 1890; the Debtors Acts, 1869, 1878, the Bankruptcy (Discharge and Closure) Act, 1887, the Deeds of Arrangement Act, 1887, and the rules and forms thereunder*, 8th edn (Sweet & Maxwell, 1904).
[60] *Broderip v Salomon* (n 45) 336 per Lindley LJ.
[61] ibid 337.
[62] ibid.
[63] Fictional long-running case in the Court of Chancery in C Dickens, *Bleak House* (Electric Book Co, 2001).
[64] Vaughan Williams J was a member of the Committee, as was the QC who acted for Salomon in the Court of Appeal.

The Davey Committee noted the high number of companies in the United Kingdom – 18,361 at the time of the Report[65] – and the ease of incorporation, which the Committee considered gave England a competitive advantage over Continental jurisdictions. The Committee commented on the trend to convert the businesses of individuals or firms into companies.[66] The rise of the small 'private' company, where incorporation was motivated by an existing business wishing to obtain the benefits of limited liability, rather than as an enterprise seeking to raise funds from the public, was discussed at length by the Davey Committee.[67] It was ultimately determined that no change to the law was necessary.[68] If the primary motivation of incorporation was to avoid liability to creditors, it was anticipated by the Committee that the corporate form would be set aside by the courts. Part of the sanguinity of the Davey Committee may have been brought about by a belief that the Court of Appeal judgments in *Salomon* would not be overturned by the House of Lords. Indeed, the Committee appended the judgments of the Court of Appeal to the Report.

The Davey Committee, therefore, clearly endorsed Lord Lindley's view in the Court of Appeal in *Broderip v Salomon* that incorporation would be upheld unless a company was established for an illegitimate purpose. Despite finding against Salomon (or, in reality, the mortgagee of the debenture), and consistent with the most recent edition of his treatise, Lindley LJ in his Court of Appeal judgment accepted that the incorporation of the company could not be disputed, citing section 18 of the Companies Act 1862.[69] However, Lindley LJ also concluded it was intended that the seven persons associate together carry on the business of the company. What was not intended was, as here, six people making it possible for the seventh person to operate the business:[70]

> There can be no doubt that in this case an attempt has been made to use the machinery of the Companies Act, 1862, for a purpose for which it never was intended. The legislature contemplated the encouragement of trade by enabling a comparatively small number of persons – namely, not less than seven – to carry on business with a limited joint stock or capital, and without the risk of liability beyond the loss of such joint stock or capital. But the legislature never contemplated an extension of limited liability to sole traders or to a fewer number than seven.[71]

[65] Board of Trade Company Law Amendment Committee, *Report of the Departmental Committee appointed by the Board of Trade, to inquire into what amendments are necessary in the Acts relating to Joint Stock Companies with limited liability under the Companies Acts, 1862 to 1890* (C 7779, 1895) (Davey Committee Report), cl 4.

[66] ibid cl 12.

[67] ibid cl 13.

[68] ibid cl 16. There was, however, a recommendation that grounds for winding up be extended to include, amongst other things, where a certificate of incorporation had been obtained to defraud, defeat or delay creditors.

[69] *Broderip v Salomon* (n 45) 337.

[70] ibid.

[71] ibid.

As we know from the debates in *Hansard*, the driving motivation behind the general incorporation statutes was not to enable small trading partnerships to become companies. It was in fact to facilitate incorporation and encourage investment by the middle classes. Whilst the first part of the Lindley LJ's statement may not therefore be correct, the second part is undoubtedly true, as seen in Lowe's statement excerpted in section V.

In the pleadings to the Court of Appeal, Buckley QC argued that the assets belonged to the corporation and the creditors needed to look to them for their security: 'The corporation has always a separate existence from the shareholders.'[72]

In the Court of Appeal Lindley LJ concluded that 'The company must, therefore, be regarded as a corporation, but as a corporation created for an illegitimate purpose.'[73] Lindley LJ had shifted to regarding a company incorporated pursuant to a general incorporation statute (Companies Act 1862) as a form of corporation. Like corporations through history, it had to be established for a purpose, with the purpose now found in the statute rather than a charter.

Lindley LJ's primary objection therefore is that the Companies Act 1862, which could be seen as akin to the charter of the company, was used to create a one-man corporation; a purpose for which it was never intended.

Lindley LJ's judgment is criticised by Lord Macnaghten in the House of Lords for describing the company as a trustee. But it was only because Lindley LJ had concluded that the company was established for an illegitimate purpose that he then regarded the company as a trustee.

> I should rather liken the company to a trustee for him – a trustee improperly brought into existence by him to enable him to do what the statute prohibits. It is manifest that the other members of the company have practically no interest in it, and their names have merely been used by Mr Aron Salomon to enable him to form a company, and to use its name in order to screen himself from liability. ... In a strict legal sense the business may have to be regarded as the business of the company; but if any jury were asked, Whose business was it? they would say Aron Salomon's, and they would be right, if they meant that the beneficial interest in the business was his.[74]

On appeal, the House of Lords rejected the previous rulings. The outcome and how the statute was now to be interpreted were clear from the first words in the speech of Lord Halsbury LC:

> My Lords, the important question in this case, I am not certain it is not the only question, is whether the respondent company was a company at all – whether in truth *that artificial creation of the Legislature* had been validly constituted in this instance; and in order to determine that question it is necessary to look at what the statute itself has determined in that respect. I have no right to add to the requirements of the

[72] ibid 333.
[73] ibid 337.
[74] ibid 338.

> statute, nor to take from the requirements thus enacted. The sole guide must be the statute itself.[75]

The company had seven shareholders as required by the Companies Act 1862, all the relevant formalities had been complied with, and the Act was silent on the question of beneficial interests and control. A Salomon and Co Ltd was different from Salomon as an individual: '[I]t seems to me impossible to dispute that once the company is legally incorporated it must be treated like any other independent person with its rights and liabilities appropriate to itself.'[76]

Lord Halsbury LC[77] saw the view of the Court of Appeal as involving a logical contradiction. Sometimes it regarded A Salomon and Co Ltd as a company and sometimes it did not, continuing:

> My Lords, the learned judges appear to me not to have been absolutely certain in their own minds whether to treat the company as a real thing or not. If it was a real thing; if it had a legal existence, and if consequently the law attributed to it certain rights and liabilities in its constitution as a company, it appears to me to follow as a consequence that it is impossible to deny the validity of the transactions into which it has entered.[78]

Lord Watson's view was that the creditors of the company could have searched the Companies Register to find out the name of the shareholders, and their failure to do so should not impute a charge of fraud against Salomon.[79] Lord Herschell largely based his speech on the intention of the statute to protect shareholders by limiting their liability,[80] observing 'both Courts treated the company as a legal entity distinct from Salomon'.[81]

Lord Macnaghten considered that the lower courts had dealt with Mr Salomon somewhat harshly, viewing his actions in a more favourable light.[82] The Act did not require the shareholders to be connected.[83] The company retains maturity at its birth.[84] Unlike the Court of Appeal, he could not see evidence of fraud:[85]

> The company is at law a different person altogether from the subscribers to the memorandum; and, though it may be that after incorporation the business is precisely the same as it was before, and the same persons are managers, and the same hands receive the profits, the company is not in law the agent of the subscribers or trustee for them. Nor are the subscribers as members liable, in any shape or form, except to the extent

[75] *Salomon v Salomon & Co Ltd* (n 44) 29 (emphasis added).
[76] ibid 30.
[77] ibid 29.
[78] ibid 33.
[79] ibid 40.
[80] ibid 45.
[81] ibid 42. Although that may not be true of Vaughan Williams J.
[82] ibid 47.
[83] ibid 50.
[84] ibid 51.
[85] ibid 52–53.

> and in the manner provided by the Act. That is, I think, the declared intention of the enactment.[86]

Lord Davey was more pragmatic.[87] His view was that the result may not have been contemplated by the legislature and that there might be a defect in the legislation. He also mentioned that it was not argued that there was no association. He was impressed with the absence of a trust and rejected the arguments based on fraud. Lord Morris simply agreed with the other Law Lords.[88]

Lopes LJ in the Court of Appeal had said:

> It would be lamentable if a scheme like this could not be defeated. If we were to permit it to succeed, we should be authorizing a perversion of the Joint Stock Companies Acts. We should be giving vitality to that which is a myth and a fiction.[89]

In effect the House of Lords, by reversing the lower courts, did in fact give life to the fiction of the modern company. It is a fiction in the sense of its inception as a creation of the law rather than being based on its shareholders.

[86] ibid 51.
[87] ibid 54.
[88] ibid.
[89] *Broderip v Salomon* (n 45) 340–41.

10

Key Milestones in the Development of the Modern Company

I. INTRODUCTION

AT THE END of the nineteenth century, the modern company had again acquired the key features first combined in the English East India Company when it acquired permanent capital in 1657. As a consequence of limited liability, the Corporate Fund was separated from shareholders.

Double-entry bookkeeping was significant again.

Some innovations were novel. The floating charge provided security over the Corporate Fund. The development of company law through the second half of the nineteenth century vacillated between contractual principles drawn from partnership law, and principles drawn from corporation law. At times, company law rules were explained using both, with a tension between the two bodies of law continuing to the present. Most significantly, the House of Lords in *Salomon v Salomon* laid out the parameters of the modern company as a legal person that is a separate legal entity from its shareholders.[1]

II. DOUBLE-ENTRY BOOKKEEPING

Chapter 9 sets out how, from 1855, the liability of shareholders of incorporated companies could be limited,[2] and from 1856 limited liability was the default position.[3] Statutory limited liability meant shareholders and their successors were liable only to the amount of capital they initially agreed to contribute when subscribing for shares. Unlike shareholders in deed of settlement companies, shareholders of incorporated companies could not be compelled to contribute more capital by either the company or the creditors of the company.

Limited liability is significant in its effects on both shareholders and the company's capital. By separating the company's fortunes from the fortunes of

[1] *Salomon v Salomon & Co Ltd* [1897] AC 22 (HL).
[2] See Limited Liability Act 1855 (18 & 19 Vict c 133).
[3] See Joint Stock Companies Act 1856 (19 & 20 Vict c 47).

its shareholders, limited liability to the company bounded the financial risk for shareholders. Also, shares became easily transferable. Fully paid-up shares could be transferred free of the risk of future liability. If shares were partly paid up, transferees knew the extent of any future liability. The liability of a shareholder in a modern limited liability company was and is no greater or less than the amount of capital the shareholder promises to contribute. That amount of capital contribution required from shareholders is fixed. Once shares are fully paid up, the shareholder or any subsequent holder of the shares cannot be asked to contribute any more money to the company.[4]

Statutory limited liability meant that capital needed to be identified and separated from shareholders. The Companies Act 1862 was described as the accountants' friend because it required the keeping of accounts at every point of a public company's life,[5] echoing the requirements forced by the generality on the governing body of the English East India Company in the first part of the seventeenth century.

Indeed, the birth (or rebirth) of the modern company has been linked to the transformation of bookkeeping into modern accounting, and the emergence of the accounting profession.[6] Accounts distinguished capital from costs and income. The requirement to keep proper and publicly available accounts that identified capital potentially available to creditors was also driven by the actions of the Railway Kings like George Hudson, who 'fiddled the books', showing costs as capital investments rather than expenses.[7] The requirement was to ensure that dividends were paid from profit and not capital – a rule set out judicially by Lord Jessel MR in *Flitcroft's case* in 1882.[8]

As Cooke, writing in 1951, pointed out:

> The importance of the double entry system of keeping books lies not in its arithmetic, but in its metaphysics. To create a capital fund which can be shown as in debit or in credit towards its owners was to do the same thing in terms of finance that the lawyers did in terms of law. The lawyers created, for essentially practical purposes, the legal entity of the corporation, a legal person separate and distinct from its members, linked with them by rights and duties. The business men created the financial entity of the business, a fund separate and distinct from its subscribers, linked with them

[4] As the 19th century progressed, the practice shifted from issuing shares with high par values that were not fully paid up to issuing shares for low par values (one pound) fully paid up. Speculatively, that may be one of the reasons why the business corporation form did not really flourish and grow until the 1880s. This point is explored in ch 12.

[5] J Gleeson-White, *Double Entry: How the merchants of Venice shaped the modern world – and how their invention could make or break the planet* (Allen & Unwin, 2011) 144. The 20th century's biggest accounting firms were established in London during this period – William Deloitte (1845), Samuel Price and Edwin Waterhouse (1849), and William Cooper (1854).

[6] BS Yamey, 'The historical significance of double-entry bookkeeping: Some non-Sombartian claims' (2005) 15 *Accounting, Business & Financial History* 77, 77–78.

[7] Gleeson-White (n 5) 143.

[8] *In re Exchange Banking Company* or *Flitcroft's case* (1882) LR 21 Ch D 519.

> by debits and credits. The most common corporate form of the twentieth century, the [modern] company, is descended from these two inventions.[9]

(Cooke does not recognise that the modern company form existed in the earlier business corporations like the English East India Company.)

III. THE FLOATING CHARGE

The floating charge emerged from a series of cases in the Chancery courts. *Re Panama, New Zealand, and Australian Royal Mail Co* is regarded as the key decision.[10] In each of these cases, debate revolved around the interpretation and legal effect of the words used in the debenture form, indicating that the drafters of these forms did not set out explicitly how the security was to operate.

Rather, as we shall see, the phrasing in the debentures was sufficiently nebulous for it to become the role of judges to give the words meaning that would allow for business efficacy. As Cairns LJ lamented in *Gardner v London, Chatham and Dover Railway (No 1)* in 1867:

> I cannot avoid feeling regret that securities such as railway debentures, upon which so many millions of money have been invested, should have been left at their creation in a state to admit of so much argument … and that their legal operation and extent should come to be defined, not at the time when they have been given as security, but [subsequently by the court].[11]

The cases tackling the problem of how debentures should be construed arise in the immediate aftermath of the Panic of 1866, suggesting the company collapses of that year first highlighted the problem. Perhaps debentures had been issued for years with boilerplate wording (such as that at issue in *Gardner*, decades-old and originally intended for mortgage deeds), without any dispute ever arising as to their effect. The seeming absence of prior case law would suggest as much.

Railway companies were issuing debenture stock to the public before the 1860s. By 1868, they had raised a total of £126 million in 'Debenture Stock and Bonds' as compared with £143 million in preference shares and £233 million in ordinary shares.[12] Up until 1867, it was assumed that such debentures gave

[9] CA Cooke, *Corporation, Trust and Company: An Essay in Legal History* (Harvard University Press, 1951) 185.

[10] *Re Panama, New Zealand, and Australian Royal Mail Co* (1870) 5 Ch App 318. AKM Masudul Haque, 'The Floating Charge as a Security Device' (2006) 10 *University of Western Sydney Law Review* 25.

[11] *Gardner v London, Chatham and Dover Railway (No 1)* (1867) LR 2 Ch App 201, 218.

[12] J Coles, 'Railway Debenture Stock considered as a Security for the Investment of the Funds of a Life Assurance Society' (1869) 15 *Journal of the Institute of Actuaries and Assurance Magazine* 1, 5–6.

the holder a legal right over the railroad's property upon any default. But in *Gardner*, it was held that unless a debenture specifically stated otherwise, it conferred only a claim to profits, not to the company's property as a whole.[13]

In *Gardner*, a railway company that was a statutory corporation had issued so-called 'mortgage debentures', using a template set out in the Companies Clauses Consolidation Act 1845,[14] whereby the company agreed to '*assign* unto [the mortgagee] the said *undertaking*, and all the tolls and sums of money arising … and all the estate, right, title, and interest of the company in the same'.[15]

Cairns LJ held that this formula did not assign the entirety of the company's property to the debenture holder, as contended by the plaintiffs. Had that been the case,

> they might, from the first, have asserted their rights as mortgagees by taking … the capital, the cash balances, the rolling stock, and even their own money advanced. … [T]he moment the company borrowed money on debentures it would depend on the will or caprice of the debenture holder whether the railway was made at all.[16]

Rather, the 'undertaking' referred to the operation of the railroad, while the 'sums of money' were the revenues arising from that operation.[17]

Behind this finding lay not just pragmatism, but also the notion that Parliament had conferred statutory powers and responsibilities on the railway company and no one else. To give debenture holders a proprietary claim over the company's assets would be potentially to hand over those powers and responsibilities to unauthorised parties.[18]

Turner LJ noted that it would not be impossible to draft a debenture that did carry the rights for which the plaintiffs contended:

> [T]he nature and extent of these rights must, of course, depend upon the construction and effect of their debentures … Had it been intended to go further, and to charge the capital of the railway-company, and the surplus lands, as it was contended

[13] JB Jefferys, *Business Organisation in Great Britain, 1856–1914* (Dissertations in European Economics History, Arno Press, 1977) 247; Coles, 'Railway Debenture Stock' 3.

[14] Companies Clauses Consolidation Act 1845 (8 & 9 Vict c 16), sch C.

[15] ibid (emphasis added). RC Nolan, 'Property in a Fund' (2004) 120 *Law Quarterly Review* 108, 118 (footnotes omitted). As Nolan describes the issue, 'Much litigation established precisely what was meant by a "mortgage of an undertaking". In particular, the courts had to resolve two issues: what assets constituted a statutory company's "undertaking" within the scope of such a mortgage; and what rights of security were conferred by the "mortgage". These questions were difficult to resolve, given that Parliament clearly did not intend a mortgage authorised by statute to paralyse an undertaking mandated by statute.'

[16] *Gardner* (n 11) 215.

[17] ibid 217: 'The tolls and sums of money ejusdem generis – that is to say, the earnings of the undertaking – must be made available to satisfy the mortgage; but, in my opinion, the mortgagees cannot [claim upon] the capital, or the lands, or the proceeds of sales of land, or the stock of the undertaking …'.

[18] ibid 212–13. See also RR Pennington, 'The Genesis of the Floating Charge' (1960) 23 *Modern Law Review* 630, 638.

> before us that it does, there can be no doubt that apt words could have been found for that purpose …[19]

Robert Pennington argues that the position of railway debenture holders was not as weak as the judgment in *Gardner* suggests. Citing other contemporaneous cases, he suggests the debenture holders did in fact possess a charge over, and a proprietary interest in, the company's assets, from which they were entitled to repayment if the company was wound up. Thus:

> The inability of the mortgagees to have the company's assets sold while it was a going concern was really only a restriction on their power to realise their security, and not a limitation on the extent of their security, despite the impression which the words of Cairns LJ … might create.[20]

The validity of this view can be seen by judgments contemporaneous with *Gardner* with alternative formulations. In *Re Marine Mansions Co*, reported in 1867, a company formed in 1865 had issued debentures in that year that stated 'we hereby *pledge the property belonging to us for the time being* during the subsistence of the said debenture'.[21]

Upon winding up, the company's liquidators argued that if the debentures truly constituted a charge on all the company's property, the company would be precluded from dealing with any of that property, thus paralysing the business. The only reasonable construction was that the debentures were nothing more than an expression of an ordinary debt, recoverable *in personam* from the company.[22]

Wood VC held that the words used indicated more than this; they demonstrated an intention to charge the real assets (land and buildings, though not the capital) of the company. He contended the directors would not be impeded in their running of the company. The company could spend and receive money freely, though it could only deal with real property with the consent of the debenture holders.[23]

To modern eyes this is an unsatisfactory result. Although total paralysis is avoided by the exclusion of capital from the charge, any dealing with land or buildings is reliant upon, in Cairns LJ's words, 'the will or caprice of the debenture holder'.[24]

Another unsatisfactory result is seen the following year. In *Re New Clydach Sheet and Bar Iron Company*, debentures that purported to assign 'the *undertaking*, and all the real and personal estate'[25] of the company were held to affect 'all personal property in existence at their respective dates'.[26]

[19] *Gardner* (n 11) 220–22.
[20] Pennington (n 18) 639.
[21] *Re Marine Mansions Co* (1867) LR 6 Eq 601, 604 (emphasis added).
[22] ibid 606–07.
[23] ibid 608–09.
[24] *Gardner* (n 11) 215.
[25] *Re New Clydach Sheet and Bar Iron Company* (1868) LR 6 Eq 514, 515 (emphasis added).
[26] ibid 516.

Lord Romilly MR noted that the wording of the debentures was not as strong as seen in *Marine Mansions*. There, debentures expressly extended to future property.[27] By contrast, these debentures affected only past and not future property:

> Assume that one set of debentures was issued in May, and a second set in August; … I think the debenture holders of May would be entitled to satisfy themselves out of all the property existing in May, so far as it will extend, but must give the debenture holders of August all that was acquired subsequently.[28]

As with *Marine Mansions*, in hindsight this seems wholly unworkable.

In the wake of these cases, with so much of the investing public's money tied up in railroad debentures, it was presumably recognised that a formula was needed that would give the debenture holder the desired security, whilst not impeding or jeopardising the operation of the company.

A key ingredient of the solution had in fact already been provided in a seemingly unrelated case. In *Holroyd v Marshall* in 1862,[29] a debtor assigned the equipment of his business to a trustee for his creditor. The deed of assignment stated that the trust created would include any further equipment acquired in future. The Court found that, though at common law property not yet existing could not be assigned in such a way, in equity it could.[30] As soon as the new property was acquired, the assignee would obtain an equitable interest in it.[31] Thus a charge could exist over the whole of an enterprise's property, and any newly acquired property would enter under the umbrella of that charge.

Pennington argues that in the wake of *Holroyd*:

> Business men and draftsmen must have apprehended the possibility promptly because mortgages and bonds began to appear during the 1860s which were secured by what we now recognise as floating charges.[32]

However, as we shall see, this argument rests on a rather flimsy foundation.

With *Re Panama, New Zealand, and Australia Royal Mail Co* the ingredients came together.[33] At issue in this case, as in *Gardner*, was the meaning of the word 'undertaking'. Yet now the Court came to a very different conclusion. The company had issued debentures in 1866 (in other words, before the decision in *Gardner* was handed down), which stated:

> By virtue of the powers contained in our articles of association we, … are held and firmly bound, and do hereby for ourselves, our successors and assigns, *charge the said*

[27] ibid 515.
[28] ibid 516.
[29] *Holroyd v Marshall* (1862) 10 HL Cas 191.
[30] ibid 219–20.
[31] Pennington (n 18), 635–36.
[32] ibid 642.
[33] *Re Panama, New Zealand, and Australia Royal Mail Co* (1870) 5 Ch App 318.

> *undertaking*, and all sums of money arising therefrom, and all the estate, right, title, and interest of the company ...[34]

The company, citing *Gardner*, argued that 'undertaking' referred to the enterprise of the company, and the only property charged would be the income from that enterprise.[35] Giffard LJ rejected this argument, distinguishing *Gardner* on the arguably specious grounds that

> in that case there was a peculiar subject matter on which the debentures operated – that is to say, a permanent railway, which it was well known to everybody was permanent, and could not be mortgaged, or sold, or dealt with in any way.[36]

Here, Giffard LJ found, 'undertaking' referred to the whole property of the company. Perhaps even more significantly, it referred to property 'not only which existed at the date of the debenture, but which might afterwards become the property of the company'.[37] This was despite a lack of express words stating that the charge would extend to future property, such as had been present in *Holroyd*. Finally, despite there being a charge over all this property, the company could continue to do business, and the debenture holder would have no right to interfere, until such time as the company defaulted or came to be wound up; '[at that] moment the rights of these parties, beyond all question, attach'.[38] These three elements, subsequently enumerated by Lord Romer in *Re Yorkshire Woolcombers Association Ltd*,[39] are the key ingredients of what we refer to today as a floating charge.

After *Panama Mail*, the courts became willing to infer an intention to create such a charge, even where the actual words used in the debenture document were 'less than wholly felicitous' to such an inference.[40] In *Re Florence Land and Public Works Co, ex parte Moor*, the company in question issued debentures in 1868 that purported to 'hereby, in pursuance and under the power of their articles of association, bind themselves, ... and all their estate, property, and effects, to pay [the debenture holder]'.[41]

On appeal from a decision that the debentures did not operate as a charge on the company's property, Jessel MR looked not only to the words of the debentures, but also to the articles of association under which they were issued:

> I think when you look at the nature of the company, the duties the directors had to perform, and the terms in which the articles of association are couched, you may arrive fairly at the conclusion ... that the bond or debenture shall be a security on

[34] ibid 318–19 (emphasis added).
[35] ibid 320.
[36] ibid 321.
[37] ibid 322.
[38] ibid 322–23.
[39] *Re Yorkshire Woolcombers Association Ltd* [1903] 2 Ch 284 (CA), 294–95.
[40] Nolan (n 15) 119.
[41] *Re Florence Land and Public Works Co, ex parte Moor* (1878) 10 Ch D 530, 532 cited in Pennington (n 18), 643–44.

> the property of the company as a going concern, subject to the powers of the directors to dispose of the property of the company while carrying on its business in the ordinary course.[42]

James LJ focused simply on the wording of the debentures themselves, finding that 'bind' had the same meaning as 'charge', and 'estate, property, and effects' the same meaning as 'undertaking' in *Panama Mail*, that is, the company's assets for the time being.[43] These words were thus intended to have the same effect as in *Panama Mail*, and as outlined above by Jessel MR.

By the late 1880s, both the concept and the language of a floating charge were firmly established. In *Government Stock and Other Securities Investment Co v Manila Railway Co*,[44] a company issued debentures in 1888 purporting to create a 'floating security [over] all its property whatsoever and wheresoever, both present and future'.[45] It was in this case that Lord Macnaghten, who was soon to determine the outcome of *Salomon v Salomon & Co Ltd*, gave the first of his famous explanations:

> A floating security is an equitable charge on the assets for the time being of a going concern. It attaches to the subject charged in the varying condition in which it happens to be from time to time. It is of the essence of such a charge that it remains dormant until the undertaking charged ceases to be a going concern, or until the person in whose favour the charge is created intervenes.[46]

This was followed in 1904 by the equally well-known and more poetic passage in *Illingworth v Houldsworth*, in which the floating charge is described as

> ambulatory and shifting in its nature, hovering over and so to speak floating with the property which it is intended to affect until some event occurs or some act is done which causes it to settle and fasten on the subject of the charge within its reach and grasp.[47]

Later, Buckley LJ said:

> A floating security is not a specific mortgage of the assets, plus a licence to the mortgagor to dispose of them in the course of his business, but is a floating mortgage applying to every item comprised in the security, but not specifically affecting any item until some event occurs or some act on the part of the mortgagee is done which causes it to crystallize into a fixed security.[48]

The floating charge has been credited with accelerating the rate of incorporations in the later part of the nineteenth century, as banks sought comprehensive

[42] ibid 540–41.
[43] ibid 545–47.
[44] *Government Stock and Other Securities Investment Co v Manila Railway Co* [1897] AC 81.
[45] ibid 81.
[46] ibid 86.
[47] *Illingworth v Houldsworth* [1904] AC 355, 358.
[48] *Evans v Rival Granite Quarries Ltd* [1910] 2 KB 979, 999.

security that the partnership form could not offer.[49] It may also have contributed to a conception of the value in a company as a going concern or dynamic entity, which is described in this book as a Corporate Fund.

The invention of the floating charge reflects the changing conception of the modern company. Viewed through the paradigm set out in this book, the Joint Stock or Corporate Fund was the security provided for a floating charge, which extended over the company as it operated in the world as an entity.

IV. COMPANY LAW

In 1999, in *O'Neill v Phillips*,[50] Lord Hoffmann said that company law developed seamlessly from partnership law. Partnership law was and is based on the idea of a firm as an association of individuals. Private law principles drawn from contract and agency law govern partnership law. Rather than seamlessly descending from partnership law, modern English company law has struggled to balance the two pre-existing bodies of law. One is derived from corporations' law, and the other from private law agency and partnership law principles as applied to deed of settlement companies.

Several fundamental principles of modern company law can be explained using a contractual basis for the company, drawing on its origins in the deed of settlement company, the partnership and the contractual Joint Stock Company. Several other fundamental principles can be explained, drawing on its roots in corporations' law and the law surrounding the business corporation and statutory corporation. The rule in *Foss v Harbottle*[51] is an example. As Wedderburn highlights, one part of the rule is that in the case of a wrong done to the company, the company, not shareholders, is the proper plaintiff. That part of the rule draws on corporations' law, where the company was treated as a separate legal entity from its shareholders. The second part of the rule, derived from *MacDougall v Gardiner*,[52] is that in the case of a wrong done to the company, there is no point having litigation about it if the shareholders could ratify the wrong. That rule is derived from the contractual and partnership origins of the company. The two rules are generally understood to say the same things in different ways, but the conceptual basis of each is entirely different.[53]

[49] A Televantos, *Capitalism Before Corporations: The morality of business associations and the roots of commercial equity and law* (Oxford University Press, 2021) 175, citing J Getzler, 'The Role of Security over Future and Circulating Capital: Evidence from the British Economy circa 1850–1920' in J Getzler and J Payne (eds), *Company Charges: Spectrum and Beyond* (Oxford University Press, 2006) 248–50; R Harris, 'The Private Origins of the Private Company: Britain 1862–1907' (2013) 33 *Oxford Journal of Legal Studies* 339.

[50] *O'Neill v Phillips* [1999] 1 WLR 1092, 1099A.

[51] *Foss v Harbottle* (1843) 67 ER 189.

[52] *MacDougall v Gardiner* (1875) 1 Ch D 13.

[53] For discussion of the rule in *Foss v Harbottle* (1843) 67 ER 189, see the discussion in KW Wedderburn 'Shareholders' Rights and the Rule in *Foss v Harbottle*' (1957) 15 *Cambridge Law Journal* 194.

The predominance of the deed of settlement company in the eighteenth-century courts means that many principles of company law are indeed based on private law. But that does not necessarily mean that the modern company is contractual. As the late nineteenth century progressed, courts increasingly drew on the body of law that applied to corporations. For example, limitations on the scope of activities in objects provisions in memoranda of association led to the adoption of the public law doctrine of ultra vires from the law governing statutory corporations.[54] Companies could not operate beyond their objects and powers set out in their memoranda of association on incorporation. It is a constitutional understanding of the powers of the company.

The effect of statutory limited liability was that the concept of a *persona ficta* or artificial legal person as a separate legal entity, derived from corporations' law, was applied to the modern company. The legal entity containing the Corporate Fund became the juridical person rather than the shareholders associated together. The shareholders then became members of the company, with constitutional rights in the company through the general meeting, explaining Lindley's statement in his treatise that shareholders were legally separate from the company of which they were part.

Echoing the approach seen in *The Charitable Corporation v Sutton*[55] discussed in chapter 6, directors were at times regarded as being akin to trustees for the company. In *Flitcroft's case*,[56] directors presented untrue accounts. The directors knew some items in the accounts were irrecoverable and that, therefore, there were no distributable profits. Based on the report, shareholders declared dividends. Lord Jessel MR considered the action by the liquidator against the directors:

> The creditor has no debtor but that impalpable thing the corporation, which has no property except the assets of the business. The creditor ... gives credit to the company on the faith of the representation that the capital shall be applied only for the purposes of the business, and he has therefore a right to say that the corporation shall keep its capital and not return it to the shareholders, though it may be a right which he cannot enforce otherwise than by a winding-up order. It follows then that if directors who are quasi trustees for the company improperly pay away the assets to the shareholders, they are liable to replace them. It is no answer to say that the shareholders could not compel them to do so. I am of opinion that the company could in its corporate capacity compel them to do so, even if there were no winding-up. ... [D]irectors in each case are to be declared jointly and severally liable and not only jointly liable.[57]

[54] *Ashbury Railway Company and Iron Co v Riche* (1875) LR 7 HL 653. For a discussion of the development of the doctrine of ultra vires in modern company law, see W Horrwitz, 'Company Law Reform and the Ultra Vires Doctrine' (1946) 62 *Law Quarterly Review* 66; H Rajak, 'Judicial Control: Corporations and the Decline of Ultra Vires' (1995) 26 *Cambrian Law Review* 9, 32.

[55] *The Charitable Corporation v Sutton* (1742) 26 ER 642.

[56] *In re Exchange Banking Company or Flitcroft's case* (n 8).

[57] ibid 533–34.

In *Broderip v Salomon* in the Court of Appeal, Lindley LJ, by describing the directors as trustees, was also echoing earlier discussion of directors as trustees of the funds of corporations.[58] Significantly, however, Lord Jessel MR in *Flitcroft's case* was somewhat more qualified, using the term 'quasi trustees' rather than trustees. Lord Jessel, perhaps, recognised that directors were trustees by analogy. Lord Jessel would not have considered the directors of a corporation to be the same as trustees for a trust established in a deed of settlement company. As discussed in earlier chapters, the concept of directors' being entrusted with the Corporate Fund pre-dated eighteenth-century developments in the law of trusts. It is clear from the discussion in *Flitcroft's case* that Lord Jessel MR considered the directors to be quasi trustees for the company and, therefore, its creditors, rather than trustees for the shareholders.

V. THE SIGNIFICANCE OF *SALOMON*

Foundational case *Salomon v Salomon & Co Ltd*[59] has its critics. The contemporaneous comment in the *Law Quarterly Review* said that the House of Lords had recognised that one trader and six dummies would suffice for a company, and that the statutory conditions were mere machinery: 'You touch the requisite button and the company starts into existence, a legal entity, an independent persona.'[60] In the twenty-first century, that statement would be seen as an uncontroversial statement about the incorporation process. The outcome of *Salomon* was a recognition that the 'one-man company' fell within the policy of the Act. Nothing startling in that. Limited liability meant the creditors must look to the company and not the shareholders for recompense.

A change took place in the understanding of the modern company form through the second half of the nineteenth century – it was no longer contractually based on the association of shareholders. Nevertheless, the outcome of *Salomon* would have been unlikely 20 or 30 years earlier. The reference in the Act to the persons' being 'associated' would then have predicated an association of shareholders with the company based on those shareholders, even though it would have been acknowledged that those shareholders might not actually know each other.

Lindley LJ, in the Court of Appeal in *Broderip v Salomon*, by questioning the purpose for which the company was established, may have drawn on principles of corporations' law where courts would look to the charter of a corporation to determine its purpose. The general incorporation statute could be viewed as equivalent to the charter. Lindley LJ accepted that Salomon & Co Ltd was

[58] *Broderip v Salomon* [1895] 2 Ch 323 (CA), 338.
[59] *Salomon v Salomon & Co Ltd* (n 1).
[60] (1897) 10 *The Law Quarterly Review* 6.

a corporation, 'but as a corporation created for an illegitimate purpose',[61] 'an instrument for cheating honest creditors'.[62]

Lindley LJ and the Court of Appeal were overturned by the House of Lords. *Salomon* determined that, as a matter of statutory interpretation, if all the requirements set out in the Companies Act 1862 were adhered to, a company would come into existence. Neither the motivation for incorporation nor an ongoing association of the shareholders mattered. Rather than expressly determining that the modern company was a form of corporation rather than a form of partnership, as the law had been tending towards through the latter part of the nineteenth century, the House of Lords determined that a company came into existence once the requirements set out in the statute were complied with. At that point, it was a separate legal person from its shareholders. Whether a company was legally a partnership or a corporation was not expressly addressed.

Holding that a company was a separate legal person from its shareholders, however, does indicate that the House of Lords considered the company to be at least akin to a corporation, in the same way Lord Jessel MR had analysed the requirements of the Companies Act 1862 by referencing corporations' law and municipal corporations in *Imperial Hydropathic Hotel Co, Blackpool v Hampson*.[63] The House of Lords did not expressly state that a modern company was a form of statutory corporation with all the incidences and characteristics of a corporation. Left open, therefore, was the possibility that the statutory rules governing a modern company could be amended in a way that would shift modern company law away from corporations' law. For example, section 168 of the Companies Act 2006 (UK) allows the removal of a director at any time through an ordinary resolution of the general meeting.

VI. CONCLUSION

Salomon v Salomon & Co Ltd is a watershed company law case in many common law jurisdictions, because it judicially established that the company is an entity that is legally separate from its shareholders.[64] Cooke says that '[i]f the application of incorporation to the joint stock fund be thought of for a moment as a chemical reaction, the decision of the House of Lords in *Salomon v Salomon* marks the end point of that reaction'.[65]

As we have seen, a form with the key features of the modern company had emerged at an earlier time. The business corporation after 1657, when the English East India Company acquired permanent capital, shared all the key features it

[61] *Broderip v Salomon* (n 58) 337.
[62] ibid 339.
[63] *Imperial Hydropathic Hotel Co, Blackpool v Hampson* (1882) 23 Ch D 1 (CA).
[64] *Salomon v Salomon & Co Ltd* (n 1) 22.
[65] Cooke (n 9) 178.

was recognised the modern company had acquired after *Salomon v Salomon & Co Ltd*. The English East India Company was a corporation and therefore a *persona ficta* or artificial legal person. As set out in chapter 2, the *persona ficta* concept entered the common law in 1612 in *The Case of Sutton's Hospital*.[66]

The *persona ficta* corporation existed in the abstract as a creation of the law. As will be discussed in chapter 13, however, the *persona ficta* corporation is not a legal fiction in the sense that it has no reality beyond the law. The *persona ficta* corporation is a legal fiction in the sense that it is a creation of the law and is artificial, not natural. Artificial creations can be real beyond the law. Money and nations still exist even though they are man-made. Like the *persona ficta* corporation, they are created in the abstract but are manifested by the impact they have on the world.

The modern company differs from other corporations. It is novel because it is a *persona ficta* corporation that has a Corporate Fund. The Corporate Fund is seeded by capital separated from shareholders both legally (because the company is a separate legal entity from its shareholders) and through the accounting mechanism of double-entry bookkeeping. The Corporate Fund fuels the company as it operates in the world. The modern company becomes an entity as it operates in the world and acquires value. These points and others are picked up in the next chapters.

[66] *The Case of Sutton's Hospital* (1612) 10 Co Rep 23a, 77 ER 960.

Part Two

Consequences of the Modern Company

11

England Compared with Other Jurisdictions

I. INTRODUCTION

THE MODERN COMPANY form first emerged in 1657, when capital became permanent in the English East India Company. The key features of the modern company re-emerged in the nineteenth century later in England than other jurisdictions. This chapter discusses the early US business corporation, and the emergence of the modern form in Germany. The form of personal capitalism practised in England is also discussed.

II. UNITED STATES AND GERMANY COMPARED WITH ENGLAND

In the late nineteenth century, the United States saw the rapid rise of the management corporation: large, multi-tiered entities that performed multiple tasks of production and marketing. Management corporations had hierarchies of salaried executives.[1] With a concentration of economic power came a subsequent dispersal of share ownership.[2] Investors no longer involved themselves in management,[3] meaning that decision-making authority over the management and direction of the company sat with boards of directors. In many ways, the key characteristics of these US management corporations resembled the English East India Company after 1657 – a point that will be developed in other chapters.

The management corporation displaced the market economy, causing power to move from individuals involved in bilateral contracting to groups such as investors, suppliers and consumers.[4] These management corporations were capable of monopolistic control of industries. Manufacturing processes benefitted from

[1] WW Bratton Jr, 'The New Economic Theory of the Firm: Critical Perspectives from History' (1989) 41 *Stanford Law Review* 1471, 1487.

[2] AA Berle and GC Means, *The Modern Corporation and Private Property*, rev edn (Harcourt, Brace & World, 1968) 11–12.

[3] ibid 11.

[4] Bratton (n 1) 1488.

economies of scale, with fixed costs reduced by maximising output.[5] Costs were reduced by bringing them within the firm, leading to 'merger mania', with the growth of corporations and aggregation of capital. By 1890, three-quarters of the wealth of the United States was controlled by corporations.

By 1900 the United States had become the world's largest economy. Why English companies were relatively less successful has been a subject of much conjecture.[6] Great Britain was fastest to urbanise, becoming the largest consumer society from as early as 1850.[7] Comparable population proportion for urban settlement did not occur until 1900 for Germany, and until after the Second World War for the United States.

England had some of the best-serviced railway systems in the world early in the nineteenth century, with railways becoming the largest business enterprise over the course of that century. English railway managers were not as challenged to innovate as their counterparts in the United States. In England, many railways could be funded through local capital. Extensive development within the financial services sector was not required.

These early advantages in England stifled rather than accelerated innovation. The English were not pioneers in modern management, finance or government regulation. Nor did they have the same impact on the organisation and process of production and distribution. Existing practices were cemented. British business did not innovate in the way it would have if there had been forced competition and a bigger domestic market.[8]

The development of railroads in the United States led to the demand for capital, fuelling the rise of many investment banks. The forced innovation and development that took place in the United States eventually advantaged US economic development.

The difference was relative: although the rate and extent of growth in England was not as great as in the United States, there was still enormous growth in England in a short period. Compared with the United States, amalgamations in the England were relatively rare until the end of the nineteenth century, when both vertical and, to a lesser extent, horizontal amalgamations became common, also leading to the rise of the management corporation.[9] Cheffins highlights the move of English companies to the stock market in the period between

[5] H Hovenkamp, *Enterprise and American Law, 1836–1937* (Harvard University Press, 1991) 241–42. (Advantages identified and exploited by Josiah Wedgwood 100 years earlier with the use of double-entry bookkeeping).

[6] An exception was the insurance industry, where over-enthusiatic amalgamations resulted in the enactment of the Life Assurance Companies Act 1870. That Act made court authorisation compulsory for transfers of life business: RM Merkin and R Colinvaux, *Colinvaux and Merkin's Insurance Contract Law*, 10th edn (Thomson Reuters, 2015) para 13-003.

[7] AD Chandler Jr, *Scale and Scope: The Dynamics of Industrial Capitalism* (The Belknap Press of Harvard University Press, 1994) 251.

[8] ibid 254.

[9] BR Cheffins, *Corporate Ownership and Control: British Business Transformed* (Oxford University Press, 2008) 188.

1880 and 1914, with the most rapid phase during the mid-1890s.[10] There were 70 companies listed on the London Stock Exchange in 1885 and 571 in 1907, with a similar exponential increase on the provincial exchanges.[11] Prior to that period, if businesses converted to companies, they remained closely held.[12]

It may or may not be coincidental that the acceleration in listings from the mid-1890s coincided with the validation of the company as a separate legal entity from its shareholders by the House of Lords in *Salomon v Salomon*,[13] and the increasing acceptance in the preceding decades that the modern company was a form of corporation. The legal separation of the entity from the direct control of current shareholders (characterised as separation of ownership from control by Berle and Means[14] and others) may have contributed to the efficacy of the modern company as a legal form for business. Chandler characterises nineteenth-century British business as being based on personal capitalism. Britain remained closely tied to a 'family-controlled enterprise', with selection to senior management positions depending as much on personal ties as it did on managerial enterprise.[15] In the same period, the United States and Germany developed 'Managerial Enterprises'.[16]

In *Scale and Scope: The Dynamics of Industrial Capitalism*, Chandler focuses on the key distinctions that led to the different economic performance and corporate development of entities respectively within Germany, Great Britain and the United States. Chandler argues that the failure to develop corporate structures beyond personal capitalism prevented British firms from accessing the three-pronged investment strategy utilised by both the United States and Germany toward the end of the nineteenth century: namely, manufacturing, marketing and management. These structures were administered by corporate boards that usually included the original founding members of the company, but which also included representatives of banks and members of any associated companies that had management powers because of past mergers or acquisitions.

Chandler terms the developments in the United States 'competitive managerial capitalism'. From the 1890s onwards, the United States was the world's leading industrial nation, and by 1913 it was producing 36 per cent of the world's industrial output, whilst Germany accounted for 16 per cent, and Britain 14 per cent.

Why did the modern, integrated, multi-unit enterprise appear in greater numbers and attain greater size in a shorter period of time in the United States than it did in England?[17] Two major factors underpinning rampant growth in

[10] ibid.
[11] ibid 176.
[12] See the discussion ibid 176–80.
[13] *Salomon v Salomon & Co Ltd* [1897] AC 22 (HL).
[14] Berle and Means (n 2).
[15] Chandler (n 7) 240.
[16] ibid 236, 242.
[17] ibid 51.

the United States up until 1930 (the Great Depression) were higher population growth and a higher per capita income growth rate. Combined, these are the necessary ingredients to fuel aggregate demand.[18] The United States was also less dependent on foreign trade, and had the advantage of a larger domestic market, meaning it was able to grow much faster than England.[19]

Another advantage suggested by Chandler is that the United States and Germany moved on from traditional family-owned or partnership business models into structures that increased opportunities for in-flows of external capital from private investors or financial institutions. Those structures, the modern corporate form, led to merger and acquisition activity – a catalyst for industry growth and international expansion.

What Chandler terms 'Managerial Enterprise' led to economies of both 'scale' and 'scope' for many corporations. British companies were unable to reap the rewards of economies of scale. Instead, management structures that benefitted controlling shareholders over the short term were maintained at the expense of sacrificing long-term gains.[20]

One of the key differentiating factors between Britain and the United States was, therefore, the enduring commitment to personal management and capitalism in Britain. This commitment can be contrasted with the evolution of the 'Managerial Enterprise' in the United States and Germany.[21] But not all controlling shareholders in England operated companies with a focus on the short term.

III. 'QUAKER' COMPANIES

Many of the founders of the nineteenth-century companies in which personal capitalism was practised were Quakers. Quakers and other Non-Conformists focused on practical means to enhance employee welfare. An example is the model villages. Thornton Hough and Port Sunlight were built by Lever Brothers in 1888 and personally supervised by William Lever, a Congregationalist. Lever's background was Liberal, non-conformist and teetotal. His abhorrence of industrial squalor prompted him to build social housing.[22] Lever may have been aware of Saltaire[23] and other predecessor towns. Certainly, he was a keen

[18] ibid 52.
[19] ibid 53.
[20] ibid 236–37.
[21] ibid 239.
[22] E Hubbard and M Shippobottom, *A Guide to Port Sunlight Village*, 2nd edn (Liverpool University Press, 2005) 1.
[23] Saltaire was built in 1850 by Sir Titus Salt, a Congregationalist and Yorkshire wool manufacturer. Saltaire was a giant Italianate mill outside Bradford, with 560 houses and public facilities. G Darley, *Villages of Vision: A Study of Strange Utopias*, 2nd rev edn (Five Leaves Publications, 2007) 131–33.

amateur student of architecture and town planning, as well as a believer in public welfare.[24]

Lever introduced shorter working hours and various benefit schemes, and as a Member of Parliament campaigned 'unceasingly' for old-age pensions and the right to strike.[25] He rejected direct profit-sharing with employees, preferring what he termed 'prosperity sharing' instead. The facilities provided at Port Sunlight were the 'prime instance' of this.[26] Port Sunlight was still reserved for employees of Unilever up until the 1980s when the first private sales occurred. Interestingly, former Unilever CEO Paul Polman has been a driver of corporate governance reform and sustainable business, both whilst in his CEO role and subsequently.

Quakers constructed many villages and used other means to enhance the lives of their workers.[27] Bourneville was built by Quaker George Cadbury, who inherited, along with his brother Richard, the chocolate business founded by their father. George conceived of the idea of building 'a factory in a garden', with pure air and healthy accommodation.[28] The new factory opened the following year, but included only a small amount of housing for key workers.[29] Unlike Port Sunlight, which Lever Brothers heavily subsidised as part of William Lever's 'prosperity sharing', Bourneville was intended to be a self-sustaining community. Bourneville thus represents a consciously less paternalistic model, with Cadbury family members stressing that village residents would not be recipients of the 'dole'.[30]

Joseph Rowntree followed Cadbury's example.[31] In 1900 Rowntree purchased the surrounding farmland and hired an architect to design a village using Bourneville as a model.[32] In 1904 he handed the land over to a Village Trust, committing half his wealth to this and two other charitable trusts.[33] Rowntree also instituted one of the first pension schemes, with £10,000 seed money coming from his own pocket.[34] Rowntree's employment policies were based on several principles, with workers' earnings, hours and working conditions reasonable,

[24] See Hubbard and Shippobottom (n 22) 5–7.

[25] Darley (n 23) 145.

[26] Hubbard and Shippobottom (n 22) 4.

[27] Trowse Newton, a pre-existing village outside Norwich built in 1805, was expanded upon by the Colman family (of mustard fame) in order to house factory workers. Much of the land is still held by the Colman family. Bourneville was built by George Cadbury in 1879, and New Earswick (1904) was built by Joseph Rowntree in 1904. After the 1919 merger between Fry's and Cadbury, the Fry arm gradually began to shift operations outside of Bristol to Somerdale, a 'factory in a village' on a similar model to Bourneville. PH Emden, *Quakers in Commerce: A Record of Business Achievement* (Sampson Low, Marston & Co, 1940) 197.

[28] D Cadbury, *Chocolate Wars: From Cadbury to Kraft: 200 Years of Sweet Success And Bitter Rivalry* (HarperPress, 2010) 103–04.

[29] M Harrison, *Bournville: Model Village to Garden Suburb* (Phillimore & Co, 1999) 34.

[30] ibid 80–83. The 'dole' was a benefit paid by the state to the unemployed.

[31] ibid 87–89.

[32] He began by building 30 houses in 1902–03. Darley (n 23) 188.

[33] Cadbury (n 28) 185–86.

[34] ibid 222.

and guaranteed economic security in old age. Workers should share in the firm's prosperity. Hence, schemes for pensions, widows' pensions, sickness and unemployment were introduced.[35]

Street, in Somerset, was home to a Quaker contingent from the seventeenth century, including the Clark family, who established Clarks Shoes in the town.[36] The firm funded social initiatives in Street, including a school, theatre, swimming pool, playing fields and low-cost housing.[37] Reckitt & Sons was incorporated as a private company in 1878 and went public in 1899. From the beginning, James Reckitt instituted a pension scheme and accident insurance.[38]

What was the impetus for model villages or other initiatives for workers? George Cadbury believed it was his duty to use his wealth to improve society. This idealism drove him to create ambitious schemes. However, he also possessed the practical skills to carry them out.[39]

Rowntree and Cadbury were examples of a new strain of thought in late-Victorian Quaker philanthropy: the idea that its first beneficiaries should be the very workers who helped created the wealth being distributed.[40] Fundamental Quaker beliefs were that no boundaries were drawn between religious and secular activities; hence trade must be conducted in consonance with their beliefs.[41] Concern for the less privileged (and thus industrial employees) was 'an absolutely normal Quaker duty'.[42]

Indeed Quakers appear to have thrived in industry from the start: they ran two-thirds of all British ironworks by the early eighteenth century. The first public railway, the Stockton and Darlington, was established by Quaker Edward Pease. Some of the most famous names in Victorian commerce belonged to Quaker companies. Quakers established 74 banks by the early nineteenth century, including Barclays and Lloyds.[43]

During the seventeenth century, the Quaker reputation for honesty and their practice, unusual during the period, of setting fixed prices, earned them public goodwill: 'to be a Friend was a kind of guarantee of business credit'.[44] Published guidelines advised Quakers on how to behave in all areas of life, including commerce. By 1861, these included advice on plain dealing, fair trading, debt, inappropriate speculation, etc.[45] Reckless debt was seen as 'shameful'.[46] This attitude may have contributed to success and longevity by deterring Quaker firms from over-leveraging in good times only to get into trouble in bad.

[35] Emden (n 27) 209.
[36] See at http://en.wikipedia.org/wiki/Street,_Somerset.
[37] Emden (n 27) 178–79. Clarks was not incorporated as a company until 1903.
[38] ibid 182–83.
[39] Harrison (n 29) 28–29.
[40] E Isichei, *Victorian Quakers* (Oxford University Press, 1970) 257.
[41] JS Rowntree, *The Society of Friends: Its Faith and Practice*, 2nd edn (Headley Brothers, 1901) 45.
[42] Cadbury (n 28) 51.
[43] ibid 43–44.
[44] Emden (n 27) 17.
[45] Cadbury (n 28) 47.
[46] ibid 3.

This would be an especial danger in the periods of frequent boom and bust that characterised the nineteenth century.

Furthermore, accumulating too much money for oneself was condemned.[47] Profit maximisation in the short term would therefore have been discouraged. In practice, the Quaker community rewarded wealth with social prestige. Wealthy Quakers dominated meetings, and bankrupts were expelled.[48]

There were few rags-to-riches tales in Quakerdom with, again, a focus on the long term. Most of the famous Quaker families in Victorian commerce built up their wealth over several generations.[49] Quakers had instinctive caution and a conviction that steady accumulation was the only way to achieve long-term success.[50] This attitude may have shielded them against disaster in an era of boom and bust.

Quakers could not hold public office.[51] One area of achievement not closed off to them was success in business.[52] The same is true of philanthropy – a wealthy Quaker could gain widespread recognition as a great benefactor.[53] Successful Quakers were also subject to pressure from within the community and their own families to be charitable. They could not ignore requests for aid if they wished to remain in good standing.[54]

Although George Cadbury gave much of his wealth away, his wife and children still inherited large sums. They became philanthropists in their own right.[55] Despite increasingly foreign competition (eg from Nestle) in the twentieth century, 'a Quakerly concern for the well-being of the workforce continued'.[56] However, the overt Quaker influence in the chocolate business had faded by the 1930s. A patent dispute between Cadbury and Rowntree, which previously might have been settled by a Quaker meeting, was instead negotiated by lawyers.[57] Nonetheless, the younger Cadbury generations continued to plough their returns into charitable trusts.[58] George's great-grandson Adrian Cadbury was the author of the Cadbury Report, the first Corporate Governance Code, which has since been adopted and replicated across the world.

IV. THE EARLY US CORPORATION

America developed comprehensive limited liability for shareholders before England did. In America, the private contractual form played a much less

[47] ibid 47.
[48] Isichei (n 40) 183–84.
[49] ibid 184–85.
[50] Emden (n 27) 18–21.
[51] Due to the Test Act 1673, until its replacement by the Sacramental Test Act 1828. See ibid 14–15.
[52] Isichei (n 40) 176.
[53] ibid 215–16.
[54] ibid 216.
[55] Harrison (n 29) 29.
[56] Cadbury (n 28) 257.
[57] ibid 257–58.
[58] ibid 258–59.

significant role than in England. Corporations were always creatures of the legislatures, meaning, significantly, the presumption that shareholders were not liable for the debts of the corporation as a separate legal entity remained in place. By the nineteenth century the United States had moved to two distinct business forms: partnerships on one hand; and corporations on the other. Ease of incorporation through a charter or general incorporation statute rendered the contractual form of company redundant.[59]

Corporations were not traditionally used for manufacturing purposes in the United States until the second half of the eighteenth century.[60] Kempin discusses the countervailing pulls on legislatures when entrepreneurs sought the corporate form. On one hand there was the desire to industrialise the new nation and free it from manufactured products from Europe and, in particular, Britain. The US system was based on equal treatment, meaning that the partiality of England when granting charters was rejected.[61] Compared with England, charters were relatively easy to obtain so long as there was a public purpose with the essentials of corporate form, such as name, place, seal, power to sue and be sued, in place.[62] On the other hand, legislatures sought to protect creditors in claims against these fictitious entities.[63]

In a similar way to the debate that took place in England several decades later, it was initially considered that the granting of corporate status with protection for shareholders from liability to third parties was a type of monopoly of legal privilege that was antidemocratic, and which would give some businessmen an unfair advantage over others.[64] Although sought after by the investing and entrepreneurial communities, for a period a limited partnership in the '*commandite*' form sufficed.[65] 'It was only when capital requirements became enormous that pressure for incorporation became overwhelming.'[66] Banks, insurance companies and infrastructure companies were the biggest corporations, with no record of losses to creditors through the effect of limited liability.[67] The opposition to limited liability was generally more muted than in England.[68]

[59] CA Cooke, *Corporation, Trust and Company: An Essay in Legal History* (Harvard University Press, 1951) 94.

[60] J Goebel Jr, *Cases and Materials on the Development of Legal Institutions* (The Vermont Printing Company, 1946) 418.

[61] Cooke (n 59) 93.

[62] ibid 93–94.

[63] FG Kempin Jr, 'Limited Liability in Historical Perspective' (1960) 4 *American Business Law Association Bulletin* 11, 15.

[64] ibid 15–16. See also Hovenkamp (n 5) 50.

[65] In the *partnership en commandite* or limited partnership, which originated in France, the general partners have joint and several liability, and the liability of the limited partners is limited to the amount, if any, unpaid on their contributions to the capital.

[66] Kempin (n 63) 16.

[67] JS Davis, *Essays in the Earlier History of American Corporations* (Harvard University Press, 1917) 297.

[68] See the discussion in Cooke (n 59) 92–93.

The reaction to the divergent pressures over granting corporate status with resulting protection from liability to third parties was legislatures' granting charters to manufacturing companies with a 'niggardly hand' in the States of New England and New York. Manufacturing was important in those States at an early stage, because the stony soils limited agricultural opportunities.[69] Davis notes that in 1789 the stockholders of the Baltimore Manufacturing Company were granted limited liability once subscriptions were fully paid.[70]

Initially limping charters, where corporate status was combined with the elimination or withholding of limited liability, were granted to 'those groups which appeared to be seeking license for operation in fields where private gains seemed to outweigh the potential public benefit'.[71] Despite the desire for equality of treatment, meaning general incorporation statutes rather than petitions for incorporation were favoured,[72] not all States permitted incorporation for purely private purposes.[73]

Interestingly and significantly, the presumption developed that unlimited liability had to be expressly provided by the legislature. This presumption supports arguments in this book that protection from liability for shareholders to third parties dealing with the corporation was the default position for shareholders of business corporations. Contemporary text writers Angell and Ames asserted in 1832:

> No rule of law we believe is better settled than that, in general, the individual members of a private corporate body are not liable for the debts, whether in their persons or in their property, beyond the amount of property which they have in the stock.[74]

The liability of shareholders to the corporation was less clear, as was the ongoing liability of transferors of shares to the corporation. Accounting practice was in a primitive state. Only banks and insurance companies had shares of fixed par value. Funds were collected by assessment against shareholders as need arose. 'A "share" signified a proportional participation in the enterprise and was, in the circumstances, highly contingent.'[75] To counter the problem, legislatures needed to spell out that assessments for shares could not exceed the amount at which each share was originally issued. Massachusetts did this in 1830.[76]

[69] Kempin (n 63) 16.
[70] Davis (n 67) 447.
[71] S Livermore, 'Unlimited Liability in Early American Corporations' (1935) 43 *Journal of Political Economy* 674, 686.
[72] Cooke (n 59) 94.
[73] Kempin (n 63) 18.
[74] JK Angell and S Ames, *A Treatise on the Law of Private Corporations Aggregate* (Hilliard, Gray, Little & Watkins, 1832) 349; cf MJ Horwitz, '*Santa Clara* Revisited: The Development of Corporate Theory' (1986) 88 *West Virginia Law Review* 174, 208–09. Horwitz did not consider that strict limited liability developed until the late 19th century.
[75] Goebel (n 60) 432; Kempin (n 63) 22.
[76] 1830 Massachusetts Corporations Act (amended in 1836). The Revised Statutes of the Commonwealth of Massachusetts (1836), ch 38, s 13, pp 327, 329–30 in Kempin (n 63) 22.

Statutory restrictions around comprehensive limited liability continued for a period. The 1828 New York statute and the 1830 Massachusetts statute provided for full limited liability once the whole amount of capital was paid up. The New York general incorporation statutes provided for limited liability for fully-paid shares, but double liability before shares were paid up.[77]

Blair highlights that it took some time for the benefits of limited liability to be realised in the United States:

> [E]ven if a business did incorporate and the terms of the charter limited the liability of the stockholders for business debts, creditors would commonly insist that the business organizers pledge their personal assets to back debt incurred by the corporations. Thus, in the early years at least, the benefits of limited liability may not have exceeded its costs.[78]

By 1840, limited liability was in place in Connecticut, New Hampshire, Maine, Vermont, Rhode Island, New Jersey and Pennsylvania.[79] Comprehensive limited liability was in place in America, therefore, some 15 years before it was in England. The benefits of the modern company were thus realised earlier in the United States than in England. Throughout, the consistent presumption was that, in the absence of a clause in the charter to the contrary, the liability of shareholders of corporations was separate from the liability of the corporation in which they held shares, because the corporation was a separate legal entity from its shareholders.

V. GERMANY

As a result of their organisational differences, Germany surpassed England's performance to become a leading industrial nation[80] by the early twentieth century. The birth of the modern industrial enterprise took place quickly, as it did in the United States, following the completion of transportation and communication networks that allowed companies to take advantage of the economies of scale and scope.[81]

A number of key factors differentiated German industrial enterprises from comparable enterprises in the United States and England. The economic differences were markets structures, sources of supply and methods of finance. By the twentieth century, education in Germany was considered among the best in the world, with many industrial enterprises having access to technical and scientific knowledge. Unlike in the United States, large multipurpose banks played a

[77] Hovenkamp (n 5) 51.

[78] MM Blair, 'Locking in Capital: What Corporate Law Achieved for Business Organizers in the Nineteenth Century' (2003) 51 *UCLA Law Review* 387, 440.

[79] Hovenkamp (n 5) 49.

[80] ibid 294.

[81] ibid 397.

major role in providing funds for initial investment in the new, capital-intensive industries – investment that was essential to achieve the economies of scale and scope.

The Stock Corporation (*Aktiengesellschaft* (AG)) structure in Germany highlghts the difference between the personal style of English management and the more impersonal, systemic and professional style of German management.[82] In 1884, a law was passed in Germany that required two supervisory boards, further reaffirming the legislative focus on ensuring that there were clearly defined management responsibilities and hierarchy. In the AG, the management board is appointed by the supervisory board, with the management board charged with 'the promotion of the interests of the company as a whole and thereby all stakeholders'.[83] Unlike in France and England, Germany has maintained adherence to the conception of the company as an artificial legal person.[84] In addition, prohibitions around monopoly did not emerge in Germany with the legalisation of cartelisation, leading to a much richer variety of inter-firm contractual relationships in Germany than in the United States or England.[85]

During the late nineteenth century, both German and US companies grew faster than English companies, primarily due to their more progressive approach to corporate management. Legal reforms that allowed large companies to leverage developing financial institutions for increased access to capital facilitated growth. Growth around the end of the nineteenth century was significant to both the United States and Germany because of their geographical size and more rugged terrain.[86] It also had a profound effect on the financial services sector in Germany, in a similar way as took place with Wall St in New York.[87]

VI. CONCLUSION

Berle and Means identify the separation of ownership (in shareholders) from control (in boards of directors) as a key characteristic of the modern

[82] ibid 399.

[83] T Baums, 'The Organ Doctrine: Origins, Developments and Actual Meaning in German Company Law' (2016) *Institute for Law and Finance Working Paper* 148/2016, 7 at www.ilf-frankfurt.de/fileadmin/user_upload/ILF_WP_148.pdf.

[84] See discussion ibid 7.

[85] Chandler (n 7) 423–24. In contrast to the United States, because cooperation was legal in Germany, there was less merger and acquisition activity early on. Therefore, there were much more complex formal ties and direct investment.

[86] ibid 411. When comparing Great Britain and Germany, it should be noted that in 1871 Germany had a population of 41.06 million whilst Britain (including Ireland) had a population of 31.5 million. It was much more easily compared to the United States, with a population of 40.9 million. However, as previously discussed, the urban population proportion in Germany was much lower during the late 19th century. Germany's largest city had 826,000 residents whilst London boasted 3,890,000: ibid 409.

[87] ibid 415.

corporation.[88] Stephen Bainbridge says 'Corporation statutes effectively separate ownership from control. Indeed this de jure separation of ownership and control is one of the chief features distinguishing the corporation from other forms of business organization.'[89]

The lack of legal and functional separation of the corporate entity from current shareholders, a key characteristic that needs to be realised for the modern company form to achieve its potential, is highlighted by the fact that in England, managerial decisions were made by large shareholders who had inherited their positions. In the United States, salaried managers with little or no equity in the enterprise, whom Marx would have termed functionaries, administered the enterprise through extensive managerial hierarchies. Those managers made critical coordinating and allocating decisions.

As the Davey Report discussed in the previous chapter shows, the English were aware of competition for capital investment from other jurisdictions by the end of the nineteenth century. They were also aware of the relative economic performance of various business forms in other jurisdictions. Although many factors contribute to the economic success of a jurisdiction, the availability and utilisation of all of the attributes the modern corporate form offers may matter for prosperity. In particular, the modern form may facilitate increases in the size and scale of enterprises. Certainly, by the end of the nineteenth century, the United States and Germany were outperforming England economically. At the beginning of the nineteenth century, England outstripped the world. The following chapter sets out possible reasons for the delay in transition to the modern form in England.

[88] Berle and Means (n 2).

[89] SM Bainbridge, *The New Corporate Governance in Theory and Practice* (Oxford University Press, 2008) 4.

12

The Transition to the Modern Company in England

I. INTRODUCTION

As SET OUT in chapter 11, Chandler highlighted that one of the key differentiating factors between Britain and the United States was the enduring commitment to personal management and capitalism in England.[1] Family-controlled companies dominated, with England slower than the United States and Germany to shift to the 'Managerial Enterprise' characterised by professional management and wide investment from the public. Managerial Enterprise unleashes the full economic potential of the modern company.

One major reason for the slower transition to managerial enterprise, discussed in chapters 9 and 10, was that it took until the second half of the nineteenth century for English companies incorporated pursuant to general incorporation statutes to acquire all the key legal features of the modern company. This chapter speculates on some of the reasons for the delay.

II. SLOW ADOPTION OF THE CORPORATE FORM

English enterprise was slower to adopt the corporate form in the second half of the nineteenth century. Free incorporation and limited liability, facilitated by the general incorporation statutes, were controversial. Even though enactment of the statutes was driven by what were perceived to be the interests of business, business was initially slow to incorporate. Apparently 'shrewd critics'[2] foresaw the outcome, that incorporation 'made no quick revolution'. It was initially limited to industries where incorporation was already the custom (eg railroads, ironworks, shipbuilding).[3]

Immediately after the enactment of the Companies Act 1862, there was a brief surge in company registrations: from 381 companies per year with total

[1] AD Chandler Jr, *Scale and Scope: The Dynamics of Industrial Capitalism* (The Belknap Press of Harvard University Press, 1994) 235–36.

[2] eg, *The Economist* (1 July 1854), as cited in JH Clapham, *An Economic History of Modern Britain*, vol 2 (Cambridge University Press, 1932) 137, fn 1.

[3] Clapham (n 2) 139.

nominal capital of £21 million (annual average between 1857 and 1861), to 975 companies with total nominal capital of £235 million in 1864. Registrations then fell back to pre-1863 levels, afterwards climbing steadily.[4]

With the passing of the 1862 Act, the stage was set for proprietors of existing businesses (rather than new ventures) to 'take them public'.[5] Owners could have used the investing public as a source of capital to fund expansion or acquisition, or to 'cash out', completely or partially, of successful enterprises, freeing up money for other purposes. But manufacturing companies did not follow the fundraising patterns that the infrastructure canal and railroad statutory corporations had followed in the period before general incorporation.

Why? Business could source loan capital from the well-developed banking sector with no need to appeal to the public for investment capital. There was, therefore, no need to offer limited liability to attract and protect shareholding investors.[6] *The Economist*, in an 1854 article, after rebutting several 'alarmist' objections to proposed limited liability reform, also poured cold water on the optimists:

> They think [limited liability] is to bring forth many hidden stores of capital, and give a great stimulus to industrious enterprise. For such expectations there is no ground. … The banking system [already] brings forth every particle of capital.[7]

There had been no groundswell of opinion amongst manufacturers in favour of limited liability. Prior to the passing of the general incorporation statutes, manufacturing firms made extensive use of bank loans as a source of capital. As a result, banks' fortunes were closely linked to industry, and there was a high rate of bank failures.[8] But manufacturers were generally satisfied with the availability of capital, and indeed tended to oppose the introduction of limited liability as they did not need it to access capital. And limited liability still bore some of the eighteenth-century stigma highlighted in earlier chapters. Instead, the drive for limited liability legislation had tended to come from the investor side.[9] Jefferys calls the legislation a 'victory of the investing classes over the industrialists'.[10]

Due to the lack of interest from industrialists, the companies that were formed during the early 1860s tended to be 'financial and speculative' rather than based on solid business foundations, leading to a bubble of investment

[4] ibid 357–58.

[5] See BC Hunt, *The Development of the Business Corporation in England 1800–1867* (Harvard University Press, 1936) 151–52.

[6] Clapham (n 2) 138.

[7] 'Limited or Unlimited Liability' *The Economist* (1 July 1854) 699 at https://go-gale-com.ezproxy.auckland.ac.nz/ps/dispBasicSearch.do?userGroupName=learn&prodId=ECON (Gale Cengage Economist Historical Archive).

[8] JB Jefferys, *Business Organisation in Great Britain, 1856–1914* (Dissertations in European Economic History, Arno Press, 1977) 15–17.

[9] ibid 48, 50, 52.

[10] ibid 53.

enthusiasm that burst in the Panic of 1866.[11] According to Clapham, 'the average sober manufacturer remained suspicious or indifferent [to incorporation] far into the "seventies and "eighties"'.[12]

In these circumstances, general incorporation 'made no quick revolution', initially being limited to infrastructure industries like railroads, ironworks and shipbuilding, where incorporation via Act of Parliament to create a statutory corporation was already the norm.[13] People who had capital to invest also acted as an initial constraint. Individual investors holding non-railway shares numbered around 50,000 in the early 1860s rising to as many as 500,000 by the 1900s.[14]

Until 1885, incorporation was driven primarily by an 'increase in the amount of fixed capital needed in … some industries and the inability of the private partnership system to supply this'.[15] It was only after that time that other factors, such as the desire of founders to cash out of their businesses, began to play an important role.[16] Existing firms were often hostile to companies intruding on their turf. Up until the 1880s, Adam Smith and William Gladstone's view[17] that companies should only be formed for enterprises to which the partnership form was unsuited (eg infrastructure projects) predominated.[18] This attitude may have dissuaded potential 'converters' from incorporating, as such hostility would have made it difficult to raise finance.

The slow emergence of the 'promotion professional' may also have contributed to the slow conversion to the modern corporate form in England. In the 1860s, companies tended to be formed without the assistance of specialised professionals other than solicitors. Outside investors, if any, were drawn from the contacts of the founders. The 'embryo promoter' first appeared in order to assist companies whose capital needs demanded a wider appeal for subscribers.[19]

Conversion of existing businesses to limited liability companies was handled by 'financial agents' or 'investing agents' drawn from the ranks of accountants. Investing agents would commission a valuation, draw up a prospectus and solicit investment from their own contacts, as well as those of the vendors. The vendors typically took 30 per cent of the shares; the agents' 'friends' the same.

[11] ibid 57.

[12] Clapham (n 2) 138.

[13] ibid 139.

[14] BR Cheffins, *Corporate Ownership and Control: British Business Transformed* (Oxford University Press, 2008) 191, citing Jefferys (n 8) 435 and RC Michie, *The London Stock Exchange: A History* (Oxford University Press, 1999) 72.

[15] Jefferys (n 8) 112.

[16] ibid 112–13.

[17] The Gladstone Committee, *First Report of the Select Committee on Joint Stock Companies; together with the Minutes of Evidence (taken in 1841 and 1843), Appendix, and Index* (HC 1844, 119-VII) and see the discussion in ch 9.

[18] Jefferys (n 8) 113–14.

[19] ibid 294–97.

This was a typical practice for companies that did not appeal to the wider public for funding and seek a Stock Exchange listing. Advertising was seldom required under this model.[20]

By the 1880s, the demand for capital necessitated wider appeals to the public. Simultaneously, a bigger class of investors was emerging. Professional intermediaries were clearly needed to match investors to opportunities. The financial agents now took a more active role, approaching firms with offers to incorporate.[21] Some evolved into professional 'promoters', who would identify and purchase businesses, arrange underwriting of the share issue, float the company, take a large commission, then exit.[22]

Marshall states:

> [The promoter] is seldom able to get a hold of those industries which are chiefly in the hands of small capitalists: they remain undeveloped largely because his help is not forthcoming, and they have not leaders of their own ready for the work. ... in relation to those industries ... in the hands of men accustomed to deal with large capitals ... the owners ... sometimes arrange a fusion without external aid. But often the initiative in starting a new company, or in fusing existing businesses to form a great concern, comes from a professional organiser.[23]

On this argument, the delay in incorporation could be down partly to underdevelopment of the promoters/agents industry, which acted as the intermediary connecting proprietors with investors, and as a facilitator of incorporation.[24]

III. FINANCING STRUCTURE

The financing structure of many companies incorporated under the general incorporation statutes in England may have contributed to the delay in the transition to the modern legal form, primarily because companies did not need

[20] Clapham (n 2) 360–61; JH Clapham, *An Economic History of Modern Britain*, vol 3 (Cambridge University Press, 1938) 206–07. Clapham's source is the evidence of a David Chadwick, a leading 'financial agent', given to a Select Committee in 1877. The most prominent of these firms was Chadwick, Adamson and Collier. Others included Richardson Chadbourn and Co, Alfred Whitworth, Clemesha and Co, and Joshua Hutchinson and Co; Jefferys (n 8) 298–99.

[21] Jefferys (n 8) 306–07.

[22] ibid 308–12; A Marshall, *Industry and Trade: a study of industrial technique and business organization: and their influences on the conditions of various classes and nations*, 2nd edn (Macmillan, 1919), as reprinted in RE Wright and R Sylla (eds), *The History of Corporate Finance: Development of Anglo-American Securities Markets, Financial Practices, Theories and Laws*, vol 6 (Pickering & Chatto, 2003) 362–63.

[23] Marshall (n 22) 361–62.

[24] Note that the role of the 'promoter' as described by Marshall, ibid 362–63, is more extensive than that of the 'agent' as described by Chadwick 40 years earlier. So we may have seen an evolution of the agent, who approaches (or is approached by) a proprietor, then sources investors and handles the formalities, perhaps investing some funds himself, into the promoter, who actually purchases (perhaps with outside finance), restructures and floats the business (with the vendor taking a large portion of the shares). With the growth of this class of businesspeople, firms ripe for incorporation would more quickly be identified; incorporation would not be dependent on the proprietor's own nous.

to appeal to the wider public for investment. This section discusses the financing infrastructure in place prior to the general incorporation statutes, with the following sections focusing on financing techniques adopted by business in the period after the general incorporation statutes were introduced.

By the beginning of the nineteenth century, England had developed an industrial urban economy.[25] In the early nineteenth century, most industry in England was on a modest scale, with correspondingly low capital requirements. Proprietors seeking extra capital could find it through local networks of wealthy individuals. Company formation was driven instead by the large infrastructure projects such as canals and railways, which were often set in motion by local industrialists seeking increased trade from improved transport links. However, the capital requirements were so large that they could not be financed by big local players alone. Promoters would petition to form statutory companies (via Acts of Parliament) and seek investment from the wider public. Canal and railway companies had heavy capital requirements, and often required ad hoc or emergency financing. As well as issuing additional equity (eg preference shares), these companies relied on debt financing, including mortgages,[26] annuities, promissory notes and, most commonly, bonds.[27]

Preference shares had originated in the period prior to the general incorporation statutes, as infrastructure companies, canal and railway companies almost invariably ran into cost overruns requiring further financing. After experimenting with various methods, such as selling shares at a discount,[28] from 1825 onwards infrastructure companies increasingly settled on the 'preference share'.[29]

Preference shares offer a guaranteed fixed dividend to shareholders. Since there was a long delay before these enterprises were profitable, shares that paid a fixed dividend out of capital acted as an inducement to further investment.[30] Preference shares were typically offered to existing shareholders pro rata; before 1850, companies rarely appealed to the wider public for extra capital.[31]

> Preference shares, thus, owe their existence partly to the specialized character of the canals and railways. Once started there was a tantalizing urge to complete them in an effort to obtain profits … The preferential features of shares were used as bait to procure the needed sums.[32]

In the early days, preference shares carried this 'bait' for a limited period, often only until the ordinary shares were capable of delivering the same return.

[25] Chandler (n 1) 252.

[26] See GH Evans Jr, *British Corporation Finance, 1775–1850: A Study of Preference Shares* (The Johns Hopkins Press, 1936) 45–50.

[27] See ibid 51–56; EV Morgan and WA Thomas, *The Stock Exchange: Its History and Functions* (Elek Books, 1962) 103–04.

[28] See Evans (n 26) 64–69.

[29] ibid 39–40.

[30] Morgan and Thomas (n 27) 103–04. Though note that in 1847, the payment of interest out of capital was prohibited: Evans (n 26) 101.

[31] Evans (n 26) 104–05.

[32] ibid 6.

After that point, the distinction between share classes would disappear.[33] That context explains why preference shares originally carried the right to vote and participate in profits.[34] However, from 1850 the fixed dividends were almost always permanent, and from 1847 they started to be issued without the aforementioned rights.[35] In America, non-voting preference shares had always been the norm,[36] perhaps influencing English practice.

Preference shares proved popular with the public. By 1848 they represented over half of new railway equity in Britain.[37] Except during periods of boom and speculation, preference shares tended to trade at a premium compared with ordinary shares.[38] Companies resorted to them particularly in bad years, such as the period following the Panics of 1837 and 1847.[39] Investors who preferred safe investments were drawn to preference shares and debentures by a 'predilection for marketability and security'.[40] Given that such investors' previous experience would have been with government bonds, it is no surprise that they would prefer apparently less speculative and risky fixed-interest shares.

Shares in canal and railway companies were at times widely held, even by modern standards.[41] Founders typically held only a small portion of the shares. Initially shareholders tended to be drawn from the local area of the undertaking. Later in the period, they came from further afield, particularly London and surrounds.[42] Shareholders in statutory corporations often had statutory limited liability, which facilitated transfer of shares. The shift in the nature of shareholders, from being akin to active partners in a partnership to passive or rentier investors, meant the statutory business corporations of the later period had the key features of modern companies.

IV. FINANCING AFTER THE GENERAL INCORPORATION STATUTES

Infrastructure companies continued borrowing practices from the period before the enactment of the general incorporation statutes, with a reliance on debt financing, and financing practices such as partly-paid shares with high par values, and non-voting preference shares.

[33] ibid 110–12.
[34] See ibid 126, 128.
[35] ibid 113, 128.
[36] RE Wright and R Sylla (eds), *The History of Corporate Finance: Development of Anglo-American Securities Markets, Financial Practices, Theories and Laws*, vol 1 (Pickering & Chatto, 2003) xl–xli.
[37] ibid xl–xli.
[38] Evans Jr (n 26) 143–48.
[39] see ibid 90–91.
[40] Cheffins (n 14) 192, citing Jefferys (n 8) 414, 209–10, 417–21.
[41] ibid 26–28.
[42] Cheffins (n 14) 192, citing Jefferys (n 8) 414, 209–10, 417–21.

The peculiar capital requirements of early canal and railway companies explain the early prevalence of the part-paid share. Since the lengthy preliminary work (surveying, land purchases) was relatively inexpensive compared to the actual construction, investors could be lured in with a small upfront payment, leaving the bulk of the capital to be called up when construction began.[43] The joint-stock banks of the late eighteenth and early nineteenth centuries also typically issued partly-paid shares,[44] perhaps due to the particular capital requirements of banks.

An 1836 House of Commons standing order had restricted railway companies to borrowing no more than one-third of their share capital. Railroads in need of emergency capital that had exhausted their allowable borrowing were forced to issue preference shares.[45] Heavy capital requirements of railways meant they tended to borrow the maximum possible. Loans became long-term affairs, renewed as soon as they fell due. Railways were vulnerable to shifts in interest rates, with rates from 2 per cent to 10 per cent above base rate between 1857 and 1867. Hence there was a strong impetus for a shift to fixed-rate debentures.[46]

Prior to general incorporation, manufacturing companies had tended to borrow from banks. In the early part of the general incorporation period, *The Economist* estimated that less than 10 per cent of the nominal capital was paid in advance,[47] suggesting that both partly-paid shares and shares held in reserve were the norm. Shares held in reserve are shares that are issued by the company but not offered to shareholders The use of debentures provided an attractive alternative to equity finance as the period progressed. Partly-paid shares and debentures are discussed in the following sections.

A. Partly-Paid Shares

Partly-paid shares are shares where only some of the actual or nominal capital subscribed for by shareholders is actually paid up. Shares were issued with nominal capital. All that nominal capital was not called up by the company on incorporation. Partly-paid shares reduced the benefits of limited liability for shareholders, as shareholders could be asked at any time by the company to contribute extra capital up to the amount of the nominal capital they subscribed for. They required shareholders to monitor the management of the company more closely and frequently rather than through the accountability mechanism of the general meeting. A separation of current shareholders from management control was delayed.

[43] Morgan and Thomas (n 27) 102, 106.

[44] See JH Clapham, *An Economic History of Modern Britain*, vol 1, 2nd edn (Cambridge University Press, 1930) 267.

[45] Jefferys (n 8) 242; Evans (n 26) 63, 150.

[46] Jefferys (n 8) 243–44.

[47] Clapham (n 2) 360.

There had been much debate in the 1840s and 1850s about the dangers of limited liability. It was widely argued that high nominal capital leaving large amounts of capital uncalled through partly-paid shares would enhance the security, and therefore the commercial standing, of the new companies.[48] That view was widely espoused by commentators in the 1860s.[49] The idea was that the uncalled capital acted as 'a continuous guarantee fund beyond the control of Directors and managers'.[50] After the 1862 Act, the practice issuing of partly-paid shares was taken in other industries. On average only around 10 per cent of the nominal capital subscribed for by shareholders was actually paid up.[51]

Creditors demanded that the companies they dealt with had a pool of uncalled capital for emergencies.[52] These demands gradually faded over the years, as the modern company form proved to be efficient and stable.[53] However, even as late as 1877, company promoter David Chadwick advocated uncalled capital of between 25 to 40 per cent; 'without that they cannot stand in the market with proper credit'.[54]

Shares were issued with high par (or pound) values, meaning high amounts of capital could be called on each share later (even though initially investors did not believe this would happen). Between the 1856 Act and the Panic of 1866, par values were high. Most companies formed had shares of between £10 and £100 of par value. Eighty-four per cent[55] of companies formed had shares of £5 or more (52 per cent between £10 and £100).[56]

Why? In the absence of any experience of general limited liability, patterns from the canal and railway companies exerted a powerful influence. Canal companies had typically had shares of £100.[57] Further, the Limited Liability Act of 1855 restricted companies to shares of £10 or higher in par value, though this was not repeated in the Joint Stock Companies Act 1856.[58] And contemporary attitudes about security had an effect. Lawyers advised that large shares ensured stability.[59] High share values and uncalled capital were also thought to

[48] JB Jefferys, 'The Denomination and Character of Shares, 1855–1885' (1946) 16 *The Economic History Review* 45, as reprinted in EM Carus-Wilson (ed), *Essays in Economic History* (Edward Arnold, 1954) 344, 347–48.

[49] ibid 347–48.

[50] *The Law of Limited Liability and its Application to Join Stock Banking Advocated* (1863) (as cited ibid 348).

[51] Hunt (n 5) 155, fn 49.

[52] Jefferys (n 48) 349–50.

[53] ibid 353.

[54] ibid 350.

[55] ibid 344.

[56] ibid 344.

[57] Morgan and Thomas (n 27) 101.

[58] Jefferys (n 48) 347; Limited Liability Act 1855 (18 & 19 Vict c 133), s 1. The rationale behind this provision is unclear, though it may be connected to contemporary attitudes about security.

[59] Jefferys (n 8) 174.

be a guard against speculation – an eternal bogeyman in the debate over limited liability.[60]

The early share model also matched the pockets of the typical early investors, who were wealthy persons known to either the founders or the financial agents incorporating the company. A small number of large shares 'placed in good hands' meant capital was easily raised.[61] Smaller investors did not yet have confidence in the new companies, 'and in any case the channels for bringing this class of investor into contact with the limited company were largely undeveloped'.[62] Thus, the expansion to a wide investing shareholder base was postponed.

The conventional wisdom was first shaken by the Panic of 1866. Company failures saw shareholders asked through calls to deliver multiples of capital in addition what they had originally paid on their shares. As a result, even shares where calls had not been made could not be sold, except at a huge discount.[63] As well as reigniting hostility towards limited liability,[64] the crisis created 'an abhorrence of large Shares' amongst the public.[65] It had become apparent that uncalled capital meant investors' liability was not so limited as they thought.[66]

In the aftermath, an 1867 Select Committee heard voices for the first time criticising high share par values and uncalled capital. It was now argued that company security came not from having a few, wealthy shareholders but from spreading shareholding as widely as possible.

However, 'the existing methods … still found defenders'.[67] No immediate revolution took place. A Select Committee 10 years later heard that wider shareholding, lower par values and less uncalled liability were becoming more common. An important factor in this trend was the entry of middle-class investors into the market, with their confidence buoyed by the stability of some of the companies. These investors wished to diversify their holdings rather than invest heavily in one company. The professional intermediaries that had arisen thus tailored shares to attract this class of investor by lowering par value and uncalled liability on partly-paid shares.[68]

Witnesses advocating lower share prices before the 1867 Select Committee still regarded £10 as the practical minimum par value.[69] Share par values trended

[60] ibid 171.

[61] L Fitz-Wygram, 'Limited Liability Made Practical. Reduction of Capital of Companies and the subdivision of Shares' (Effingham Wilson, 1867), as reprinted in RE Wright and R Sylla (eds), *The History of Corporate Finance: Development of Anglo-American Securities Markets, Financial Practices, Theories and Laws*, vol 3 (Pickering & Chatto, 2003) 213.

[62] Jefferys (n 48) 351.

[63] ibid 351.

[64] See Hunt (n 5) 154–55.

[65] Fitz-Wygram (n 61) 213–15.

[66] Hunt (n 5) 155.

[67] Jefferys (n 48) 351–52.

[68] ibid 352–53.

[69] Jefferys (n 8) 160.

downwards only gradually; it has been suggested that it took the City of Glasgow Bank crash of 1878 to 'drive the lesson home'.[70] However, after cotton and ship companies had success with £5 or £1 shares in the 1870s, the practice spread to other industries.[71] By 1890 'the triumph of the £1 share was complete'.[72]

Another delaying factor in realising the benefits of statutory liability by reducing the practice of partly-paid shares was the habit of using the uncalled capital as security for borrowing or the issuing of debentures. Only by using the company's fixed assets as security instead could the pool of uncalled capital be done away with.[73] The innovation of the 'floating charge', legitimised by the courts from 1870 onward, as discussed in chapter 10, made this practicable.[74]

By the 1880s, the trend was clear. 'A small share fully paid began to suit most companies and their investors.'[75] There were exceptions in some industries. Banking, finance and insurance companies, having little in the way of fixed assets, left large amounts of capital uncalled in order to inspire the confidence of creditors and the public.[76] Nonetheless,[77] from 1885 onwards there was increasing standardisation across industries.[78] By 1900, it was settled across all industries that the optimal share value was £1, fully paid-up, and the debate had moved on to the issue of classes of shares.[79]

Practice varied across industries according to the needs of companies and investors.[80] These variables, along with the practice of using uncalled capital as security for credit, may explain the slowness of the shift to the £1 share.[81] Nevertheless, after 1885 the trend became more uniform across industries, reflecting the increasing power of middle-class investors.[82] Private companies that were closely held bucked the trend.[83]

[70] HA Shannon, 'The Limited Companies of 1866–1883' (1933) 4 *The Economic History Review* 290, as reprinted in EM Carus-Wilson (ed), *Essays in Economic History* (Edward Arnold, 1954) 380, 389–90.

[71] Jefferys (n 48) 345–47. Practices varied across industries. In non-ferrous mining, the £1 fully-paid share was practically universal by the 1880s. In shipping, share values were higher for large shipping lines, whilst 'single ship' companies usually had low-value, fully-paid shares. Iron, steel, coal, engineering and shipbuilding, on the other hand, continued to issue £10 to £50 shares into the 1880s. Banking and insurance continued to leave large amounts of capital uncalled. These variations were influenced largely by the needs of companies in different industries, and the types of people investing. Mining investors were 'small local men', whilst iron, steel, etc investors were 'chiefly the original owners, local men of some standing and a few town investors'.

[72] Jefferys (n 8) 160–61.

[73] Jefferys (n 48) 353–54; Jefferys (n 8) 199.

[74] Jefferys (n 8) 273.

[75] Jefferys (n 48) 356.

[76] Jefferys (n 8) 194.

[77] See ibid 167–68, 205.

[78] ibid 157.

[79] Jefferys (n 48) 344.

[80] See ibid 346–47.

[81] Jefferys (n 8) 181.

[82] ibid 177–79.

[83] Private companies often continued to issue large shares, with the exception of 'one-man' companies, where the six dummy shareholders 'were rarely down on the share register for more than

B. The Shift to Debentures

Debentures provided an alternative to shares for investors. They therefore diverted investment from equity capital to debt capital, again contributing to the delay in a shift to a widely-held shareholder base that is a feature of a Managerial Enterprise. The shift to debentures largely took place between 1865 and 1880.[84] Railway companies had prepared the ground by familiarising the investing public with the debenture form. The practice of issuing debentures was then carried over to companies formed under the general incorporation statutes. They 'carried the idea ... to its logical conclusion of issuing them simultaneously with share capital at the formation of the company'.[85]

The divisibility of debentures (as opposed to standard loans) made them more marketable, and hence popular with investors. Railway debentures filled a niche one step up from government bonds (in both risk and reward), and thus attracted investors at the conservative end but not the extreme of it.[86] Their popularity was boosted by the downturn in the 1870s when ordinary shares were considered risky and speculative. 'This was the first depression period in which it had been possible for investors to switch over from the ordinary shares bought in prosperity to fixed interest bearing securities.'[87]

Like the railway companies, companies formed under the general incorporation statutes initially used debentures to raise supplementary capital. It was only later that debentures became a source of initial capital issued at the formation of the company. Some companies issued debentures as early as the 1860s, though this was a rarity.[88] The 1867 Select Committee heard from a barrister that the rationale behind issuing debentures was to avoid the need to make calls on shares.[89] The debentures were themselves often raised on the security of the uncalled share capital.[90]

In the 1870s debentures became a substitute for loans.[91] Companies requiring extra capital, could raise it through debentures more easily than through a bank loan, and (unlike shares) whether the company was prosperous or not. In addition, in a profitable company, debentures would have a beneficial effect on share dividends.[92] The 1870s also saw the novel practice of debentures' being

a £1 share each'. (Salomon & Co Ltd (n 162) is the most famous example). Another major exception was banking and finance companies. Shannon (n 70) 390.

[84] Jefferys (n 8) 245.

[85] ibid 246.

[86] ibid 248–49.

[87] ibid 264.

[88] ibid 251.

[89] Report of the Select Committee on Limited Liability Acts (28 May 1867), question 1235, David Salomons to George Lathom Browne, *Hansard* (HC 1867, 187) col 5.

[90] Jefferys (n 8) 184.

[91] ibid 255–56.

[92] ibid 119, 259.

issued as part payment to vendors of existing businesses being converted into companies.[93] Salomon & Co Ltd is a famous example.

By the 1880s, debentures were accepted as a common method of raising additional capital. From 1885, they started to be used to raise initial capital as well. By 1897 the latter practice was described as 'universal', with debentures typically supplying around one-third of a company's capital.[94] The extent of debenture issue varied from industry to industry, though.[95]

Debentures provided a source of debt finance for companies. Relying on debt finance meant English companies did not need to raise money from the wider public. The significance for our purposes in the context of the discussion in chapter 11 is that a wide shareholder base is one of the characteristics of US corporations in the period. A wide shareholder base facilitates a functional separation of shareholders from the company.

C. Preference Shares

At first, non-infrastructure companies rarely issued preference shares in the period after the enactment of the general incorporation statutes.[96] From 1885, they increasingly began to do so, and as a source of initial, rather than supplementary, capital.[97] By 1898, dividing capital into one-third ordinary shares, one-third preference shares and one-third debentures, in order to appeal to as wide a class of investors as possible, was 'almost universal' among public companies. Part of the impetus was the desire of vendors to maintain control of their companies. In small private companies, debentures were issued for this purpose, rather than preference shares.[98] Thus, the use of preference shares cemented control by founders in English companies, contributing to the delay in the transition to managerial enterprise.

V. CONTEMPORANEOUS COMMENTARY ON ENGLISH FINANCING OF COMPANIES

Commentators tended to respond to rather than drive innovation in financing techniques. In England, company law commentators, and it can be assumed some lawyers advising companies, were slow to critique current financing techniques. If shifts in practice were being spearheaded by lawyers, it is not apparent from the major company law treatises of the day. Most of the commentary,

[93] ibid 252.
[94] ibid 265–66, 269, 271.
[95] See ibid 268, 458–60.
[96] ibid 216–17.
[97] ibid 222.
[98] ibid 227–30.

from Lord Lindley, Baron Thring and Sir Francis Palmer, is descriptive, rather than offering practical advice. Further, what they have to say on these matters changes little, if at all, from edition to edition over the course of this period, despite the evolution in practice we have seen.

For example, on share values, Lindley merely states that small shares are 'more marketable'.[99] From 1898, Palmer's *Company Law* describes £1 shares as 'very common. So are £10 shares and £5 shares.'[100] These are usual values; sometimes, though rarely, shares are smaller.[101] Palmer gives no advice as to what value is appropriate in any particular circumstance. His *Company Precedents* is more helpful on this front. By at least 1881, Palmer advocates lower share values (£5 or £10, or even £1) for public companies, as there is a better demand for smaller shares.[102]

On uncalled capital, Thring suggests if the company's business will be heavily dependent on credit, a large uncalled capital should be left to stand as security.[103] Lindley simply states it is 'not usual' to issue paid-up shares.[104] Palmer's *Company Precedents* says it is 'generally expedient not to leave much, if any liability on the shares', in order not to impair their marketability. However, for specialised industries, such as banking or insurance, uncalled capital may be required in order to confer security.[105]

[99] N Lindley, *A Treatise on the Law of Partnership, including its application to Companies*, 2nd edn (William Maxwell & Son, 1867) 617; 3rd edn (William Maxwell & Son, 1873) 634; 4th edn (William Maxwell & Son, 1878) 613; N Lindley, *A Treatise on the Law of Companies, considered as a branch of the Law of Partnership*, 5th edn (Sweet & Maxwell, 1889) 393; 6th edn (Sweet & Maxwell, 1902) 546. H Thring, *The Law and Practice of Joint-Stock and Other Public Companies*, 2nd edn (Stevens & Sons, 1867–1868) 104; 3rd edn (Stevens & Sons, 1875) 133; 4th edn (Stevens & Sons, 1880) 108 states 'If the objects of the company be popular, it may be advisable to make the shares of small amount, with the view of attracting numerous applicants. Shares of large amount cannot so easily be got rid of, but, when in good hands, afford great facilities for raising money, and are much to be preferred in companies conducting a business of a private nature, and involving a large expenditure.'

[100] FB Palmer, *Company Law: A Practical Handbook for Lawyers & Business Men*, 2nd edn (Stevens & Sons, 1898) 17; 3rd edn (Stevens & Sons, 1901) 18; 5th edn (Stevens & Sons, 1905) 23.

[101] FB Palmer, *Company Law: A Practical Handbook for Lawyers & Business Men*, 2nd edn (Stevens & Sons, 1898) 53; 3rd edn (Stevens & Sons, 1901) 57; 5th edn (Stevens & Sons, 1905) 64.

[102] FB Palmer, *Company Precedents for use in relation to Companies subject to the Companies Acts 1862 to 1880*, 2nd edn (Stevens & Sons, 1881) 54; FB Palmer, *Company Precedents for use in relation to Companies subject to the Companies Acts 1862 to 1883*, 4th edn (Stevens & Sons, 1888) 139; FB Palmer, *Company Precedents for use in relation to Companies subject to the Companies Acts, 1862 to 1890*, vol 1, 6th edn (Stevens & Sons, 1895–96) 218.

[103] H Thring, *The Law and Practice of Joint-Stock and Other Public Companies*, 2nd edn (Stevens & Sons, 1867–68) 104; 3rd edn (Stevens & Sons, 1875) 132; 4th edn (Stevens & Sons, 1880) 108.

[104] N Lindley, *A Treatise on the Law of Partnership, including its application to Companies*, 2nd edn (William Maxwell & Son, 1867) 618; 3rd edn (William Maxwell & Son, 1873) 634; N Lindley, *A Treatise on the Law of Companies, considered as a branch of the Law of Partnership*, 6th edn (Sweet & Maxwell, 1902) 547.

[105] FB Palmer, *Company Precedents for use in relation to Companies subject to the Companies Acts 1862 to 1880*, 2nd edn (Stevens & Sons, 1881) 54; FB Palmer, *Company Precedents for use in relation to Companies subject to the Companies Acts 1862 to 1883*, 4th edn (Stevens & Sons, 1888) 139; FB Palmer, *Company Precedents for use in relation to Companies subject to the Companies Acts, 1862 to 1890*, vol 1, 6th edn (Stevens & Sons, 1895–96) 218; FB Palmer, *Company Precedents for use*

On voting rights, Thring suggests that, for founders to retain control, companies should either institute pro rata voting, or alternatively issue two classes of shares, 'for example, £1000 shares and £50 shares', giving voting rights only to the former.[106] Palmer says 'very commonly' voting will be one per share, but does not proffer any advice on the best arrangement.[107]

On classes of shares, Palmer simply says it is 'not unusual' to issue preference shares;[108] and 'not uncommon', though becoming more so, to issue founders shares, with the rights attaching thereto varying considerably.[109] Again, Palmer offers little concrete advice, simply saying the classes of shares that should be offered depend on 'the special needs and circumstances of the company and on the condition of the market'.[110] Lindley consistently describes preference shares as a source of supplementary capital,[111] the shift in their use seemingly having bypassed him.

Edward Cox was a lawyer who was apparently more prescient about the potential of the modern corporate form. Even before the Companies Act 1862 had come into effect, he was advocating the issue of small shares, fully paid-up, as best allowing the company to operate at no further risk to the shareholder.[112] For a private company, he suggested shares with a par value as low as five shillings, and for a Joint Stock Company on a large scale, £5.[113] The actual pattern was that private companies tended to retain higher share values for longer.

VI. THE PRIVATE COMPANY

The advent of Joint Stock did not diminish the importance of the simple mercantile partnership, which remained the preferred structure for small businesses

in relation to Companies subject to the Companies Acts, 1862 to 1900, vol 1, 8th edn (Stevens & Sons, 1902) 396.

[106] H Thring, *The Law and Practice of Joint-Stock and Other Public Companies*, 2nd edn (Stevens & Sons, 1867–68) 111; 3rd edn (Stevens & Sons, 1875) 140; 4th edn (Stevens & Sons, 1880) 115.

[107] FB Palmer, *Company Law: A Practical Handbook for Lawyers & Business Men*, 2nd edn (Stevens & Sons, 1898) 113; 5th edn (Stevens & Sons, 1905) 144.

[108] FB Palmer, *Company Law: A Practical Handbook for Lawyers & Business Men*, 2nd edn (Stevens & Sons, 1898) 17; 3rd edn (Stevens & Sons, 1901) 18; 5th edn (Stevens & Sons, 1905) 23.

[109] FB Palmer, *Company Law: A Practical Handbook for Lawyers & Business Men*, 2nd edn (Stevens & Sons, 1898) 57; 3rd edn (Stevens & Sons, 1901) 61; 5th edn (Stevens & Sons, 1905) 68.

[110] FB Palmer, *Company Law: A Practical Handbook for Lawyers & Business Men*, 2nd edn (Stevens & Sons, 1898) 58–59; 3rd edn (Stevens & Sons, 1901) 62–63; 5th edn (Stevens & Sons, 1905) 70.

[111] N Lindley, *A Treatise on the Law of Partnership, including its application to Companies*, 2nd edn (William Maxwell & Son, 1867) 780; 3rd edn (William Maxwell & Son, 1873) 817; 4th edn (William Maxwell & Son, 1878) 796; N Lindley, *A Treatise on the Law of Companies, considered as a branch of the Law of Partnership*, 5th edn (Sweet & Maxwell, 1889) 435; 6th edn (Sweet & Maxwell, 1902) 607.

[112] EW Cox, *The Law and Practice of Joint Stock Companies and Other Associations, as Regulated by the Companies Act, 1862*, 6th edn (John Crockford, 1862) 27–28.

[113] ibid 40.

until the late nineteenth century. The French *commandite* form of limited liability partnership, with inactive investing partners and active partners operating the business, was not made available as an option for small English businesses. The Limited Liability Act 1855 (UK) afforded limited liability only to companies with at least 25 shareholders,[114] although the Joint Stock Companies Act 1856 reduced this number to seven.[115]

The architects of the general incorporation legislation saw companies as providing an opportunity for investment by the rising middle class. The idea that simple partnerships, which were based on a legal relationship between the partners as owners, might be given corporate status was considered and rejected. But the very freedom around internal regulation and the ease of incorporation by registration meant that partnerships could incorporate if they wanted to. Popular books, such as *Private Companies and Syndicates: Their Formation and Advantages* by Francis Beaufort Palmer, not only provided reassurance to the owners of the trading partnerships that incorporation would not necessitate disclosure of sensitive business information, but also set out the process of incorporation.[116] Palmer's accompanying *Company Precedents for use in relation to Companies subject to the Companies Acts 1862 to 1880* was used to assist in the drafting of the internal rules, the articles of association, of numerous companies during the period.[117]

Some of Palmer's texts included sets of precedents that modified the opt out articles of association determining the internal constitutions of companies[118] so that they would work better for private companies. One was entitled *Private Companies, or How to Convert Your Business into a Private Company, and the Benefit of So Doing*. These texts by Palmer contributed to, or perhaps even caused, the adoption of the corporate form for small business. As Palmer himself pointed out, somewhat immodestly but probably accurately in his precedent text:

> During the last ten years the conversion, under the Companies Act, 1862, of business concerns into private companies, ie, companies started without any appeal to the public for capital, has made extensive progress and, as the writer has good reason to know, in a very large number of cases the conversion has resulted from a perusal of this little book.[119]

[114] Limited Liability Act 1855 (18 & 19 Vict c 133), s 1(4).

[115] Joint Stock Companies Act 1856 (19 & 20 Vict c 47).

[116] FB Palmer, *Private Companies and Syndicates, Their Formation and Advantages; being a Concise Popular Statement of the Mode of Converting a Business into a Private Company, and of Establishing and Working Private Companies and Syndicates for Miscellaneous Purposes*, 17th edn (Stevens & Sons, 1902) 33, 37–63.

[117] FB Palmer, *Company precedents for use in relation to companies subject to the Companies Acts 1862 to 1880*, 2nd edn (Stevens & Sons, 1881).

[118] ibid.

[119] FB Palmer, *Company precedents for use in relation to companies subject to the Companies Acts, 1862 to 1907*, 10th edn (Stevens & Sons, 1910) preface.

Palmer recognised that all companies registered under the Companies Act 1862 were, in contemplation of law, public companies, that is, companies intended to be carried on with capital obtained from the public.[120] The use of the private company was novel not just within England, but also internationally. It was not contemplated by the legislature in 1862. The 1862 legislature had intended companies to be investment vehicles incorporated to raise money from the public for big concerns. The fact that articles of association could be amended and thus permitted the creation of the private company was a happy (or some might say, not so happy,) chance.

A major difference between nineteenth-century English companies and nineteenth-century US corporations was the prevalence of private companies with founder control in England that would have been partnerships in the United States. 'One-man' companies like Salomon & Co Ltd, with one shareholder and 'six dummies', could be formed. Edward Cox foresaw 'the technique and the fraudulent possibilities' as early as 1856, but businessmen were not yet so canny. Shannon states a few private companies were formed in the 1860s, but only in the 1870s did they appear in large numbers.[121] During 1875–83,[122] private companies (those not offering shares to the general investing public) accounted for 20 per cent of companies 'actually formed' (as opposed to merely registered). In 1890, they numbered half the actual formations according to one estimate,[123] or one-third of registrations according to the registrar's estimate.[124] An analysis made in that year of 415 'private or family' company registrations revealed 82 per cent had fewer than 10 shareholders; the biggest had 20.[125] Shannon finds that 1,391 out of 6,240 'effective' (ie not 'abortive or small') formations between 1875 and 1883 were private companies.[126]

Private companies that were operated like partnerships came to be known later as quasi-partnerships (Maitland quipping that 'quasi' was one of the few Latin terms English lawyers were happy to adopt!). The conflation of the functional partnership with the corporate form may have contributed to the long after-life of partnership law principles in English law. Those principles were already in place, because the immediate antecedent of the modern English limited liability company was the contractual deed of settlement company

[120] ibid 1.

[121] Shannon (n 70) 380.

[122] FB Palmer, *Private Companies and Syndicates, Their Formation and Advantages; being a Concise Popular Statement of the Mode of Converting a Business into a Private Company, and of Establishing and Working Private Companies and Syndicates for Miscellaneous Purposes*, 10th edn (Stevens & Sons, 1892) 32.

[123] Clapham (n 2) 204–05.

[124] Shannon (n 70) 391.

[125] Board of Trade Company Law Amendment Committee, *Report of the Departmental Committee appointed by the Board of Trade, to inquire into what amendments are necessary in the Acts relating to Joint Stock Companies with limited liability under the Companies Acts, 1862 to 1890* (C 7779, 1895) (Davey Committee Report) 56 (as cited in Clapham (n 2) 205).

[126] Shannon (n 70) 398–99.

based at common law on a partnership. Using the same form may also have strengthened arguments that the modern company was associative and based on shareholders, rather than an artificial legal person separate from shareholders, because functionally the private company as a quasi partnership was based on its shareholders.

The widespread use of the private company for half a century before it was overtly recognised by the law in the 1907 Act shows 'how well adapted it was to British business habits and conditions'.[127] It essentially took over from the old private partnerships, where partners would source extra capital (if any) from friends and family. Reformers had long called for Britain to introduce the Continental *en commandite* partnership,[128] which had limited liability for sleeping partners but not for active ones. But the private company rendered this unnecessary. And in theory at least, a private company could easily transform into a public company where necessary.[129] Most significantly, the private company enshrined personal capitalism where founders retained control. Private companies reinforced the practice that had developed in British business not to draw on a wider network of investors. Unlike the United States, functional separation of ownership and control did not emerge as quickly, or to the same extent.

VII. FOUNDERS AND FAMILIES RETAINING CONTROL

The retaining of control by founders and families may have delayed the transition to the management corporation with widely dispersed shareholding and functional separation of ownership and control discussed in chapter 11. When the decision was made to go public, many proprietors wished to retain control of the businesses they had founded. The obvious way for founders to retain control would have been to relinquish only a minority stake in the company, but the Stock Exchange's 'two-thirds rule' prevented this. The rule was designed to improve liquidity in the market by requiring two-thirds of a listed security to be offered to the public.

One way for a proprietor to evade the two-thirds rule would have been to repurchase a controlling share on the open market subsequent to listing, which is what the proprietor of Guinness did. However, a rising market for shares would make this an unattractive proposition. A better way is simply to split the shares into two classes, and list only one. A founder could retain all shares in one class and one-third of shares in the other, leaving the founder with a controlling share. Splitting the shares into two classes became the pattern, with founders

[127] Clapham (n 2) 205.

[128] See Hunt (n 5) 79–82; 'Manufacturing Corporations' (1829) 2 *American Jurist and Law Magazine* 92, as reprinted in RE Wright and R Sylla (eds), *The History of Corporate Finance: Development of Anglo-American Securities Markets, Financial Practices, Theories and Laws*, vol 2 (Pickering & Chatto, 2003) 366.

[129] Clapham (n 2) 290.

keeping control by retaining all 'ordinary shares' and issuing two-thirds of the 'preference shares'.

The only problem with this model is that, in order to retain control, founders could relinquish no more than 50 per cent of the share capital. If founders wanted to bring in larger amounts of capital, or release more of their own capital, whilst still retaining control, they had to skew the relative voting power of the share classes. This could be done either by enhancing the power of 'insider' shares (eg by issuing 'founders' or 'management' shares, which carry extraordinary power) or by reducing the power of 'outsider' shares (eg by making preference shares non-voting). The consequence of these tactics was that in English companies, some founding shareholders retained control over management. The Managerial Enterprise could not emerge.

Founders retained control through voting rights. The default schema for voting rights with voting caps when a holding of a certain number of shares was reached was found in the opt-out rules for articles of association.[130] Thring, a commentator who was also involved in drafting the legislation, suggested retaining the schema for large companies with objects of a public nature.[131] Similarly Cox calls the voting schema in the opt-out provisions for articles of association in Table A 'a proportion which has been found to work well in practice … proposed in the former edition of this work, and has been adopted by the new statute'.[132] In the second edition of *Company Precedents*, Palmer also suggests a scale.[133]

VIII. DELAYS IN MANAGEMENT POWER SHIFTING FROM SHAREHOLDERS TO THE BOARD

One of the features of the Managerial Enterprise corporations described by Chandler is that decision making over the management of the company, broadly

[130] Table A, cl 44 of the Companies Act 1862 was also found in the previous Companies Act 1856, at cl 38 of Table B. H Thring, *The Law and Practice of Joint-Stock Companies* (Stevens & Sons, 1861) 90 says that this schema is 'arranged on the model of the Companies Clauses Act [1845]'.

[131] Thring (n 130) 92, 'if the company be large, and its objects of a public nature, the rule of table B is more likely to be acceptable and to conciliate shareholders'. Thring suggests modifying it to a one vote per share model, for 'a company … formed by a small number of capitalists for the purpose of carrying on a particular business' (ie a private company) 'thus making the holder of a great number of shares exercise a predominant influence over the company, or by creating two classes of shares, for example, £1000 shares and £50 shares, and giving the power of voting only to the £1000 shareholders'.

[132] Cox (n 112) 82.

[133] FB Palmer, *Company precedents for use in relation to companies subject to the Companies acts 1862 to 1880*, 2nd edn (Stevens & Sons, 1881) 117 sets out the following clause as an example: 'Every member shall have one vote for every share held by him [up to ten, and he shall have an additional vote for every … shares beyond the first ten shares, but no member shall more than … votes.]' He then states that 'Not uncommonly the words in brackets are omitted … Sometimes a class of members is given no voting power. And where a large proportion of the capital is to be issued to a vendor his rights of voting … are sometimes limited.'

defined, sits with the board. The long legacy of the eighteenth century, with the prominence in case law of the contractual deed of settlement company, led to uncertainty in the nineteenth century around the balance of decision-making powers between shareholders, acting either constitutionally through the general meeting or informally, on one hand, and directors, acting either individually or as the board, on the other.

Another form of corporation remained significant during the period. Statutory corporations, formed through a discrete statute, existed in parallel with companies incorporated pursuant to general incorporation statutes. The Companies Clauses Consolidation Act 1845 provided a set of standard sections for statutory corporations that differed in some significant ways from the Joint Stock Companies Act 1856 and the Companies Act 1862, which were general incorporation statutes. The Companies Clauses Consolidation Act 1845 for statutory corporations made directors subject to the control and regulation of the general meeting. In the general incorporation statutes, decisions around the allocation of powers between the general meeting and the board were made by shareholders through the articles of association.

For companies incorporated pursuant to the general incorporation statutes, the uncertainty around whether they were contractually based on an association of shareholders, in the same way as contractual deed of settlement companies, contributed to uncertainty around the nature of the legal relationship between shareholders collectively and directors as part of the board. Could shareholders override decisions made by directors either constitutionally through the general meeting, or because directors were considered to be the legal agents of the shareholders?

Agency-based conceptions of the relationship between directors and shareholders were derived in part from the private law principles governing the deed of settlement company. At common law, the shareholders in a deed of settlement company were partners and the directors were the legal agents of the shareholders. Directors were subject to the instructions of the shareholders as principal. As discussed in chapter 9, in an attempt to negate the legal position and to make these companies as much like corporations as possible, deeds of settlement consistently contractually allocated the management and superintendence of the affairs of the company to directors in the deed of settlement. In fact, as discussed in chapter 8, shareholders in both forms of companies were gradually disempowered by the approach first taken in the contractual form and then followed in the incorporated form.

As company law developed in the nineteenth century, it was not clear if management decisions of directors could be overridden by shareholders in the general meeting. The decision of the English Court of Appeal (Cotton, Lindley and Fry LLJ) in *Isle of Wight Railway Co v Tahourdin*[134] in 1883 is

[134] *Isle of Wight Railway Co v Tahourdin* (1883) 25 Ch D 320 (CA).

sometimes considered[135] to be authority for the assertion that nineteenth-century courts continued to view directors as agents of the shareholders in general meeting for companies incorporated pursuant to the general incorporation statutes. The Court did state that a meeting of the shareholders of the company had a power to direct and control the board in the management of the company.[136]

The courts of the period may not have held that view for companies incorporated pursuant to a general incorporation statute.[137] A year before *Tahourdin* was decided, in *Imperial Hydropathic Hotel Co Blackpool v Hampson*,[138] the Court of Appeal (which included Lord Jessel MR) had considered the nature of the board and the relationship of the board to the company. The Court of Appeal categorically stated that, for a company registered under the Companies Act 1862,[139] directors 'are not exactly agents nor exactly servants ... nor exactly trustees, nor exactly managing partners ... they are persons invested with strictly defined powers of management under the articles of association of a statutory corporation'.[140]

Interestingly, the Court described a company incorporated pursuant to a general incorporation statute as a statutory corporation. Also interesting is how the statement echoes Lord Hardwicke in *Charitable Corporation v Sutton*, where a director of a business corporation is said

> to be of a mixed nature. It partakes of the nature of a publick office, as it arises from the charter of the crown. ... committee-men are most properly agents to those who employ them in this trust, and who empower them to direct and superintend the affairs of the corporation.[141]

As discussed in chapter 6, read in the eighteenth-century context, Lord Hardwicke did not consider directors to be legal agents of shareholders. Modern agency principles had not emerged at that time.

And finally, the unresolved tension between whether companies incorporated through general incorporation statutes were contractual or were corporations is seen in the Court's terming directors as akin to agents, servants (employees), trustees, managing partners, before landing on a description of them as

[135] eg M Stokes, 'Company Law and Legal Theory' in W Twining (ed), *Legal Theory and Common Law* (Blackwell Publishing, 1986) 160; PL Davies, *Gower and Davies' Principles of Modern Company Law*, 7th edn (Sweet & Maxwell, 2003) 300; RP Austin and IM Ramsay, *Ford's Principles of Corporations Law*, 13th edn (LexisNexis Butterworths, 2007) ch 7.120. It is the prevailing view.

[136] *Isle of Wight Railway Co v Tahourdin* (n 134) 331.

[137] *Tahourdin* was followed in one case, *Barron v Potter* [1914] 1 Ch 895. The articles of association had given to the board of directors the power to appoint additional directors. When, due to differences between the directors, no directors' meeting could be held, the Court held that the company retained the power to appoint additional directors in general meeting. The notable fact in *Barron* is that the power allocated to the board was not a management power but a power to appoint directors, a power that ordinarily resides with the shareholders. The decision can be rationalised on that basis.

[138] *Imperial Hydropathic Hotel Co, Blackpool v Hampson* (1882) 23 Ch D 1 (CA).

[139] Companies Act 1862 (25 & 26 Vict c 89).

[140] *Imperial Hydropathic Hotel Co, Blackpool v Hampson* (n 138) 12–13.

[141] *The Charitable Corporation v Sutton* (1742) 2 Atk 400, 405; 26 ER 642, 644.

managers of a statutory corporation. It follows that the Court considered the allocation of powers to be constitutional.

How can the apparent inconsistency between *Tahourdin* and *Hampson* be explained? Rather than inconsistency, there may interpretation by the Court of Appeal of two different statutes governing two different legal forms. *Tahourdin* was a case about a statutory corporation.[142] Under the Companies Clauses Consolidation Act 1845, a standard set of rules for companies created by statute, such as railway and public utility companies, were set out. Section 90 of that Act stated that the powers of directors would be subject to the control and regulation of the general meeting.[143] *Wordsworth on Joint Stock Companies*, in the sixth edition of 1851, refers to the general rule that directors were subject to the general meeting. This continued to be the position for statutory corporations formed after 1845 using provisions drawn from the Companies Clauses Consolidation Act 1845.[144]

An equivalent of section 90 of the 1845 Act was not included in any of the general incorporation statutes.[145] The company that was the subject of the litigation in *Hampson* was incorporated under the Companies Act 1862, a general incorporation statute. The internal management rules were determined by the shareholders of the company and set out in the articles of association rather than in the statute itself. The allocation of the powers to the board shifted from being partners as the signatories of the deed (in a contractual deed of settlement company) to shareholders through the articles of association. This distinction was recognised by Cozens-Hardy LJ in *Automatic Self-Cleansing Filter Syndicate Co Ltd v Cuninghame*.[146] That case, discussed below, addressed the constitutional division of powers between the two organs of the company. The allocation of the board's powers also shifted from the statute itself, as seen in the

[142] Companies Clauses Consolidation Act 1845 (8 & 9 Vict c 16).

[143] The exact wording of s 90 was 'The directors shall have the management and superintendence of the affairs of the company and they may lawfully exercise all of the powers of the company, except to such matters as are directed by this or the Special Act to be transacted by a general meeting of the company; but … and subject to the provisions of this and the Special Act; and the exercise of all such powers shall be subject also to the control and regulation of any general meeting specially convened for the purpose, but not so as to render invalid any act done the directors prior to any resolution passed by such general meeting.'

[144] C Wordsworth, *The law of railway, canal, water, dock, gas, and other companies, requiring express authority of Parliament: together with the law of abandonment and winding-up, and that of parliamentary costs, with forms and all the statutes, including the Consolidation acts of 1845*. 7, 6th edn (William Benning & Co, 1851).

[145] Joint Stock Companies Act 1844 (7 & 8 Vict c 110); Joint Stock Companies Act 1856 (19 & 20 Vict c 47); Companies Act 1862 (25 & 26 Vict c 89). The long title to the Joint Stock Companies Act 1844, the first of the general incorporation statutes, included an intention to invest companies with the qualities and incidents of corporations. The long title said (in full, emphasis added) 'After reciting that it is expedient to make provision for the due registration of joint stock companies during the formation and subsistence thereof; and also, after such complete registration as is hereinafter mentioned, to invest such companies with *the qualities and incidents of corporations*, with some modifications, and subject to certain conditions and regulation.'

[146] *Automatic Self-Cleansing Filter Syndicate Co Ltd v Cuninghame* [1906] 2 Ch 34 (CA), 46.

1844 Act, and in the discrete Acts creating statutory corporations. What then was the significance of the new source of the board powers?

The wording of the opt-out articles of association in Table A in the appendix to the Companies Act 1862 was drawn from deeds of settlement.[147] As discussed in chapter 8, the tendency in deeds of settlement had been for founding shareholders who would become the directors of the company to allocate powers to the directors. Article 55 of the opt-out Table A of the Companies Act 1862[148] allocated management decision-making powers to the directors.[149] The article said in part that the management power of directors was 'subject to any regulations from time to time made by the company in general meeting', leading to a possible argument that the powers of the directors were subject to the direction of the general meeting.[150] However, that is to misunderstand the meaning of the word 'regulations' used in this context. The Articles themselves are regulations.[151] The power to prescribe regulations, which remains in modern companies with the power of shareholders to determine the constitution of the company, is 'the vestigial remains of the power to make by-laws'[152] that existed

[147] The default articles in Table B of the Joint Stock Companies Act 1856 (later Table A in the Companies Act 1862) were in content clearly direct descendants of the deeds of settlement drafted by lawyers in the 18th century: CA Cooke, *Corporation, Trust and Company: An Essay in Legal History* (Harvard University Press, 1951) 88. The form of words used to empower the board or equivalent was remarkably similar and consistent. Article 46 of Table B of the Joint Stock Companies Act 1856 read 'The Business of the Company shall be managed by the Directors, who may exercise all such Powers of the Company as are not by this Act, or by the Articles of Association, if any, declared to be exercisable by the Company in General Meeting'. Article 55 of Table A of the Companies Act 1862 was almost identical. A typical clause in a deed of settlement, the Deed of Settlement of the Nottingham and Nottinghamshire Banking Company (1834) read 'That the business, affairs, and concerns of the Company shall, from time to time, and at all times, be under the control of five Shareholders (as Directors), who shall have the entire ordering, managing and conducting of the Company, and of the capital, stock, estate, revenue, effects, affairs, and other concerns thereof …'. The clauses in deeds of settlement were drafted to be as similar as possible to the clause empowering boards in charters. In the Charter of the Company of Clothworkers of London (1648), the empowering clause stated that '[t]he Freemen … may chuse and make themselves three Wardens to support the business of the same Mistery or Art, and Comminalty and Fraternity or Gild aforesaid, to oversee, Rule and Governe the Mistery or Art and Comminality aforesaid'. The Charter of the Corporation of the Amicable Society for a Perpetual Assurance-Office (1710) stated 'And it shall and may be lawful to and for the Directors of the said Amicable Society, or the major Part of them, from time to time assembled in Court as aforesaid, to order, manage and direct the Affairs and Business of the said Corporation …'.

[148] Companies Act 1862 (5 & 26 Vict c 89).

[149] The Article provided 'The business of the company shall be managed by the directors who may pay all expenses incurred in getting up and registering the company, and may exercise all such powers of the company as are not by the foregoing Act or by these articles required to be exercised by the company in general meeting, subject nevertheless to any regulations of the Articles, to the provisions of the foregoing Act and such regulations being not inconsistent with the aforesaid regulations, or provisions as may be prescribed by the company in general meeting; but no regulation made by the company in general meeting shall invalidate any prior act of the directors which would have been valid if such regulation had not been made.'

[150] See *Dowse v Marks* (1913) 13 SR (NSW) 332 (NSWSC).

[151] KA Aickin, 'Division of Power Between Directors and General Meeting as a Matter of Law, and as a Matter of Fact and Policy' (1967) 5 *Melbourne University Law Review* 448, 459.

[152] RR Pennington, *Company Law*, 8th edn (Butterworths, 2001) 698.

for chartered business corporations. The general meeting could not therefore reallocate management powers to itself other than prospectively and constitutionally through the general meeting itself.

Where did the idea of empowering directors through the articles of association rather than the statute itself come from? The answer may lie across the Atlantic. For some US corporations of the period, the clause empowering directors was included in the by-laws rather than in the statutory instrument itself.[153] The fact that for a period boards obtained their powers from the by-laws rather than the statutory instrument was not ultimately significant, as in almost all US States statutes provide that a corporation shall be managed by or under the direction of its board of directors.[154] This model is the norm in most jurisdictions,[155] where decisions have made it clear that the power of management control of the board is original and undelegated and derived directly from the Act itself.[156]

Nevertheless, it must be acknowledged that the shift to leaving the allocation of management powers to shareholders in the 1856 and 1862 Acts, rather than the powers' being allocated to boards through the statute, may mark a significant and intentional point of departure in England. That departure can be seen as a legacy of the deed of settlement form. The most plausible explanation is that it was an adoption of the practice in contractual deed of settlement companies.

Is the departure more significant, showing a clear intention to make the governance of companies incorporated pursuant to the general incorporation statutes contractual, with directors the agents of shareholders?[157] Lowe, the chief architect of the 1856 Act, referred to modern incorporated companies as 'little republics' in the Parliamentary debates discussed in chapter 9.[158] Lowe may have been influenced by developments in France after the 1789 Revolution, where the

> deconstruction of the old legal persons and the reduction of the formerly chartered corporations to a partnership contract between the members [led to] the

[153] eg, Art 2 of the By-laws of the Maine Atlantic Granite Company states that 'The business of the Company shall be conducted by seven Directors who shall be annually elected by the Stockholders.' See Maine Atlantic Granite Company, *The charter and by-laws of the Maine Atlantic Granite Company* (GW & FW Nichols, 1836) 4.

[154] FA Gevurtz, 'The Historical and Political Origins of the Corporate Board of Directors' (2004) 33 *Hofstra Law Review* 89, 92. Missouri is, apparently, the exception; Model Business Corporation Act (US) § 8.11.

[155] Germany is an exception, with a dual board structure. A supervisory board appoints and oversees a managing board that operates the company.

[156] See *Peoples Department Store Inc (Trustee of) v Wise* [2004] 3 SCR 461, [34]: 'For the directors of CBCA corporations, this power originates in s 102 of the Act.'

[157] Section 14 of the Companies Act 1862 stated that all or any of the provisions included in Table A could be adopted, but that subscribers to the memorandum of association could prescribe such regulations for the company as deemed expedient. It was thus theoretically possible to incorporate a company without a board of directors, or without directors' being given the power to manage the company.

[158] *Hansard* (HC 1856, 139) col 134.

> empowerment of the members to appointing and dismissing the administrators at will, and the treatment of those as mere mandataries or agents of the members.[159]

The use of the word '*mandataire*' in the French Code de Commerce of 1808 implied that the administrators (directors) could be given instructions by the members.[160]

Companies incorporated pursuant to general incorporation statutes were intended to be a continuation of the deed of settlement form. The deed of settlement company was contractually based on its shareholders, with directors the agents of shareholders. However, part of the shift that took place in the second half of the nineteenth century, where the modern company shed some of the characteristics of the partnership and acquired some of the characteristics of a corporation, was the courts' upholding the constitutional allocation of management powers to the board in articles of association.

The issue of whether shareholders in general meeting could override management decisions made by boards, in situations where the power to make management decisions was allocated to boards in the articles of association, was not considered by the courts until the early part of the twentieth century. Cozens-Hardy LJ in 1906, in *Automatic Self-Cleansing Filter Syndicate Co Ltd v Cuninghame*,[161] apparently aware of the significance of the issue he was being asked to determine, described the late consideration of such an interesting and important question as remarkable but brought about simply because that issue had not come before the courts until that date. The delay is less remarkable once it is recognised that the precondition for the powers of boards' being derived constitutionally from the articles rather than contractually from the shareholders was judicial acceptance that a company incorporated pursuant to the general incorporation statutes was a separate legal entity from its shareholders, and not therefore contractually based on its shareholders. The separate legal entity concept had only gained definitive judicial acceptance in *Salomon v Salomon & Co Ltd*[162] some 10 years earlier.

In *Cuninghame*, the articles of association of the company stated that the general management of the company and the power to deal with the company's assets were vested in the directors. The shareholders instructed the directors to sell the business of the company to a particular buyer. The directors refused, in the belief that the proposed sale was not in the best interests of the company. The English Court of Appeal said that once the power had been allocated to the directors, the shareholders could not take it back again (other than presumably

[159] T Baums, 'The Organ Doctrine: Origins, Developments and Actual Meaning in German Company Law' (2016) *Institute for Law and Finance Working Paper* 148/2016, 4 at www.ilf-frankfurt.de/fileadmin/user_upload/ILF_WP_148.pdf.

[160] Art 31, as cited ibid.

[161] *Automatic Self-Cleansing Filter Syndicate Co Ltd v Cuninghame* (n 146).

[162] *Salomon v Salomon & Co Ltd* [1897] AC 22 (HL).

prospectively through changing the articles of association). It was, therefore, a question of construction of the articles in each case whether the directors have a particular power. In this case, the articles gave power to the directors to sell the company's assets. Therefore, the shareholders through the general meeting did not have the powers either to sell the business to the buyer, or to compel the directors to do so.

Cuninghame was distinguished in a later decision of a lower court, *Marshall's Valve Gear Co Ltd v Manning Wardle & Co Ltd*, as turning on the contents of the particular articles of association of the company.[163] However, the non-intervention principle set out in *Cuninghame* was interpreted as applying to the provision in the standard Articles of Association in Table A in a number of subsequent cases.

In *Gramophone and Typewriter Ltd v Stanley* (and consistent with his arguments as counsel for the appellant in the Court of Appeal), Lord Buckley followed *Cuninghame* and explained:

> The directors are not servants to obey directions given by the shareholders as individuals; they are not agents appointed by and bound to serve the shareholders as their principals. They are persons who may by the regulations be entrusted with the control of the business, and if so entrusted they can be dispossessed from that control only by the statutory majority which can alter the articles. Directors are not, I think, bound to comply with the directions even of all the corporators acting as individuals.[164]

The words of Lord Buckley echo the Court of Appeal in *Hampson* discussed above. Directors are not employees or agents of shareholders (with the term 'agent' given the narrow modern meaning.) Their powers are constitutional, being derived from the articles of association as the regulations of the company and the vestiges of the by-laws of chartered corporations.

The House of Lords in 1909, in *Quin & Axtens Ltd v Salmon*, stated that 'the directors should manage the business; and the company, therefore, are not to manage the business unless there is provision to that effect'.[165] The Privy Council in *Howard Smith Ltd v Ampol Petroleum Ltd* also adopted this approach, stating that

> directors, within their management powers, may take decisions against the wishes of the majority of shareholders, and indeed the majority of shareholders cannot control them in the exercise of these powers while they remain in office.[166]

Thus, the original incorporators in the articles of association constitutionally allocated the decision-making authority to the decision-making bodies – the

[163] *Marshall's Valve Gear Co Ltd v Manning, Wardle & Co Ltd* [1909] 1 Ch 267.
[164] *Gramophone and Typewriter Ltd v Stanley* [1908] 2 KB 89 (CA), 105–06. See also similar comments by Fletcher Moulton LJ at 98.
[165] *Quin & Axtens Ltd v Salmon* [1909] AC 442 (HL) 443.
[166] *Howard Smith Ltd v Ampol Petroleum Ltd* [1974] AC 821 (PC) 837 (citations omitted).

shareholders in general meeting and the board. As the board was the corporate organ responsible for the relationship between the operating company and the outside world, the practice was to allocate to the board decision-making authority over the management of the company. Once a power was allocated to the directors, a general meeting of shareholders could not revoke that allocation or purport to exercise that power.

The judgments are a consequence of the company's not being contractually based on its shareholders but a separate legal entity from its shareholders, with shareholders as members then having a constitutional role within the company in the general meeting. As the English Court of Appeal explained in *John Shaw and Sons (Salford) Ltd v Shaw*:

> A company is an entity distinct alike from its shareholders and its directors. Some of its powers may, according to its articles, be exercised by its directors, certain other powers may be reserved for the shareholders in general meeting. If powers of management are vested in the directors, they and they alone can exercise these powers. The only way in which the general body of shareholders can control the exercise of the powers vested by the articles, is by altering their articles, or, if opportunity arises under the articles, by refusing to re-elect the directors of whose actions they disapprove. They cannot themselves usurp the powers which by the articles are vested in the directors any more than the directors can usurp the powers vested by the articles in the general body of shareholders.[167]

The ultimate significance of the allocation of powers to directors through the articles of association rather than the statute itself, may have been the uncertainty around the managerial authority of directors, which may have contributed to delaying the shift to managerial control by boards in the modern company in England and therefore to Managerial Enterprise. The notion that in a conceptual sense the corporate structure allows current shareholders to exercise ultimate authority over management decisions of the board is seen as a constraint on the powers of boards of directors of UK companies. The statement in a 1909 text on investment cited by Brian Cheffins is typical: 'The shareholder, therefore, although he surrenders the control of his capital to his directors, is still in a position to exercise a very effective control over his directors …'.[168] As we have seen, the role of the regular general meeting in business corporations in the seventeenth and eighteenth centuries extended to approving broad policy and holding the board accountable for the performance of the company. It did not extend to the shareholders in general meeting's controlling the managerial decision making of directors. The relationship was constitutional, not contractual: between the general meeting on one hand, and the board of directors on the other.

[167] *John Shaw and Sons (Salford) Ltd v Shaw* [1935] 2 KB 113 (CA), 134.

[168] H Lowenfeld, *Investment Practically Considered* (The Financial Review of Reviews, 1908), 406 (as cited in Cheffins (n 14) 30).

IX. CONCLUSION

This chapter has set out possible reasons for the slower transition to the managerialist corporation in England. Reasons may have included slower adoption of the corporate form by business, widespread debt financing through debentures and the use of hybrid instruments like preference shares. In addition, the use of financing techniques like partly-paid shares with high par values meant that investors did not gain the full benefits of statutory limited liability. It took some time for the issue of fully paid-up small shares to be recognised as the best means to allow a company to operate at no further risk to the shareholder.[169] When future liability is not attached to shares, they become a more attractive investment for outside investors, facilitating the ready transfer of shares and a wide shareholder base.

A widely-held shareholder base is not essential for the board of a company to operate with a perpetual perspective. A smaller shareholder base with individual shareholders holding bigger blocks of shares does, however, increase the likelihood that those shareholders will intervene and be influential over, or even control, the management decisions of the board, especially if corporate participants believe shareholders are entitled to exercise that control.

One consequence of actual or possible current shareholder involvement in management decision making may be the board's adoption of an undue focus on current shareholders' short-term interests, rather than a long-term perspective focusing on the interests of the corporate entity as a whole. The initial uncertainty around the contractual rather than constitutional approach to governance in the mid-nineteenth century may have caused current shareholders to retain control over directors whom they regarded as their legal agents. Constitutional governance still allows shareholders, through the mechanism of the regular general meeting, to hold the board accountable, and may facilitate the adoption of a perpetual perspective by the board. Constitutional governance, and the consequences of current shareholders' driving managerial decision making, will be discussed in the last four chapters of this book.

***

Chapter 1 highlighted how Nicholas Murray Butler described the modern company as 'the greatest single discovery of modern times'.[170] When Butler continued to say that 'even steam and electricity would be reduced to comparative impotence without it',[171] he was highlighting the incredible efficacy of the features combined in the modern company as an organisational form. Put simply, the modern company has enabled value to be created from ideas.

[169] Cox (n 112) 27–28.
[170] WM Fletcher, *Cyclopedia of the Law of Corporations* (Callaghan 1917–20) vol 1, pt 21.
[171] ibid.

The first 12 chapters of this book have outlined the making of the modern company, in an attempt to discover the origins and significance of the key features that combine in the modern company. It has focused on developments in England in the period leading up to the end of the nineteenth century, and the recognition in *Salomon v Salomon* that the modern company as a legal person was a separate legal entity from its shareholders.[172] The concluding chapters of the book will focus on the consequences of these insights.

Chapter 13 considers the key features of the modern company through theoretical lenses. To reiterate, the key features identified in the preceding chapters are a Corporate Fund seeded by capital contributed by shareholders, but separated from those shareholders for accounting purposes through double-entry bookkeeping. The Corporate Fund is also separate for legal purposes, as it is held by a *persona ficta* or artificial legal person that is a separate legal entity from its shareholders. The modern company can exist in perpetuity, making size and scale possible over time.

Chapter 14 adopts an eversion in perspective, shifting from considering the company from the perspective of its shareholders or its stakeholders to considering the company itself as an entity. Although the entity is amorphous, it captures and creates value and has impact as it operates in the world.

The last two chapters consider the significance of the insights derived from the historical and conceptual analysis for corporate governance (in chapter 15) and for evolving debates around the role of the modern company in a society beset with grand challenges around climate change, pandemics and inequality (in chapter 16).

[172] *Salomon v Salomon & Co Ltd* (n 161).

13

Conceptions of the Components and Characteristics of the Company

SO FAR, THIS book has focused on developments in England in the period leading up to the end of the nineteenth century and the recognition in *Salomon v Salomon & Co Ltd* that the modern company was a corporation and a separate legal entity from its shareholders.[1] The concluding chapters of the book will focus on the consequences of these insights.

This chapter considers the key features of the modern company through theoretical lenses. To reiterate, the key features identified in the preceding chapters are a Corporate Fund seeded by capital contributed by shareholders, but separated from those shareholders for accounting purposes through double-entry bookkeeping. The Corporate Fund is also separate for legal purposes, as it is held by a *persona ficta* or artificial legal person that is a separate legal entity from its shareholders.

I. THE CORPORATE FUND AND ENTITY SHIELDING

The advantage of the corporate form in locking in and partitioning value has long been acknowledged. David Gindis highlights that Ernst Freund, in 1897 in *The Legal Nature of Corporations*,[2] was perhaps the first modern scholar to recognise that the corporate form secures property from outsiders, and from insider defection.[3] Margaret Blair argues that the critical advantage of the corporate form is 'the ability to *commit* capital, once amassed, for extended periods – for decades and even centuries'.[4]

Margaret Blair and Henry Hansmann and Reiner Kraakman[5] have set out compelling arguments for the essential role of organisational law. The first

[1] *Salomon v Salomon & Co Ltd* [1897] AC 22 (HL).

[2] E Freund, *The Legal Nature of Corporation* (University of Chicago Press, 1897).

[3] D Gindis, 'Ernst Freund as Precursor of the Rational Study of Corporate Law' (2020) 16 *Journal of Institutional Economics* 597, 615–16.

[4] MM Blair, 'Locking in Capital: What Corporate Law Achieved for Business Organizers in the Nineteenth Century' (2003) *UCLA Law Review* 387, 390.

[5] H Hansmann and R Kraakman, 'The Essential Role of Organizational Law' (2000) 110 *Yale Law Journal* 387.

essential aspect is that incorporation gives the enterprise 'entity' status under the law. The second is that incorporation requires governance rules that legally separate business decision making from contributions of financial capital.

Hansmann and Kraakman recognised that economic theory does not explain why productive activity is commonly organised in nexuses of contracts, 'in which a single central actor contracts simultaneously with employees, suppliers, and customers who may number in the thousands or even millions'.[6] That single organisational actor is the company. Why, they ask, are organisational employment relationships not constructed in the form of contractual cascades, in which each employee contracts not directly with the firm, but instead with their immediate superior, so that the pattern of contracts corresponds to the authority relationships we see in a standard pyramidal organisation chart?

Hansmann and Kraakmaan proceed by assuming such structures are essential for modern market economies. The focus of their discussion is on the separation between the firm's assets and the personal assets of the firm's owners and managers as the core defining characteristic of a legal entity, 'and establishing this separation is the principal role that organizational law plays in the organization of enterprise'.[7]

Hansmann and Kraakmaan have explored the issue of the single organizational actor in other work. *The Anatomy of Corporate Law*, which Hansmann and Kraakman co-author with others, describes the company as a nexus for contracts, rather than the typical law-and-economics depiction of a firm as a nexus of contracts. *Anatomy* draws on the civil law concept of patrimony (used in earlier work by Hansmann and Kraakmaan – see below) to define the demarcation of a pool of assets in the company. The company is owner in law of the assets. The company's assets are distinct from the shareholders' assets, with *Anatomy* terming shareholders the company's owners, but not directly at least the owners of the assets of the company.[8] 'What has been termed a separate patrimony drawing on the civil law means that the company is viewed in law as having property rights in a demarcated pool of assets.'[9] Entity shielding gives creditors of the company priority over creditors of the shareholders. Capital lock-in also protects the assets of the company from the creditors of the shareholders.[10]

[6] ibid 391.

[7] ibid 393.

[8] R Kraakman et al, *The Anatomy of Corporate Law: A Comparative and Functional Approach*, 3rd edn (Oxford University Press, 2017) 5, fn 12. The authors are careful to qualify their use of the term 'owner' when describing shareholders, stating 'We use the term "owners" simply to refer to the group who have the entitlement to control the firm's assets.'

[9] In explaining what is meant by property rights, Armour and Whincop highlight that participants' entitlements to control are protected not just against other participants but against third parties generally: J Armour and MJ Whincop, 'The Proprietary Foundations of Corporate Law' (2007) 27 *Oxford Journal of Legal Studies* 429, 448.

[10] Kraakman et al (n 8) 6.

In the earlier work, Hansmann and Kraakman recognised that the concept of a separate fund exists in civil law:

> While the Anglo-American legal literature has heretofore had no name for the concepts that we term entity shielding and asset partitioning and has – surprisingly – largely neglected these concepts in general, the civil law literature is more self-conscious about the issue. In particular, the civil law has long deployed the concept of a separate fund or separate patrimony. This concept comprises a broad and somewhat vague category of arrangement commonly described – in the most general terms – as involving a group of assets set apart for a particular purpose. Creditors' rights are an important consideration in determining the presence (or consequences) of a separate fund, and the presence of a separate fund is commonly considered an aspect of the much-disputed concept of a juridical person. However, the presence of a separate fund does not necessarily indicate a distinct juridical person.[11]

Whilst recognising the existence of a separate fund, Hansmann and Kraakman attach minimal significance to the concept of corporate legal personhood: the *persona ficta*. This means that they do not consider the implications of the insight of the separate patrimony as it relates to the modern company as an artificial legal person and contracting party in its own right. Hansmann and Kraakman question why the company is a single, organisational actor rather than there being contractual cascades. Could it be that the modern company is the single central actor because the modern company is an artificial legal person from the moment of incorporation? That artificial legal person can contract with employees and third parties dealing with the company. That artificial legal person is based on the Corporate Fund that is seeded by capital contributed by shareholders.

What Hansmann and Kraakman term the 'separation' of the firm's assets is initiated by the separation of the capital contributed by shareholders. That capital forms the seed of the Corporate Fund of the modern company.The modern company is a separate legal entity from its shareholders from the moment of incorporation. Organisational law endows the modern company with the status of an artificial legal person or *persona ficta*. Status as a juridical person gives the *persona ficta* based on the Corporate Fund the potential of perpetual life as the company operates in the world, becoming an entity as it acquires value.

The company can grow the value of the Corporate Fund by extracting, aggregating, generating and transacting for forms of value. The *persona ficta* based on the Corporate Fund is an active participant when it transacts for value. The *persona ficta* is not the passive nexus of contracts between participants that many contractual theorists classify it as. Financial value can be valorised from the entity through the Corporate Fund. That value is separated from the company using double-entry bookkeeping, and is distributed to shareholders.

[11] H Hansmann, R Kraakman and R Squire, 'Law and the Rise of the Firm' (2006) 119 *Harvard Law Review* 1135, fn 9.

The financial value of the Corporate Fund 'crystallises' and is realised by creditors and shareholders if the company is liquidated.

II. THE CORPORATE FUND IN HISTORY

The historical discussion in Part One of this book reveals that the Corporate Fund is a core component of the company, not some marginal characteristic.

This book outlines the development of shared funds for enterprise. As discussed in chapter 2, in the Middle Ages owners of excess funds contributed funds for short-term ventures because usury laws prevented them from lending those funds. The use of shared funds was driven by the need for longer-term investment of capital in ventures such as mines, privateering ventures or trading voyages. When Joint Stock Funds first appeared, investors were partners who could contribute stock in the form of assets or money. The Joint Stock Fund did not persist beyond the venture. Proceeds were divided up at the end of a venture based on the ex ante agreed value of the contribution made by each stockholder. In England by the late sixteenth century, the shared fund was separated from the partners using double-entry bookkeeping. This is the origin of the contractual Joint Stock Company, which legally was a partnership in which partners shared in a Joint Stock Fund.

Joint Stock Funds were also used in corporations. In the first half of the seventeenth century, developments in the English East India Company led to the abandonment of the idea that stockholders had a claim on specific assets, leading to capital contributions rather than asset contributions. The use of double-entry bookkeeping separated the capital account of the Company from shareholders. Shareholders were legally separate in their private capacities from the corporation.

By 1657, there was a shift in the English East India Company, away from a series of Joint Stock Funds that were terminated at the end of each voyage or series of voyages and to permanent capital. That permanent fund became the basis of the English East India Company as a corporation and, therefore, a *persona ficta*. At the same time, obligations of directors developed to act in the interests of shareholders. It has been argued in this book that those interests were held in the Corporate Fund. The governing body continued to have significant management powers over the Corporate Fund. However, through the first half of the seventeenth century, investing shareholders had won rights to monitor and hold management accountable by measuring a return on capital. A secondary market where shares were traded was another way in which the performance of management could be evaluated.

The Corporate Fund is a feature of the modern company that has been 'hiding in plain sight', obscured by contemporary theoretical conceptions that marginalise the significance of the Corporate Fund, the *persona ficta* and the entity that develops as the company operates in the world. Companies were called Joint

Stock Companies until the second half of the nineteenth century, highlighting the significance of the Joint Stock Fund. Amongst historical commentators, Karl Marx recognised a modern company was essentially a combination of capitals separated from shareholders, rather than a combination of shareholders. Marx also recognised that the formation of companies produces an enormous expansion of the scale of production and of businesses. That expansion was impossible for individual capitals.[12]

Recognition of the significance of the Corporate Fund is scattered historically, with examples set out in this book. Through an anonymous pamphlet, Josiah Child, the Governor of the English East India Company, recognised in 1701 that the East India trade could become an instrument of capital accumulation that was a 'Fund of Wealth'.[13]

III. THE CORPORATE FUND AND CREDITORS

The concept of an equitable fund for creditors developed as early as the seventeenth century, although it may have depended on the presence of particular facts. In 1673, in *Naylor v Brown*, the Court held that 'there was still an equitable fund appertaining to the company for the benefit of creditors'.[14]

Shareholders in modern companies have limited liability to the company. This means that the Corporate Fund of the company is liable for the debts of the company. Creditors of the company cannot recover debts owed to them by the company from its shareholders. This principle arose because the corporation was a separate person at law from the shareholders of the company. In 1784, Lloyd Kenyon (in a private opinion) said that 'the Corporate Stock alone would be answerable to the engagements, and the individuals who may compose the Corporation could not be liable in their private characters'.[15] Kenyon also adopts this view from the Bench in *Russell v The Men of Devon*.[16] The general incorporation statutes reinforce this principle with statutory limited liability for shareholders.

The modern company can also generally not be required to make extra calls of capital on shareholders to meet the obligations of the company to creditors

[12] K Marx, *Das Kapital*, vol III (Verlag von Otto Meisner, 1894) ch 27, 'The Role of Credit in Capitalist Production'.

[13] J Child, *The great honour and advantage of the East-India Trade to the Kingdom* (Thomas Speed, 1697) 4–5 at https://quod.lib.umich.edu/e/eebo/A32830.0001.001/1:3?rgn=div1;view=fulltext.

[14] CA Cooke, *Corporation Trust and Company: An Essay in Legal History* (Harvard University Press, 1951) 78, citing *Naylor v Brown* (1673) Rep Temp Finch 83, 23 ER 44.

[15] Lord Kenyon, Case of Opinion of 29 January 1784, Boulton & Watt Mss, Birmingham Collection, Assay Office, as cited in AB DuBois, *The English Business Company after the Bubble Act, 1720–1800* (The Commonwealth Fund, 1938) 95–96.

[16] *Russell v The Men of Devon* (1778) 2 TR 667, 672; 100 ER 359, 362.

of the company.[17] Lord Hardwicke LC, in *The Case of the York-Buildings Company* in 1740, laid down:

> Where the companies are obliged to make calls, this court will not decree them to make such a call, upon a bill brought by a creditor for that purpose, in favour of that particular creditor, unless under very extraordinary circumstances.[18]

The modern company's being conceived of as akin to a trust holding a fund for creditors emerged for a period early in the nineteenth century in the United States. In *Wood v Dummer* in 1824,[19] Justice Story stated:

> It appears to me very clear upon general principles, as well as the legislative intention, that the capital stock of banks is to be deemed a pledge or trust fund for the payment of the debts contracted by the bank. The public, as well as the legislature, have always supposed this to be a fund appropriated for such purpose. The individual stockholders are not liable for the debts of the bank in their private capacities. The charter relieves them from personal responsibility, and substitutes the capital stock in its stead.[20]

The trust fund doctrine was one of the legal developments that facilitated the legal separation of the Corporate Fund in the corporation from shareholders in the United States:

> Ironically the effect of the trust fund doctrine in effecting that separation led to its eventual effective demise by the early twentieth century with the separate identity of the corporation where the corporation held its property like any individual stressed by contemporary writers. The residual place of the doctrine was only in insolvency when the distinct corporate identity disappeared.[21]

IV. THE CORPORATE FUND AS A CONCEPT

The concept of separated capital in the company, which in this book is called the Corporate Fund, has long been understood to be a different concept from that of capital contributed by shareholders, even though the Corporate Fund is seeded by capital contributed by founding shareholders. As discussed in chapter 5, once the English East India Company had permanent capital, it returned capital to its shareholders in subsequent years. The word 'capital' has multiple meanings, both generally and as a term connected with companies.[22] Capital was understood to be fluctuating. In England, the capital maintenance

[17] Statutory provisions may negate or qualify these principles in certain circumstances.

[18] *The Case of the York-Buildings Company* (1740) 2 Atk 57, 26 ER 432.

[19] *Wood v Dummer* 30 F Cas 435 (1st Cir 1824).

[20] ibid.

[21] H Hovenkamp, *Enterprise and American Law: 1836–1957* (Harvard University Press, 1991) 55, discussing SD Thompson, *Commentaries on the Law of Private Corporations*, 2nd edn (The Bobbs-Merrill Company, 1909) 29, 33, 34.

[22] LCB Gower, *Gower's Principles of Modern Company Law*, 4th edn (Stevens, 1979) 214.

rules developed, but these were designed to protect creditors[23] and should not be understood to mean that the Corporate Fund of the company is the same as the capital contributed by shareholders. The only time the two are always the same is at the moment of incorporation, with the capital contributed by shareholders seeding the Corporate Fund. The seeding capital gives shareholders 'an interest' in the company through the Corporate Fund on which the company is based.

Some scholars have recognised that the modern company or corporation has a type of fund, without necessarily exploring the implications of that insight. Berle and Means' *The Modern Corporation and Private Property* contains the following discussion:

> It should be noted that the term 'assets' as used by lawyers and others appears to have a multiple personality. At times it refers to the particular objects (and rights) which in their organised relationship make up an enterprise. A pro-rata share in such assets (for instance, one millionth of a factory building plus one millionth of a series of machines plus one millionth of a fleet of delivery trucks, etc) would have almost no meaning to a shareholder. It would be practically impossible to have new capital added through sale of securities to outsiders and yet each former stockholder maintain his asset portion. Only when the term assets is used to refer to a fund of value, – perhaps a sum of values, measured in a chosen unit (money), does pro-rata share come to have meaning. The introduction of value, however, brings with it a multitude of meanings which attach to that concept and the fund of value referred to 'assets' may, therefore, refer to quite different things. Most commonly, the value fund referred to is 'book value,' ie, the assets as arrived at by the accountant through the application of his statistical technique and frequently 'book value,' or something closely analogous, is the concept back of assets in much of legal thinking. When the question is pushed, however, it usually appears that the value fund may bear little relation to book value, being rather the value fund which the whole enterprise represents – still involving a vague concept, but one which frequently leads to results different from 'book value'.[24]

Rather than developing the 'value fund … the whole enterprise represents'[25] concept further, Berle and Means adopted the definition of assets as a fund of value. They confined their discussion to a footnote on the basis that the actual definition would only occasionally affect their current study.

V. UNDERSTANDING THE CORPORATE FUND THROUGH THE FLOATING CHARGE

Chapter 10 contains a discussion of the floating charge. The collective rights of shareholders to the Corporate Fund are not dissimilar to the rights of a debt creditor holding a floating charge.

[23] ibid 216.

[24] AA Berle and GC Means, *The Modern Corporation and Private Property*, rev edn (Harcourt, Brace & World, 1968) 141, fn 1.

[25] ibid.

As Richard Nolan terms it:

> The floating charge is a charge over a fund of assets, in the sense that the chargee has an immediate security interest in identified assets owned by the chargor, which is nevertheless subject to, and restricted by, the superior but limited power of the chargor (as owner) to manage and alienate those assets free of the chargee's interest.[26]

The floating charge is a charge over the entity and the Corporate Fund. The rights of shareholders in the Corporate Fund underpinning the company align to some extent with the rights of a chargee of a floating charge, in the sense that they 'float … with the property which it is intended to affect until some event occurs or some act is done which causes it to settle and fasten on the subject of the charge within its reach and grasp'.[27] For shareholders, that event would be the solvent liquidation of a company with no creditors. At that time, the entity and the *persona ficta* would cease to exist, and shareholders would fasten on and lay claim to the crystallised financial value of the Corporate Fund. If the company has creditors, the shareholders' collective rights to the Corporate Fund rank behind the creditors of the company.

VI. PROPERTY RIGHTS IN THE COMPANY

Shareholders' having limited liability to the company and not being liable to third parties meant that shares came to be recognised as property in their own right. As an outcome of the judgment of Lord Jessel MR in *Pender v Lushington*:[28]

> Shareholders not only had a right not only to dividends, they could now readily assign their shares 'for value' [sic]. It was this, above all else, which established shares as an autonomous form of property, independent of the assets of the company. Their legal redefinition reflected not only the fact that they had become essentially rights to profit – in many instances, this had long been the case – but rights to profit with a value of their own which could be freely and easily bought and sold in the marketplace. With this, shareholders were no longer 'tied' to their shares, nor to the companies of which they were members or its assets.[29]

Shareholders own shares. The share gives the shareholder a bundle of rights. The *persona ficta*, as the fundholder, holds the assets of the company. The *persona ficta* is based on the Corporate Fund. Who therefore owns the company?

Whilst in existence, the status of the company as a *persona ficta* and a separate legal entity offers it entity shielding from the claims of shareholders and the

[26] RC Nolan, 'Property in a Fund' (2004) 120 *Law Quarterly Review* 108, 117.
[27] ibid 128.
[28] *Pender v Lushington* (1877) 6 Ch D 70.
[29] P Ireland, 'Capitalism without the Capitalist: The Joint Stock Company Share and the Emergence of the Modern Doctrine of Separate Corporate Personality' (1996) 17 *Journal of Legal History* 41, 68 (citations omitted).

creditors of shareholders.[30] Armour and Whincop agree with Hansmann and Kraakman that the critical contribution of organisational law is entity partitioning. Armour and Whincop consider, however, that limiting the impact of organisational law to entity partitioning understates the role of property law:

> Proprietary rights protect their holders' claims better than do contractual ones, thereby enabling their more effective use as governance mechanisms within the firm, but at the same time, create costs for third parties. The law must balance the goal of facilitating flexibility in partitioning of entitlements between participants in the firm, whilst at the same time minimizing costs for third parties.[31]

Armour and Whincop distinguish the 'proprietary foundations' of the company from the 'contractarian superstructure'.[32] Whilst the authors acknowledge that the law works differently if the corporate form is used, they do not attribute those differences to legal personality or corporate personhood, but instead to a different balancing of third-party rights.[33]

Might the proprietary foundations Armour and Whincop set out simply be the *persona ficta* itself based on the Corporate Fund? The most efficient and effective way of creating proprietary rights is for the law to create an artificial legal person. That artificial legal person will have property rights over the entity. As the *persona ficta* has the status of a juridical person, it can enforce rights against parties interacting with the companies that are third parties from the perspective of the shareholders.

For this argument to be accepted, it must first be acknowledged that the form of legal personality that a modern company has means it is a *persona ficta* or artificial legal person. That argument is set out in the balance of the chapter.

VII. CONCEPTIONS OF THE COMPANY

Herbert Hovenkamp, in *Enterprise and American Law 1837–1937*, explains how, historically, the jurisprudential concept of the modern corporation passed through three broad views: an 'associational' perspective, a 'fictional' view that developed during the nineteenth century, and a 'personal' or 'entity' view that became important at the end of that century.[34] The associational, fictional and entity perspectives of the modern company were all drawn from the law and

[30] Hansmann and Kraakman (n 5) 440.

[31] Armour and Whincop (n 9) 431.

[32] ibid 449.

[33] ibid 460. The example of the Scots law partnership is used. The example may not be apt. As discussed in section XI, the absence of perpetual succession in the Scottish form of partnership weakens the form of entity partitioning functionally available to partners.

[34] Hovenkamp (n 21) 14. Despite a divergence in the history of the development of the US corporation from the English company after American independence, and despite the more rapid re-emergence of the modern form in the United States, conceptions of the modern company shifted in similar ways in both jurisdictions.

principle surrounding earlier corporate forms: they were not built on new principles but on ancient foundations.[35]

These views can be used to track how the modern company was perceived in the period after general incorporation. First, immediately after the enactment of the general incorporation statutes, a company was understood to be based on its shareholders in the same way as a contractual Joint Stock Company (the associational perspective). Second, with the impact of incorporation giving the modern company the status of a legal person, the company was understood to be a legal fiction. (the fictional view). That legal fiction could be understood in one of two ways. Did the fiction cloak the underlying shareholders? Or was the modern company, like a corporation, a *persona ficta* or artificial legal person existing in the abstract? Finally, as the impact of the operation of the company in the world became apparent, a modern company was understood to be an entity (the 'personal' or 'entity' view).

Associational ideas relate to contractual Joint Stock Companies and the deed of settlement companies of the eighteenth century. A company is based on its shareholders. As discussed in chapter 11, with a focus on the economic aspects of the company, both companies and business corporations were viewed by commentators as associations of natural persons akin to partnerships and as the private property of shareholders.

The legal fiction idea was drawn from two sources. First, it came from corporations law derived from canon law and Roman law, as introduced to the common law by Coke CJ in *The Case of Sutton's Hospital*.[36] The corporation as a *persona ficta* existed as an artificial creation or fiction of the law. The corporation was incorporeal, existing entirely in the abstract. Second, from the eighteenth and nineteenth centuries, a group of natural persons connected contractually would be treated by the law as if they were a legal person. It was a legal fiction as a type of convenient shorthand for the purposes of the law, with no other veracity.

Real entity ideas came from German jurists such as Gierke, Dernberg and Mestre, and also from early conceptions of guilds and fellowships. Gierke argued that 'the real and social existence of a group makes it a legal person'.[37] As such, the corporation was not created by the law but was pre-legal or extra-legal, and a real thing.[38] The real entity is greater than the sum of its parts (meaning the

[35] Cooke (n 14) 138–39.

[36] *The Case of Sutton's Hospital* (1612) 10 Co Rep 23a, 77 ER 960.

[37] O Gierke, *Political Theories of the Middle Age*, tr FW Maitland (Cambridge University Press, 1913). See the discussion in R Harris, 'The Transplantation of the Legal Discourse on Corporate Legal Personality Theories: From German Codification to British Political Pluralism and American Big Business' (2006) 63 *Washington and Lee Law Review* 1421, 1424.

[38] Harris (n 37); M Petrin, 'Reconceptualising the Theory of the Firm – From Nature to Function' (2013) 118 *Penn State Law Review* 1, 6.

people who are part of it.) Even though the law did not create the corporation, Gierke argued that the law was bound to recognise its existence.[39]

All these ideas can be drawn on to understand the complex modern company. Is the company an entity? Entity concepts, as they relate to the modern company, help to explain the impact of the company as it operates in the world. The entity concept is explored further in chapter 14. Is the company associational? The modern company owes its existence to founding shareholders, who follow the statutory process for incorporation and agree to make the financial contributions of capital that seed the Corporate Fund. In that sense the modern company is associational. Is the company a legal fiction? At the moment of incorporation the modern company is a legal person. But what type of legal fiction is that legal person? Whether the modern company is a legal fiction in the sense of a convenient form of legal shorthand cloaking the underlying association of shareholders, or whether the modern company is a legal fiction in the sense of being an artificial legal person (as asserted in this book) is explored in sections VIII and IX.

VIII. THE NATURE OF LEGAL PERSONHOOD

Could an understanding of the source of legal personality assist in an understanding of the nature of legal personality and personhood? Eric Orts outlines the main legal theories of the firm that focus on the possible sources of the legal personality of the modern company.[40] Real entity theory is discussed in chapter 14. Concession theory takes a top-down view that political states 'grant' companies the right to exist, with the primary focus on government as law-giver. In participant theory, firms are created by the individual persons who comprise them, the shareholders, with the primary focus on those individual participants.[41]

The concession principle was in place when peititioners were required to apply and make a case to be granted the right to form a corporation. The corporation was only permitted to exist by, and therefore owed its existence to, the state in some form – initially the Crown, later the Crown and Parliament, and then just Parliament. In 1612, in *The Case of Sutton's Hospital*, discussed in chapter 2, Coke CJ[42] stated that 'the incorporation cannot be created without the King'.[43] Concession theory explained the origins of juridical personhood for

[39] See Gierke (n 37); MJ Phillips, 'Reappraising the Real Entity Theory of the Corporation' (1994) 21 *Florida State University Law Review* 1061; Harris (n 37) 1424; Petrin (n 38) 6–8.

[40] EW Orts, *Business Persons: A Legal Theory of the Firm* (Oxford University Press, 2013) 12.

[41] ibid 12–13.

[42] M Koessler, 'The Person in Imagination or Persona Ficta of the Corporation' (1949) 9 *Louisiana Law Review* 435, 441.

[43] *The Case of Sutton's Hospital* (n 36) 77 ER 960, 964–65.

corporations created by a charter. It extended to include corporations created by discrete statutes or letters patent, and to business corporations with Joint Stock funds and then permanent capital, like the English East India Company. Concession theory focuses on the inception of the corporation. The source of legal personhood was not shareholders or other corporate participants.

Participant theories hold that a modern company is based contractually on its individual shareholders. In a liberal economy based on natural persons and on transactions between natural persons as actors, corporate personality is then a convenient form of legal shorthand, which enables a company to transact. A company based on an atomistic aggregate of participating shareholders can transact *as if it were* a natural person. Corporate legal personality is, therefore, not significant.

Concession theory and participant theory of the corporation are of long standing, perhaps originating, respectively, in the Roman *Universitas* and the atomistic Roman *societas*. The *Universitas* owed its existence to the state and was a juridical person. The Roman *societas* owed its existence to contracting individuals and was an early version of the partnership. As the great legal historian FW Maitland apprehended the distinction in his introduction to Gierke, 'the *Universitas* is a person; the *societas* is only another name, a collective name, for the *socii*'.[44]

Were modern companies incorporated pursuant to a general incorporation statute based on an association of the initial shareholders set out in the memorandum of association? The modern company would then have been a continuation of the private contractual deed of settlement form that was a variation on the contractual Joint Stock Company. The modern company would be contractually based on shareholders and registered following a general incorporation statute. Registration through following the statutory process would mean that the law would allow the incorporators to transact as a legal person. As we have seen, this was probably the view held by parliamenterians like Robert Lowe and by commentators like Lindley LJ in the period immediately after the general incorporation statutes were enacted.

Alternatively, did the general incorporation statutes make the modern company akin to a corporation and therefore a *persona ficta* – an artificial legal person? As we have seen, by the end of the nineteenth century, the conception had developed that the company was a person separate from other persons. Status as a juridical person might, therefore, have been a concession *permitted* by the state when the process set out in the general incorporation statute was followed.

As discussed in chapter 9, the modern company was considered akin to a partnership and to be based on an association of shareholders for a period in the nineteenth century. But the understanding of the legal form of the modern

[44] Maitland, 'Introduction' in Gierke (n 37) xxii.

company changed in the second half of the nineteenth century. As seen in chapter 10, this shift was largely as a result of statutory limited liability and the resulting increased importance of the use of double-entry bookkeeping to ensure the identification and separation of the Corporate Fund for the benefit of creditors. (As discussed in chapter 12, that shift was delayed in England for a range of reasons.) Statutuory limited liability and the resulting shifts made the modern company more like a business corporation. The legal separation of the Corporate Fund from shareholders meant that by the end of the nineteenth century, a modern company at the moment of incorporation was no longer based on an association of shareholders. The modern company was a separate legal person from its shareholders. The outcome of *Salomon v Salomon & Co Ltd*[45] in the House of Lords and the consistent application of the law since that date has made it clear that, for the legal personhood of the company to be upheld, an ongoing association of shareholders, either at or following incorporation, is not necessary. A company is a separate legal entity from its shareholders at the moment of incorporation. (As we shall see, that does not necessarily mean that legal personality is a concession of the state.)

A legal fiction is a mechanism adopted by the law that does not have reality outside the law. The notion of the modern company as just a legal fiction lost favour when its size, reality and impact, and its importance in national affairs, made describing it as a fiction seem unrealistic. In Hovenkamp's outline of the three stages of jurisprudential understanding of the modern company, whilst association is superseded by legal fiction, legal fiction is then superseded by entity theory. Entity theory is discussed in chapter 14.

It is true that the impact of the modern company on the world makes it inapt to decribe it just as a legal fiction. As a second stage, the company develops to become an entity as it operates in and has an impact in the world.[46] However, if that company never operated in the world and had no impact, it would still be incorporated, and remain a *persona ficta*. At the moment of incorporation, the company is a *persona ficta*; an artificial legal person formed according to legal rules.

The initial source of legal personhood can be considered separately from the ongoing basis of that personhood. We have established that legal personality and legal personhood are not dependent on an ongoing association of shareholders. The modern company is an artificial legal person that is separate from all other persons. But is the initial *source* of legal personhood the shareholders through the process of incorporation? Or is the initial source the state through the general incorporation statute? Does the initial source of the legal personhood of the company necessarily affect the type of legal fiction it becomes on incorporation? Section IX considers these questions.

[45] *Salomon v Salomon & Co Ltd* (n 1).
[46] Orts (n 40) 14.

IX. THE MODERN COMPANY AS A LEGAL FICTION

Incorporation transitioned from being a concession to being a right, if a process set out in the statute is followed. As discussed in this section, incorporation's being a right probably means that concession theory did not survive general incorporation. Maitland said that if 'the Concession Theory has notice to quit, [it] may carry the whole Fiction Theory with it'.[47] Maitland was suggesting that if, after the general incorporation statutes, incorporation is no longer a concession of the state, the legal fiction concept of the company may also now be redundant. As set out in section VIII, the modern company may still be a legal fiction at the moment of incorporation, in that it is a creation of the law that will not necessarily become an entity if it is not operated in the world. But what type of legal fiction would a modern company then be?

Maitland identified that, concerning the company, there are two sorts of legal fiction at play:

> Both alike exhibited a certain unity in plurality; both alike might be called 'moral persons'; but in the one case as in the other this personality was to be thought of as a mere labour-saving device, like stenography or the mathematician's symbols. What we may call the Bracket Theory or Expansible Symbol Theory of the Corporation really stands in sharp contrast with the Fiction Theory as Savigny conceived it, though sometimes English writers seem to be speaking of the one and thinking of the other.[48]

Maitland was right to highlight the confusion over the Fiction Theory. Lon Fuller terms a fiction as 'either (1) a statement propounded with a complete or partial consciousness of its falsity, or (2) a false statement recognised as having utility'.[49]

Fuller later writes:

> Most of what has been written about the supposedly profound question of corporate personality has ignored the possibility that the question discussed might be one of terminology merely. No one can deny that the group of persons forming a corporation is treated, legally and extralegally, as a 'unit.' 'Unity' is always a matter of subjective convenience. I may treat all the hams hanging in a butcher shop as a 'unit' – their 'unity' consists in the fact that they are hanging in the same butcher shop.[50]

To Fuller, therefore, the modern company is the second type of legal fiction: a false statement recognised as having utility. The corporate legal person is then a mere labour-saving device, based on the corporate participants as shareholders within it.

[47] Maitland, 'Introduction' in Gierke (n 37) xxxviii; see also D Runciman, *Pluralism and the Personality of the State* (Cambridge University Press, 1997) 94.

[48] ibid xxiv.

[49] LL Fuller, *Legal Fictions* (Stanford University Press, 1967) 9.

[50] ibid 12–13 (citations omitted).

If the modern company is based on its shareholders as members, participant or contractual theory does not consider the effect of the changing composition of shareholders. Roger Scruton writes that Wilhelm von Humboldt's belief that a company as a composite person '"should be regarded as nothing more than the union of the members at a given time" has been the gut-reaction of liberal thinkers ever since'.[51] Scruton points out that von Humboldt's suggestion does not recognise that the membership of companies changes all the time:

> Those who are members at the time when a decision is executed may not have been members when the decision was made; while a wholly new membership may have replaced them before the legal and moral consequences of the decision are felt. If we were to follow von Humboldt, then we should adjudicate the affairs of corporations by holding the present membership individually liable for the deeds of those to whom they have succeeded, and who may be already dead. This is both legally absurd and contrary to natural justice.[52]

Even more compellingly, arguments that a modern company is based on participating shareholders fall apart at the centre. After the outcome of *Salomon v Salomon & Co Ltd*, a company is a separate legal entity from its shareholders from the moment of incorporation. As set out in this book and as discussed in the previous sections of this chapter, the modern company is not based on an association of shareholders after incorporation. It is a *persona ficta* that exists separately from shareholders. It does not derive its ongoing status as an artificial legal person from its shareholders.

What, therefore, becomes of juridical personhood as a concession? Maitland described concession theory as 'its personality must have its commencement in some authoritative act, some declaration of the State's will'.[53] The declaration of the state's will could be viewed as the requirement that the incorporation process is followed and the provision in every incorporation statute that once the incorporation process happens, the company will exist from that point on as a juridical person. However, incorporators previously petitioned for a charter for a corporation. The granting of the charter was discretionary and a concession from the Crown or Parliament when declaring the state's will. Under the general incorporation statutes, the state cannot deny incorporation if the process set out in the statute is followed. Incorporation is, therefore, now a right, not a concession.

As well as referring to the Bracket Theory (contractual or participant theory, where the company is based on shareholders as participants), Maitland refers to Fiction Theory as Savigny conceived it. When the German Fredrich Carl von Savigny set out his version of Fiction Theory in 1840, his starting point was that human beings were rights-and-duties-bearing units. The capacity of a

[51] R Scruton and J Finnis, 'Corporate Persons' (1989) 63 *Proceedings of the Aristotelian Society, Supplementary Volumes* 239, 246 (citations omitted).
[52] ibid.
[53] Maitland, 'Introduction' in Gierke (n 37) xx.

human being could be taken away in part or in whole. Also, the capacity of a separate legal entity could be given to something that was not a human being. The ideal person had to be sundered from those natural persons who were its members.[54]

Rather than agency, Savigny used the Roman concept of guardianship as the analogy that best expresses the role of those natural persons who animate the ideal person.[55] For a company, it is suggested that it is the board. Savigny's understanding has links to canon law and the *persona ficta* conception introduced into the common law by Coke CJ in *Sutton's Hospital*.[56] Explaining the concept, Maitland said 'The guardian is no "member" of his ward; and how even by way of fiction could a figment be composed of real men? We had better leave body and members to the vulgar.'[57]

The source of juridical or legal personhood of the modern company may not, therefore, be a concession, as incorporation is a right if a statutory process is followed. Nor is ongoing legal personhood based on participating shareholders associated together, as the company is a separate legal entity from its shareholders from the moment of incorporation.[58] A more tenable argument is that the company is incorporated because of the actions taken by participating shareholders, following the process of incorporation set out in a statute. After the general incorporation statutes, incorporation shifted from being a concession to being a right that it is only possible to exercise through participating shareholders' compliance with process requirements set out in a statute. Founding shareholders' actions, by following a process set out in a general incorporation statute, bring about incorporation and the creation by the law of a *persona ficta* or artificial legal person that exists in the abstract separately from its shareholders and from all other persons.

In summary, participant theory informs us about the source of legal personhood. The modern company is a legal fiction in the sense that it is a creation of the law. The source of its legal personhood is its participants (shareholders). At the moment of incorporation, the modern company is an artificial legal person that exists separately from shareholders.

Ongoing legal personhood is based not on participants but on the Corporate Fund in which the interests of participants are held. The existence of the Corporate Fund differentiated the modern company and the earlier business corporation from the *persona ficta* corporation of the sixteenth century. The modification of the *persona ficta* is discussed in section X.

[54] ibid.

[55] ibid xx–xxi.

[56] *The Case of Sutton's Hospital* (n 36).

[57] Maitland, 'Introduction' in Gierke (n 37) xxi.

[58] Even though shares give shareholder membership rights as part of the general meeting, it is not realistic to say legal personhood is based on shareholders in their constitutional capacities when they participate in the general meeting as members.

X. THE *PERSONA FICTA* MODIFIED

As discussed in chapter 2, Coke CJ, in *The Case of Sutton's Hospital*,[59] introduced into the common law the concept of *persona ficta*, where a corporation is an artificial legal person separate from all natural persons. The basis of the case that was brought by the heirs in 1612 was that the Hospital's land did not belong to the Charitable Corporation at the moment of incorporation, and that therefore the Corporation did not validly exist as there was nothing corporeal for it to base its existence on at the moment of incorporation.[60] Coke CJ's significant progression to the common law was to determine that the Charitable Corporation could nevertheless exist in the abstract as an artificial legal person or *persona ficta*.

The Charitable Corporation was not based on anything at the moment of incorporation. The modern company is more than just a *persona ficta*. Modern companies are incorporated based on the Corporate Fund seeded by shareholders. That Corporate Fund fuels the *persona ficta* as it operates in the world.

Hobbes considered the business corporation in *Leviathan* in 1653. 'Those bodies which were constituted by subjects among themselves, or by authorities from a stranger' were private.[61] Hobbes saw trading corporations like the English East India Company as public, not private. Bodies politique (politic) for the ordering of trade were corporations that must be authorised by the state (by a concession). They were persons in the law.[62]

Hobbes therefore shared a conception of the trading corporation as a *persona ficta* or artificial legal person permitted to exist by the state as a concession. However, Hobbes developed the idea of the *persona ficta* in a manner that allows it both to survive the general incorporation statutes and be based on a Corporate Fund that can operate in the world, becoming an entity.

David Runciman writes:

> Hobbes preferred State – the concessionary State – all freedoms inevitably rest with the author of the drama, who is sovereign. But even in a liberal state, where groups acquire masks as and when desired, it is not the groups themselves who do the acquiring; rather, it is done for them by those individuals who have decided to provide the group with a personality of its own. Nor does the group wear the mask itself; it is worn for it by an actor, its appointed representative.[63]

Applying this analogy means there are three components to the incorporation and operation of the modern company. These are, first, the individuals who

[59] *The Case of Sutton's Hospital* (n 36).

[60] ibid.

[61] Runciman (n 43) 26, citing T Hobbes, *Leviathan*, ed R Tuck (Cambridge University Press, 1991) 156.

[62] Runciman (n 43) citing Hobbes (n 61) 160.

[63] Runciman (n 43) 237–38.

acquire the mask of incorporation, the *acquirers*; second, the *group* that has the mask acquired for it; and, third, the *representative* that wears the mask.

Groups as participants can acquire masks (incorporate) as and when desired through following the statutory process set down in the general incorporation statute. Using a Hobbesian analysis, the *acquirers* obtain the mask of incorporation for the company. Rather than petitioning for a charter and seeking a concession from Parliament or Crown, as in the past, the mask is acquired by the founding shareholders' following the process necessary to meet the requirements for incorporation set out in a statute, including contributing the initial capital that seeds the Corporate Fund. (Until relatively recently, the distinct role of the *acquirers* was recognised in corporate law: they were described as promoters.)

Once incorporated, the company becomes *a persona ficta*, an artificial legal person. The board bridges the *persona ficta* and the world. It is the primary decision-making body that determines the operation of the company in the world. By appointing the chief executive officer (CEO) it establishes the cascading corporate hierarchy of people that are the *representatives* wearing the mask for the *persona ficta* as it operates in the world.

The other requisite component is the *group* that has the mask acquired for it. David Runciman says '[t]he group itself does nothing, which is what makes it a fiction, and depends for everything on the natural persons (its members) who give it a mask and the artificial person (its representative) who wears it'.[64] The final question is, therefore, who or what is the *group* given the mask of incorporation?

If we accept, as we must, that a modern company is a separate legal entity from its shareholders then the shareholders cannot be the *group*. The shareholders are the natural persons who are the members, who give the company the mask as *acquirers*. The people who operate the company in the world are not the *group*, they are the *representatives*. The *group* need not necessarily be persons. Inanimate objects like idols and rivers can be *persona ficta* or artificial legal persons.[65] For a modern company, the *group* can only be the Corporate Fund that, at and from the moment of incorporation, is a *persona ficta* – an artificial legal person – and becomes an entity as it operates in the world.

XI. THE SIGNIFICANCE OF THE *PERSONA FICTA*

How significant is corporate legal personality? Despite being placed first by most commentators writing about the company, the significance attached to the legal personhood of the company varies greatly. As we have seen, to some commentators legal personality is a utility fiction – a convenient form of legal shorthand,

[64] ibid 238.
[65] Te Awa Tupua (Whanganui River Claims Settlement) Act 2017 (NZ), s 14.

like a collective noun for the contractually-combined shareholders underpinning the companies. Hart argued that the rights and duties of companies are created by the law to adjudicate the independent legal interests of individuals. For Hart, the concept of the juridical person, with its own rights and duties, was a procedural device, which made the adjudication more manageable.[66]

If classic liberal economics is based on transactions between participants, to be shoehorned within this framework, the company must be one of two things. The company must either be a transacting participant or be made up of participants that transact *as if* they were a single participant. Law-and-economics adherents generally favour the second. The starting point for conventional law-and-economics adherents is to conceive of the firm, including the modern company, as a network or nexus of contracts.[67] Corporate law therefore becomes a specialist branch of contract law.[68] For Easterbrook and Fischel, the modern company is an outcome of private ordering.[69] The focus is consequently wholly on the contractual relationships between corporate participants.[70]

Easterbrook and Fischel[71] attach minimal importance to corporate legal personality in the modern company. They classify the company as a financing device that is not otherwise distinctive.[72] Corporate personhood creates a legal identity, allowing a corporation to have a name in which it may sue and be sued conveniently – an 'it' just as business trusts are an 'it'.[73] For Easterbrook and Fischel, '[t]he "personhood" of a corporation is therefore a matter of convenience rather than reality'[74] and legal personality no more than a collective noun for shareholders as participants.

Although also adhering to a law-and-economics framework to understand the modern company, Hansmann and Kraakman concede that legal personality is acquired from organisational law rather than contractually.[75] They do not specify whether the source of corporate personality need be statutory, or whether it could be derived from legal rules.

[66] HLA Hart, 'Definition and Theory in Jurisprudence' in HLA Hart, *Essays in Jurisprudence and Philosophy* (Oxford University Press, 1983) 40–46.

[67] FH Easterbrook and DR Fischel, *The Economic Structure of Corporate Law* (Harvard University Press, 1991).

[68] See the discussion in Armour and Whincop (n 9) 429.

[69] FH Easterbrook and DR Fischel, 'The Corporate Contract' (1989) 89 *Columbia Law Review* 1416.

[70] The term 'contractual' is not used in a legal sense but in an economic sense, although there is obviously a relationship between the two concepts.

[71] Easterbrook and Fischel (n 69); Easterbrook and Fischel (n 67).

[72] Easterbrook and Fischel (n 67) 10.

[73] ibid 11. See also MC Jensen and WH Meckling, 'Theory of the Firm: Managerial Behaviour, Agency Costs, and Ownership Structure' (1976) 10 *Journal of Financial Economics* 305; O Williamson, 'Transaction Cost Economics' in R Schmalensee and R Willig (eds), *Handbook of Industrial Organization*, vol 1 (Elsevier, 1989); O Hart, *Firms, Contracts, and Financial Structure* (Oxford University Press, 1995).

[74] Easterbrook and Fischel (n 67) 12.

[75] Hansmann and Kraakman (n 5) 406.

Hansmann and Kraakman are two of the authors of *The Anatomy of Corporate Law*. *Anatomy* sets out the core components of a company as '(1) legal personality, (2) limited liability, (3) transferrable shares, (4) centralized management under a board structure, and (5) shared ownership by contributors of equity capital'.[76] Despite placing legal personality first on the list of core components,[77] the authors consider that legal personality is not a necessary precondition for any of the other characteristics.[78] Therefore, the legal personality of the modern company is efficient but not particularly special; a common law partnership that lawyers consider to lack legal personality can, the authors suggest, enjoy each foundational characteristic.[79]

A consequence of status as a legal person is characteristics including entity shielding, authority to transact and procedures for legal action.[80] Could these characteristics be replicated using contracting? The deed of settlement companies of the eighteenth century were an historical attempt to replicate these key characteristics of business corporations. As established through this book, business corporations like the English East India Company had all the key features of the modern company.

First, entity shielding. As discussed in chapter 8, the deed of settlement company, as legally a form of partnership, had weak-form entity shielding. Weak-form entity shielding means that the creditors of the firm (partnership) have priority over the personal creditors of the partners.[81] Modern companies have a stronger form of entity shielding. Liquidation protection means shareholders' personal creditors cannot foreclose on assets in the company.[82] Because of capital lock-in of shareholders, shareholders cannot withdraw their capital at will,[83] or be forced by their creditors to withdraw their capital.[84] Partners in partnerships, in contrast, can withdraw their capital at will, or be forced by their creditors to withdraw their capital. The deed of settlement company was legally a partnership. Entity shielding was therefore effective against shareholders and the personal creditors of shareholders of such a company. The deed of settlement company did not have strong-form entity shielding. It was theoretically possible for shareholders by contract to agree to lock in their capital. But such a contract would not bind creditors of shareholders, who could force the shareholders to withdraw their capital.

[76] Kraakman et al (n 8) 4–5.

[77] ibid 5.

[78] ibid 8.

[79] ibid 8, fn 27. The authors cite *Burnes v Pennell* (1849) 2 HLCas 497, 521; 9 ER 1181, 1191. However, in 1849, the House of Lords compared the deed of settlement company form with the partnership. The House of Lords did not consider the modern company incorporated pursuant to a general incorporation statute.

[80] ibid 7.

[81] Hansmann, Kraakman, and Squire (n 11) 1379.

[82] Kraakman et al (n 8) 6.

[83] ibid 6. See Blair (n 4).

[84] Hansmann, Kraaakman and Squire (n 11) 1349.

Second, procedures for legal action. Procedures for legal action were problematic using the contractual deed of settlement company form, because of the requirement by the courts that all shareholders join in the action. That requirement came about because, legally, the shareholders were partners in a partnership.

Finally, authority to transact. The eighteenth-century courts accommodated the deed of settlement companies' transacting as if they were juridical persons. However, as discussed in chapters 8 and 9, while the courts accommodated the form as much as possible, they consistently did not resile from their fundamental position that deed of settlement companies were legally, if not economically, a form of partnership. Shareholders remained liable for the debts incurred by the company.

The Scottish form of partnership is frequently used to support arguments that the form of corporate personhood enjoyed by the modern company is of minimal significance. The Scottish partnership has had separate legal personality since at least the nineteenth century.[85] Although the foundational characteristic of entity shielding is the most efficient factor in running a business, Laura Macgregor argues that it is not enough. Hansmann and Kraakman do not consider perpetual succession to be foundational, but rather an inconvenience fixed by contractual workarounds.[86] The Scottish partnership does not have perpetual succession. Every time a partner retires, the partnership ends and a new partnership with a new legal personality is formed.

Mcgregor demonstrates the challenges for efficiency and continuity due to changes in partners caused by the absence of perpetual succession. Contractual workarounds have not resolved these challenges as partnership agreements do not apply to third parties. In particular, the jingle rule does not fully apply. (The jingle rule is a partnership law rule under which partnership assets are first distributed to the creditors of the partnership and each partner's assets are first distributed to that partner's creditors.) The jingle rule does not apply to the extent that personal creditors do not take priority over partnership creditors in relation to personal partner assets. The consequence is that Scottish partnerships do not even have weak-form entity shielding.[87] Macgregor concludes that resolution for Scottish partnerships can only come through statutory amendment: it is not possible through contracting.[88]

Perpetual succession of shareholders is related to the perpetuity of the company as a legal form that can potentially exist forever. Both perpetual succession and the perpetuity of the company are, it is suggested, key characteristics of the company that cannot be replicated by contracting participants. In a

[85] See the discussion in L Macgregor, 'Partnerships and Legal Personality: Cautionary Tales From Scotland' (2020) 20(1) *Journal of Corporate Law Studies* 237.

[86] Hansmann and Kraakman (n 5) 413; Kraakman et al (n 8) 1394 discussed by Macgregor (n 85).

[87] Macgregor (n 85) 247.

[88] ibid 261.

partnership, every time a partner leaves the partnership ends. Even if that legal consequence were to be contracted out of in some way, the fact that a partnership is based on its partners means its basis and nature shifts whenever a partner leaves or a new partner joins the partnership.

As Schwartz highlights, perpetual existence has long been considered a leading attribute of corporations.[89] In Blackstone's *Commentaries*, Blackstone described the corporation as 'a person that never dies'. Its shareholders and managers may change, but it is still the same corporation, just 'as the river Thames is still the same river, though the parts which compose it are changing every instant'.[90] As Mcgregor discusses, and as the deed of settlement form of company demonstrated in the eighteenth century, the underlying changes to the organisation with the withdrawal of a partner are problematic, even if the legal form endures somehow. And many of the advantages of the corporate structure relating to size and scale are linked to the potential of the corporation to exist in perpetuity.

Maitland interestingly suggested that if the legislature had not capitulated to demands for general incorporation statutes in the mid-nineteenth century, contractual Joint Stock Companies might have continued to contract using the word 'limited' in their names. Third-party creditors might then have been precluded from claiming from shareholders, having recourse only to the Joint Stock or Corporate Fund. Shareholders would have had limited liability.[91]

The protection for shareholders could only have extended to voluntary creditors the company contracted with who had notice of the limited liability of the company and its shareholders. The protection would not have extended to involuntary creditors, such as tort victims of the company. Whatever strong policy arguments might exist in favour of shareholders' being liable for the torts that their company commits,[92] shareholders would not have had comprehensive limited liability. Any comprehensive limitation of liability of shareholders would have required the courts to recognise that the contractual Joint Stock Company was legally separate from its shareholders. In effect, corporate personhood would have remained significant, with its source not the incorporation statutue but the common law. Corporate personhood through organisational law.

An explanation of the origins and central significance of status as a juridical person in the history of the modern company strengthens arguments that corporate legal personality cannot be explained away as an instance of contracting

[89] AA Schwartz, 'The Perpetual Corporation' (2012) 80 *George Washington Law Review* 764.

[90] W Blackstone, *Commentaries on the Laws of England*, vol 1 (Clarendon Press, 1765–69) ch 18, 456. In the Dartmouth College case, Chief Justice Marshall observed that the genius of the corporate form was that it allowed 'a perpetual succession of individuals' to act 'for the promotion of the particular object, like one immortal being'. *Trs of Dartmouth Coll v Woodward*, 17 US 518 (1819) (as cited by Schwartz (n 89).

[91] FW Maitland, 'The Corporation Sole' in HAL Fisher (ed), *The Collected Papers of Frederic William Maitland* (Cambridge University Press, 1911) vol 3.

[92] H Hansmann and R Kraakman, 'Towards Unlimited Liability for Corporate Torts' (1991) 100 *Yale Law Journal* 1879.

and thus of private ordering. The modern company cannot be wholly private and solely a consequence of contracting. One of its crucial characteristics, being a *persona ficta* or artificial legal person, cannot be acquired through contracting. No amount of contracting can create a legal person.

XII. SEPARATE LEGAL ENTITY AND LEGAL PERSONHOOD

The modern company is not just a juridical person. As a *persona ficta*, the modern company is a juridical person that is a separate legal person from its shareholders and from all other persons. Legal personality and separate legal personality are two related, but different, concepts.

The company's status as a separate legal entity from its shareholders and from all persons is the central and foundational tenet of corporate law. In 2013 in the United Kingdom, in the Supreme Court case of *Prest v Petrodel Resources Ltd*, Lord Sumption SCJ said:

> The separate personality and property of a company is sometimes described as a fiction, and in a sense it is. But the fiction is the whole foundation of English company and insolvency law. As Robert Goff LJ once observed, in this domain 'we are concerned not with economics but with law. The distinction between the two is, in law, fundamental': Bank of Tokyo Ltd v Karoon (Note) [1987] AC 45, 64. He could justly have added that it is not just legally but economically fundamental, since limited companies have been the principal unit of commercial life for more than a century. Their separate personality and property are the basis on which third parties are entitled to deal with them and commonly do deal with them.[93]

As endowed entities, modern companies are juridical persons. Status as a juridical person distinguishes modern companies from trusts and partnerships.[94] However, the significance attached to modern companies' legal personhood and its source remains contested. *Salomon v Salomon & Co Ltd* was a watershed case for a range of reasons. Its outcome sounded the death knell for the associative basis of legal personality derived from an ongoing underpinning of shareholders. The approach adopted by the House of Lords in *Salomon* was also the final stage in the process of the legal separation of shareholders from the Corporate Fund. The separation had existed previously in business corporations like the English East India Company. The process of legal separation of shareholders from the company or corporation took place in jurisdictions across the world in the nineteenth century.

Separate legal entity, some argue, does not necessarily mean that the juridical personhood of the company is significant. From Arthur Machen:

> Now, in respect to the nature of a corporation, there are two basic propositions, (1) that a corporation is an entity distinct from the sum of the members that

[93] *Prest v Petrodel Resources Ltd* [2013] UKSC 34, [2013] 2 AC 415, [8].
[94] Unless legal personality is bestowed on a partnership through a statute.

> compose it, and (2) that this entity is a person. These propositions are often confused; but they are properly quite distinct from one another. For example, one who denies that a corporation is really a person, or who accepts that proposition merely as a figurative statement or fiction of law, is not at all bound by logical consistency to deny the reality of the corporation as an entity distinct from the sum of the members.[95]

Other commentators consider that corporate personality combines characteristics, or rights and attributes. Salmond's basic view was:

> Persons are the substances of which rights and duties are the attributes. It is only in this respect that persons possess juridical significance, and this is the exclusive point of view from which personality receives legal recognition.[96]

Everting perspective to the *persona ficta*, that *persona ficta* at the moment of incorporation has the right to call on amounts subscribed for by shareholders for the Corporate Fund. As a juridical person, the company has attributes such as the ability to enter into contracts and own property.

The authors of *The Anatomy of Corporate Law* consider that legal personality bundles together *characteristics* (entity shielding, authority to transact, procedures for legal action) rather than *participants*. The significance of legal personality or separate legal personality is as a term that bundles the three foundational characteristics together. It is a 'convenient heuristic formula for describing organizational forms which enjoy the benefit of each of the three foregoing "foundational" rule types.'[97]

The *characteristics* do not exist before, or independently of, the existence of the company as a *persona ficta*. The artificial legal person first comes into existence, and the characteristics of entity shielding, authority to transact and procedures for legal action are attributes of the artificial legal person. In other words, the characteristics are not in existence and then bundled together in the *persona ficta*. Instead, the artificial legal person comes into existence and in doing so acquires the rights and attributes as a consequence of being a *persona ficta*. At the very moment of incorporation, the modern company is a *persona ficta* that exists separately from its shareholders and all other persons. It has the three characterisitics named, as well as other characteristics such as the potential to exist in perpetuity.

XIII. CONCLUSION

The modern company is unique as an organisational form for business. None of the other organisational forms, such as individual proprietorships, partnerships

[95] AW Machen, 'Corporate Personality' (1911) 24 *Harvard Law Review* 253, 258 (citations omitted).

[96] JW Salmond, *Jurisprudence, or, The Theory of the Law*, 2nd edn (Stevens and Haynes, 1907) 275.

[97] Kraakman et al (n 8) 8.

and deed of settlement companies, available to entrepreneurs and commonly used at the beginning of the nineteenth century, created organisations with 'entity' status, in the sense that property could be held in the name of the entity rather than in the name of the individuals involved in the enterprise. None established governance mechanisms that were separate from the participants.[98] Capital is legally separated from shareholders and forms the basis of the artificial legal person. These features make the modern company a fundamentally different form from sole traders and partnerships. That point is often forgotten when companies are characterised as sitting on a spectrum of business forms that includes partnerships. As Gower pointed out in 1979:

> The concept of capital is of fundamental importance to a proper understanding of company law in general, and in particular to an appreciation of the distinction between individual traders and partnerships on the one hand, and incorporated limited liability companies on the other.[99]

The forms' being seen as sitting on the same spectrum may be a consequence of their economic conflation in the eighteenth century and their legal conflation for a period in the mid-nineteenth century.

The modern company is a *persona ficta*. As such, the modern company is both an artificial legal person and a separate legal entity from its shareholders. The Corporate Fund forms the basis of the *persona ficta*. The *persona ficta* has property rights in the entity that develops as the company operates in the world (as further discussed in chapter 14). Thus the modern company may provide better entity shielding than is currently understood. Hansmann and Kraakman identify three forms of entity shielding. Weak entity shielding grants firm creditors priority over personal creditors of contributors in the division of firm assets, meaning that the personal creditors of contributors of capital may only levy on firm assets if the firm creditors have been paid in full. Partnerships have weak-form entity shielding. Strong entity shielding adds a rule of liquidation protection, which restricts the ability of both the contributors of capital and their personal creditors to force the payout of a contributor's share of the firm's net assets. Complete entity shielding means non-firm creditors cannot make any claim on firm assets.

Hansmann and Kraakman categorise the modern company as an example of strong entity shielding, as corporate creditors enjoy a prior claim to the corporation's assets. Corporate creditors are also protected from attempts by shareholders or personal creditors to liquidate those assets. Any form of claim is only possible, however, if the company is in liquidation. But while it is in

[98] Blair does not consider that shareholders as the contributors of capital that seed the Corporate Fund might therefore have claims that are superior to other corporate participants or stakeholders In other work with Stout, Blair views the modern company as based on team production between corporate participants: MM Blair and LA Stout, 'A Team Production Theory of Corporate Law' (1999) 85 *Virginia Law Review* 247.

[99] Gower (n 22) 214.

existence, the *persona ficta* provides complete entity shielding. Non-firm creditors cannot make any claim on firm assets, nor can they force liquidation if the company complies with the terms of its loan. Only if the company is placed into liquidation, either by creditors of the firm or by shareholders of the firm, and the 'life' of the *persona ficta* ends can personal creditors make claims on the company's assets. At that time, the forms of value held in the entity will be realised, will crystallise and become part of the Corporate Fund that is no longer cloaked by the *persona ficta*.

Replicating the potential longevity of the modern company through contracting or through using other private law forms is challenging. Partnerships end when a partner leaves the partnership. Contractual work-arounds do not alter the fact that the partnership is based on the partners, and when a partner leaves the basis of the partnership changes. Whereas beneficiaries of a trust cannot be an undefined class, shareholders can, because the company is not based on shareholders. The company is seeded by initial capital that then becomes the Corporate Fund that underpins the *persona ficta*. The company is not based on current shareholders at any time after the moment of incorporation. The complete legal separation of the *persona ficta* based on the Corporate Fund, from shareholders and from all other persons makes the company a potent vehicle for business.

The Corporate Fund is a critical component of the modern company. It is is more than the initial cash subscriptions of shareholders. It captures value created when the company uses the initial subscribed capital to operate in the world and become an entity.

The Corporate Fund is locked in or permanent, in the sense that shareholders have no right per se to extract their subscribed capital or make a claim on assets acquired by the company while the *persona ficta* is extant. The Corporate Fund is managed by directors who are constitutionally separate from shareholders and who act in the interests of the entity based on the Corporate Fund.

Although entity shielding means that creditors may make claims on the Corporate Fund rather than on shareholders, the Corporate Fund is not a fixed sum of money that equates to the sum of money contributed by shareholders as initial capital. Instead, it is the unrealised value of the entity the Corporate Fund underpins. Value from the entity can be valorised for shareholders and distributed as dividends. In that way, the Corporate Fund is similar to a floating charge held over a company that crystallises on liquidation. Shareholders own shares. Shareholders cannot require the return of the initial capital they contributed. Shareholders also cannot require that value be valorised as a dividend. Shares have rights attached while the company is solvent that usually, but need not, include the right to receive a pro rata share of dividends on a distribution. If the company becomes insolvent, creditors may realise any remaining financial value in the Corporate Fund. Any residual value in the Corporate Fund remaining after creditors are paid becomes the property of shareholders.

The modern company may be the first type of fiction identified by Lon Fuller – 'a statement propounded with complete or partial consciousness of its falsity'.[100] Legally the company is a *persona ficta* or artificial legal person that exists in the abstract. The fiction may be our shared belief and acceptance that the company exists,[101] meaning we interact with the company as a real thing that extends beyond the law as a mere legal fiction.

As Roger Scruton and John Finnis put it:

> 'Personality' is a distracting metaphor in a realistic moral and political analysis of human associations and their actions. The metaphor is always tugged between its two historic sources. On the one hand, there is persona as mask; to this corresponds the law's carefree attribution of legal personality to anything that figures as the subject of legal relations, particularly litigious and/or property relations: idols, funds, parcels of property on the quayside, ships, the Crown … On the other hand, there is persona as individual substance, of a rational nature (Boethius); to this corresponds nothing (save metaphorically) in the many orderings of human association which we call groups – nothing except the people who are members.[102]

As set out in this chapter, the first, not the second, type of personality is a fundamental characteristic of the modern company. The persona masks the Corporate Fund.

[100] Fuller (n 49) 9.
[101] R Cooke, *Turning Points of the Common Law* (Sweet & Maxwell, 1997) 11–12.
[102] Scruton and Finnis (n 51) 274.

14

The Modern Company as an Entity

I. INTRODUCTION

ERIC ORTS, IN *Business Persons: A Legal Theory of the Firm*, sets out an institutional theory that takes an intermediate view that firms are formed according to legal rules and organised by natural persons.[1] Chapter 13 focuses on the key attributes of the modern company as a *persona ficta* based on the Corporate Fund. The focus of chapter 15 is on corporate governance. The subject of this chapter is the firm itself as an entity, which is a focus of institutional theory.[2] But what type of entity is a modern company?

II. THE ROLE OF REAL ENTITY THEORY

Sociological theories of corporate legal personality, where it is posited that a company derives legal personality from the natural persons who are part of the company, relate to real entity and institutional theories. These theories were initially used to explain German fellowships (*Genossenschaft*), where corporate status could be obtained by a resolution of members. That resolution was given recognition by the Crown or the state. The theories explain early forms of organisation, such as the towns, boroughs and guilds of the twelfth and thirteenth centuries, which sought recognition from the king or other lords,[3] discussed in chapter 2.

The German academic Otto von Gierke argued that the real and social existence of a group justifies recognition as a legal person. As such, the corporation was not created by the law but was pre-legal or extra-legal.[4] Even though the

[1] EW Orts, *Business Persons: A Legal Theory of the Firm* (Oxford University Press, 2013) 14.

[2] ibid 15.

[3] CA Cooke, *Corporation, Trust and Company: An Essay in Legal History* (Harvard University Press, 1951) 20.

[4] O Gierke, *Political Theories of the Middle Age*, tr FW Maitland (Cambridge University Press, 1913) 611; R Harris, 'The Transplantation of the Legal Discourse on Corporate Legal Personality Theories: From German Codification to British Political Pluralism and American Big Business' (2006) 63 *Washington and Lee Law Review* 1421, 1424; M Petrin, 'Reconceptualising the Theory of the Firm – From Nature to Function' (2013) 118 *Penn State Law Review* 1, 6.

law did not create the real corporation, Gierke argued that the law was bound to recognise its existence.[5]

This aspect of real entity theory cannot apply to the legal personhood of a modern company. A group of people cannot assert that they are a limited liability company and therefore a juridical person. Maitland highlights how 'from saying organisation is corporateness, English lawyers were precluded by a long history'.[6]

As Orts sets out in his intermediate institutional theory, a company is formed according to legal rules. The contemporary relevance of real entity theory does not relate to the *source* of the juridical personhood of the modern company but instead to the reality of the modern company as it operates in the world.

III. THE CONTRIBUTION OF REAL ENTITY THEORY TO THE UNDERSTANDING OF THE MODERN COMPANY

During the late nineteenth and early twentieth centuries, the growth in its size and importance led to a focus on the modern company as a real entity. Adherents of German 'new school' economic ideas were challenging neoclassical economics, where the economy is understood to be based on transactions between individuals.[7]

Lord Halsbury may have been influenced by real entity ideas of the company, describing the company as a 'real thing' in *Salomon*.[8] He may have adopted an adapted version of real entity theory, as he was careful to say that the company is an artificial creation of the law. Lord Halsbury did not limit the existence of the company once it was created though. 'Once a company is legally incorporated it must be treated like any other independent person with its rights and liabilities appropriate to itself …'[9] After the acceptance in *Salomon v Salomon & Co Ltd* that the modern company was a separate legal entity from its shareholders that was a legal person, the next logical question had to be what and who comprised the entity.

Some adherents to real entity theory posited that the organisation is a living organism that is itself a person 'possessed of a real will of its own, and capable of actions and responsibility for them, just as a man is'.[10]

[5] See MJ Phillips, 'Reappraising the Real Entity Theory of the Corporation' (1994) 21 *Florida State University Law Review* 1061, 1068–69; Harris, 'Transplantation of the Legal Discourse' 1424.

[6] FW Maitland, 'Trust and Corporation' in HAL Fisher (ed), *The Collected Papers of Frederic William Maitland*, vol 3 (Cambridge University Press, 1911) 390.

[7] H Hovenkamp, *Enterprise and American Law, 1836–1937* (Harvard University Press, 1991) 298.

[8] *Salomon v Salomon & Co Ltd* [1897] AC 22 (HL), 33. See the discussion in R Cooke, *Turning Points of the Common Law* (Sweet & Maxwell, 1997) 11.

[9] *Salomon v Salomon & Co Ltd* (n 8) 30.

[10] JW Salmond, *Jurisprudence, or, The Theory of the Law*, 2nd edn (Stevens and Haynes, 1907) 288.

The corporation, under 'real entity' theory, would have its own life in the sense that it has a sociological or psychological existence:[11] in the words of Machen, a 'corporation is an entity – not imaginary or fictitious, but real, not artificial but natural'.[12] Whilst some real entity theorists considered the corporation to be an organism,[13] others saw it as a system comprised of human and non-human elements: a network or a machine.[14]

Real entity theory gathered such traction in England in the early years of the twentieth century that, in an article reproduced in the *Law Quarterly Review* in 1911 from a *Festschrift* for Professor von Gierke, Frederick Pollock argued not just that the legal fiction theory had been officially discarded by the English courts, but also that it had never been adopted.[15]

When FW Maitland introduced Gierke to the English-speaking world, his description of the 'German Fellowship' clearly reveals the origin of organic theory and the later twentieth-century identification theory in English law:

> [It] is no fiction, no symbol, no piece of the State's machinery, no collective name for individuals, but a living organism and a real person, with body and members and a will of its own. Itself can will, itself can act; it wills and acts by the men who are its organs as a man wills and acts by brain, mouth and hand. It is not a fictitious person; ... it is a group-person, and its will is a group-will.[16]

Others were less convinced. Salmond, writing in 1906, was scathing about real entity theory, talking about German jurists, such as Gierke, Dernberg and Mastre, attempting to establish a new theory that treats corporate personality as a reality and not a fiction,[17] being given 'sympathetic exposition, if not express support from Prof Maitland'.[18] Salmond argues that the will of the company is, in fact, the wills of a majority of its directors or shareholders, and that when men associate together, they do not become one person 'any more than two horses become one animal when they pull the same cart'.[19]

[11] Harris (n 4) 1473; Petrin (n 4) 6.

[12] AW Machen, 'Corporate Personality' (1911) 24 *Harvard Law Review* 253, 262; Phillips (n 5) 1068.

[13] GF Deiser, 'The Juristic Person. III' (1909) 57 *University of Pennsylvania Law Review* 300, 310 (as cited in Phillips (n 5) 1069, fn 50) (corporate body is a 'composite organism'); GA Mark, 'The Personification of the Business Corporation in American Law' (1987) 54 *The University of Chicago Law Review* 1441, 1469 (as cited in Phillips (n 5) 1069, fn 50) (discussing the organicism of, amongst others, Gierke and Maitland). Organic theory may have had its origins in Germany. It still dominates German conceptions of the company. T Baums, 'The Organ Doctrine: Origins, Developments and Actual Meaning in German Company Law' (2016) *Institute for Law and Finance Working Paper* 148/2016, 1 at www.ilf-frankfurt.de/fileadmin/user_upload/ILF_WP_148.pdf.

[14] Phillips (n 5) 1069–70.

[15] F Pollock, 'Has the Common Law Received the Fiction Theory of Corporations?' (1911) 27 *Law Quarterly Review* 219, 235.

[16] Maitland, 'Introduction' in Gierke (n 4) xxvi. E Freund, *The Legal Nature of Corporations* (University of Chicago Press, 1897) was also influential in the United States; see Harris (n 4) 1431–35.

[17] Salmond (n 10) 288.

[18] ibid 288, fn 1.

[19] ibid 288.

Salmond's analogy, however, can be nuanced. Although two horses do not become one animal when they pull the cart, they collectively contribute the horsepower for the cart. The two horses do not act autonomously, with the way each behaves in pulling the cart affected by the other. Like the cart, the company as an artificial and inanimate Corporate Fund by analogy requires decision-making 'organs' or bodies to operate in the world. One organ is the board, comprised of individual directors who collectively make decisions about the direction of the company in the world. The directors in a meeting contribute to joint decisions as part of a collective process. Those decisions will differ from the decisions each director as an individual would make.

Denning LJ explored the notion that while the acts, knowledge and state of mind of servants (employees) and agents of a company are legally separate from the company, those who are the directing mind and will of the company are acting *as* the company for those purposes:

> A company may in many ways be likened to a human body. It has a brain and nerve centre which controls what it does. It also has hands that hold the tools and act in accordance with directions from the centre. Some of the people in the company are mere servants and agents who are nothing more than hands to do the work and cannot be said to represent the mind or will. Others are directors and managers who represent the directing mind and will of the company, and control what it does. The state of mind of these managers is the state of mind of the company and is treated by the law as such.[20]

Less colourful than considering the company as analogous to a person with organs is to look back to the early corporation and consider the organs as constitutional decision-making bodies for the company. The board as a collective decision-making body steers the company through the world as its management body. (To govern means to steer.) The general meeting is the constitutional body that determines the board's composition. The general meeting is a collective decision-making body that can make 'life-and-death' decisions about the company, including whether or not to keep the corporate vessel afloat or liquidate it. Of course, persons for these purposes comprise the board and persons, either directly or ultimately, participate in the general meeting. That does not mean that those persons are part of the corporate entity for all purposes, just that they make decisions in their constitutional capacities. To return to Salmond's analogy, no one would suggest that the two horses are part of the cart; the collective efforts of the horses provide the horsepower that pulls the cart down the path. The directors and shareholders who make decisions for the company as part of its decision-making bodies are not part of the company but their decisions determine the direction of the company.

[20] *HL Bolton (Engineering) Co Ltd v TJ Graham and Sons Ltd* [1957] 1 QB 159 (CA), 172.

IV. THE MODERN COMPANY AS A REAL ENTITY

Is the company real, or is it just a legal fiction? It seems a nonsense to characterise a multinational corporation like Amazon, or the companies that dominate the skylines of every major city of the world, either atomistically, as nothing more than a nexus-of-contracts, or merely as a fiction with no reality outside the law.

A company can have a physical presence through its building and assets. Correctly understood, though, those physical assets are property of the company that comprises part of its value, rather than part of the company itself. In the twenty-first century, much of the value of a company may exist in intangible assets like data and intellectual property. We have learned with Big Tech corporations that they can have minimal physical presence within a jurisdiction but have an enormous impact. Real entity and institutional theories of the modern company most usefully identify, recognise and describe the reality of the impact of the modern company as an entity as it operates in the world.

V. THE PERSONA OF THE CORPORATE ENTITY

As the company based on the Corporate Fund initially contributed by shareholders operates, it acquires a form of intangible persona connected with its externally perceived reputation and brand. The intangible persona will relate to the activities of the company as it operates in the world. As the company is a separate legal entity from its shareholders, that persona attaches to the modified *persona ficta* containing the Corporate Fund.

What distinguishes the persona of a modern company from the persona that institutional or organisational groupings of natural persons like cities, nations, or clubs might develop? This persona or form of group personality should be differentiated from the status of the modern company as a *persona ficta* or artificial legal person. Speculatively, as the modern company is a separate entity that is an artificial legal person, the persona might attach more closely to the modern company than other forms of organisation that are not legal persons. People come and go from organisations. While the basis and nature of a partnership changes if one partner leaves the partnership, the artificial legal person based on the Corporate Fund remains constant.

VI. THE MODERN COMPANY AS A FIRM

Institutional and real entity theories recognise that the collective decisions and energies of natural persons connected with a company lead to its developing a corporate persona. The corporate persona develops after incorporation, as the company operates in the world. The energies of the natural persons who serve in the capacities of employees and agents acting in and on behalf of the company lead to the growth of the reputation and brand of the company. These are all aspects of its corporate persona. That reputation is not wholly attached to any natural persons connected with the company, even though reputation and brand derive in part from the actions of all of those natural persons. Instead, the persona transcends the people connected with the company and is attached to the *persona ficta*.

What about employees? Employees contribute knowledge and skills to the company. The company derives value from employees, both individually and collectively, that is part of the entity and which ultimately becomes part of the Corporate Fund.

Economics is founded on market forces and classical economics on transactions between individuals. Coase's question in the theory of the firm in 1937 was why, therefore, do firms exist at all? His answer was that it is cheaper at times to direct employees rather than negotiate and enforce separate contracts for each transaction.[21]

Specifying all that is required of a business relationship is difficult. For that reason, some contracts are necessarily 'incomplete'.[22] In Oliver Williamson's transaction cost economics, the firm is a governance structure. As companies grow in size, it becomes more efficient for firms to undertake transactions internally rather than externally. Once the firm reaches a certain size, though, this dynamic changes, and it may then become cheaper to undertake contracts externally.[23]

Alfred Chandler argued against the analysis of the firm as being through transactions by the firm:

> I am convinced that the unit of analysis must be the firm, rather than the transactions or contractual relations entered into by the firm. Only by focusing on the firm can microeconomic theory explain why this legal, contracting, transacting entity has been the instrument in capitalist economies for carrying out the processes of production and distribution, for increasing productivity and for propelling economic growth and transformation. Only by focusing on the firm can theory predict the firm's continuing role as an instrument of economic growth and transformation, and assist in developing policies and procedures for maintaining industrial productivity and competitiveness in an increasingly global economy.[24]

[21] RH Coase, 'The Nature of the Firm' (1937) 4 *Economica* 386; RH Coase, 'The Problem of Social Cost' (1960) 3 *Journal of Law and Economics* 1.

[22] OD Hart, 'Incomplete Contracts and the Theory of the Firm' in OE Williamson and SG Winter (eds), *The Nature of the Firm Origins: Evolution, and Development* (Oxford University Press, 1993) 138.

[23] OE Williamson, 'Transaction-Cost Economics: The Governance of Contractual Relations' (1979) 22 *Journal of Law and Economics* 233.

[24] AD Chandler, 'Organizational Capabilities and the Economic History of the Industrial Enterprise' (1992) *Journal of Economic Perspectives* 79, 99. It is clear that Chandler was writing about the modern corporation.

Chandler, therefore, considered the firm itself to be more significant than just a transacting party.

For Armen A Alchian and Harold Demsetz, the firm is the central contractor in a team production process. Measuring the contribution of each member to the work of the team, and therefore allocating rewards to team members fairly, is difficult. Thus it is challenging to put tasks out to the market when the output results from a team effort. So the role of the firm is to act as both coordinator and monitor of the team.[25] Margaret M Blair and Lynn A Stout, in a team production theory of company law, argue that shareholders should not be preferred over other stakeholder groups like employees who make firm-specific investments.[26]

What do we mean when we talk about a firm? The theory of the firm is agnostic about the legal form of the firm. However, it is suggested that the legal form that the firm takes is of fundamental importance. Commentators may be operating with differing conceptions about what a firm is. A partnership is contractually based on its partners. The contractual Joint Stock Company was contractually based on shareholders. The modern company is a separate legal entity from its shareholders based on the Corporate Fund. Is each of these legal forms the same sort of firm?

The modern company is a *persona ficta* severed from its shareholders. The role of shareholders in the general meeting does not make shareholders part of the company, any more than directors participating in the other decision-making body as part of the board are thereby part of the company. Recognising that severance compels us to ask whether the internal transactions of the company are synonymous with the internal transactions of a firm like a partnership that includes its owners as participants. Whether the legal form of the firm is either based on persons or separate from them would seem to be primarily important when answering this question. In fact, if the modern company is a personified Corporate Fund that is an artificial legal person, how can it undertake transactions internally? The modern company is fundamentally different from the partnership, which, as a firm, can have transactions between individual partners, and between individual partners and third parties. In other words, the modern company is itself a legal person. One of its attributes is the ability to transact *as* a legal person. The *persona ficta* is itself a contracting party, whereas in a partnership, one participant contracts on behalf of the other participants.

Chandler and the team production theorists are, it is suggested, writing about the modern company rather than the partnership when they write about the firm. Similarly, referring to the company as a nexus *for* contracts that encloses key characteristics assumes that the company does not contain persons.

[25] AA Alchian and H Demsetz, 'Production, Information Costs, and Economic Organization' (1972) 62 *American Economic Review* 777, 782ff.

[26] MM Blair and LA Stout, 'A Team Production Theory of Corporate Law' (1999) 85 *Virginia Law Review* 247, 288, 305.

Referring to a company as a nexus of contracts is no mere semantic difference. To Coase, and Williamson and others, firms include their employees. Sitting behind that depiction is an understanding of the modern company as just a legal fiction that has no reality beyond the legal dimension. Like the partnership, the contractual conception of the company includes persons. To paraphrase Maitland, when you crack open a partnership or contractual company, you find a firm made up of contract-bound men. When you crack open the artificial legal person, you do not find people, you find a Corporate Fund. The fact that the Corporate Fund holds the interests of shareholders as initial capital contributed does, it is suggested, privilege shareholders over other participants in the team production.

VII. THE MODERN COMPANY AS AN ORGANISATION

In a review of Meir Dan-Cohen's *Organizational Jurisprudence*, Richard B Stewart agreed with Dan-Cohen's criticism of the failure of current legal theory to take sufficient account of the organisation:

> [P]revailing legal theory is ultimately based on a two-tier conception of society that comprehends only individuals and government. This model of political individualism tends either to personify organizations, investing them with the same rights and responsibilities as individuals or to dissolve them into a mere aggregation of individuals that lacks independent jurisprudential significance. This approach, however, fails to address the distinctive and important characteristics of organisations such as corporations.[27]

Baums traces that rejection back to the French Revolution and 'the abrupt and radical abolition of all privileged guilds, corporations, and intermediary associations between the individual and the State'.[28] The French Revolution in 1789 meant that a *société anonyme* of the French Code de Commerce of 1808 transitioned from being a chartered corporation exempted from applying general laws to

> a *société* based on a partnership contract between its members like other forms of private partnerships … The principle of equality, the demand of the physiocrats for the freedom of the business under the same laws for everybody as well as negative experiences with chartered companies fostered this development.[29]

One rationalisation is to separate the understanding of the company at the moment of incorporation from its ongoing operation in the world. At the moment of incorporation the modern company is an artificial legal person based on a Corporate Fund seeded by the capital of shareholders. As the company

[27] RB Stewart, 'Organizational Jurisprudence' (1987) 101 *Harvard Law Review* 371, 371.
[28] Baums (n 13) 4.
[29] ibid 4.

operates in the world, the artificial legal person contracts and transacts for value, with those forms of value becoming part of the entity. Employees are not part of the company in their private capacities. Does that mean that employees are part of the corporate entity in their working lives? At least as conceptualised in this book, the entity, like the *persona ficta*, exists in the abstract, separate from natural persons with the entity comprised of forms of value.

Employees do, however, become part of an organisation. The modern company differs from other firms and organisations because the central contracting and transacting party is a single artificial legal person. Does that firm and organisation, with the *persona ficta* at its centre, include employees?

Before Berle and Means identified the phenomenon they termed 'separation of ownership and control' in large corporations, Walther Rathenau described what was happening in large German corporations. Rathenau was an industrialist and political essayist. He was responsible for the organisation of the German war economy during the First World War, and later became German Foreign Minister in the Weimar Republic.[30] Rathenau describes German corporations as depersonalised – their own entity. Corporations have a concentration of power and a wide variety of interests. There are 'owners', workers, consumers and those in control, with a constant struggle to make this power the servant of the bulk of individuals it affects.

Germany responded by introducing co-determination on boards in the 1920s. At that time, the legal doctrine that the company was an 'enterprise as such' ('*Unternehmen an sich*') meant it was not the property of shareholders and therefore should not be charged with pursuing their interests exclusively. It should also pursue the interests of its employees, creditors, suppliers, clients and the nation as a whole. It is the social entity conception of the corporation set out by Chancellor Allen and discussed in chapter 1.

The expression of the obligation in the Stock Corporation Act in 1937 stated that 'the management board has under its own responsibility to lead the corporation in such a way as [promotes] the welfare of the enterprise and its followers [*Gefolgschaft*; employees] as well as the common benefit for the nation and the Reich'.[31] The fact that the doctrine found its legal expression in a Stock Corporation Act promulgated during the Nazi Reich may have affected the wider dissemination and consideration of its application to large corporations outside Germany.

Within Germany, the principle survives, but in a modified form, where only employees are involved in governance. Corporations have two-tier boards, with a supervisory board that includes employee representation. The management board has management responsibility. It cannot be instructed by either the supervisory board or the shareholders' meeting. The management board is charged with acting in the 'interest of the enterprise' (*Unternehmensinteresse*).

[30] ibid 6.
[31] Quoted in § 70(1) Stock Corporation Act of 1 October 1937 (as cited in Baum (n 13) 6).

Rather than the maximisation of shareholder value being the primary goal, the focus is on the value of the enterprise in the interests of all stakeholders.[32]

The German conception considers that in companies that have employees, those employees become part of the corporation as an organisation. However, in German law the unique position of shareholders is ignored. The conception of the corporation underpinning German company law does not appear to recognise the existence of the Corporate Fund holding the interests of shareholders. Speculatively, the influence of Gierke may mean that the Roman and canon law *persona ficta* conception may be less significant. Nevertheless, by expressly charging the management board to focus on the interests of the entity, the legislation does set the obligations of the management board in a way that will ensure shareholders are enriched as the forms of value in the entity (and resultingly share value) increase.

The common law modern company based on the *persona ficta* does not include employees in the same way as the German corporation does. Employees are part of the organisation. They might even be part of a firm, with the company as a *persona ficta* at its centre as a nexus for contracts. But employees are not part of the entity. Like the the *persona ficta*, the entity exists in the abstract, separate from all natural persons.

VIII. THE MODERN COMPANY AS AN ENTITY

In the United States in the late nineteenth century, the emergence of the modern corporate form led to the rapid rise of the management corporation. These were large multi-tiered entities that performed multiple tasks of production and marketing, containing hierarchies of salaried executives.[33] Shareholders no longer involved themselves in management. That phenomenon was identified by Berle and Means as separation of ownership from control.[34] It is discussed in chapter 11.

Karl Marx had identified the phenomenon at an earlier time. By the nineteenth century, when Marx was writing, the capitalist mode of production had reached a point where supervision work, entirely separate from ownership of capital, was available. Marx recognised that the wages of management for the manager were isolated from the profits of the enterprise in cooperative factories and companies, and this separation was constant. Companies, in general, had an increasing tendency to separate management work from ownership of capital. Hence, a manager who had no entitlement to capital performed all the

[32] Baum (n 13) 7.

[33] WW Bratton, 'The New Economic Theory of the Firm: Critical Perspectives from History' (1989) 41 *Stanford Law Review* 1471, 1475, 1487.

[34] AA Berle and GC Means, *The Modern Corporation and Private Property*, rev edn (Harcourt, Brace & World, 1968).

real functions of the functioning capitalist, with the capitalist (the shareholder) disappearing as superfluous from the production process.[35]

These US management corporations were capable of monopolistic control of industries. By 1890, three-quarters of the wealth of the United States was controlled by corporations.[36] The phenomenon of enclosure and aggregation of value within the *persona ficta* mirrored the dominance of the English East India Company after 1657, and mirrors the twenty-first-century dominance of Big Tech corporations like Amazon that enclose data as a form of value.

Oliver Weinstein argued that the firm forms a coherent whole, with skills and organisational learning fundamentally social and collective. Weinstein identified four characteristics that are features of this collective dimension:

(1) The capacities and knowledge of the organisation are greater than the sum of the knowledge of the people who work for or who are connected with the organisation. 'The skills of the firm exist, replicate and develop, even though the individuals that make up the firm change and its structures evolve.'[37]
(2) The skills and knowledge of each participant, as fragments of the knowledge and skills of the organisation, can only be significant and effective within a particular context, which is related to the skills and knowledge of other participants.
(3) The processes of learning and production of knowledge are based on shared codes, beliefs and representations: 'any form of durable organisational learning requires mechanisms for the codification of knowledge and interaction procedures'.[38]
(4) The organisational architecture (the organisation's structure and its system of relations) is necessary for organisational capabilities.[39]

The collective dimension aligns with real entity theory, where it is recognised that the sum is greater than the parts.

The skills and organisational learning contributed by employees provide value to the entity. Its legal form facilitates the codification of knowledge and the development of organisational architecture and systems. Fragments of knowledge and skills contributed by employees become part of the entity. The potential longevity of the modern company, existing in perpetuity, when compared with natural persons and with legal forms such as partnerships based on natural persons, means that the company as a legal form is better equipped to

[35] K Marx, *Das Kapital*, vol III (Verlag von Otto Meissner, 1894) ch 23, 'Interest and Profit of Enterprise'.
[36] MJ Horwitz, '*Santa Clara* Revisited: The Development of Corporate Theory' (1986) 88 *West Virginia Law Review* 173, 180, 185–86.
[37] O Weinstein, 'The Current State of the Economic Theory of the Firm: Contractual, Competence-based and Beyond' in Y Biondi, A Canziani, T Kirat (eds), *The Firm as an Entity: Implications for Economics, Accounting and the Law* (Routledge, 2007) 42–43.
[38] ibid 42–43.
[39] ibid.

capture or extract these forms of value from its employees over time. Longevity matters, because greater value will be aggregated and realised over time.

What is considered to be value may change over time. We live in the information age. Anne Branscomb argues that information, in particular personal information, is the primary asset in advanced economies. New technologies give value to previously worthless aggregations of information that are now worth more than the sum of their parts.[40]

The modern company is also equipped to capture the value from the persona consisting of attributes of the company perceived externally, such as reputation and brand. However, unlike some other forms of value like, for example, property rights in land the company owns, deriving value from the persona depends on the ongoing existence of the entity operating in the world. If a company is liquidated, if it ceases to exist as a dynamic entity and as a *persona ficta*, the forms of value attached to the persona may be lost. Also, the value connected to brand and reputation can be lost if the persona, which is how the company is perceived externally, is found not to be an authentic representation of the company as an organisation. For example, a company with a reputation for sustainable practices that is exposed for dumping toxic waste will lose reputational value in its persona. The loss of value in the persona may exceed the former reputational value of the persona.

The work of Alfred Chandler on nineteenth-century US corporations graphically illustrated how the modern company did not just capture value from employees and other corporate participants but, through scale and scope, was able to generate wealth to a level never seen before. The epoch was called the Gilded Age for that reason. The wealth-generation potential of the corporation may have been realised once it acquired the modern form. Chandler writes about the period from the 1880s, when management corporations first appeared in the United States, through to the Second World War. It may be drawing too long a bow to attribute the successes of, for example, Standard Oil solely to the modern corporate form. But that re-emergence made perpetual growth possible, and the capture of organisational capabilities and other forms of value in the dynamic entity, as well as valorisation of that value through the Corporate Fund for investing shareholders.

The entity's status as a *persona ficta* that could exist in perpetuity made possible scope and scale over time. Chandler shows how the distinctive feature of firms in the new capital-intensive industries of the late nineteenth century was their ability to use new production technologies to exploit advantages of scale and scope in a way that firms in older labour-intensive industries could not. As Chandler depicted it:

> The individuals come and go, the organization remains. On the basis of these capabilities many of the enterprises that a century ago helped to fashion the Second

[40] AW Branscomb, *Who Owns Information? From Privacy to Public Access* (Basic Books, 1994) 4.

> Industrial Revolution have prospered and grown during a century of global wars, deep economic depressions, dramatic political changes and continuing profound technological transformations.[41]

Chandler identified four attributes of the firm as an entity from the theoretical literature. (As discussed previously, when referring to 'firms', Chandler clearly meant modern corporations.) The firm is a legal entity, an administrative (or managerial) entity (because teams of managers must coordinate and monitor its different activities), a productive entity ('a pool of physical facilities, of learned skills and liquid capital')[42] and, finally, 'the primary instrument in capitalist economics for the production and distribution of current goods and services and for the planning and allocation for future production and distribution'.[43] Weinstein added a fifth attribute, noting that firms are primarily an instrument for the valorisation of capital. Firms are a financial entity, a bundle of non-human assets subject to a unified control right.[44] Weinstein's categorisation of the financial entity as the repository for non-human assets is similar to the depiction of the Corporate Fund and the entity set out in this book.

IX. THE ACCOUNTING ENTITY

The legal separation of capital from investors when the company was recognised as a separate legal entity from its shareholders, first in the seventeenth century, in the English East India Company and other business corporations, and then in the late nineteenth century, was 'supported (or perhaps led) by the notion of the business as a separate accounting entity'.[45] The alchemy of accounting through double-entry bookkeeping led to the legal alchemy that conceived of the modern company's existing as a legal entity even though it did not necessarily have a physical or 'real' counterpart.

The word 'company' was originally a collective noun describing a combination of natural persons. William Shakespeare was part of a company of players. To lawyers, who reason using words, the fact that the word 'company' means a collective of human beings may have delayed recognition that the modern company is a *persona ficta* based on a Corporate Fund that, at the moment of incorporation, exists separately from its shareholders and all persons. For accountants, the idea of the company as a financial entity involves less of a paradigm shift: some accountants have long practised entity accounting.

[41] Chandler (n 24) 87.
[42] ibid 79.
[43] ibid.
[44] Weinstein (n 37) 45.
[45] Cooke (n 3) 48.

Entity accounting treats the company as an entity that is separate for accounting purposes. One paper from *The Accounting Review* describes the economic entity as

> an aggregate of assets, directed by human intelligence and effort, committed to, and engaged in, an economic undertaking. By assets we mean property and rights in property, whether real or personal, tangible or intangible.[46]

In entity accounting:

> [T]here is no real owner of the economic entity, but instead an entity itself, which maintains relationships with various (and usually conflicting) groups … [T]he responsibility of management (which is the entity's governing group) must be not to any one of those groups but to the entity itself. This is the long-run best interests of all of the groups. …
>
> The responsibilities of management are, therefore …: (1) To maintain the economic strength of the entity so that it may continue to function into the indefinite future, and (2) to maximize its ability to produce goods or render services (ie, to fulfil the entity's purpose in even existing). These are not responsibilities of management to the stockholders, nor to creditors, nor to its employees, nor to society as a whole. They are management's responsibilities to the entity.[47]

Integrated reporting, which combines information taken from financially orientated reports prepared in the traditional way with the material parts of corporate sustainability reports related to stakeholder issues, is a modern example of entity accounting.[48]

As discussed in chapter 13, at the moment of incorporation, a company is a *persona ficta* that exists separately from its shareholders and from all natural persons, with its status as a juridical person derived from the state through incorporation by founding shareholders following a process set out in a statute.[49] That *persona ficta* on incorporation has the right to call the capital, subscribed for by shareholders, that seeds the Corporate Fund. As a juridical person, that company has attributes, such as the ability to enter into contracts and own property.

[46] WML Raby, 'The Two Faces of Accounting' (1959) 34 *The Accounting Review* 452, 453 (emphasis omitted).

[47] ibid 454–55.

[48] See RG Eccles and T Youmans, 'Materiality in Corporate Governance: The Statement of Significant Audiences and Materiality' (2016) 28 *Journal of Applied Corporate Finance* 39. The International Integrated Reporting Council (IIRC) is a global coalition of regulators, investors, companies, standard setters, the accounting profession and non-governmental organisations. Together, this coalition shares the view that communication about value creation should be the next step in the evolution of corporate reporting: '10 Years of the IIRC' (*Integrated Reporting*) at www.integratedreporting.org.

[49] From Maitland, 'its personality must have its commencement in some authoritative act, some declaration of the State's will': Maitland, 'Introduction' in Gierke (n 4) xx.

The fact that the company, as an entity, is separate from other persons may facilitate the separation and extraction of value from the natural persons who work for the company as employees. A Marxist perspective views capitalism and the holders of capital (shareholders) as extracting value from employees, with the company as 'a particularly effective mechanism for achieving this'.[50]

The English East India Company succeeded once it had acquired all the characteristics of the modern company, ultimately outperforming the Dutch East India Company (VOC).[51] After it acquired permanent capital in 1657, the English East India Company experienced an economic boom for the next three decades. Between 1657 and 1691, proprietors received 840 per cent in dividends on their original investment.[52]

As Baskin and Miranti describe it:

> The success of the English East India Company derived from a combination of organizational and financial advantages inherent in the persona ficta form. The Company evolved effective means for concentrating substantial capital that consisted of liabilities of varying maturities supported by a permanent core of transferrable equity shares. Its strong, permanent capital base in turn gave the firm sufficient financial flexibility to be able to exploit economies deriving from an increased scale of operations and a broader scope of trading activities. The creation of an effective administrative structure for coordinating and controlling far-flung business ventures yielded other competitive advantages, including the reduction of agency, information, transportation, and other transaction costs.[53]

Chandler and Williamson argue that the multidivisional firm invented in the United States in the 1920s was an organisational innovation. As discussed in chapter 5, in fact, the English East India Company was a multidivisional firm. That development has been attributed to its monopoly status.[54] It could also be attributed to the form: both the English East India Company after 1657, and US corporations and English companies in the nineteenth century, evolved to become entities that were *persona ficta* based on Corporate Funds equipped to lock in organisational architecture over the long term.

Granted, the success of the English East India Company cannot be attributed just to the legal and accounting form it took after 1657. But the significance of the emergence of permanent capital in the *persona ficta* form in the

[50] L Talbot, *Great Debates in Company Law* (Palgrave Macmillian, 2014) 16 (referring to K Marx, *Capital*, vols 1–3 (Penguin, 2004)).

[51] In the late 17th century, the English East India Co was overshadowed by the VOC. Not until the 1780s did it catch up on the volume of ships. But in country trade, Chaudhuri considers the English East India Co rivalled the Dutch in a period of rapid expansion. In the 18th century, '[t]he East India Company went from strength to strength'. KN Chaudhuri, *The Trading World of Asia and the English East India Company: 1660–1760* (Cambridge University Press, 1978) 82.

[52] ibid 49.

[53] JB Baskin and PJ Miranti Jr, *A History of Corporate Finance* (Cambridge University Press, 1997) 57.

[54] GM Anderson, RE McCormick and RD Tollison, 'The Economic Organization of the English East India Company' (1983) 4 *Journal of Economic Behavior and Organization* 221.

seventeenth century, and its re-emergence in the nineteenth century, making it possible for the corporation to lock in value, should be recognised. The complete legal and accounting separation of capital from natural persons has made possible scope and scale over time.

Supporting the argument that the separation mattered is Chandler's work comparing the English company of the late nineteenth century with its US counterpart. United States corporations grew and prospered compared with their English company counterparts, as discussed in chapter 12. The US corporation achieved legal separation earlier than its English counterpart. As noted in chapter 10, during that late nineteenth century, following general incorporation and statutory limited liability, the English company transitioned. It shifted from the contractual Joint Stock Company form based on shareholders, to its separation as a legal entity and *persona ficta* recognised in *Salomon v Salomon & Co Ltd*[55] in 1897. Separation as a legal entity facilitates a consequential shift in focus by boards. That shift is from current shareholders to the interests of the entity itself. A long-term perspective is possible because the modern company can exist in perpetuity. Chandler shows that pressure by current shareholders before that separation took place, to convert value to dividends, meant in these English companies that the 'three-pronged investment in production, distribution, and management essential to exploit economies of scale and scope' did not occur.[56]

[55] *Salomon v Salomon & Co Ltd* (n 8).

[56] AD Chandler Jr, *Scale and Scope: The Dynamics of Industrial Capitalism* (The Belknap Press of Harvard University Press, 1994) 286.

15

Corporate Governance

I. INTRODUCTION

THE MODERN COMPANY can be considered through multiple lenses. We tend to consider the company using eighteenth- and nineteenth-century legal and economic theory.[1] As set out in this book, the 'second-best' unincorporated contractual form dominated much of the law and discourse during that period, casting a distorted perspective on the modern form. When considering the modern company in the twenty-first century, we can look back further to when the governance principles of business corporations was thrashed out by the generality and the elite in the English East India Company.[2] We can remind ourselves that the power sat with the governing body, with investing shareholders forcing a gradual relinquishing of some power by the governing body. Accountability mechanisms were also developed.

We can also recall the origins of the legal form of the corporation as a body politic. As bodies politic, corporations are powerful and prominent actors in corporate life.[3] John Parkinson highlighted that they make private decisions that have public results. That kind of power should be justified, forming the basis of the argument that corporations must act in the public interest. '[I]t is not the legal qualities of limited liability or separate personality in themselves that justify intervention [by the state], but the concentration of power in private hands that has come about partly as a result of their existence.'[4] Developments rooted in accounting around ESG (Environmental, Social, Governance) disclosures and integrated reporting force companies to identify and set out the externalities they cause as they operate in the world. Protecting society and the environment may require more. These points are explored in the concluding chapter.

Each corporation is also itself a body politic with its own internal system of governance. The focus on economic analysis has led to a one-dimensional picture of corporate governance where 'there can be no privileged or ultimate

[1] S Bottomley, *The Constitutional Corporation: Rethinking Corporate Governance* (Ashgate Publishing, 2007) 11.

[2] That development is set out in in ch 4.

[3] Bottomley (n 1) 36.

[4] JE Parkinson, *Corporate Power and Responsibility: Issues in the Theory of Company Law* (Clarendon Press, 1993) 30, which is also cited in Bottomley (n 1) 48.

analytical framework for studying the complexity of corporate organisations'.[5] Stephen Bottomley identifies four limitations to the application of the solely contractual paradigm to corporate governance. First, complex relationships between many people tend to be reduced to bilateral agreements between legal or economic actors.[6] The organisation is ignored.[7] Second, the economic analysis of corporate governance issues excludes other perspectives.[8] Third, the contractual frameworks are orientated towards end results rather than their impact on the rights or interests of the persons involved.[9] Finally, 'corporations and the things they do are treated as essentially private phenomena', meaning external regulation of corporate activity, or public-law like concepts, must be justified.[10]

Descriptions of general meetings as 'little Parliaments' (in the seventeenth century)[11] and of modern companies as 'little Republics' (by Robert Lowe in the general incorporation debates of the nineteenth century) may therefore be apt if the modern company is a body politic. Considering the internal governance of the company from a constitutional perspective better reflects the origins of corporate governance in the Courts (meetings) of the English East India Company in the seventeenth and eighteenth centuries. The relationship between the two organs of the company, the general meeting and the board, and the extent to which directors are either legally or economically the agents of shareholders, can be re-examined.

II. ARE DIRECTORS THE LEGAL AGENTS OF SHAREHOLDERS?

This book sets out how features drawn from the early corporation and from the Joint Stock Fund were combined in the modern company first in the seventeenth century and then again in companies incorporated pursuant to the general incorporation statutes of the mid-nineteenth century. Corporations were constitutional, and the Joint Stock Fund was contractual and economic. Shareholders have both an economic relationship with the company through their investment of capital in the Joint Stock Fund, and a constitutional relationship with the company as members with rights, including the rights to attend, participate in and vote at the general meeting.

Some shareholder rights are constitutional in nature. Membership rights relate to the right to receive notice of and attend general meetings of the company, to vote for the directors who comprise the board and so forth. As discussed in

[5] Bottomley (n 1) 47.
[6] ibid 30.
[7] ibid 31.
[8] ibid 31.
[9] ibid 32.
[10] ibid 33.
[11] AB Levy, *Private Corporations and Their Control* (Routledge, 1950) 40.

chapters 4 and 5, those constitutional rights were fought for by the generality, the small investors, in the English East India Company in the seventeenth and early eighteenth centuries. Powers were divided constitutionally between the two governance organs: the general meeting and the board. As shown in chapter 12, when the modern form re-emerged in the late nineteenth century, in cases such as *Automatic Self-Cleansing Filter Syndicate Co Ltd v Cuninghame*,[12] the courts enforced the constitutional division of powers in the company by not permitting shareholders to override management decisions allocated to the board.

As discussed in chapter 5, in the governance of the English East India Company in the late seventeenth and early eighteenth centuries, the victories won by the generality in the century before were maintained. Each shareholder had voting rights so long as they had a minimum holding of shares.[13] Quarterly meetings of the 'little Parliaments' were held to hear directors' reports and to vote on corporate policy. In practice the General Court rarely refused to follow the proposals of the governing body.[14] The annual meeting in April regularly attracted over a thousand shareholders, brought together to elect 24 directors to office for 12 months.[15] (Provisions for rotation of directors were never applied, with some directors and governors holding office for long periods.)[16] Directors had to swear an oath they would act in the interests of the shareholders.

Levy summarised the governance of business corporations in the period after the Bubble Act 1720, as follows:

> The structure typical of earlier companies was on the whole maintained. The supreme authority was vested in the General Court (general meeting) of shareholders ... The management was entrusted to the Court of Directors ... The General Court dealt only with matters reserved to it by the charter or by-laws.[17]

As discussed in chapter 12, in the period before it was clear that the company incorporated pursuant to general incorporation statutes was a separate legal entity from its shareholders, questions arose about whether shareholders could at will override management decisions allocated to boards in articles of association or similar. If directors were the legal agents of shareholders, the answer would be that shareholders could override management decisions allocated to boards at will (subject always to the application of the principles of agency law as they affected third parties dealing with the company). The uncertainty arose because it was not clear for a period whether companies incorporated pursuant to general incorporation statutes were contractually based on their

[12] *Automatic Self-Cleansing Filter Syndicate Co Ltd v Cuninghame* [1906] 2 Ch 34 (CA).
[13] Levy (n 11) 27–28.
[14] ibid 40.
[15] N Robins, *The Corporation that Changed the World: How the East India Company Shaped the Modern Multinational*, 2nd edn (Pluto Press, 2012) 27.
[16] Levy (n 11) 28.
[17] ibid 51.

shareholders in the same way as a contractual Joint Stock Company. The question was settled in 1902 in *Automatic Self-Cleansing Filter Syndicate Co Ltd v Cuninghame*.[18] The English Court of Appeal said that once the power had been delegated to the directors, the shareholders could not take it back again (other than presumably prospectively and constitutionally though the articles of association). Constitutional decision making was upheld. It is therefore not tenable to argue that directors of modern companies are the legal agents of shareholders. Shareholders as members participate in the decision-making organ of the general meeting, and directors participate in the decision-making organ of the board. Each organ is allocated decision-making powers that cannot be overridden.

In the modern company, directors are not legally the agents of the shareholders. Economically, though, directors could be viewed as agents of the shareholders. However, shareholders give up ownership of the capital they contribute to the company while the company is a *persona ficta* in return for a bundle of rights. Thus, arguments that the directors are the economic agents of the shareholders while the company exists as an artificial legal person, can also be tested.

III. ARE DIRECTORS THE ECONOMIC AGENTS OF SHAREHOLDERS?

In a seminal 1976 article, Jensen and Meckling drew on the theory of the firm, as well as theories of agency, finance and property rights, to argue that corporate governance mechanisms are needed in modern corporations to monitor those in control and protect the interests of shareholders as principals.[19] Other concerns, described as agency costs, are the imbalance of information between management as controllers and the shareholders as owners.[20] The article is based on a contractual understanding of the modern company based on shareholders, with directors and managers the economic agents of those shareholders.

The article was prefaced by a quote from Adam Smith, which says, in part, that directors'

> being the managers rather of other people's money than of their own, it cannot well be expected, that they should watch over it with the same anxious vigilance with which the partners in a private copartnery frequently watch over their own.[21]

Jensen and Meckling's work has provided the foundation for much law-and-economics and finance scholarship, and has also influenced understanding of

[18] *Automatic Self-Cleansing Filter Syndicate Co Ltd* (n 12).

[19] MC Jensen and WH Meckling, 'Theory of the Firm: Managerial Behavior, Agency Costs and Ownership Structure' (1976) 3 *Journal of Financial Economics* 305.

[20] Agency theory does not differentiate between directors and executive management.

[21] A Smith, *An Inquiry into the Nature and Causes of the Wealth of Nations*, vol 3, 5th edn (W Strahan and T Cadell, 1789) 124.

corporate law and the modern company itself.[22] Smith called directors 'managers', but the theory is known as 'agency theory', because directors are assumed to be the economic agents of shareholders. Applications of agency theory use corporate law and governance to align the interests of directors and executive management with those of current shareholders, treating the entity as the private property of current shareholders.

Strategies that enforce an economic agency model on the relationship between investing shareholders and directors as managers can be problematic. Closely aligning the interests of the entity solely with the short-term interests of current shareholders has the potential to lead to management decisions that will damage the interests of corporate constituents like employees, society more widely and even the longer-term interests of shareholders themselves. Incentivising corporate management to maximise profits for current shareholders in the short term may be the expense of prioritising the long-term value creation possible with the perpetual company. Excessive risk taking may be encouraged, potentially damaging the economic value of the entity and therefore the Corporate Fund that holds the interests of shareholders. Risk may also threaten the continued existence of the company – it may fail financially, its legitimacy may be questioned if it is believed it has lost its social licence to operate, or regulation may threaten its very viability.

A longer-term perspective has not been problematic for current shareholders through history. In fact the reverse is true. In the periods through history when that shift has taken place, corporations have become unparalleled aggregators and generators of value. The modern company or corporation can be so potent a form that in the late nineteenth century, antitrust (competition) law was a response by the US legislature to the unrestrained growth of corporations. Twenty-first-century tech corporations are equally dominant, with indications of litigious or legislative responses again from states.

Why has loss of management focus on their short-term interests paradoxically enriched shareholders? Modern agency theory was a response to the managerialism of the mid-twentieth century, when the shirking and self-maximising behaviour identified by Adam Smith seemed to have become a feature of the management of US corporations. That may not be the 'fault' of the modern corporate form per se; it may be that boards in that period were captured by the interests of senior management.

One of the flaws of agency theory is that it risks ignoring the role of boards in companies by conflating boards with senior management. The use of the term 'management' by Adam Smith does not help. As discussed earlier, until the twentieth century and the emergence of management science, the word 'managing'

[22] SSRN shows that the article has been cited 4,379 times, with Jensen's work having been cited over 10,000 times. See MC Jensen and WH Meckling, 'Theory of the Firm: Managerial Behavior, Agency Costs and Ownership Structure' *Social Science Research Network* (1998) at www.papers.ssrn.com/sol3/papers.cfm?abstract_id=94043.

related to directing and supervising. Boards are a constitutional organ setting the direction for the company. Problems arise when boards do not manage the company in its interests as an entity. Malign control of boards by senior management could indeed lead to the shirking and the self-maximising behaviour that Adam Smith predicted, harming the interests of the entity and therefore the shareholders. However, the constitutional internal governance structure of the modern company with its accountability mechanisms, if operated well and combined with external monitoring by gatekeepers and secondary markets, may be enough to ensure this does not happen.

As Smith says, directors are the managers of other people's money. That money is shareholders' capital held in the Corporate Fund. While the *persona ficta* is extant, the Corporate Fund forms the basis of the entity. One of the roles of boards is to protect the corporation from being driven by the interests of one or more stakeholder constituents rather than in the interests of the entity itself in the long term. Current shareholders are a stakeholder constituent, albeit a constituent with rights attached to their shares, and senior management is also a constituent, as a class of employee.

As well as the agency problem, Adam Smith was concerned about short-termism. A perpetual perspective is possible if boards ensure that the company acts in its own interests as an entity in perpetuity, rather than on behalf of and in the interests of its current shareholders or current management. Strengthening the overall management powers of boards, with ex-ante obligations to the company, and ex-post accountability to shareholders if those obligations are not met, combined with direction and oversight management by boards independent of corporate constituents, has been a mechanism that has in periods through the history of corporations facilitated the operation of the company for the long term.

Mechanisms used to resolve the perceived agency problem by aligning the interests of directors and managers with those of current shareholders may be counterproductive and disrupt the governance balance in the modern company that has evolved. Involvement by current shareholders in decision making, by treating directors as the agents of shareholders, may shift to those shareholders' exercising undue influence and even indirect control, leading to short-termism. Short-term incentives for management, linking current shareholder interests around profitability with manager remuneration, may have contributed to short-termism and excessive risk taking in the period leading up to the 2008 Global Financial Crisis.

The current dominance of agency theory, and the predominance of contractual theories that focus on corporate participants rather than the corporate entity itself, may have skewed corporate decision making. Further, that dominance may have obscured the underlying fundamental characteristic of the company that has enriched investors and entrepreneurs since the English East India Company acquired permanent capital in 1657: that the modern company is a *persona ficta* based on a Corporate Fund that has the potential to operate as an entity in perpetuity.

Most often, with application of a contractual paradigm, the separation of 'ownership' (in shareholders) from control (in managers) is pathologised as an agency problem for shareholders, with that problem mitigated by aligning the interests of controlling managers with those of current 'owner' shareholders. Those interests are assumed to be either profit maximisation or financial value maximisation, often in the short term.[23]

Returning to Chancellor Allen's framing of the debate around the nature of companies set out in chapter 1, we can see that the modern company is not in fact the private property of shareholders, or at least not directly. Instead, shareholders own transferrable shares that have bundles of rights attached to them. Direct proprietary rights over the Corporate Fund are only realisable by shareholders once the *persona ficta* ceases to exist on the liquidation of the company. Even then, those collective rights of shareholders are subject to the rights of creditors of the company.

While the company is an extant *persona ficta*, shareholder' rights attached to shares are constitutional (for example, the right to vote at general meetings as a member of one of the governing bodies of the company) and financial (the right to receive a pro-rata share of dividends when value is valorised by the company). Potential exists for the governance of companies to operate constitutionally. Shareholders collectively can hold the board accountable through the election and removal of directors, and through active participation in the general meeting. Shareholders are heterogeneous. As members of a company, shareholders can constitutionally challenge decision making by boards that may harm the prospects of the entity in the long term or cause the entity to create externalities such as environmental damage. Shareholders may have an ethical obligation to participate actively as members. Although the days are gone where more than a thousand shareholders would gather together at Leadenhall for quarterly meetings of the English East India Company, virtual meetings may again make it practicable for the shareholder voice to be heard.

Boards' overly focusing on the perceived property rights of current shareholders, when understood to be solely financial as profit maximisation in the short term, can mean a failure to realise the potential of the perpetual corporation in the long term. Shareholders elect a board entrusted with control over the Corporate Fund. The primary obligation of the board is to act in the *interests* of the shareholders, which, in a modern company with permanent capital, are held in the Corporate Fund that becomes an entity as it operates in the world. A perpetual perspective adopted by boards facilitates a realisation of the potential inherent in the perpetual *persona ficta* in the ultimate interests of its shareholders.

[23] Jensen and Meckling (n 22).

IV. BERLE AND MEANS

In *The Modern Corporation and Private Property*, Berle and Means described control, like sovereignty, its counterpart in the political sphere, as an elusive concept, as 'power can rarely be sharply segregated or clearly defined'.[24] Gevurtz tracks a history of boards running parallel with the history of corporations. The vesting of normative managerial control in a board or equivalent governing body has been a defining characteristic of corporations since their inception.[25] Control allocated to governing bodies in business corporations pre-dated the general meeting. It has continued uninterrupted in US corporate law through general incorporation statutes. The statutory allocation of management powers to boards as the default is now the practice in most common law jurisdictions except England, where power is allocated in the constitution of the company.

Although management control over the entity is allocated to boards, boards have not always exercised that control in the interests of the company. Corporations have been operated either in the interests of current shareholders, with the risk of resulting short-termism, or in the interests of senior corporate employees, with the risk of resulting problems like the shirking and self-interested behaviour by managers identified by agency theory.[26] How might control of the corporate entity by the board contribute to modern companies' realisation of their potential? What checks and balances might be put in place to protect the interests of the company, and therefore its shareholders and wider stakeholders?

In a structural and normative sense, the board controls the overall management of the modern company,[27] with' management' having the wider meaning of 'direction'. As the decision-making organ that sits at the company's apex, the board animates the inanimate *persona ficta*, making critical strategic decisions. The board navigates the corporate entity through the world with oversight over its strategic direction. The board decides how much of the entity's value should be valorised, separated and distributed to shareholders.

Does the *persona ficta* form offer potential for the board to do more? Berle and Means' *The Modern Corporation and Private Property*[28] was the most influential book written on the corporation in the twentieth century. The authors focused on the *consequences* of the (perceived) loss of management control by shareholders, and on the role and purpose of the corporation. Berle and Means

[24] AA Berle and GC Means, *The Modern Corporation and Private Property*, rev edn (Harcourt, Brace & World, 1968) 66.

[25] FA Gevurtz, 'The Historical and Political Origins of the Corporate Board of Directors' (2004) 33 *Hofstra Law Review* 89, 121.

[26] Agency theory focuses on shareholders as principals, with management as their agents; corporate law focuses on resolving the resulting agency problems. Jensen and Meckling (n 19) 305.

[27] SM Bainbridge, *The New Corporate Governance in Theory and Practice* (Oxford University Press, 2008) 4.

[28] Berle and Means (n 24).

asked in whose interest corporations should be operated. Whilst the traditional logic of private property dictated that it should be the shareholders,[29] the authors recognised that the role of shareholders had shifted in the modern company.

For Berle and Means, corporations started small and then got bigger, meaning that, originally, shareholders were both the owners of the company and the owners of the assets held in the company. This is not correct. As set out in this book, in the first cycle of development of the modern company, business corporations were historically used to raise investment for big enterprises. In England in the nineteenth century, modern companies started big and were adapted as a business form by small enterprises previously operated as partnerships, primarily to obtain the benefits of limited liability. However, for a period in the nineteenth century, before the accounting and legal separation of the company from its shareholders, shareholders were considered to be owners of both the company and the assets of the company.

Berle and Means highlighted that by 1932, shareholders no longer had 'title' to the property of the company. Shareholders could benefit through participation in the corporation. The role of shareholders could therefore be described as constitutional. With this transition, Berle and Means identified that the role of management had shifted. From a technical (profit-making) role, which included the distribution of profits,[30] the power of management had expanded. Management could therefore exercise its power in a way that was not in the apparent interests of current shareholders.[31] Although this shift seemed to legalise the diversion of profits to management as the controlling group, powers had to be used to benefit the whole corporation.[32] Thus, there could be situations where management seized a portion of profits and shielded them from current shareholders, saying it was 'in the company's best interests'.[33]

In contrast with Adam Smith's idea of wealth focused on tangible things, Berle and Means refer to passive wealth in shares (also identified by Karl Marx) and active wealth.[34] Active wealth in the modern company is a complex set of relationships between property, workers and consumers. Echoing real entity theory, Berle and Means describe the modern company as an organism that only has value if it continues to function[35] – with success coming from coordination, not personal initiative.[36] In this book, these characteristics are linked with the operation of the entity in the world as an organisation, and the generation of value.

[29] ibid 294.
[30] ibid 294. See ch 4 for a discussion of the change in the role of management in the English East India Co and in the English company throughout the 19th century.
[31] Berle and Means (n 24) 295.
[32] ibid 295. See the discussion of the evolution of duty of good faith in ch 6.
[33] ibid 295.
[34] ibid 304–05.
[35] ibid 306.
[36] ibid.

Berle and Means argued for a new concept of the corporation focusing on corporate enterprise. They identified that modern corporations[37] have a concentration of power and a wide variety of interests, with a constant struggle to make this power the servant of the bulk of the individuals it affects. The same kind of struggle led to the reformation of the Catholic Church in religious power, and constitutional law regarding political power.[38] How to make the bulk of capital serve the bulk of the people is the same question that communism and socialism were trying to answer.[39]

How was the demand for public benefit to be met? Berle and Means concluded that a convincing system of community obligations would need to be worked out, but that societal interests supersede the passive property right of shareholders. For example, fair wages, security to employees, reasonable service to the public and stabilisation of business divert a portion of the profits away from passive property owners. In the twenty-first century, we would add externalities such as protecting the environment to the list of societal interests, and class these as ESG (environmental, social, governance) goods. The Total Value Framework puts a tangible financial value on the material negative and positive impacts a company has.[40] The community would accept that these societal goods outweigh the profit maximisation interests of shareholders.[41]

In Chancellor's Allen's categorisation, the modern company was understood either to be the private property of current shareholders or to be a social entity. A focus on the entity itself could change the understanding of the board's role to one that aligns more closely with Berle and Means' original thesis than applications of agency theory. The caveat is that the entity is based on a Corporate Fund seeded by the capital of shareholders, meaning that shareholders have constitutional and financial rights that distinguish them from other stakeholders in the modern company.

V. ENTITY PRIMACY

In 1932, Berle and Means presciently predicted that corporations would become the dominant social institution in society, meaning that corporations should act more like states, with corporation law the new constitutional law and businesspeople the new statesmen.[42] In the twenty-first century, Berle and Means' prediction of the dominance of corporations has indisputably come to pass, as we live through a second gilded age dominated by technology corporations.

[37] ibid 309–10.
[38] ibid 310.
[39] ibid 310.
[40] C Penner, 'A New Way of Seeing Value' (*Harvard Law School Forum on Corporate Governance*, 24 September 2021) at corpgov.law.harvard.edu/2021/09/24/a-new-way-of-seeing-value/.
[41] Berle and Means (n 24) 312.
[42] ibid 313.

Berle and Means set out a compelling case for operating the modern company as a social entity. However, no account is taken of the modern corporate entity's being based on a Corporate Fund seeded by the financial contributions of shareholders. Although shareholders can no longer be said to own the modern company, shareholders, through ownership of shares, have constitutional and financial rights that other corporate constituents or stakeholders do not have. Shareholders do not have direct management control rights, but they do have ultimate authority, in the sense that they can appoint and remove the directors on the board. They can end the existence of the entity and the *persona ficta*, crystallising and realising the value of the Corporate Fund. It might be naive to believe that investing shareholders would not exercise these rights if they formed the view that the entity was not generating sufficient value over time.

An alternative, but related approach is to accept that the board's fundamental obligation is to act in the company's interests as an entity, rather than in its stakeholders interests per se. That entity is based on the Corporate Fund. Accommodating stakeholders' interests may be legitimate and, in fact, tolerated by investing shareholders if it enhances the entity's value, including its reputation and the protection of its persona,[43] in perpetuity. This gives boards considerable scope to accommodate broader constituent, stakeholder and societal interests in the perpetual interests of the entity.

Paying attention to societal goods may enhance the reputation and, therefore, the persona of the corporation. The persona is a shell or mask protecting the dynamic entity and ensuring the longevity of the artificial legal person. If the entity loses the shell of protection provided by the persona, that value is also lost to shareholders, and the corporation may not survive as a *persona ficta*. Decisions around persona are contextual. In the third decade of the twenty-first century, the societal context in which modern companies are operating means institutional and other investors increasingly expect overt attention be paid to ESG externalities, with ESG shifting beyond disclosure towards measurement of impact, addressing concerns of investors around materiality, impact and long-term financial performance. These forms of value can be measured.[44]

Can boards legitimately distribute value to corporate constituents other than shareholders whilst acting in the entity's interests? Blair and Stout argue that shareholders' interests should not be favoured over those of other corporate stakeholders, and that the role of corporate law is to create value, broadly defined, for all corporate stakeholders.[45] Berle and Means argue that control would be a neutral technocracy where claims by groups in the community are brought, assigning income on the basis of public policy rather than private cupidity.[46]

[43] For a discussion of corporate persona, see MM Blair, 'Corporate Personhood and the Corporate Persona' [2013] *University of Illinois Law Review* 785, 798 and 809–14.

[44] Penner (n 40).

[45] MM Blair and LA Stout, 'A Team Production Theory of Corporate Law' (1999) 85 *Virginia Law Review* 247.

[46] ibid 312.

However, in terms of weighing up relative contributions to the value held by the corporate entity, determining claims based on public policy may be problematic.

Corporate constituents like employees may have legitimate claims to share in the value they contribute to the entity as part of the employment relationship. Adopting a perpetual perspective, providing financial or other benefits to employees may induce loyalty and enhance reputation and, therefore, the company's persona. Companies both compensate for externalities they create by extracting value and enhance their reputation, and therefore value, through growing their personas. The approach adopted by the 'Quaker Companies' around housing and other benefits for workers discussed in chapter 11 may have contributed to the prosperity and longevity of those companies.

VI. SHOULD COMPANIES MAXIMISE WEALTH FOR SHAREHOLDERS?

Stephen Bainbridge distinguishes between the means and ends of corporate governance, arguing that the means should be governance through the board rather than through shareholders. Bainbridge claims that shareholders are the appropriate beneficiaries of directors' fiduciary duties on the 'ends axis'. For Bainbridge, director accountability to maximise shareholder wealth is an essential component of director primacy.[47]

> Along the other axis (the 'Ends Axis'), models can be plotted according to the interests the corporation is said to serve. At one end of the spectrum are models contending that corporations should be run so as to maximise shareholder wealth. At the other end are stakeholder models arguing that directors and managers should consider the interests of all corporate constituencies in making corporate decisions.[48]

The term 'shareholder wealth' could apply to current shareholders, adopting a contractual paradigm, or it could apply to the wealth of shareholders as a class held in the Corporate Fund. Arguments supporting the wealth maximisation of current shareholders as the end of corporate governance may have two bases. They may be predicated on an understanding of companies as based on shareholders, with directors then their agents. Alternatively, these arguments may be based on current shareholders' having the strongest claim for their interests to be equated with the interests of the company as residual claimants. As previously discussed, directors are not the legal agents of shareholders, and few modern commentators would advance that first argument. Nevertheless, an understanding that the modern company is still based on shareholders retains potency,[49] with these ideas having the advantage of apparently being congruent with economically based contractual paradigms like shareholder primacy and

[47] ibid 550.
[48] ibid 549.
[49] P Watts, N Campbell and C Hare, *Company Law in New Zealand*, 2nd edn (LexisNexis, 2016) 230.

agency theory. The congruence is superficial, though. Shareholder primacy arose much later than the contractual conception of the company and is economically based. Proponents argue for the interests of shareholders to be primary either as owners, or as residual claimants. Proponents would not necessarily say that the company is based on its shareholders.[50]

A stronger related argument is that the interests of current shareholders, at least when a company is solvent, should be treated as the interests of the company,[51] either because shareholders are residual claimants or because considering the interests of multiple stakeholders creates indeterminacy and complexity for boards, and risks directors' being accountable to no one.[52]

An argument that current shareholders are residual claimants is flawed. The shareholding of a company can change all the time. Shareholders only have claims if a sequence of events first occurs, with the liquidation of the company and then the meeting of all prior claims of creditors. Current shareholders cannot be assumed to be residual claimants, but shareholders as a class can be.

The indeterminacy and accountability objections, which are governance problems, are stronger. Why should the 'ends' of corporate governance relate to corporate participants, whether shareholders or stakeholders, and not to the interests of the entity itself? Approaches prioritising either current shareholders or all corporate stakeholders risk overemphasising the importance of corporate constituents, when it is the interests of the entity itself that should be the focus. When considering the company's interests and complying with statutory and fiduciary obligations, a board should consider the company as an entity underpinned by a Corporate Fund holding the interests of shareholders, which a board is charged with navigating through the world in perpetuity. Value extends beyond the financial to other forms, such as organisational systems, the corporate entity's persona[53] and ESG value, which can feature as part of the Total Value Framework.[54] The board's role is then to operate the company in the world as an entity, with the end of creating value in perpetuity. Conceiving the ends of the entity in this manner resolves the dichotomous debate on Bainbridge's 'ends axis', between those who argue corporations should be operated for all their stakeholders and those who consider shareholder wealth maximisation to be the ultimate goal.

[50] D Millon, 'Theories of the Corporation' [1990] *Duke Law Journal* 201. Associational thinking, where a company is based on current shareholders, may persist in relation to closely-held and private companies because it appears to make practical sense where shareholders are also directors and with little or no functional separation of ownership and control. But despite the tendency for shareholder directors of companies to treat the company like an incorporated partnership, the law is clear: a company is a separate legal entity from its shareholders.

[51] Watts, Campbell and Hare (n 49) 35.

[52] ibid 230, 386–89; F Dawson, 'Acting in the Best Interests of the Company – For Whom are Directors Trustees?' (1984) 11 *New Zealand Universities Law Review* 68.

[53] See further SM Watson, 'The Corporate Legal Person' (2019) 19 *Journal of Corporate Law Studies* 137; and SM Watson, 'The Corporate Legal Entity as a Fund' [2018] *Journal of Business Law* 467.

[54] Penner (n 40).

History teaches us, first with the English East India Company and then with the form of the modern company that emerged at the end of the nineteenth century, that companies and corporations legally separated from current shareholders and freed from the shackles of short-termism to operate in perpetuity can generate, capture, aggregate and transact for value, which grows the value of the entity and thereby enriches shareholders by increasing the value of their shares.

The modern corporate form facilitated the shift by boards away from acting in the short-term interests of current shareholders towards acting in the interests of the company conceived of as an entity. The shift away from a focus on short-term profit maximisation for current shareholders makes value creation possible for the perpetual corporate entity. The role of boards in creating value in perpetuity need not necessarily mean that value must just be separated as profits for existing shareholders or other current corporate constituents. Uniquely, the modern business corporation can exist in perpetuity long past the lifetimes of current shareholders. Therefore, strategic decisions and actions are available as options to boards that are not available to natural persons or organisations such as partnerships based on natural persons.

Andrew Keay argues that the role of the board encompasses both entity maximisation and sustainability:

> This allows the directors to make decisions which are best for the entity and not for any shareholder or stakeholder. Under [the entity maximisation and sustainability model] the company is not run for the benefit of the shareholders or any other stakeholders, but for itself. So, in making any decisions, the directors must ask: what will benefit the company?[55]

This book has argued that adopting a perpetual perspective maximises the value creation for the entity and therefore the Corporate Fund over time. At the time of writing, evidence is emerging that an increase in stakeholder value by corporations' minimising negative externalities also grows shareholder value. Putting a tangible value on ESG impacts through a data-driven approach can allow those impacts to be identified and tied to long-term value creation. Interestingly, it may also support shareholders' engaging when a problem arises rather than divesting.[56]

VII. OBLIGATIONS OF DIRECTORS

In considering the interests of the entity, the ultimate end for the board might be both the entity's guardianship and value creation for the corporate entity in perpetuity. What are the obligations of directors?

[55] AR Keay, *The Corporate Objective* (Edward Elgar, 2011) 174–75, 276.
[56] Penner (n 40).

A duty to act in good faith and the best interests of the company exists in the company law of most jurisdictions. To whom or what is that duty owed? A contractual understanding of the modern company, drawing on the contractual Joint Stock Company conception, would support the duty of directors as being to the company's current shareholders. Stakeholder capitalism or a social entity conceptualisation would support the conception of the duty as a public duty owed to society as a whole, or to the company's stakeholders who transact with the company or who are impacted in some way by the company as it operates in the world. But if we accept the model of the modern company set out in this book, the duty to act in good faith and in the best interests of the company may be owed neither to current shareholders nor to stakeholders of the company. Instead the duty is owed to the entity itself. That entity is based on a Corporate Fund seeded by the capital contributions of shareholders. The impact of the entity on stakeholders as it operates in the world legitimatises not just disclosure, but also measurement of externalities, with emerging evidence that growing ESG value (primarily through minimising negative externalities) grows the value of the entity and therefore the Corporate Fund.

The origins and nature of the good faith obligation in modern corporate law, and the relationship between the duty of good faith and the fiduciary duties around conflicts and profit from office, are contested. This debate matters, because a fiduciary may not act for its own benefit or the benefit of a third person without the principal's informed consent. For some commentators, far from exhorting moral behaviour, fiduciary obligations are 'far more cynical, functional and instrumentalist in outlook, focusing on lessening the danger that a fiduciary's undertaking will not be properly performed'.[57] The positive good faith duty would not then be fiduciary.

The alternative argument, cogently set out by Rosemary Langford, is that while the duties to avoid conflicts and profits

> aim to prevent directors from being swayed from exercising their powers and duties in the interests of the company … [t]he duty to act bona fide in the interests of the company ensures that when those powers and duties are exercised they are exercised in the interests of the company.[58]

While the prevailing view is that the duty of good faith is subsidiary,[59] as suggested in chapter 6 it may in fact be the duties around conflicts and profits

[57] M Conaglen, 'The Nature and Function of Fiduciary Loyalty' (2005) 121 *Law Quarterly Review* 452, 453–54.

[58] RT Langford, 'Best interests: multifaceted but not unbounded' (2016) 75 *Cambridge Law Journal* 505, 508.

[59] On this understanding, the duty exists to ensure that in certain sensitive situations, self-interest will not interfere with correct performance of the duties of the fiduciary 'to preserve and promote'. See P Finn, 'The Fiduciary Principle' in TG Youdan (ed), *Equity, Fiduciaries, and Trusts* (Carswell, 1989) 1; and Conaglen (n 57).

that are subsidiary, with those duties having developed as a reaction to specific fact situations. Dine and Koutias point out:

> It was traditional under the common law to give a list of the breaches of fiduciary duties of directors under headings such as: misappropriation of company property; exercise of powers for an improper purpose; fettering discretion; and permitting interest and duty to conflict. While no one would dispute that these are all areas where directors have been found to be in breach of duty, the listing of the duties in this way has tended to obscure the fundamental point that a director is under one overriding duty and that is to act bona fide [in good faith] in the interests of the company.[60]

That conceptualisation is supported by the discussion of the evolution of the subsidiary duties set out in the historical analysis in the book. In *Keech v Sandford*, a strict approach was taken to conflicts of interest of those in a position of trust, with the principles around fiduciary obligations apparently later finding their way into corporate law.[61] But did an earlier form of the duty to act in good faith and the best interests of the company, represented by the ethical duty signified by the oath, pre-date the situation-specific fiduciary obligations? Does the regarding of the duty of good faith as the overarching duty, to the extent that in the United States it can override the strict approach to conflict found in *Keech v Sandford*, point to its earlier origin? If so, it may inform the current debate on whether the duty is subsidiary and whether it is fiduciary. The oath sworn by the Governor and committees in business corporations like the English East India Company may have been a source of the duty of good faith. That oath related to safeguarding the interests of all the shareholders. Those interests were the capital contributed by shareholders seeding the Corporate Fund. It therefore follows that the primary obligation of boards relates to the interests of shareholders held in the Corporate Fund in the entity. Once a perpetual perspective is adopted, we can broaden our understanding of value that attaches to the Corporate Fund.

History can also inform the modern debate, with many of the apparently cutting-edge concepts emerging around corporate law and corporate governance in fact intentionally or unintentionally drawing on established concepts. All duties come from somewhere. Take the debate on corporate purpose led by Colin Mayer and others.[62] Although ultimately overturned, Lindley LJ considered purpose in his judgment in *Broderip v Salomon*.[63] Lindley LJ questioned the purpose for which the company was established. He applied principles of corporations' law where courts would look to the charter of a corporation to

[60] J Dine and M Koutsias, *Company Law*, 6th edn (Palgrave MacMillan, 2007) para 11.5.

[61] *Keech v Sandford* (1726) 2 Eq Cas Abr 741, 25 ER 223; J Getzler, 'Rumford Market and the Genesis of Fiduciary Obligation' in A Burrows and A Rodger (eds), *Mapping the Law: Essays in Memory of Peter Birks* (Oxford University Press, 2006) 577.

[62] CP Mayer, *Prosperity: better business makes the greater good* (Oxford University Press, 2018).

[63] *Broderip v Salomon* [1895] 2 Ch 323 (CA), 337.

determine its purpose. Corporations historically were established for a public purpose set out in their charter. They could not obtain a charter without having a public purpose, albeit that with business corporations it was accepted that at the same time there were private benefits for shareholders. Lindley LJ accepted that Salomon & Co Ltd was a corporation, 'but a corporation created for an illegitimate purpose'.[64]

The use of the term 'purpose' in this way echoes commentary around Lord Hardwicke's discussion in *The Charitable Corporation v Sutton* set out in chapter 6. The anonymous author of the pamphlet, like Lord Hardwicke, views directorship as a 'mixed office'.[65] Lord Hardwicke suggested two duties. The first duty was to consider the charter and the *purpose* for which it was granted by the Crown.[66] The second duty was to act in the best interests of the shareholders. Where those duties conflicted, the purpose of the corporation took precedence.[67]

Instances may exist where a director may not breach a specific fiduciary duty but may nevertheless still not be acting in good faith and in the company's best interests. An example might be a director who does not exercise independent judgement in decision making. Another example might be a director who does not intervene in a board decision when the director knows that the other directors' primary motivation is not to act in the interests of the company.

Drawing on the origins of the obligations of governing bodies of perpetual corporations in charters, the board must ensure that the entity remains dynamic. In other words, the board should ensure through its decision making, acting in the interests of the entity, that the company continues to be able to operate in the world. The board must also sustain the entity, and therefore Corporate Fund, through good decision making. Part of the role of the board is to ensure that distributions to current shareholders at any time are not so excessive that they drain the value of the entity and therefore the Corporate Fund.

Ensuring perpetuity necessitates, therefore, that decision making is in the long-term interests of the entity. So, for example, a company may build and provide housing for its employees to retain them in the long term, as was seen with the model villages built by the 'Quaker' companies. Corporate constituencies such as employees and other stakeholders will almost certainly benefit from these decisions. Still, the primary reason for making these decisions need not be altruistic. The focus is on the dynamic entity, including protecting and enhancing its persona and growing ESG value.

[64] ibid.

[65] *The Charitable Corporation v Sutton* (1742) 26 ER 642; *A Short History of the Charitable Corporation* (A Millar, 1732) 7.

[66] *The Charitable Corporation v Sutton* (n 65).

[67] *A Short History of the Charitable Corporations* (n 65) 17, see 'In most cases the design and interest of the proprietors is to pursue that purpose (of the charter), and their directors ought *therefore* keep this continually in view'.

VIII. OPERATIONALISING ENTITY PRIMACY

In Bainbridge's director primacy, the corporation is a vehicle by which the board hires factors of production.[68] In entity primacy, the dynamic entity is based on a Corporate Fund that is an artificial legal person. The *persona ficta* is animated by the board of directors, which, as its primary representative, hires various production factors. As an artificial legal person, the company can transact for value. At the same time, the company is based on a Corporate Fund that can hold, extract, aggregate and generate value. The company through its impact on the world creates externalities. Minimisation of negative externalities and maximisation of positive externalities are ESG value.

How does a board operate a company in the company's own interests? A company as a *persona ficta* operates in the world, transacting for value with other persons. Relationships with some classes of corporate constituents or stakeholders will involve both a transaction (the employment relationship) and an extraction of value. It can be assumed that a company will not employ an individual unless it considers that it will extract more value from the work of the employee than the value it passes to the employee in terms of salary and other benefits. That value might be extracted from the employee individually, perhaps from the employee in conjunction with others, or perhaps in the contributions of the employee to the organisational architecture. Even passing on value to the employee in terms of higher wages or other benefits can also benefit the company. The company can create positive externalities and social value by taking care of its employees.

As it operates in the world, the company will also seek to enhance its persona. As well as increasing the value of the entity through growing its brand and reputation, the persona may also protect the company by ensuring its continuing viability. Therefore, a board of a company will be acutely sensitive to the context in which the company operates and the 'stakeholders' which which it interacts. For example, an airline corporation will be conscious that its right to operate in a world increasingly focused on climate change risks becoming tenuous. Also, its consumers as purchasers of flights may be mindful of the environmental impacts of flying. So airline companies may choose to focus on environmental sustainability. These initiatives can be reported through ESG reporting. The reputation and persona may protect airline company from regulation, so have value. These initiatives may also ensure that consumers purchase travel through that airline corporation rather than other airlines, choosing alternative ways to travel, or not travelling at all – another form of value.

Boards will seek to reduce risk around the entity caused by creating negative externalities for which the company may be forced to compensate, and

[68] Bainbridge (n 27) 550.

also creating the danger of regulatory constraints. The board will seek to strengthen its persona to protect the entity and induce firm-specific investments by constituents. So, for example, if environmental concerns are perceived by the board to matter to corporate constituents like investors and consumers and regulatory bodies, the board will pay overt attention to environmental concerns in the entity's interests. Paying attention to environmental concerns will also enhance the reputation and, therefore, the corporate entity's value.

Conversely, a decision to carry out, for example, an activity that will harm the environment may offer immediate financial benefits for the company. It may even grow the financial value of the entity in the short term. But that decision may adversely affect the reputation and, therefore, the company's persona in perpetuity, affecting the value of the entity and making it more difficult for the company to induce firm-specific investments from constituents in the future. The company may be forced to compensate for the externality. It also risks industry-wide regulation.

Focusing on the entity in perpetuity offers a conceptually robust mechanism for boards, as they enter into relationships and transactions with corporate constituents,[69] to look beyond the interests of existing shareholders and to look beyond the present. It also creates challenges of complex decision making and accountability risks when considering multiple stakeholders. Like a jury, a board is a collective decision maker that should draw on multiple perspectives. A diverse board that offers diverse perspectives may strengthen decision making. The governance component of ESG reporting on a diverse board will also enhance the persona and value of the entity.

Corporate constituents influence directors on boards in their decision making. The influence constituents actually have depends on several factors. First, board dynamics and the relationships between directors will affect how boards can be influenced in their decision making. Second, the board's composition, the directors' characteristics and the approach adopted by directors in their decision making will affect the degree to which constituents influence respective directors. Finally, the degree of influence of a constituent will depend on the degree of relative power a constituent has, and on the level of independence a board is empowered or prepared to exercise. For example, a shareholder with a majority holding risks influencing decision making by directors to a great extent, because that controlling shareholder can remove directors at any time. That influence risks short-termism if the board focuses unduly on the interests of a current majority shareholder.

[69] See Blair and Stout (n 45) 248. The argument differs from Blair and Stout's discussion of the 'team' making firm-specific investments, in that there is an eversion in perspective to the entity itself through its board's inducing firm-specific investments with the end of generating value in the corporate fund.

IX. CONCLUSION

Contemporary corporate governance scholarship about the role of the board is split. Some consider the board's role is to maximise profits and value for current shareholders. This is Chancellor Allen's property conception. Some believe that the board's role is to consider the interests of all corporate stakeholders: stakeholder capitalism, where the company is deemed to be a social entity. Recognising that the board's role relates directly to the dynamic entity operating in the world, rather than to current shareholders, provides clarity.

Conceptualising the modern company as an entity based on a Corporate Fund comprising forms of value provides a middle ground in the debate that can accommodate both conceptions. On incorporation, the company is comprised of financial capital contributed by shareholders. That Corporate Fund is separated from shareholders collectively as a class through double-entry bookkeeping. The Corporate Fund on incorporation has the status of a *persona ficta* or juridical person. That *persona ficta* can transact and operate in almost the same way as a natural person. As it operates in the world, the *persona ficta* becomes an entity with a persona. The entity acquires forms of value. Some of that value becomes forms of capital that the company can then use to generate more value – the financial value of the Corporate Fund increases or decreases in line with the entity's value. As Keay explains, the board, in its decision making, will seek to sustain and maximise the value of the corporate entity.[70] The board may make decisions that favour the interests of corporate constituents who contribute value, such as employees and consumers, with those decisions potentially creating positive externalities that increase the value of the entity.

This entity conceptualisation of the modern company might appear to support a stakeholder understanding of the company. But this understanding must be qualified and realistic. Although the board and its delegates may seem to favour the interests of stakeholders, from an entity perspective these interests will be legitimately accommodated only to the extent that they either ultimately grow the various forms of value held by the corporate entity, or strengthen its persona through positive ESG value. Ultimately, creation of value will benefit shareholders. One benefit is through valorisation (the separation and conversion of value that is distributed as dividends to shareholders.) Another benefit is the increase in the value of the entity, leading to the growth in the value of the Corporate Fund. For listed companies, the share price of shares owned by shareholders will increase.

In the modern company, shareholders have lost direct control over the management of the entity but have retained the constitutional rights to participate in the appointment and removal of directors on the board. Shareholders

[70] Keay (n 55).

also have ultimate authority, with the collective right to end the life of the *persona ficta*. These rights ensure accountability from directors. In the constitutional division of powers between shareholders collectively exercised notionally through the general meeting and directors exercised through the board, control over the company's management, broadly defined, rests with the board.[71]

Shareholders give up control rights over the Corporate Fund in that, while the company remains a legal person, shareholders have no right to demand a distribution. The proprietary rights of shareholders over the Corporate Fund are residual rights of ownership that 'crystallise' and only come into play when the company is liquidated and no longer exists as a juridical person.

The 'mixt nature' of directorship referred to by Lord Hardwicke in *The Charitable Corporation v Sutton*[72] remains, with directors having both a (constitutional) representative role to act in the interests of shareholders held in the Corporate Fund, and a governance role relating to guardianship of the entity. The board sits at the intersection between shareholders and the corporate entity. The dual role reflects the hybrid origins of the board. As discussed in chapter 4, the committees (directors) of contractual Joint Stock Companies were the representatives of shareholders. In business corporations, committees (directors) represented the interests of shareholders in Joint Stock Funds. The governing bodies of corporations, which had governors and also included committees (directors), had a guardianship and stewardship role derived from canon law and set out in early charters.

The board serves several purposes through the life-cycle of the modern company. After incorporation, the board animates the inanimate *persona ficta* or artificial legal person based on the initial capital contributed by shareholders that is the Corporate Fund. In its decision making, the board exercises direct management control over the entity. The board's fundamental fiduciary and statutory obligations relate to the guardianship of the Corporate Fund and the entity that develops as the board navigates the company through the world. But the board's role extends beyond functions akin to trusteeship. The board will seek to create value for the entity, and therefore of the Corporate Fund. The company can operate in perpetuity, so that value creation can extend beyond short-term realised financial value that is valorised and distributed to shareholders as profits. Secondary markets, such as share markets, base share value on the projected future value of shares more than valorised value distributed to shareholders. The primary competitive advantage that the *persona ficta* form has over natural legal persons is its potential longevity. Boards can adopt a perpetual perspective on the creation of value.

[71] If shareholders retain or usurp management powers, they will be deemed or shadow directors in most jurisdictions. C Noonan and SM Watson, 'The nature of shadow directorship: ad hoc statutory intervention or core company law principle' [2006] *Journal of Business Law* 763.

[72] *The Charitable Corporation v Sutton* (n 65).

At the same time, creating value is contextual, as the company operates in a world where expectations of investors and other corporate constituents shift – in the twenty-first century, that long-term perspective legitimises the consideration, recording and measurement of ESG components of value that ensure the enduring viability of the company. The loss of direct control over decision making about the direction of the company benefits current shareholders. Although current shareholders may sacrifice short-term profits realised through dividends, the value of the Corporate Fund will be reflected in the value of their shares.

16

The Modern Company: Perils and Potential

I. CORPORATE MORALITY

CAPITALISM MAKES IT possible to derive value from capital. Societal changes post-pandemic and pressures around inequality, climate change and sustainability mean there are calls to reimagine capitalism.[1] As the primary tool for capitalism, can the modern company be reimagined as a force for good?

The wealthiest people in the world are not natural persons but corporations. Invisible, immortal beings are amongst us, determining and controlling many aspects of our lives. Reverend Reynolds exhorted the English East India Company in 1657 to base its values on Nehemiah. The motives of the founders of the tech behemoths, at least ostensibly, are not what Big Tech has become. Is perpetual life a good thing for any person, natural or artificial?

Whether an action is socially irresponsible will depend on what and who an organisation is responsible to. If it is considered that a company is responsible only to its current shareholders then any action that derogates from maximising existing shareholder wealth might be considered socially irresponsible. As Milton Friedman famously put it, the only social responsibility of a company is then to maximise profits.[2]

In their article about corporate morality, Mitchell and Gabaldon argue that the 'organisational context changes the perceived moral framework for individual decision making, and that powerful psychological forces push good people to turn bad without their even realising it'.[3] Princeton psychologist John Darley considers that most evil is accomplished by people acting through corporations, as a type of organisational pathology.[4]

[1] R Henderson, *Reimagining Capitalism in a World on Fire* (Public Affairs, 2020).

[2] M Friedman, *Capitalism and Freedom* (University of Chicago Press, 1962) 133; see the case of *Dodge v Ford Motor Company* (1919) 170 NW 668 (SC) in the United States; and see also *Parke v Daily News* [1962] Ch 927, 2 All ER 929 involving cakes and ale.

[3] LE Mitchell and TA Gabaldon, 'If I Only Had a Heart: Or, How Can We Identify a Corporate Morality' (2002) 76 *Tulane Law Review* 1645, 1654.

[4] JM Darley, 'How Organizations Socialize Individuals into Evildoing' in DM Messick and AE Tenbrunsel (eds), *Codes of Conduct: Behavioral Research into Business Ethics* (Russell Sage Foundation, 1996) 13.

Darley discusses the work of Milgram on the agentic State:

> From a subjective standpoint, a person is in a state of agency when he defines himself in a social situation in a manner that renders him open to regulation by a person of higher status. In this condition the individual no longer views himself as responsible for his own actions but defines himself as an instrument for carrying out the wishes of others.[5]

In a corporate setting, an individual will consider himself or herself responsible to those higher in the hierarchy. In a modern company, the directors who comprise the board are the most elevated in the hierarchy. Directors may consider themselves accountable to the company. A company may be conceived of as current shareholders as its owners. The directors on the board may believe all shareholders require the company to maximise value and extract profits in the short term. An agentic state limiting conscience and morality may then come into being. As Mitchell and Gabaldon put it, 'the profit motive and the complex interactions among organizational participants make it possible for any corporation to do harm'.[6]

Evidence exists that the profit maximisation imperative may affect behaviour by individuals within the corporation. Marks describes an internal audit carried out by BP following a refinery explosion, where 33 per cent of Texas City operators and 42 per cent of Toledo operators agreed that process safety was of secondary importance to meeting production goals.[7] So whether generated internally by the nature of groups or externally mandated by the perceived requirement to maximise profits in the short term, corporations may be constitutionally incapable of operating with fully functioning consciences as moral entities.

The picture may not be as black as painted. First, the perceived profit maximisation imperative is weakening. Increasing numbers of investors, either individually or through ethical investment funds, expect corporations to consider ESG (Environmental, Social, Governance) issues in their decision making. The profit maximisation imperative is itself based on an outmoded conceptualisation of the company in which directors are solely the economic agents of current shareholders. Recognising that the board's primary role relates to the entity itself in perpetuity provides scope to legitimise decision making by boards that is not driven by the perceived short-term profit maximisation imperative for current shareholders.

Second, the central role of the board and the autonomy given to the board through the recognition of business judgement rules or equivalent in different

[5] S Milgram, *Obedience to Authority: An Experimental View* (Harper and Row, 1974) 134, discussed in Darley (n 4) 206–12.

[6] Mitchell and Gabaldon (n 3) 1653.

[7] *The Report of the BP Refineries Safety Review Panel* (17 January 2007), discussed in CP Marks, 'Jiminy Cricket for the Corporation: Understanding the Corporate "Conscience"' (2008) 42 *Valparaiso University Law Review* 1129, 1153–54.

jurisdictions, gives scope for boards to move beyond agentic decision making. Boards will be pressured, will be influenced by corporate constituents. That influence may be deleterious to moral decision making. However, influence from corporate constituents can also lead to moral decision making. Institutional investors and ethical investment funds attract capital that is then directed to companies that align with their projected values. Governmental pressure in various jurisdictions and the threat of regulatory constraints cause corporations to alter their behaviour. So cautious optimism tinged with realism: corporations will change their practices not because they are inherently 'good', but because boards are aware of the risks around loss of reputation. Loss of reputation can affect persona, potentially the ability of corporations to attract investment, or even their social licence to operate if they do not shift behaviours. In other words, with reputation the board is protecting the persona of the entity, and with investment it is safeguarding the Corporate Fund. In the quest to make the modern company 'good', perhaps it is the least – and the most – we can expect. And the recent actions by jurisdictions over minimum tax rates for Big Tech (discussed in section III), or even changing the rationale behind jurisdictional domicile, show the potential for jurisdictions to influence corporate decision making if those jurisdictions choose to exercise that power.

Recollect Chancellor Allen's two conceptions of the modern corporation, the private property conception and the social entity conception, set out in chapter 1. The social entity conception of the company is apt in the sense that the board has direct control over the management and operation of the entity as it operates in the world. The entity is, however, constitutionally controlled by two governing bodies, the board and the shareholders' meeting, with directors elected by shareholders and shareholders' rights to appoint directors and participate in general meetings attached to their shares.

In this hybrid form, the social entity conception can prevail as the company operates. From Chancellor Allen:

> The corporation comes into being and continues as a legal entity only with governmental concurrence. The legal institutions of government grant a corporation its juridical personality, its characteristic limited liability, and its perpetual life. This conception sees this public facilitation as justified by the State's interest in promoting the general welfare. Thus, corporate purpose can be seen as including the advancement of the general welfare. The board of directors' duties extend beyond assuring investors a fair return, to include a duty of loyalty, in some sense, to all those interested in or affected by the corporation. … The corporation itself is, in this view, capable of bearing legal and moral obligations.[8]

What can be done to cultivate optimal decision making by the board? Constraints on board decision making can be generated externally or internally. They can

[8] WT Allen, 'Our Schizophrenic Conception of the Business Corporation' (1992) 14 *Cardozo Law Review* 261, 265.

also be legitimate in the sense that they are legal. Constraints may be legislative or derived from case law. They may be constitutional, involving those who operate in various capacities in and around the company. Examples of 'legitimate' constraints are legislative and common law obligations (duties) of loyalty and care on directors, binding them to the entity as it operates in the world. Another constraint may be a resolution by shareholders at a meeting over a decision constitutionally allocated to shareholders that relates to the management of the company.

Constraints can also be 'illegitimate' or illegal. A board that is being pressured by a major shareholder to valorise value from the Corporate Fund for current shareholders, thereby prioritising short-term profit maximisation ahead of other factors that might ultimately benefit the entity, may be facing an illegitimate constraint. An undue focus on short-term profits for current shareholders might come at the expense of due consideration of other factors, such as reputational concerns that affect the corporate persona, and ESG concerns such as considering the interests of the employees whose contributions create value for the Corporate Fund. Another factor might be the long-term relationship of the company with the consumers it transacts with and the community of which the company is part. Pressure applied by current shareholders around short-term profit maximisation may ultimately affect the social licence to operate that the company holds. Again, these are value held by or attached to the entity.

In more egregious cases, undue influence may morph into control by a shareholder and may cause the board not to comply with its legal duties to the entity. Shareholders who involve themselves in decision making by the board over the management of the company act beyond the role of a shareholder; jurisdictions recognise this implicitly by deeming such shareholders to be shadow directors or equivalent.[9] In the most extreme and egregious cases of unconstitutional shareholder intervention in management decision making, shareholders who control decision making by boards can face liability in the same way as de jure directors. Minimising forms of constraint on board decision making, sometimes termed 'fettering discretion', should therefore be prioritised.[10] Directors and boards of modern companies are not the agents of shareholders.

Constraints might also be internal and may relate to the composition and operation of the board, the character and aptitude of directors, and, most notably, the perception by directors of their roles. Directors' developing a deeper understanding of the nature of the modern company may improve corporate behaviour. Boards may accept that creating value beyond financial value is a legitimate exercise of discretion. But ultimately a company will be 'selfish'.

[9] C Noonan and SM Watson, 'The nature of shadow directorship: ad hoc statutory intervention or core company law principle' [2006] *Journal of Business Law* 763.

[10] This argument consciously contradicts agency theory, where it is argued that mechanisms should be used to align the interests of management with the interests of shareholders.

In the end, the board will always make decisions that preserve the entity and create value, either in the short term or in the long term. The fundamental obligation of directors in their decision making is to act in the company's best interests. It is well established that entirely altruistic decisions by directors that deplete the value of the entity are not legitimate.[11]

Accepting that a company will be legitimately selfish by acting in its own interests does nevertheless give considerable scope in decision making, once it is accepted that the obligations of boards are owed to the perpetual entity rather than to current shareholders.

The company does not operate in a vacuum. Directors will be aware of the context in which a company operates. Individuals with whom the company seeks to transact, such as consumers, will, in deciding whether or not to deal with it, be affected by factors beyond price, such as brand and reputation, that are part of the company's persona. If a company acquires a reputation for acting unethically, consumers may not transact with it.

Societal norms have also shifted, so that increasingly, consumers and investors expect that companies in their decision making take account of ESG factors by minimising negative externalities and maximising positive externalities. Consumers will assess companies using these factors, with disclosure and measurement of ESG likely to increase.

Integrated reporting aims for 'a holistic understanding of the value creation process'.[12] As set out on its website, Value Reporting Foundation UK states that it

> aims to:
>
> - Improve the quality of information available to providers of financial capital to enable a more efficient and productive allocation of capital
> - Promote a more cohesive and efficient approach to corporate reporting that draws on different reporting strands and communicates the full range of factors that materially affect the ability of an organization to create value over time
> - Enhance accountability and stewardship for the broad base of capitals (financial, manufactured, intellectual, human, social and relationship, and natural) and promote understanding of their independencies
> - Support integrated thinking, decision-making and actions that focus on the creation of value over the short, medium and long term.[13]

The conception of the modern company set out in this book aligns with integrated reporting. The six capitals (financial, manufactured, intellectual, human, social and relationship, and natural) in integrated reporting become value attached to the entity.

[11] *Parke v Daily News* (n 2).

[12] F Rijkse, 'NN Group redefines its purpose through integrated thinking' (Value Reporting Foundation UK, 18 August 2021) at https://integratedreporting.org/news/nn-group-delivers-value-for-all-stakeholders-through-integrated-thinking. Value Reporting Foundation: Integrated Reporting Framework accessed from integratedreporting.org, 20 August 2021.

[13] Value Reporting Foundation UK, 'About Us' at https://integratedreporting.org/the-iirc-2/.

Integrated reporting and ESG disclosure and reporting show us that evidence of attention to these factors will enhance the persona of the company and become forms of value creation. They also tell us that value is contextual. Twenty years ago, consumers would have attached little or no value to these factors. Similarly, a focus on sustainable finance and sustainable investment means evidence of sustainable practices within a company will encourage investment and is itself a form of value. The speed of the transition by companies to recognition of changing societal norms around the environment and sustainability shows the adaptability of the *persona ficta* form to the context in which it operates.

Environmental, Social, Governance and sustainability practices are forms of value in the third decade of the new millennium, even though these practices had little or no value in the first or even second decades. And therein lies a limitation of the modern company as a force for good. Anecdotally, companies in industries with the greatest potential to cause environmental harm pay the greatest attention to sustainability. Companies that do not have consumers may be less concerned with reputation, brand and other aspects of value that relate to the persona. Sustainable finance is significant, because societal expectations around sustainable practices are channelled through investors as shareholders of funds. But not all investors care about sustainability.

Environmental, Social, Governance and integrated reporting consider the impact of a company from the perspective of the company itself. They presuppose that the modern company has legitimacy as an artificial legal person. They are transactional. As we have seen, status as a legal person offers enormous advantages. We are comfortable with personifying funds based on capital contributed by shareholders. Might we level the playing field for the stakeholders on which the company has an impact?

One idea is to give nature some form of legal standing. Christopher Stone's famous 1972 article proposed legal rights for nature.[14] In Aotearoa New Zealand, legal personhood has been bestowed on mountains and rivers. The Whanganui River has been recognised as Te Awa Tupua – an integrated living whole.[15] Two guardians, one Maori and one a state representative, are charged with acting and speaking on behalf of the River, upholding its recognition and values as an indivisible entity and legal person, promoting and protecting the environmental, social, cultural and economic health and well-being of the River, and, finally, taking any other action reasonably necessary to achieve its purpose and perform its functions.[16]

The River is therefore a legal person. As a legal person, it is a subject of rights and duties. The River, unlike the Corporate Fund on which the modern company is based, has always existed. Its personhood is based on an underlying

[14] CD Stone, 'Should Trees Have Standing? – Toward Legal Rights for Natural Objects' (1972) 45 *Southern California Law Review* 450.

[15] Te Awa Tupua (Whanganui River Claims Settlement) Act 2017 (NZ).

[16] ibid s 20.

reality: the River itself as Te Awa Tupua. This recognition of legal personhood is unlike the legal personhood of the modern company. The modern company as a *persona ficta* is artificial in the sense that it is created by a statute. The modern company becomes real through its operation in and impact on the world. There are, however, similarities The modern company has the board; the River similarly has guardians that represent it in the world. The guardians of the River have a legal right to act and speak on its behalf as a living entity. If another legal person, natural or artificial, caused harm to the River, the River through its guardians presumably could litigate. Applying the Coase theorem, with improved rights for the personified River, true compensation for externalities caused by the modern company becomes possible.[17]

Giving nature legal personhood may facilitate true compensation for harm caused by other legal persons, including companies. It will disincentivise, but it may not prevent harm. The limitations of corporate conscience may necessitate appropriate external regulatory constraints on the activities of some companies and some industry sectors. Companies will seek to prevent legislative interventions because of their inevitable negative impact on the entity's value. The risk of regulation also drives corporate decision making. In the game of corporate control, where control over the Corporate Fund sits with boards and control over the selection of the board sits with shareholders, it is states that have ultimate control. A regulatory environment that mandates and restricts particular behaviour and activities by corporations may be a legitimate trade-off for the privileges of incorporation. Those privileges include status as a juridical person and statutory limited liability for shareholders. These attributes could not be acquired other than through being enabled by states through general incorporation statutes. We need not resile from an acceptance that a corporation's primary purpose is to create value in perpetuity and accept, at the same time, that a modern company can be a good citizen.

II. SUSTAINABILITY REALISED

A board that considers sustainability issues only to the extent that the entity's value is enhanced might be vulnerable to criticism if the focus is just on financial value. Notwithstanding the eversion in focus to the entity itself, that would be a consequence of entity maximisation and sustainability if the ultimate objective remains increasing the financial value of the entity and prolonging the life of the company. Environmental, Social, Governance interests will be accommodated only to the extent that they ultimately increase the entity's financial value in either the short term or the long term. The purpose of corporate governance remains wealth maximisation by the growth of the economic value of the

[17] RH Coase, 'The Problem of Social Cost' (1960) 3 *The Journal of Law and Economics* 1.

Corporate Fund for the ultimate benefit of shareholders. This approach does not prioritise creating environmental and social value of the entity beyond the extent to which it enhances the company's persona.

Existing language around long-term interests and value for shareholders masks the reality that boards have *always* focused on creating economic value for the entity. When boards make decisions, they may describe those decisions as being in the interests of shareholders in the short term or the long term, in stakeholders' interests or even as sustainable decisions. In fact, boards are generally working to create value. Boards may develop relationships with stakeholders and address stakeholder concerns only so far as suits the ultimate end, which is to maximise the economic value of the entity. Therefore, the shift to recognition of ESG factors as forms of value legitimises their consideration by a board but may not necessarily change decision making by boards. Accommodating ESG interests may be considered legitimate to the extent it enhances the reputation of the corporate legal person through its persona and generates economic value for the entity in the short term or long term. Boards may also consider sustainability issues when assessing risk. But if the focus is on entity value maximisation in the long term, boards may continue to discount the risks to the entity from negative externalities. The impact of these externalities on the outside world may be ignored or minimised.

The danger is that the concept of sustainability may be hijacked and used to legitimise value maximisation in perpetuity rather than in the short term. That value in the entity may then be passed on to those constituents who control the corporation – senior management through excessive remuneration, or shareholders in the form of dividends. Corporate sustainability may become a 'woke' synonym for corporate longevity, where virtue signalling masks the reality that nothing has changed. After all, the English East India Company was a sustainable company if sustainability is equated with longevity. True sustainability asks more of boards:

> *Corporate sustainability* [is] a state when business and finance on aggregate create value in a manner that is (a) *environmentally* sustainable in that it ensures the long-term stability and resilience of the ecosystems that support human life, (b) *socially* sustainable in that it facilitates the respect and promotion of human rights and other basic social rights as well as good governance, and (c) *economically* sustainable in that it satisfies the economic needs necessary for stable and resilient societies.[18]

If a company is to exist in perpetuity, the world in which it operates must also exist recognisably without the ravages brought about by extreme climate change or reactions to inequality.[19] The top 50 richest human beings own more than

[18] B Sjåfell and CM Bruner, 'Corporations and sustainability' in B Sjåfell and CM Bruner (eds), *Cambridge Handbook of Corporate Law, Corporate Governance and Sustainability* (Cambridge University Press, 2019).

[19] Henderson (n 1) 8. Much of that wealth is held in shares in companies.

the poorest half of humanity. That wealth is mostly held in shares in modern companies. Once we accept that modern companies, as *persona ficta*, are a type of person, we recognise that the wealthiest people living among us are not human beings.

The conceptualisation of the company set out in this book may assist in ensuring genuine corporate sustainability. First, acknowledging that the company as it operates in the world is a dynamic entity accommodates recognition that the dynamic entity comprises forms of value contributed not just by shareholders but by other corporate stakeholders too, such as employees and consumers. Traditionally we have measured financial value, but integrated accounting measures other forms of value. We treasure what we measure. Measuring ESG value is an expansion of value.

This acknowledgement legitimises two things. First, it legitimises the extension of the sustainability role of boards to preserving all the forms of the value attached to the entity. The entity can develop long-term relationships with constituents, and can protect and enhance the corporate persona. More contentiously, it may also legitimise the return of value to constituents who contribute value to the company. Just as the means and ends of corporate governance need not be the same, the ends can themselves also be unpacked once an entity-focused understanding is adopted. It is entirely possible to conceive of the board's role in creating value as separate from the board's role when it makes decisions about how the value generated by the entity is distributed. In particular, if the entity extracts value from employees, some of that value could be distributed to employees in some form. The return of value need not be financial. The Quaker companies discussed in chapter 11 built model villages to house their employees. Companies can benefit in the long term through enhancing their personas and growing ESG value.

If the value is obtained contractually by the company through a transaction, the case for return of value to stakeholders is less strong. If the value is reputational and part of the contextual persona of the company, that value could be returned. For example, arguably, the entity should not be enriched overall due to environmentally driven initiatives that enhance its reputation, persona and, therefore, value.

Second, sustainability practices that look beyond economic value maximisation of the entity would require boards to move beyond decision making that will benefit the company through growth in the financial value of the entity in the short term or long term. It would require the company as a legal person to practise good environmental and social citizenship, to the extent that the company would create environmental and social value as well as economic value. The company, through its board, would recognise it has moral obligations to the communities in which it operates that are a corollary to the benefits it receives through organisational law –most particularly, being granted status as a legal person and the benefits of complete entity shielding for the Corporate Fund. These benefits make wealth generation possible for shareholders through the Corporate Fund. Continuing legitimacy may depend on conscious decisions by boards to minimise environmental and social externalities, even if that minimisation means that the financial value of the entity is not maximised. From the entity's perspective, these decisions can be rationalised from a distributional perspective as a return to society, for society's granting the modern company a social licence to operate.

Some emerging approaches align with requiring the company as an entity to compensate for the value it extracts. The European Commission has said that 'it is an internationally agreed principle that profit should be taxed where value is created'.[20] The OECD's Base Erosion and Profit Sharing Project aims to ensure that 'profits are taxed where economic activities occur and value is created'.[21] At the time of writing, the G7 had agreed to support a minimum tax rate of 15 per cent, to deter multinational companies, particularly Big Tech companies, from avoiding taxes by stashing profits in countries that charge low tax rates. More interestingly, the G7 ministers also endorsed proposals requiring multinational companies to pay tax in countries where they have high sales but no physical headquarters – a type of impact tax that aligns with a conception of the modern company as an amorphous entity that manifests itself primarily by the impact it has on the world.

A rationale for the shift is that for tech corporations, the means of production and what is produced are indeed amorphous. Previously, corporate activity was understood to be based around capital and labour. That understanding may be a long-standing misconception. Capital, in a company as the Corporate Fund, is itself an abstract concept, even though companies traditionally owned real property and physical assets. The *persona ficta* contracts for labour but has never been comprised of that labour or the people who perform that labour as its employees. Buildings were a physical manifestation of value held in the Corporate Fund. Impact taxes may therefore be a conceptually sounder way to tax corporations.

Three proposals set out by the OECD in the Inclusive Framework's Public Consultation document 'Addressing the Tax Challenges of the Digitalisation of the Economy' adopt a unified approach. All relate to impact. The user participation proposal is based on 'the concept that the active and sustained engagement of users creates significant value for certain highly digitalised businesses'.[22]

The marketing intangibles proposal

> recognises a link between the market jurisdiction and marketing intangibles which enables successful multinational businesses to establish and develop marketing intangibles even though they might have a limited local presence (such as a limited risk distributor) or no local physical presence at all.[23]

[20] C Elliffe, *Taxing the Digital Economy: Theory, Policy and Practice* (Cambridge University Press, 2021) 34.
[21] ibid.
[22] ibid 169.
[23] ibid 171–72.

In the significant economic presence proposal, the key concept is that

> technological advances have enabled businesses to be involved in the economic life of another jurisdiction without physical presence. Accordingly, the new business developments have rendered the rules largely useless. This proposal focuses on 'expanding' the concept of what constitutes a taxable presence in a jurisdiction away from the traditional permanent establishment. Instead, 'factors that evidence a purposeful and sustained interaction with the jurisdiction via digital technology and other automated means' could constitute a 'significant economic presence' when combined with revenue generated on a sustained basis.[24]

Recognition of the potential inherent in the perpetual entity offers enormous competitive advantages. As Lina Khan highlighted when explaining the Amazon phenomenon, where ongoing shareholder investment was attracted despite Amazon's never turning a profit. Amazon's trajectory reflects the business philosophy that Jeff Bezos outlined from the start. In his first letter to shareholders, Bezos wrote 'We believe that a fundamental measure of our success will be the shareholder value we create over the *long term*. This value will be a direct result of our ability to extend and solidify our current market leadership position.'[25] Now chair of the US Federal Trade Commission, Khan advocates reframing antitrust/competition law beyond the current focus on the short-term interests of consumers predicated on the rationale of profit-maximising actors.

Khan draws on the initial rationale for antitrust regulation.[26] 'Congress enacted antitrust laws to rein in the power of industrial trusts, the large business organisations that had emerged in the late nineteenth century. Responding to a fear of concentrated power, antitrust sought to distribute it.'[27] Echoing Chandler:

> [T]he premise of Amazon's business model was to establish scale. To achieve scale, the company prioritized growth. Under this approach, aggressive investing would be key, even if that involved slashing prices or spending billions on expanding capacity, in order to become consumers' one-stop-shop. This approach meant that Amazon 'may make decisions and weigh tradeoffs differently than some companies,' Bezos warned. 'At this stage, we choose to prioritize growth because we believe that scale is central to achieving the potential of our business model'.[28]

The approach taken by Amazon and its investors demonstrates both the potential inherent in the perpetual corporate form when the horizon extends beyond the generation of short-term profits. It also illustrates, as was seen with the English East India Company and the corporations of the first gilded age, the

[24] ibid 175.
[25] JP Bezos, 'Letter to Shareholders' (30 March 1998) at http://media.corporate-ir.net/media_files/irol/97/97664/reports/Shareholderletter97.pdf 1, quoted in LM Khan, 'Amazon's Antitrust Paradox' (2017) 126 *Yale Law Journal* 710.
[26] Khan (n 25).
[27] ibid 739–40.
[28] ibid 749–50 (footnotes omitted).

extent of the potential wealth and power through size and scale that can be generated by unleashing the full potential of the perpetual entity.

III. PERSONAL CAPITALISM

The argument set out in this book is that value creation in the entity has been maximised when current shareholders have not exercised management control over the entity. The primary advantage of the board's control of the management of the perpetual entity is that it can choose to focus on the long term, thereby realising the potential in the perpetual entity. Current shareholders, like partners in a partnership, may adopt a more short-term perspective. However, controlling shareholders can choose to focus on the long term. An interesting alternative narrative is developing around personal capitalism, where current shareholders retain and exercise management control and act in the entity's long-term interests. Personal capitalism practised in this way may ensure corporate longevity by creating value beyond the financial through the company's persona and through ESG value. The Quaker companies of the nineteenth century, discussed in chapter 11, in which attention was paid to employees' interests, and German corporate governance, also discussed in chapter 11, are examples.

Received wisdom tells us that long-term corporate prosperity is linked with functional separation of ownership from control with widely held companies. In the absence of agency theory-driven incentives on directors and managers to maximise profitability in the interests of current shareholders, dispersed shareholding may ensure control by boards and scope to focus on long-term value. However, it may well be that it is the focus on value over a long-term time horizon that ultimately drives prosperity, rather than the ownership or governance structure of the company.

IV. THE MODERN COMPANY

The study of the modern corporation across disciplines[29] mainly concentrates on considering the corporation externally, either from the perspective of shareholders[30] or from the perspective of other constituent stakeholders.[31] From the perspective of the entity itself, the company is an artificial legal person separate

[29] AA Alchian and H Demsetz, 'Production, Information Costs, and Economic Organization' (1972) 62 *American Economic Review* 777; FH Easterbrook and DR Fischel, 'The Corporate Contract' (1989) 89 *Columbia Law Review* 1416.

[30] J Hill, 'Visions and Revisions of the Shareholder' (2000) 48 *American Journal of Comparative Law* 39; R Kraakman et al, *The Anatomy of Corporate Law: A Comparative and Functional Approach*, 3rd edn (Oxford University Press, 2017).

[31] MM Blair and LA Stout, 'A Team Production Theory of Corporate Law' (1999) 85 *Virginia Law Review* 247, 253; RE Freeman, *Strategic Management: A Stakeholder Approach* (Pitman Publishing, 1984).

from all other persons. As an endowed entity, the company owes its status as an artificial legal person or *persona ficta*[32] to its initial shareholders' following a process of incorporation set out in a statute.[33] That entity is normatively controlled by its board.

This conceptualisation of the modern company compels us to reconsider corporate law and corporate governance, most notably the guardianship role of the board[34] and the ownership claims of shareholders.[35] Modern corporate law focuses on minimising the perceived disadvantage for shareholders when they entrust a company with their capital. This issue underpins Jensen and Meckling's agency theory; it is the imperative for much modern corporate law.[36]

Adam Smith identified the agency problem for shareholders.[37] Interestingly, it was recognised earlier in the debate in the mid-seventeenth century between shareholders in the English East India Company over the benefits of free trade compared with permanent capital. For that reason, a close examination of both the development of the English East India Company and the work of Adam Smith assists in an understanding of the modern corporate form. This book engages with the paradox that, despite the agency problem for shareholders, the corporate form in fact greatly enriches shareholders.[38] Why this happens may be linked in part to the attributes of the corporate form that facilitate the modern company's creation of value by transacting for, locking in, generating and protecting value in perpetuity. Success is also linked to a board charged with acting in the entity's interests, rather than management control exercised by current shareholders who may adopt a short-term perspective.

The modern company is a legal entity that is a *persona ficta*, an artificial legal person separate from shareholders. Recent scholarship has shown that legal rules like the legal separation of the modern company from shareholders in the late-nineteenth century facilitated the locking in of capital in the corporate form.[39]

[32] SM Watson, 'The Corporate Legal Person' (2019) 19 *Journal of Corporate Law Studies* 137.

[33] Companies Act 1993 (NZ).

[34] SM Bainbridge, 'Director Primacy: The Means and Ends of Corporate Governance' (2003) 97 *Northwestern University Law Review* 547.

[35] J Armour and MJ Whincop, 'The Proprietary Foundations of Corporate Law' (2007) 27 *Oxford Journal of Legal Studies* 429; cf P Ireland, 'Company Law and the Myth of Shareholder Ownership' (1999) 62 *Modern Law Review* 32.

[36] MC Jensen and WH Meckling, 'Theory of the Firm: Managerial Behavior, Agency Costs and Ownership Structure' (1976) 3 *Journal of Financial Economics* 305; Kraakman et al (n 30).

[37] A Smith, *An Inquiry into the Nature and Causes of the Wealth of Nations*, vol 3, 5th edn (W Strahan and T Cadell, 1789).

[38] T Piketty, *Capital in the Twenty-First Century*, tr A Goldhammer (Harvard University Press, 2014).

[39] MM Blair, 'Locking in Capital: What Corporate Law Achieved for Business Organizers in the Nineteenth Century' (2003) 51 *UCLA Law Review* 387; H Hansmann and R Kraakman, 'The Essential Role of Organizational Law' (2000) 110 *Yale Law Journal* 387; H Hansmann, R Kraakman and R Squire, 'Law and the Rise of the Firm' (2006) 119 *Harvard Law Review* 1333; SM Watson, 'How the Company Became an Entity: A New Understanding of Corporate Law' [2015] *Journal of Business Law* 120.

Work by Blair[40] and by Hansmann and Kraakmann[41] has shown that organisational law locks in capital and partitions the entity from shareholders. The argument developed in this book is that endowed status as a *persona ficta* or artificial legal person enables the company to transact for value in the same way as a natural person. As it operates in the world, the company based on the Corporate Fund comprising the interests of shareholders becomes an entity equipped to capture, create and valorise value for shareholders and, arguably, other corporate constituents. The lock-in of the Corporate Fund in the entity potentially in perpetuity has made size, scope and scale possible through utilisation of the corporate form.[42]

Other persons have roles in and perform functions for the modern company. They make decisions as members of its decision-making bodies, or as its employees or agents. Beyond the various capacities in which they act, those persons are not part of the modern company. The accounting[43] and later legal separation[44] of the Corporate Fund in the *persona ficta* from all other persons facilitated the growth of the entity's value in perpetuity.[45]

The attribute of its being a separate legal entity, combined with its status as a juridical person based on a Corporate Fund, equips the company to acquire forms of value over time that become part of the entity or the Corporate Fund.[46] Value is derived from the people who transact with the company as a *persona ficta*, and is also extracted from the knowledge and skills of the natural persons who are its employees and are part of the dynamic entity for those purposes.[47] The company's longevity as an artificial legal person beyond the lifespan of any natural person uniquely enables the company as an organisation to develop, replicate and scale up managerial systems that reduce production costs and make possible rapid growth and generation of more value.[48]

As the corporate legal person operates in the world as an entity, it develops a persona determined by how it is perceived externally. The persona, comprising aspects such as brand and reputation, will be based on how the company operates and the nature of its business. The persona will also depend on the context in which the company operates. The company will adapt its persona to protect

[40] Blair (n 39).

[41] Hansmann and Kraakman (n 39).

[42] AD Chandler, Jr, *Scale and Scope: The Dynamics of Industrial Capitalism* (The Belknap Press of Harvard University Press, 1994).

[43] BS Yamey, 'The historical significance of double-entry bookkeeping: Some non-Sombartian claims' (2005) 15 *Accounting, Business & Financial History* 77.

[44] *Salomon v Salomon & Co Ltd* [1897] AC 22 (HL).

[45] SM Watson, 'The Corporate Legal Entity as a Fund' [2018] *Journal of Business Law* 467.

[46] ibid.

[47] Y Biondi, A Canziani and T Kirat, *The Firm as an Entity: Implications for Economics, Accounting and the Law* (Routledge, 2007).

[48] AD Chandler, 'Organizational Capabilities and the Economic History of the Industrial Enterprise' (1992) 6 *Journal of Economic Perspectives* 79; Chandler (n 42); L Fink, 'Larry Fink's 2021 letter to CEOs' (*BlackRock*) at www.blackrock.com/corporate/investor-relations/larry-fink-ceo-letter.

itself from regulation and to ensure the continuing viability of its mode of business – its social licence to operate. A persona is itself a form of value that can be valorised. The impact of the company in the world means it creates externalities. The increasing practice of disclosing ESG impacts means that minimising negative externalities and maximising positive externalities also become forms of value for the company.

Separation and the locking in of capital in the *persona ficta* occurred early in the history of the corporation. In 1657, Oliver Cromwell granted the English East India Company a charter where the Joint Stock became permanent capital. Simultaneously, realising value from land shifted from the feudal system to the capitalist system. Both were facilitated by the separation of value and its conversion into capital through double-entry bookkeeping.

From its inception, once the company operated in the world, the Corporate Fund was not the same as the dollar (or sterling) value of the capital contributed by founding shareholders. Although the contributions of founding shareholders seed the Corporate Fund and give the shareholders, through the holding of shares, various proprietary and decision-making rights in the company, the financial value of the Corporate Fund is linked to the value enclosed in the *persona ficta* as an entity. It is also linked the value attached to the dynamic entity as it operates in the world. Trading of shares in secondary markets gave an indication of the perceived financial value of the *persona ficta* as a dynamic entity.

Shareholders do not own the *persona ficta* that operates as an entity in the world. Shareholders own shares that have financial value. In addition, financial value is valorised and separated from the *persona ficta* through double-entry bookkeeping and distributed to shareholders as dividends.

La Porta, Lopez-de-Silanes, Shleifer and Vishny (LLSV)[49] introduced an index of six shareholder protection rules in 49 countries, known as the 'antidirector rights index'. They found that common law countries provide more robust investor protection than civil law countries,[50] and that stronger investor protection is associated with bigger capital markets.[51]

Of the six components of the 'antidirector rights index', three are concerned with shareholder voting (voting by mail, voting without blocking of shares, and calling an extraordinary meeting) and three are concerned with minority protection (proportional board representation, pre-emptive rights, and judicial remedies).[52] In a later paper, the authors consider the economic consequences of legal origins, concluding that the relative economic success of common law countries could be attributed to stronger property and contract rights.[53] The form of rights attached to shares that relate to the Corporate Fund means that if

[49] RL Porta et al, 'Law and Finance' (1998) 106 *Journal of Political Economy* 1113.
[50] ibid.
[51] ibid.
[52] ibid 1122.
[53] RL Porta, F Lopez-de-Silanes and A Shleifer, 'The Economic Consequences of Legal Origins' (2008) 46 *Journal of Economic Literature* 285.

the appropriate legal rules are in place, capital providers do not need to control management decisions made about the pooled capital held in the corporate entity. As well as ultimate authority, in the sense that they can make the collective decision to end the life of the company, shareholders have constitutional rights as members of the company that they can exercise to make corporate management accountable. The 'antidirector index' highlights how the strengthening of those rights contributes to bigger capital markets.

One of the critical characteristics of the modern company is that boards are charged with acting in the best interests of the company and, as part of that role, overseeing and monitoring the management of the company. Also essential is that those who control the management of the company act in the interests of the entity. Attempts to 'solve' the agency problem by aligning the interests of management with current shareholders, risks boards' focusing on the short term. As the work of LLSV shows, company law is most effective when it strengthens the constitutional rights of shareholders rather than strengthening shareholder control over management decision making.

In the mid-twentieth century, Cooke said of the modern company:

> This fund is used for economic purposes through the medium of many relationships which find their expression in such words as ownership, employment, contract, profit, dividends. All of these concepts which connect men with other men, are both juridical and economic … Yet this great fund of invested capital which has appeared through the economic operation of a legal institution raises problems which are not within the scope either of pure legal or of pure economic theory. From the economic side it falls to be asked whether this fund is operated efficiently in the interest of the community; whether, in the extreme case, a vast privately owned fund of capital is the best way ethically and politically as well as economically, of conducting the economic life of a nation.[54]

Historical experience has shown that the combination of key characteristics in the modern company makes it an unbeatable legal form for the creation of value in the long term.

The following from Roger Scruton and John Finnis may capture the perils and the potential of the form:

> Let us return in thought, therefore, to the world of thing-institutions, and try to discover what the individual lacks in that world. The primary thing that is missing, I believe, is the long-term view. No obligation endures there – not even the obligations of love and friendship – beyond the lifetime of the individuals who undertake them; nor does any obligation exist towards those who are not present to reciprocate it. The unborn and the dead are not only disenfranchised: they have lost all claim on the living. Their claims can be acknowledged only if there are persons who endure long enough to enter into personal relation, both with us, the living, and with them.

[54] CA Cooke, *Corporation, Trust and Company: An Essay in Legal History* (Harvard University Press, 1951) 13.

> The true public spirit – the spirit from which civil society and all its benefits derives – requires just such a projection of our duties beyond the grave. The care for future generations must be entrusted to persons who will exist when they exist: and if there are no such persons surrounding me, how can I have that care, except as a helpless anxiety? I can enter into no personal obligation that will bind me to past and future souls, nor can you. Only a corporate person can enter such an obligation, and only through corporate persons, therefore, can the relation to the unborn and the dead be made articulate and binding. … In the broadest sense, then, the corporate person is necessary to the ecology of rational agency, and without it our aims will be as truncated as our lives.[55]

The normative argument set out in this book is that a modern company is a Corporate Fund that is an artificial legal person existing in perpetuity. The potential of the modern corporate form for creating perpetual value that can potentially extend beyond financial value is fully realised when the board manages the company in its own interests as it operates in the world as a dynamic entity. The book argues for an eversion in perspective so that the company is considered from its own perspective, not the perspective of shareholders, corporate constituents or stakeholders. Using a historical lens, evidence exists that when the corporate form is operationalised in this way, enormous value creation can eventuate over time. That value can be separated using double-entry bookkeeping and valorised for shareholders as financial value distributed as dividends. Shareholders are also enriched through owning shares with rights attached, with the value of the shares linked with the value of the Corporate Fund.

We need not consider the modern company solely from its own perspective. Potentially immortal persons exist amongst us that exist primarily to aggregate wealth over time. The growth in the wealth of tech titans such as Jeff Bezos and Mark Zuckerberg, and the wealth inequality that follows, results from the value capture and aggregation in the Corporate Fund. Corporate governors and managers who directly control the Corporate Fund also benefit through excessive remuneration. Distribution of value to corporate constituents such as employees may reduce the unequal benefits derived from the modern company. Ironically, the benefits to the *persona* from minimising or compensating for negative externalities may result in growth in the value of the Corporate Fund in the long term.

With corporate wealth comes corporate power and the ability of corporations to exert political influence over states. States may not require corporations to compensate for the externalities they create. The law may not even recognise that the essential characteristics that make the corporate form so potent, in particular status as a legal person, are ultimately derived from the state. This matters, because it relates to the rights of states in relation to modern companies. It provides a rationale for state regulation of corporations through, for example,

[55] R Scruton and J Finnis, 'Corporate Persons' (1989) 63 *Proceedings of the Aristotelian Society, Supplementary Volumes* 239, 266.

antitrust/competition laws. It also relates to the requirement that financial value be extracted in taxation to benefit society as a whole.

The lessons of history are instructive. The English East India Company, in its modern form, was at least launched in a context of Puritan idealism. The entity's success operating as a modern company growing value was for 100 years, more than a natural lifetime. In that time, though, the entity morphed into a rapacious monster directly responsible for the Bengal famine and the loss of millions of lives. In the first gilded age, the resulting wealth and power of the Rockefellers and their ilk, on the back of corporations that had again acquired the modern form, resulted in the ultimate break-up of those corporations by the state through anti-trust regulation.

We live in the second gilded age driven by Big Tech platform companies, with resulting wealth inequality and corporate power. Until recently, states have seemed powerless to regulate or control them. The veil must fall from our eyes. It is only when we understand what modern companies really are and potentially can become, once we recognise that these amorphous entities impact and even control our lives, that we can regain agency. Capitalism is both one of humanity's greatest inventions, and the greatest source of prosperity the world has ever seen, and a menace on the verge of destroying our planet and destabilising society.[56] Engaging with that paradox by reimagining capitalism compels us to reimagine its primary tool: the modern company. Corporations have been described as Frankenstein's monsters, and in many ways they are artificial persons created by Man. Just as we make them, we can unmake them or remake them in a form that serves us all rather than the gilded few, as we engage in the grand challenges the world confronts.

[56] Henderson (n 1) 7.

Bibliography

BOOKS AND CONTRIBUTIONS TO EDITED VOLUMES

A Short History of the Charitable Corporation (A Millar, 1732).

Considerations upon the management of the Bank of England (1697).

Observations upon the constitution of the Company of the Bank of England, with a narrative of some of their late proceedings (London, 1694).

The Bible, 1 Corinthians, 12 King James Version.

The Case of the Charitable Corporation (1732).

Alborn, TL, *Conceiving Companies: Joint Stock Politics in Victorian England* (Routledge, 1998).

Andrews, KR, *English Privateering Voyages to the West Indies, 1588–1595* (Cambridge University Press for the Hakluyt Society, 1959).

Angell, JK and Ames, S, *A Treatise on the Law of Private Corporations Aggregate* (Hilliard, Gray, Little & Watkins, 1832)

—— and ——, *A Treatise on the Law of Private Corporations Aggregate*, 7th edn (Little, Brown, 1861).

Armour, J et al, 'What Is Corporate Law?' in R Kraakman (ed), *The Anatomy of Corporate Law*, 3rd edn (Oxford University Press, 2017) 1.

Austin, RP and Ramsay, IM, *Ford's Principles of Corporations Law*, 13th edn (LexisNexis Butterworths, 2007).

Bainbridge, SM, *The New Corporate Governance in Theory and Practice* (Oxford University Press, 2008).

Bainbridge, SM and Henderson, MT, *Limited Liability: A Legal and Economic Analysis* (Edward Elgar Publishing, 2016).

Ballantine, HW, *Manual of Corporation Law and Practice* (Callaghan and Company, 1930).

Baskin, JB and Miranti Jr, PJ, *A History of Corporate Finance* (Cambridge University Press, 1997).

Berle, AA and Means, GC, *The Modern Corporation and Private Property*, rev edn (Harcourt, Brace & World, 1968).

Berle, AA, *Studies in the Law of Corporation Finance* (Callaghan and Company, 1928).

Biondi, Y, Canziani, A and Kirat, T, *The Firm as an Entity: Implications for Economics, Accounting and the Law* (Routledge, 2007).

Blackstone, W, *Commentaries on the Laws of England*, vol 1 (Clarendon Press, 1765–69).

——, *Commentaries on the Laws of England, in Four Books*, vol 1, 14th edn (A Strahan, 1803).

Bottomley, S, *The Constitutional Corporation: Rethinking Corporate Governance* (Ashgate Publishing, 2007).

Branscomb, AW, *Who Owns Information? From Privacy to Public Access* (Basic Books, 1994).

Bray, W, *Memoirs Illustrative of the Life and Writings of John Evelyn* (Henry Colburn, 1818)

Brenner, R, *Merchants and Revolution: Commercial Change, Political Conflict, and London's Overseas Traders, 1550–1653* (Verso, 2003).

Burrough, E, *A just and righteous plea presented unto the King of England and his Council, being the true state of the present case of the people, called Quakers* (Robert Wilson, 1661).

Cadbury, D, *Chocolate Wars: From Cadbury to Kraft: 200 Years of Sweet Success And Bitter Rivalry* (HarperPress, 2010).

Carr, CT, *The General Principles of the Law of Corporations: (Being the Yorke Prize Essay for the Year 1902)* (Cambridge University Press, 1902).

——, *Select Charters of Trading Companies, AD 1530–1707*, vol XXVIII (B Quaritch, 1913).

Cawston, G and Keane, AH, *The Early Chartered Companies (AD 1296–1858)* (Edward Arnold, 1896).
Chambers, DDC and Galbraith, D (eds), *The Letterbooks of John Evelyn*, vol 1 (University of Toronto Press, 2014).
Chandler Jr, AD, *The Visible Hand: The Managerial Revolution in American Business* (The Belknap Press, 1977).
——, *Scale and Scope: The Dynamics of Industrial Capitalism* (The Belknap Press of Harvard University Press, 1994).
Chaudhuri, KN, *The Trading World of Asia and the English East India Company: 1660–1760* (Cambridge University Press, 1978).
Cheffins, BR, *Corporate Ownership and Control: British Business Transformed* (Oxford University Press, 2008).
Child, J, *The Great Honour and Advantage of the East-India Trade to the Kingdom* (Thomas Speed, 1697).
Chitty, J (ed), *Commentaries on the Laws of England by the late Sir W Blackstone*, vol 1 (W Walker, 1826).
Clapham, JH, *An Economic History of Modern Britain* (Cambridge University Press, 1930–1938).
Collyer, J, *A Practical Treatise on the Law of Partnership: With an Appendix of Forms* (S Sweet, 1832).
Condren, C *Argument and Authority in Early Middle England: The Presupposition of Oaths and Offices* (Cambridge University Press, 2006).
Cooke, CA, *Corporation, Trust and Company: An Essay in Legal History* (Harvard University Press, 1951).
Cooke, R, *Turning Points of the Common Law* (Sweet & Maxwell, 1997).
Cory, I, *A Practical Treatise on Accounts*, 2nd edn (W Pickering, 1837).
Cox, EW, *The Law and Practice of Joint Stock Companies and Other Associations, as Regulated by the Companies Act, 1862*, 6th edn (John Crockford, 1862).
Dalrymple, W, *The Anarchy: The Relentless Rise of the East India Company* (Bloomsbury Publishing, 2019).
Darley, G, *John Evelyn Living for Ingenuity* (Yale University Press, 2006).
——, *Villages of Vision: A Study of Strange Utopias*, 2nd rev edn (Five Leaves Publications, 2007).
Darley, JM, 'How Organizations Socialize Individuals into Evildoing' in DM Messick and AE Tenbrunsel (eds), *Codes of Conduct: Behavioral Research into Business Ethics* (Russell Sage Foundation, 1996) 13.
Daunton, M, *Progress and Poverty: An Economic and Social History of Britain 1700–1850* (Oxford University Press, 1995).
Davies, PL, *Gower and Davies' Principles of Modern Company Law*, 7th edn (Sweet & Maxwell, 2003).
—— (ed), *Gower and Davies: Principles of Modern Company Law*, 8th edn (Sweet & Maxwell, 2008).
Davis JP, *Corporations: A Study of the Origin and Development of Great Business Combinations and of Their Relation to the Authority of the State*, vol 1 (GP Putnam's Sons, 1905).
Davis, JS, *Essays in the Earlier History of American Corporations* (Harvard University Press, 1917).
Dickens C, *Bleak House* (Electric Book Co, 2001).
Dine, J and Koutsias, M, *Company Law*, 6th edn (Palgrave MacMillan, 2007).
DuBois, AB, *The English Business Company after the Bubble Act, 1720–1800* (The Commonwealth Fund, 1938).
Duff, PW, *Personality in Roman Private Law* (AM Kelley, 1971).
Easterbrook, FH and Fischel, DR, *The Economic Structure of Corporate Law* (Harvard University Press, 1991).
Elliffe C, *Taxing the Digital Economy: Theory, Policy and Practice* (Cambridge University Press, 2021).
Emden, PH, *Quakers in Commerce: A Record of Business Achievement* (Sampson Low, Marston & Co, 1940).

Erikson, E, *Between Monopoly and Free Trade: The English East India Company, 1600–1757* (Princeton University Press, 2014).
Evans, Jr GH, *British Corporation Finance, 1775–1850: A Study of Preference Shares* (The Johns Hopkins Press, 1936).
Evelyn, J, *The Diary of John Evelyn*, vol 1, ed W Bray (M Walter Dunne, 1901).
——, *The Diary of John Evelyn*, vol 1, ed J Bowle (Oxford University Press, 1983).
Finn, P, 'The Fiduciary Principle' in TG Youdan (ed), *Equity, Fiduciaries, and Trusts* (Carswell, 1989).
Fitz-Wygram, L, *Limited Liability Made Practical. Reduction of Capital of Companies and the subdivision of Shares* (Effingham Wilson, 1867), as reprinted in Wright RE and Sylla R (eds), *The History of Corporate Finance: Development of Anglo-American Securities Markets, Financial Practices, Theories and Laws*, vol 3 (Pickering & Chatto, 2003).
Fletcher, WM, *Cyclopedia of the Law of Corporations*, vol 1 (Callaghan, 1917–1920).
Formoy, RR, *The Historical Foundations of Modern Company Law* (Sweet & Maxwell, 1923).
Freeman M, Pearson R, and Taylor J, *Shareholder Democracies? Corporate Governance in Britain & Ireland before 1850* (University of Chicago Press, 2012).
Freeman, RE, *Strategic Management: A Stakeholder Approach* (Pitman Publishing, 1984).
Freund, E, *The Legal Nature of Corporations* (University of Chicago Press, 1897).
Friedman, LM, *A History of American Law*, 3rd edn (Simon & Schuster, 2005).
Friedman, M, *Capitalism and Freedom* (University of Chicago Press, 1962).
Fuller, LL, *Legal Fictions* (Stanford University Press, 1967).
Getzler J, 'Rumford Market and Genesis of Fiduciary Obligations' in Burrows A and Rodger A (eds), *Mapping the Law: Essays in Memory of Peter Birks* (Oxford University Press, 2006) 577.
——, 'The Role of Security over Future and Circulating Capital: Evidence from the British Economy circa 1850–1920' in J Getzler and J Payne (eds), *Company Charges: Spectrum and Beyond* (Oxford University Press, 2006) 227.
Gierke, O, *Political Theories of the Middle Age*, tr FW Maitland (Cambridge University Press, 1913).
Gleeson-White, J, *Double Entry: How the merchants of Venice shaped the modern world – and how their invention could make or break the planet* (Allen & Unwin, 2011).
Goebel Jr, J, *Cases and Materials on the Development of Legal Institutions* (The Vermont Printing Company, 1946).
Gower, LCB, *Principles of Modern Company Law*, 4th edn (Sweet & Maxwell, 1979).
Gower, LCB, Prentice, DD and Pettet, BG, *Principles of Modern Company Law*, 5th edn (Sweet & Maxwell, 1992).
Harari, YN, *Sapiens: A Brief History of Humankind* (Vintage Books, 2014).
Harris, R, *Industrializing English Law: Entrepreneurship and Business Organization, 1720–1844* (Cambridge University Press, 2000).
Harrison, M, *Bournville: Model Village to Garden Suburb* (Phillimore & Co, 1999).
Hart, HLA, 'Definition and Theory in Jurisprudence' in HLA Hart, *Essays in Jurisprudence and Philosophy* (Oxford University Press, 1983) 21.
Hart, OD, 'Incomplete Contracts and the Theory of the Firm' in OE Williamson and SG Winter (eds), *The Nature of the Firm Origins: Evolution, and Development* (Oxford University Press, 1993) 138.
Hart, O, *Firms, Contracts, and Financial Structure* (Oxford University Press, 1995).
Helmholz, RH, *The Oxford History of the Laws of England: The Canon Law and Ecclesiastical Jurisdiction from 597 to the 1640s*, vol 1 (Oxford University Press, 2004).
Henderson, R, *Reimagining Capitalism in a World on Fire* (PublicAffairs, 2020).
Holdsworth, WS et al, *A History of English Law*, vol VIII (Sweet & Maxwell, 1903–1972).
Hovenkamp, H, *Enterprise and American Law, 1836–1937* (Harvard University Press, 1991).
Hubbard, E and Shippobottom, M, *A Guide to Port Sunlight Village*, 2nd edn (Liverpool University Press, 2005).
Hunt, BC, *The Development of the Business Corporation in England 1800–1867* (Harvard University Press, 1936).

Hunter, WW, *History of India: The European Struggle for Indian Supremacy in the Seventeenth Century*, ed AVW Jackson (Grolier Society, 1907).

Ireland, P, 'Triumph of the Company Legal Form 1856–1914' in J Adams (ed), *Essays for Clive Schmitthoff* (Professional Books, 1983).

Isichei, E, *Victorian Quakers* (Oxford University Press, 1970).

Jacob, G, *New Law-Dictionary: Containing, the Interpretation and Definition of Words and Terms Used in the Law* (London, 1729).

Jefferys, JB, *Business Organisation in Great Britain, 1856–1914* (Dissertations in European Economics History, Arno Press, 1977).

Keay, A, *The Corporate Objective* (Edward Elgar, 2011).

Khan, SA, *The East India Trade in the XVIIth Century in its Political and Economic Aspects* (S Chand & Co, 1923).

Kingsbury, SM (ed), *The Records of the Virginia Company of London: The Court Book, from the Manuscript in the Library of Congress*, vol 2 (Washington Printing Office, 1906).

Kraakman, R et al, *The Anatomy of Corporate Law: A Comparative and Functional Approach*, 3rd edn (Oxford University Press, 2017).

Kyd, S, *A Treatise on The Law of Corporations*, vol 1 (J Butterworth, 1793).

Levy, AB, *Private Corporations and their Control* (Routledge, 1950).

Lindley, N, *A Treatise on the Law of Companies, considered as a branch of the Law of Partnership*, 5th edn (Sweet & Maxwell, 1889).

——, *A Treatise on the Law of Companies, considered as a branch of the Law of Partnership*, 6th edn (Sweet & Maxwell, 1902).

——, *A Treatise on the Law of Partnership: Including its Application to Joint-Stock and Other Companies*, vol 1 (T & JW Johnson, 1860).

——, *A Treatise on the Law of Partnership, Including its Application to Companies*, vol 1, 2nd edn (William Maxwell & Son, 1867)

——, *A Treatise on the Law of Partnership Including its Application to Companies*, vol 1, 3rd edn (W Maxwell, 1873).

——, *A Treatise on the Law of Partnership Including its Application to Companies*, vol 1, 4th edn (William Maxwell & Son, 1878).

——, *Supplement to a Treatise on the Law of Partnership Including its Application to Joint-Stock and Other Companies*, 5th edn (W Maxwell, 1863).

Lowenfeld, H, *Investment Practically Considered* (The Financial Review of Reviews, 1908).

Lynch, M, *Mining in World History* (Reaktion Books, 2002).

Maine, HS, *Ancient Law: Its Connection with the Early History of Society, and its Relation to Modern Ideas: with an Introduction by Theodore W Dwight 3rd American, from 5th London edn* (Henry Holt and Company, 1873).

Maitland, FW, 'The Corporation Sole' in HAL Fisher (ed), *The Collected Papers of Frederic William Maitland*, vol 3 (Cambridge University Press, 1911) 210.

——, 'The Unincorporate Body' in HAL Fisher (ed), *The Collected Papers of Frederic William Maitland*, vol 3 (Cambridge University Press, 1911) 271.

——, 'Trust and Corporation' in HAL Fisher (ed), *The Collected Papers of Frederic William Maitland*, vol 3 (Cambridge University Press, 1911) 321.

Marshall, A, *Industry and Trade: a study of industrial technique and business organization: and their influences on the conditions of various classes and nations*, 2nd edn (Macmillan, 1919), as reprinted in RE Wright and R Sylla (eds), *The History of Corporate Finance: Development of Anglo-American Securities Markets, Financial Practices, Theories and Laws*, vol 6 (Pickering & Chatto, 2003).

Marx, K, *Das Kapital* (Verlag von Otto Meissner, 1867).

——, *Das Kapital*, vol III (Verlag von Otto Meissner, 1894).

Mayer, CP, *Prosperity: better business makes the greater good* (Oxford University Press, 2018).

McQueen, R, *A Social History of Company Law: Great Britain and the Australian Colonies 1854–1920* (Ashgate Publishing, 2009).

Merkin, RM and Colinvaux, R, *Colinvaux and Merkin's Insurance Contract Law*, 10th edn (Thomson Reuters, 2015).
Michie, RC, *The London Stock Exchange: A History* (Oxford University Press, 1999).
Miligram, S, *Obedience to Authority: An Experimental View* (Harper and Row, 1974).
Mishra, R, *A Business of State: Commerce, Politics, and the Birth of the East India Company* (Harvard University Press, 2018).
Mitchell, W, 'Early Forms of Partnership' in *Select Essays in Anglo-American Legal History*, vol III (Little, Brown, 1909).
Morgan, EV and Thomas, WA, *The Stock Exchange: Its History and Functions* (Elek Books, 1962).
Neal, L, *The Rise of Financial Capitalism: International Capital Markets in the Age of Reason* (Cambridge University Press, 1990).
Orts, EW, *Business Persons: A Legal Theory of the Firm* (Oxford University Press, 2013).
Outhwaite, RB, *The Rise and Fall of the English Ecclesiastical Courts, 1500–1860* (Cambridge University Press, 2006).
Palmer, FB, *Company Law: A Practical Handbook for Lawyers & Business Men*, 2nd edn (Stevens & Sons, 1898).
——, *Company Law: A Practical Handbook for Lawyers & Business Men*, 3rd edn (Stevens & Sons, 1901).
——, *Company Law: A Practical Handbook for Lawyers & Business Men*, 5th edn (Stevens & Sons, 1905).
——, *Company Precedents for Use in Relation to Companies subject to the Companies Acts 1862 to 1880*, 2nd edn (Stevens & Sons, 1881).
——, *Company Precedents for Use in Relation to Companies subject to the Companies Acts 1862 to 1883*, 4th edn (Stevens & Sons, 1888).
——, *Company Precedents for Use in Relation to Companies subject to the Companies Acts, 1862 to 1890*, vol 1, 6th edn (Stevens & Sons, 1895–96).
——, *Company Precedents for Use in Relation to Companies subject to the Companies Acts, 1862 to 1900*, vol 1, 8th edn (Stevens & Sons, 1902).
——, *Company Precedents for Use in Relation to Companies subject to the Companies Acts, 1862 to 1907*, 10th edn (Stevens & Sons, 1910).
——, *Private Companies and Syndicates, Their Formation and Advantages; being a Concise Popular Statement of the Mode of Converting a Business into a Private Company, and of Establishing and Working Private Companies and Syndicates for Miscellaneous Purposes*, 10th edn (Stevens & Sons, 1892).
——, *Private Companies and Syndicates, Their Formation and Advantages; being a Concise Popular Statement of the Mode of Converting a Business into a Private Company, and of Establishing and Working Private Companies and Syndicates for Miscellaneous Purposes*, 17th edn (Stevens & Sons, 1902).
Parkinson, JE, *Corporate Power and Responsibility: Issues in the Theory of Company Law* (Clarendon Press, 1993).
Peck, LL, *Women of Fortune: Money, Marriage, and Murder in Early Modern England* (Cambridge University Press, 2018).
Pennington, RR, *Company Law*, 8th edn (Butterworths, 2001).
Piketty, T, *Capital in the Twenty-First Century*, tr A Goldhammer (Harvard University Press, 2014).
Pollock, F and Maitland, FW, *A History of English Law*, 2nd edn, vol 1 (Cambridge University Press, 1898).
Pufendorf, S, *De Jure Naturae et Gentium Libri Octo*, vol 2, trs CH Oldfather and WA Oldfather (Clarendon Press, 1934).
Reynolds, E, *The Comfort and Crown of Great Actions Preached, December 4, 1657, Before the Honorable East-India Company* (The Ratcliffe for George Thomason, 1659).
Robins, N, *The Corporation that Changed the World: How the East India Company Shaped the Modern Multinational*, 2nd edn (Pluto Press, 2012).

Rowntree, JS, *The Society of Friends: Its Faith and Practice*, 2nd edn (Headley Brothers, 1901).
Rubin, GR, 'Aron Salomon and His Circle' in J Adams (ed), *Essays for Clive Schmitthoff* (Professional Books, 1983) 99.
Runciman, D, *Pluralism and the Personality of the State* (Cambridge University Press, 1997).
Sainsbury, EB, *A Calendar of the Court Minutes etc of the East India Company, 1644–1649* (Clarendon Press, 1912).
——, *A Calendar of the Court Minutes etc of the East India Company, 1650–1654* (Clarendon Press, 1913).
——, *A Calendar of the Court Minutes etc of the East India Company, 1655–1659* (Clarendon Press, 1916).
——, *A Calendar of the Court Minutes etc of the East India Company, 1660–1663* (Clarendon Press, 1922).
Salmond, JW, *Jurisprudence, or, The Theory of the Law*, 2nd edn (Stevens and Haynes, 1907).
Savigny, FC, *System des heutigen Romischen Rechts*, vol 2 (Veit, 1840).
Scott, WR, *The Constitution and Finance of English, Scottish, and Irish Joint-Stock Companies to 1720*, vol 1 (Cambridge University Press, 1912).
——, *The Constitution and Finance of English, Scottish, and Irish Joint-Stock Companies to 1720*, vol 2 (Cambridge University Press, 1910).
Seipp, DJ, 'Formalism and Realism in Fifteenth-Century English Law: Bodies Corporate and Bodies Natural' in PA Brand and J Getzler (eds), *Judges and Judging in the History of the Common Law and Civil Law: From Antiquity to Modern Times* (Cambridge University Press, 2012) 37.
Shannon, HA, 'The Limited Companies of 1866–1883' (1933) 4 *The Economic History Review* 290, as reprinted in EM Carus-Wilson (ed), *Essays in Economic History* (Edward Arnold, 1954) 380.
Shapiro, B, 'Law and the Evidentiary Environment' in L Hutson (ed), *The Oxford Handbook of English Law and Literature, 1500–1700* (Oxford University Press, 2017) 257.
Shaw, J, *Charters Relating to the East India Company: From 1600 to 1761* (R Hill at the Government Press, 1887).
Sjåfell, B and Bruner, CM, 'Corporations and sustainability' in Sjåfell B and Bruner CM (eds), *Cambridge Handbook of Corporate Law, Corporate Governance and Sustainability* (Cambridge University Press, 2019) 3.
Smith, A, *An Inquiry into the Nature and Causes of the Wealth of Nations*, vol 3, 5th edn (W Strahan and T Cadell, 1789).
——, *An Inquiry into the Nature and Causes of the Wealth of Nations*, vol 2, eds R Campbell and A Skinner (Clarendon, 1976).
——, *The Wealth of Nations*, ed A Skinner (Penguin, 1970).
Solinas, M, *Legal Evolution and Hybridisation: The Law of Share Transfers in England* (Intersentia, 2014).
Stokes, M, 'Company Law and Legal Theory' in W Twining (ed), *Legal Theory and Common Law* (Blackwell Publishing, 1986) 155.
Talbot, L, *Great Debates in Company Law* (Palgrave Macmillian, 2014).
Televantos, A, *Capitalism Before Corporations: The morality of business associations and the roots of commercial equity and law* (Oxford University Press, 2021).
Thring H, *The Law and Practice of Joint-Stock Companies* (Stevens & Sons, 1861).
——, *The Law and Practice of Joint-Stock and Other Public Companies*, 2nd edn (Stevens & Sons, 1867–1868).
——, *The Law and Practice of Joint-Stock and Other Public Companies*, 3rd edn (Stevens & Sons, 1875).
——, *The Law and Practice of Joint-Stock and Other Public Companies*, 4th edn (Stevens & Sons, 1880).
Thompson, SD, *Commentaries on the Law of Private Corporations*, 2nd edn (The Bobbs-Merrill Company, 1909).
Watts, P, Campbell, N and Hare, C, *Company Law in New Zealand*, 2nd edn (LexisNexis, 2016).

Weber, M, *The Protestant Ethic and the Spirit of Capitalism*, tr T Parsons (Routledge, 2001).
——, *The History of Commercial Partnerships in the Middle Ages: The First Complete English Edition of Weber's Prelude to The Protestant Ethic and the Spirit of Capitalism and Economy and Society*, tr L Kaelber (Rowman & Littlefield Publishers, 2003).
Weinstein, O, 'The Current State of the Economic Theory of the Firm: Contractual, Competence-based and Beyond' in Y Biondi, A Canziani, T Kirat (eds), *The Firm as an Entity: Implications for Economics, Accounting and the Law* (Routledge, 2007) 21.
Whishaw, J, *New Law Dictionary; Containing a Concise Exposition of the Mere Terms of Art, and Such Obsolete Words as Occur in Old Legal, Historical and Antiquarian Writers* (J & WT Clarke, 1829).
Williams, RLV et al, *The Law and Practice in Bankruptcy, comprising the Bankruptcy Acts, 1883 to 1890; the Bankruptcy Rules and Forms, 1886, 1890; the Debtors Acts, 1869, 1878, the Bankruptcy (Discharge and Closure) Act, 1887, the Deeds of Arrangement Act, 1887, and the rules and forms thereunder*, 8th edn (Sweet & Maxwell, 1904).
Williamson, O, 'Transaction Cost Economics' in R Schmalensee and R Willig (eds), *Handbook of Industrial Organization*, vol 1 (Elsevier, 1989) 135.
Williamson, OE, *Markets and Hierarchies: Analysis and Antitrust Implications* (The Free Press, 1975).
Wordsworth, C, *The law of railway, canal, water, dock, gas, and other companies, requiring express authority of Parliament: together with the law of abandonment and winding-up, and that of parliamentary costs, with forms and all the statutes, including the Consolidation acts of 1845–7*, 6th edn (William Benning & Co, 1851).
Wright, RE and Sylla, R (eds), *The History of Corporate Finance: Development of Anglo-American Securities Markets, Financial Practices, Theories and Laws*, vol 1 (Pickering & Chatto, 2003).

JOURNAL ARTICLES

Anon, (1897) 13 *Law Quarterly Review* 6.
'Manufacturing Corporations' (1829) 2 *American Jurist and Law Magazine* 92, as reprinted in Wright RE and Sylla R (eds), *The History of Corporate Finance: Development of Anglo-American Securities Markets, Financial Practices, Theories and Laws*, vol 2 (Pickering & Chatto, 2003).
Aickin, KA, 'Division of Power Between Directors and General Meeting as a Matter of Law, and as a Matter of Fact and Policy' (1967) 5 *Melbourne University Law Review* 448.
Alchian, AA and Demsetz, H, 'Production, Information Costs, and Economic Organization' (1972) 62 *American Economic Review* 777.
Allen, WT, 'Our Schizophrenic Conception of the Business Corporation' (1992) 14 *Cardozo Law Review* 261.
Allen, WT and Strine Jr, LE, 'When the Existing Economic Order Deserves a Champion: The Enduring Relevance of Martin Lipton's Vision of the Corporate Law' (2005) 60 *The Business Lawyer* 1383.
Anderson, GM, McCormick, RE and Tollison, RD, 'The Economic Organization of the English East India Company' (1983) 4 *Journal of Economic Behavior & Organization* 221.
Anderson, GM and Tollinson, RD, 'Adam Smith's Analysis of Joint-Stock Companies' (1982) 90 *Journal of Political Economy* 1237.
Armour, J and Whincop, MJ, 'The Proprietary Foundations of Corporate Law' (2007) 27 *Oxford Journal of Legal Studies* 429.
Bainbridge, SM, 'Director Primacy: The Means and Ends of Corporate Governance' (2003) 97 *Northwestern University Law Review* 547.
Baums, T, 'The Organ Doctrine: Origins, Developments and Actual Meaning in German Company Law' (2016) *Institute for Law and Finance Working Paper* 148/2016.

Bebchuk, LA and Tallarita, R, 'The Illusory Promise of Stakeholder Governance' (2020) 106 *Cornell Law Review* 91.
Beer, GL, 'Cromwell's Policy in its Economic Aspects' (1901) 16 *Political Science Quarterly* 582.
Blair, MM, 'Locking in Capital: What Corporate Law Achieved for Business Organizers in the Nineteenth Century' (2003) 51 *UCLA Law Review* 387.
——, 'Corporate Personhood and the Corporate Persona Persona' [2013] *University of Illinois Law Review* 785.
Blair, MM and Stout, LA, 'A Team Production Theory of Corporate Law' (1999) 85 *Virginia Law Review* 247.
Bowen, H, 'The "Little Parliament": The General Court of the East India Company, 1750–1784' (1991) 34 *The Historical Journal* 857.
Bratton Jr, WW, 'The New Economic Theory of the Firm: Critical Perspectives from History' (1989) 41 *Stanford Law Review* 1471.
Bryer, RA, 'The History of Accounting and the Transition to Capitalism in England: Part 2 Evidence' (2000) 25 *Accounting, Organizations and Society* 327.
Cannan, E, 'Early History of the Term Capital' (1921) 35 *Quarterly Journal of Economics* 469.
Chandler, AD, 'Organizational Capabilities and the Economic History of the Industrial Enterprise' (1992) 6 *Journal of Economic Perspectives* 79.
Ciepley, D, 'Corporate Directors as Purpose Fiduciaries: Reclaiming the Corporate Law We Need' (2019) *Social Science Research Network*.
Clemens, PGE, Review of 'Merchants and Revolution: Commercial Change, Political Conflict, and London's Overseas Traders, 1550–1653' (1993) 21 *Reviews in American History* 575.
Coase, RH, 'The Nature of the Firm' (1937) 4 *Economica* 386.
——, 'The Problem of Social Cost' (1960) 3 *Journal of Law and Economics* 1.
Coles, J, 'Railway Debenture Stock considered as a Security for the Investment of the Funds of a Life Assurance Society' (1869) 15 *Journal of the Institute of Actuaries and Assurance Magazine* 1.
Conaglen, M, 'The Nature and Function of Fiduciary Loyalty' (2005) 121 *Law Quarterly Review* 452.
Dari-Mattiaci, G et al, 'The Emergence of the Corporate Form' (2017) 33 *The Journal of Law, Economics and Organization* 193.
Dawson, F, 'Acting in the Best Interests of the Company – For Whom are Directors Trustees?' (1984) 11 *New Zealand Universities Law Review* 68.
Easterbrook, FH and Fischel, DR, 'The Corporate Contract' (1989) 89 *Columbia Law Review* 1416.
Eccles, RG and Youmans, T, 'Materiality in Corporate Governance: The Statement of Significant Audiences and Materiality' (2016) 28 *Journal of Applied Corporate Finance* 39.
Farnell, JE, 'The Social and Intellectual Basis of London's Role in the English Civil Wars' (1977) 49 *The Journal of Modern History* 641.
Gevurtz, FA, 'The Historical and Political Origins of the Corporate Board of Directors' (2004) 33 *Hofstra Law Review* 89.
Gindis, D, 'Conceptualizing the Business Corporation: Insights from History' (2020) 16 *Journal of Institutional Economics* 569.
Gindis, D, 'Ernst Freund as Precursor of the Rational Study of Corporate Law' (2020) 16 *Journal of Institutional Economics* 597.
Hansmann, H and Kraakman, R, 'Towards Unlimited Liability for Corporate Torts' (1991) 100 *Yale Law Journal* 1879.
—— and ——, 'The Essential Role of Organizational Law' (2000) 110 *Yale Law Journal* 387.
Hansmann, H, Kraakman, R and Squire, R, 'Law and the Rise of the Firm' (2006) 119 *Harvard Law Review* 1333.
Harris, R, 'The Private Origins of the Private Company: Britain 1862–1907' (2013) 33 *Oxford Journal of Legal Studies* 339.
Harris, R, 'The Transplantation of the Legal Discourse on Corporate Legal Personality Theories: From German Codification to British Political Pluralism and American Big Business' (2006) 63 *Washington and Lee Law Review* 1421.

Hill, J, 'Visions and Revisions of the Shareholder' (2000) 48 *American Journal of Comparative Law* 39.

Horrwitz, W, 'Company Law Reform and the Ultra Vires Doctrine' (1946) 62 *Law Quarterly Review* 66.

Horwitz, MJ, '*Santa Clara* Revisited: The Development of Corporate Theory' (1986) 88 *West Virginia Law Review* 173.

Ireland, P, 'Capitalism without the Capitalist: The Joint Stock Company Share and the Emergence of the Modern Doctrine of Separate Corporate Personality' (1996) 17 *Journal of Legal History* 41.

——, 'Company Law and the Myth of Shareholder Ownership' (1999) 62 *Modern Law Review* 32.

——, 'Limited Liability, Shareholders Rights and the Problem of Corporate Irresponsibility' (2010) 34 *Cambridge Journal of Economics* 837.

Ireland, PW, 'The Rise of the Limited Liability Company' (1984) 12 *International Journal of the Sociology of Law* 239.

Jefferys, JB, 'The Denomination and Character of Shares, 1855–1885' (1946) 16 *The Economic History Review* 45, as reprinted in EM Carus-Wilson (ed), *Essays in Economic History* (Edward Arnold, 1954) 344.

Jenkins, D, 'Skinning the Pantomine Horse: Two Early Cases on Limited Liability' (1975) 34 *Cambridge Law Journal* 308.

Jensen, MC and Meckling, WH, 'Theory of the Firm: Managerial Behavior, Agency Costs and Ownership Structure' (1976) 3 *Journal of Financial Economics* 305.

Kempin Jr, FG, 'Limited Liability in Historical Perspective' (1960) 4 *American Business Law Association Bulletin* 11.

Kershaw, D, 'The Path of Corporate Fiduciary Law' (2012) 8 *New York University Journal of Law & Business* 395.

Khan, LM, 'Amazon's Antitrust Paradox' (2017) 126 *Yale Law Journal* 710.

Koessler, M, 'The Person in Imagination or Persona Ficta of the Corporation' (1949) 9 *Louisiana Law Review* 435.

La Porta, R et al, 'Law and Finance' (1998) 106 *Journal of Political Economy* 1113.

La Porta, R, Lopez-de-Silanes, F, and Shleifer, A, 'The Economic Consequences of Legal Origins' (2008) 46 *Journal of Economic Literature* 285.

Langford, RT, 'Best interests: multifaceted but not unbounded' (2016) 75 *Cambridge Law Journal* 505.

Livermore, S, 'Unlimited Liability in Early American Corporations' (1935) 43 *Journal of Political Economy* 674.

Macgregor, L, 'Partnerships and Legal Personality: Cautionary Tales From Scotland' (2020) 20(1) *Journal of Corporate Law Studies* 237.

Machen, AW, 'Corporate Personality' (1911) 24 *Harvard Law Review* 253.

Marks, CP, 'Jiminy Cricket for the Corporation: Understanding the Corporate "Conscience"' (2008) 42 *Valparaiso University Law Review* 1129.

Masudul Haque, AKM, 'The Floating Charge as a Security Device' (2006) 10 *University of Western Sydney Law Review* 25.

Millon, D, 'Theories of the Corporation' [1990] *Duke Law Journal* 201.

Mitchell, LE and Gabaldon, TA, 'If I Only Had a Heart: Or, How Can We Identify a Corporate Morality' (2002) 76 *Tulane Law Review* 1645.

Morley, J, 'The Common Law Corporation: The Power of the Trust in Anglo-American Business History' (2016) 116 *Columbia Law Review* 2145.

Müller-Freienfels, W, 'Legal Relations in the Law of Agency: Power of Agency and Commercial Certainty' (1964) 13 *The American Journal of Comparative Law* 193.

Nolan, RC, 'Property in a Fund' (2004) 120 *Law Quarterly Review* 108.

Noonan, C and Watson, SM, 'The nature of shadow directorship: ad hoc statutory intervention or core company law principle' [2006] *Journal of Business Law* 763.

Pennington, RR, 'The Genesis of the Floating Charge' (1960) 23 *Modern Law Review* 630.

Petrin, M, 'Reconceptualising the Theory of the Firm – From Nature to Function' (2013) 118 *Penn State Law Review* 1.
Phillips, MJ, 'Reappraising the Real Entity Theory of the Corporation' (1994) 21 *Florida State University Law Review* 1061.
Pollock, F, 'Has the Common Law Received the Fiction Theory of Corporations?' (1911) 27 *Law Quarterly Review* 219.
Raby, WM L, 'The Two Faces of Accounting' (1959) 34 *The Accounting Review* 452.
Rajak, H, 'Judicial Control: Corporations and the Decline of Ultra Vires' (1995) 26 *Cambrian Law Review* 9.
Reynolds, RL, 'Origins of Modern Business Enterprise: Medieval Italy' (1952) 12 *Journal of Economic History* 350.
Robbins, C, 'Selden's Pills: State Oaths in England, 1558–1714' (1972) 35 *Huntingdon Library Quarterly* 303.
Schmitthoff, M, 'The Origin of the Joint-Stock Company' (1939) 3 *The University of Toronto Law Journal* 74.
Schwartz, AA, 'The Perpetual Corporation' (2012) 80 *George Washington Law Review* 764.
Scruton, R and Finnis, J, 'Corporate Persons' (1989) 63 *Proceedings of the Aristotelian Society, Supplementary Volumes* 239.
Smith, HE, 'Complexity and the Cathedral: Making Law and Economics More Calabresian' (2019) 48 *European Journal of Law and Economics* 43.
Stewart, RB, 'Organizational Jurisprudence' (1987) 101 *Harvard Law Review* 371.
Stone, CD, 'Should Trees Have Standing? – Toward Legal Rights for Natural Objects' (1972) 45 *Southern California Law Review* 450.
Strine Jr, LE, 'Restoration: The Role Stakeholder Governance Must Play in Recreating a Fair and Sustainable American Economy – A Reply to Professor Rock' (2021) 76 *The Business Lawyer* 397.
Watson, SM, 'The Significance of the Source of the Powers of Boards in UK Company Law' [2011] *Journal of Business Law* 597.
——, 'How the Company Became an Entity: A New Understanding of Corporate Law' [2015] *Journal of Business Law* 120.
——, 'The Corporate Legal Entity as a Fund' [2018] *Journal of Business Law* 467.
——, 'The Corporate Legal Person' (2019) 19 *Journal of Corporate Law Studies* 137.
Wedderburn, KW, 'Shareholders' Rights and the Rule in *Foss v Harbottle*' (1957) 15 *Cambridge Law Journal* 194.
Werner, W, 'Corporation Law in Search of its Future' (1981) 81 *Columbia Law Review* 1611.
Williamson, OE, 'Transaction-Cost Economics: The Governance of Contractual Relations' (1979) 22 *Journal of Law and Economics* 233.
Yamey, BS, 'Closing the Ledger' (1970) 1 *Accounting and Business Research* 71.
——, 'The historical significance of double-entry bookkeeping: Some non-Sombartian claims' (2005) *Accounting, Business & Financial History* 77.

PARLIAMENTARY AND GOVERNMENT MATERIALS

Hansard

Hansard, HC Deb 2 June 1825, vol 13, col 1019.
Hansard (HC 1854, 134) cols 752–60.
Hansard (HC 1855, 139) cols 310–20.
Hansard (HC 1856, 140) cols 111–26.
Hansard (HC 1867, 187) col 5.
Hansard (HC 1853, 129) cols 1598–99.
Hansard (HL 1855, 139) cols 2039–42.

Committee Reports

Board of Trade Company Law Amendment Committee, *Report of the Departmental Committee appointed by the Board of Trade, to inquire into what amendments are necessary in the Acts relating to Joint Stock Companies with limited liability under the Companies Acts, 1862 to 1890* (C 7779, 1895) (Davey Committee Report).

The Gladstone Committee, *First Report of the Select Committee on Joint Stock Companies; together with the Minutes of Evidence (taken in 1841 and 1843), Appendix, and Index* (HC 1844, 119VII).

COMPANY CHARTERS, BY-LAWS AND CONSTITUTIONS

'Charters of the East India Company with related documents: the parchment records' (The National Archives, 1600–1947).

A Copy of the Charter of the Corporation of the Governor and Company of the Bank of England (Bank of England, 1758).

A Copy of the Kings Majesties Charter for Incorporating the Company of the Massachusetts Bay in New England in America (Printed by S Green for Benj Harris, 1689).

Charter granted by Queen Elizabeth to the East India Company (Parliament of England, 1600).

The Charter of the Corporation of the Amicable Society for a Perpetual Assurance-Office (Geo Sawbridge, 1710).

The East-India companies charter, granted by the Kings most excellent Majesty Charles the second, under the great seal of England, dated the third day of April, in the 13th. year of his Majesties reign, 1661 (The Making of the Modern World, 1759).

The Royal Charter for Incorporating the Hudson's Bay Company (Printed by R Causton & Son, 1816).

Bank of England, *A Copy of the Charter of the Corporation of the Governor and Company of the Bank of England* (Printed by H Teape, 1758).

Bank of England, *Rules, orders, and by-laws; for the good government of the corporation of the governor and company of the Bank of England* (Bank of England, 1697).

East India Company, *Abstract of by-laws made by the general court of adventurers of the East India company, the 17th January* (East India Company, 1694).

England and Wales *The East-India companies charter, granted by the Kings most excellent Majesty Charles the second, under the great seal of England, dated the third day of April, in the 13th. year of his Majesties reign, 1661* (The Making Of The Modern World, 1759).

Maine Atlantic Granite Company, *The charter and by-laws of the Maine Atlantic Granite Company* (GW & FW Nichols, 1836).

South Sea Company, *By-laws, orders and rules, for the good government of the Corporation of the governor and company of merchants of Great Britain, trading to the South Seas and other parts of America, and for encouraging the fishery, and for the better carrying on and managing the trade of the said company* (J Barber, 1712).

South Sea Company and Great Britain, *An abstract of the several acts of Parliament, commission for taking subscriptions, charter, and by-laws of the honourable South-sea company* (Richard Mount, 1718).

Index

www.ingramcontent.com/pod-product-compliance
Ingram Content Group UK Ltd.
Pitfield, Milton Keynes, MK11 3LW, UK
UKHW020239290926
15470UKWH00002B/616

9 781509 923625